Dorothy Healey Remembers

DOROTHY HEALEY

MAURICE ISSERMAN

Dorothy Healey Remembers

A Life in the American Communist Party

NEW YORK · OXFORD

OXFORD UNIVERSITY PRESS

1990

Oxford University Press

Oxford   New York   Toronto
Delhi   Bombay   Calcutta   Madras   Karachi
Petaling Jaya   Singapore   Hong Kong   Tokyo
Nairobi   Dar es Salaam   Cape Town
Melbourne   Auckland

and associated companies in
Berlin   Ibadan

Published by Oxford University Press, Inc.,
200 Madison Avenue, New York, New York 10016

Oxford is a registered trademark of Oxford University Press

Library of Congress Cataloging-in-Publication Data
Healey, Dorothy.
Dorothy Healey remembers : a life in the American communist party /
Dorothy Healey, Maurice Isserman.
p.   cm.
ISBN 0-19-503819-3
1. Healey, Dorothy.   2. Communists—United States—Biography.
I. Isserman, Maurice.   II. Title.
HX84.H43A3   1990
335.43'092—dc20   89-28394

2 4 6 8 9 7 5 3 1

Printed in the United States of America
on acid-free paper

For Dorothy's mother, Barbara Nestor
and for her son, Richard Healey

And for Maurice's uncle, Abraham Isserman

ACKNOWLEDGMENTS

This work is based substantially on a series of interviews conducted by the UCLA Oral History Program from 1972 to 1974. These interviews appear in a three-volume work titled *Tradition's Chains Have Bound Us* (© 1982 The Regents of The University of California. All Rights Reserved. Used with Permission).

Less formally, let me say that I am grateful to Joel Gardner, whom I never met but whose skillful interviewing of Dorothy for *Tradition's Chains Have Bound Us* inspired this work and saved me endless hours of duplicated effort a decade later, and to Dale E. Treleven, director of the UCLA Oral History Program, who gave me permission to draw freely upon the material in *Tradition's Chains Have Bound Us*, and who offered helpful suggestions and expressions of support throughout this project.

John Ahouse, curator of the Dorothy Ray Healey collection in the library archives at California State University, Long Beach, and his assistant Irene Still went out of their way to make my visit there productive. The Healey collection was obviously invaluable to this project; the 10,000-plus books, pamphlets, magazines, broadsides, letters, and other items it contains will be of interest to anyone researching U.S. radicalism or Southern California politics in the 1930s–1960s.

In addition to books and articles cited as the source of excerpts in the text of this book, the following published sources were useful to me: Victor B. Nelson-Cisneros, "UCAPAWA and Chicanos in California: The Farm Worker Period, 1937–1940," *Aztlan*, VII (Fall of 1976); Devra Anne Weber, "The Organizing of Mexicano Agricultural Workers: Imperial Valley and Los Angeles, 1928–34: An Oral History Approach," *Aztlan*, III (Summer 1972); Cletus E. Daniel, *Bitter Harvest: A History of California Farmworkers, 1870–1941* (1981); and Vicki Ruiz, *Cannery Women, Cannery Lives: Mexican Women, Unionization and the California Food Processing Industry, 1930–1950* (1987).

Michael Furmanovsky allowed me to read some of the unpublished chapters of his dissertation on the Communist Party in Los Angeles and also had suggestions to make on research possibilities. I also found it helpful to read Leonard Joseph Leader's unpublished dissertation "Los Angeles and the Great Depression" (UCLA 1972). Sherna Berger Gluck, Director of the Oral History program at California State University, Long Beach, sent me copies of the transcripts of oral interviews with Dorothy Healey's mother, Barbara Nestor. She also shared her knowledge of oral history theory and bibliography with this newcomer to the field, as did Michael Frisch of the History Department of the University of Buffalo. Eve Goldberg sent me a copy of her excellent film documentary "Dorothy Healey: American Red."

I'm grateful to all the people who shared their memories of Dorothy with me: Bettina Aptheker, Jim Berland, Jack Berman, Ben Dobbs, Elizabeth Eudey, Edward and Marta Goldstucker, Richard Healey, Ellenore Hittelman, Paul Jarrico, Phil Kirby, Terry Kupers, Ben Margolis, John McTernan, Carol Jean Newman, Jack and Tillie Olsen, Al Richmond, Ethel Shapiro-Bertolini, Delfino Varela, and Donna and Frank Wilkinson. (Regrettably, Al Richmond and Jack Olsen both died before this book could be published).

The Smith College Committee on Faculty Compensation and Development provided the funding that made possible my two research trips to California. Susan Rabiner shepherded this project through the early editorial stages at Oxford University Press; when she left Oxford for other employment, Valerie Aubry ably and enthusiastically took her place. Marcia Williams, to whom I have the good fortune of being married, transcribed the tapes of my interviews with Dorothy Healey—a task for which, I hasten to add, she was generously compensated by Oxford. (Would that all my debts to her were so easily repaid).

Ashfield, Massachusetts   M.I.

Dorothy Healey Remembers

INTRODUCTION

Dorothy Ray Healey joined the Young Communist League (YCL) as a teenager in Berkeley, California, in 1928. She was to remain a member of the Communist movement in California for the next forty-five years, an era which spanned the most important events in the history of American Communism. She rose to a position of leadership within the Party that was rare for a woman and particularly unusual given her increasingly critical views of the movement's dogma, practice, and allegiances. In the 1930s Dorothy was a farm and cannery union organizer in the fierce California labor struggles immortalized in John Steinbeck's novels *In Dubious Battle* and *The Grapes of Wrath*; in the 1940s she became county organizer of the Los Angeles Communist Party, an organization whose membership and influence within the American Communist movement were second only to that of the Party in New York City; in the 1950s she was indicted and convicted under the Smith Act, a conviction ultimately overturned by a Supreme Court decision; in the 1960s she was an active participant in civil rights, civil liberties, and antiwar protests, and in the process became mentor and confidant to a new generation of young radicals including such figures as Angela Davis. In many ways Dorothy exemplified the aspirations, commitment, illusions—and, ultimately, disillusionment—of a generation of young Communists who joined the movement just before and during the Great Depression, experienced the exhilaration of the Party's growing power and influence during the Popular Front era of the 1930s and the Grand Alliance era of the Second World War, and then watched in dismay as the Party was reduced to a remnant of its former strength through the battering it received in the McCarthy era and through its own sectarian mistakes. But Dorothy differed from most of her contemporaries within the Party because she chose to remain in it long after they had departed. The most significant turning point in her long political career came with the Communist movement's de-Stalinization crisis of 1956–1958, during which she emerged as one of the leading apostles of political unorthodoxy within the Communist Party. Fully three-quarters of the Communist Party membership, people who had stuck with the movement through the worst of McCarthyism, chose to leave in that two-year period, disgusted with the Party's apologies for the crimes of the Stalin era in the Soviet Union and despairing of the Communist movement's prospects in the United States. Dorothy chose to stay. And for the better part of the next two decades she found herself in constant conflict with the New York–based national leaders of the Party for whom the authority of the Soviet Union remained inviolate—it was in good measure through her influence that the Communist Party in California came to be referred to in those years as the "Yugoslavia" of the American Communist movement. Whatever one thinks about her decision to remain in the Party through the 1960s and into the early 1970s, it did give her a unique vantage point from which to observe an era in the history of American Communism that has been little studied or understood. Why she stayed, what she hoped to accomplish, what lessons she drew from her own and the Party's past achievements and failures, and why she finally decided to leave, are questions which the chapters that follow will attempt to answer.

Dorothy's life story illuminates some of the central issues in the continuing historical debate over the character of the Communist movement in the United States. During the cold war a consensus emerged among the leading historians of the movement that regarded the question of Soviet control as the key to understanding the evolution of American Communism. Theodore Draper gave this interpretation its classic statement in his 1957 book *The Roots of American Communism*:

> The periodic rediscovery of "Americanization" by the American Communists has only superficially represented a more independent policy. It has been in reality merely another type of American response to a Russian stimulus. A Russian initiative has always effectively begun and ended it. For this reason, "Americanized" American Communism has been sporadic, superficial, and short-lived. It has corresponded to the fluctuations of Russian policy; it has not obeyed a compelling need within the American Communists themselves.

In the course of the 1970s and 1980s a new generation of historians, many of whose political inclinations had been shaped by the upheavals of 1960s, challenged this consensus in such works as Mark Naison's *Communists in Harlem During the Depression*, Ellen Schrecker's *No Ivory Tower*, Bruce Nelson's *Workers on the Waterfront*, Nell Painter's *The Narrative of Hosea Hudson*, and Steve Nelson, James Barrett, and Rob Ruck's *Steve Nelson, American Radical* (the last two works representing collaborations between veterans of the Communist movement and younger, non-Communist historians). These books offered both a new interpretation and a new focus for the history of American Communism. In contrast to the top-down institutional emphasis of the earlier approach, concerned as it was first and foremost with the contacts between the national Party leadership in New York and the Soviet leadership in Moscow, the new history of Communism examined particular communities, particular unions, particular professions, particular working-class and ethnic cultures, and other subgroupings within the Party. My own writings on the Party, *Which Side Were You On? The American Communist Party during the Second World War* and the introductory chapter to *If I Had a Hammer . . . The Death of the Old Left and the Birth of the New Left*, took a "generational" approach to the history of the CP from the 1930s through the 1950s, emphasizing the lessons young Communists of the 1930s learned from the experience of those years and how those lessons ultimately contributed to the most internally devastating event in CP history, the de-Stalinization crisis of 1956–1958. These works did not so much reject the Draperian consensus as seek to ask new questions that did not fit easily within its confines. Though critical of the CP's authoritarian internal structure and its subservience to the Soviet Union, the new historians have been interested in the ways in which the American CP was shaped by the national environment in which it operated and by the people who enlisted under its banners.

This new interpretation did not sweep the field of opponents by any means. Harvey Klehr's 1984 book *The Heyday of American Communsim: The Depression Decade* took a very Draperian approach to its subject. And Draper himself returned to the fray with a scathing critique of the revisionist interpretation of American Communism in a two-part article in the *New York Review of Books* in 1985 (reprinted the following year as an afterword to a new edition of his second book on the American CP, *American Communism and Soviet Russia*). Draper expressed indignation at what he characterized as the tendency among the younger generation to romanticize the Popular Front, the period in the late 1930s when the Communists set aside the sectarian trappings of their earlier policies and achieved their widest influence:

> The new historians of American Communism have been invoking the Popular Front as if they were rediscovering a once promised land. It appeals to them as the one time American Communists had really and truly Americanized themselves, had taken on the features of a mass party, and had shown promise of becoming a major force in American life and politics—the long awaited apotheosis of American radicalism.

In Draper's opinion, this reading of the era was "historically myopic." The Popular Front, he still insisted, was nothing but a charade undertaken at Moscow's behest with no long-term impact on the views and values of American Communists themselves.

But some quarters have proved more receptive to the issues and perspectives raised in the recent histories of the Party. In *The American Communist Party: A Critical History*, the 1957 book he wrote with Lewis Coser, Irving Howe dismissed the Popular Front as a "brilliant masquerade." Returning to the subject in his 1985 book *Socialism and America*, he repeated that characterization. And yet, as he elaborated his argument, a new tone of at least grudging respect for Popular Front Communism emerged. Where once Howe portrayed all Communist cadres as "malleable objects," subordinated to a totalitarian movement and capable of "little more than a series of predictable and rigidly stereotyped responses," he now conceded:

> The most interesting group of party members consisted of people with some standing and experience who, almost against their will and perhaps to their own surprise, came to value the Popular Front as both a shrewd maneuver and more than that—indeed, may even have come to believe that, for Amer-

ica at least, this was the way radicals should go . . . . We may doubt that many of them went so far as to recognize that the Popular Front really signified a break from classical Leninism and even, perhaps, the start of an adaptation to the special circumstances of American life. But most changes of thought occur hesitantly, and language always lags behind impulse and feeling.

Though he had by no means abandoned anti-Stalinism as the centerpiece of his own democratic socialist politics, Howe conceded that contemporary radicals could learn some positive and valuable lessons from the Communist experience with the Popular Front:

> The irony of it all, a bitter enough irony, is that the most promising approach of the American left, one that apparently came closest to recognizing native realities, derives from the very movement that has done the most to discredit and besmirch the whole idea of the left . . . . If ever we are to see a resurgent democratic left in America, it will have more to learn tactically from the Popular Front initiated by the Stalinists than from the political ancestors whose integrity we admire.

Dorothy Healey's life is a case in point of changes in "thought and language" lagging behind "feeling and impulse." Sometimes, when I told people I was working on a book about a woman who had made a principled break with American Communism after forty-five years of active involvement in the movement, they were incredulous, amused, and even outraged. "Why on earth didn't she leave earlier?" was the common response. I have to confess that there were times when I was sitting down at the word processor, recording the story of yet another in the seemingly endless succession of Dorothy's losing battles with the Party's stolidly Stalinist general secretary Gus Hall, when I wanted to step back in time and confront her in the guise of suprahistorical advice columnist: "Dorothy! Wake up and smell the coffee! You'll never succeed. Why not get out and save yourself a lot of grief and wasted effort?"

Why not, indeed. That seems to me to be the crux of the story that follows: why did Dorothy choose to remain as long as she did? It was a question I posed to her on many occasions and to which she offered many different answers, depending on what period of her life we were discussing. Her own memory of herself as a young woman is of someone who was singularly unreflective (I should add, however, that most of her friends from that period take strenuous exception to that self-portrait). She had an outgoing personality, loved contact with people, and threw herself into the public activities of the Young Communist League and the Communist Party. For decades her life was a constant round of meetings, picket lines, soap boxing and organizing, a regimen that she thrived upon. As a result she had little time available to her for either personal or political introspection. The personal inclinations that led her to a life of unreflective activism meshed with the requirements of the Party's authoritarian internal structure. Questions and dissent were not encouraged by Party leaders, to say the least.

By the late 1940s, as she moved into the leadership of the Los Angeles movement, she began to accumulate nagging doubts about aspects of Party policy but found it difficult to shed the inhibitions that kept Communists from questioning their leaders or the leaders of the Soviet Union. The fact that she was under threat of imprisonment for most of the years from late 1948 through 1966 for her Communist membership did not make a critical reexamination of the movement's underlying assumptions any easier. Her loyalty and social ties to old friends and her belief that she could not be effective as a Party leader if she moved too far out of the fold of common beliefs also checked her willingness to carry her dissent to its logical conclusion. But most important of all, until the very end of the 1960s, Dorothy retained a fierce loyalty to her memory of what the Party at moments had been and her vision of what she felt it could become again—the means by which ordinary people could learn to challenge the received wisdom and established authorities who kept them in ignorance, subservience, and poverty. Her close friend Edward Goldstucker, a Czech Communist leader who had been imprisoned during the Stalinist purges of the early 1950s and forced into exile after the 1968 Warsaw Pact invasion, offered a poignant expression of the dreams that kept Communists around the world believing in and sacrificing for the movement long after it may have seemed to outsiders that their Parties had forfeited all right to their continuing allegiance:

There was always the urge to explain away the unpleasant things, and to cling to every little bit of hope. There were hopeful things, the great victory in the war, there was the renewal of the Czechoslovak state, our return from exile. There was the 20th Congress. There was the Prague Spring. We hoped that the movement could be directed into a channel towards the goal we dreamed of, that is socialism with freedom.

Dorothy's story is worth retelling both because she was in many ways typical of her generation of Communists, and because she is in many ways an extraordinary individual, as the character of both the praise and condemnation she has attracted over the years would suggest. Since she was a teenager, Dorothy has always been in the public eye. She always made good newspaper copy. Her diminuitive stature, as well as her status as a sworn enemy of the status quo, seemed to invite hyperbole; before she reached her twentieth birthday California newspapers had taken to referring to her as "ninety pounds of dynamite." Promoted to the "Red Queen of Los Angeles" by the House Un-American Activities Committee and by headline writers in the tabloid press during the McCarthy era, Healey was reviled for defying prevailing conventions of gender as well as politics. "Dorothy Healey is a bitter woman," the Los Angeles *Mirror* declared in 1952, when she was on trial for violating the Smith Act, "hard as nails and with the vocabulary of a longshoreman. She is known as 'the Little Dictator,' with good reason." The *Mirror*'s reporter found it especially galling that this tough-talking, poker-playing subversive was also an attractive woman. "If the occasion demands," he noted darkly, "she can turn on the charm."

Others found Dorothy's toughness and charm a more appealing combination. If her politics from the mid-1950s on anticipated in many ways what was known as Eurocommunism in the 1970s and *glasnost* in the 1980s, so her style of carrying and asserting herself anticipated the new feminism of a younger generation of activists. Bettina Aptheker (daughter of the Communist historian Herbert Aptheker, herself a well-known student activist at the University of California at Berkeley) was among those inspired by Dorothy's example in the 1960s. She remembers encountering Dorothy in those years at Party conventions amidst a sea of cigar smoke, puffing on the little cigarillos that were her trademark:

> I had seen many women in the Party who worked very hard, and were intelligent, and developed theoretically and politically, but I hadn't seen anyone with quite Dorothy's energy and charisma . . . . She'd barge into these circles of men conversing on something or other, whatever caucus it was, she'd barge in there, and I just loved it. I thought that was great, just great. I didn't care what she said.

Even Dorothy's most hard-bitten opponents were forced to concede, if only on occasion, and then only grudgingly, some of her virtues. It was a sure sign of the waning of the worst of McCarthyism when tabloid writers in Los Angeles began to acknowledge Dorothy's "femininity"—as in a famous *Mirror* editorial in 1958 defending "our homegrown Madame Defarge" against "national Commie bosses" critical of Dorothy's policies. "Mrs. Healey happens to be one of the very few female Reds who doesn't look like an irrefutable argument for celibacy," the *Mirror* huffed in a most peculiar expression of local boosterism. A more substantial tribute came, secretly, in an internal memorandum from the Federal Bureau of Investigation in 1969. Casting off ideological blinkers, an FBI analyst offered his superiors a shrewd assessment of Dorothy's strengths as a radical leader. She was, he wrote:

> a decisive and logical thinker . . . . An excellent speaker with an extensive vocabulary and good diction, she can speak at length on almost any topic without notes. She has considerable appeal to intellectuals and young people . . . . She speaks plainly on her stand on Party issues, a trait which has evoked criticism from other Party leaders . . . .

Noting that Dorothy believed that socialism should be a "democratic world system," and that she had "vigorously opposed" Soviet intervention in Czechoslovakia, the report concluded with apparent regret that "her political views are too deeply based to expect them to be changed in any fundamental way"—which was to say that despite her disagreements with other communist leaders, she would not prove a likely candidate for aiding the FBI's continuing effort to infiltrate and undermine the Party. Notwithstanding Dorothy's declaration, when she resigned from the Party in 1973, that her "hatred of capitalism . . . is as intense now as it was when I joined the Young Communist League in 1928," her name became anathema to loyal Communists in the years that followed. She was denounced in the Party press as an arch-revisionist, an enemy of the working class, a cold warrior and red-baiter. A few friends and comrades whom she had known for decades, people with whom she had shared jail cells, crossed the street to avoid greeting her; when she left Los Angeles in 1983 to move to Washington, D.C., one or two called to say good-bye and wish her well, but they begged her not to mention to anyone that they had called.

As befits a woman whose life and reputation have taken such complicated twists and turns over the years, the origins of this account of her life are similarly tangled. When Dorothy was getting ready to leave Los Angeles for the last time, some of her friends got together and threw a party for her. Hundreds of people turned out to reminisce about and celebrate her years of political activism and to say good-bye. Many bought space to record their own sentiments in a tribute booklet distributed to everyone who came that evening. One of the messages, sent anonymously "from one revisionist to another," offered Dorothy some succinct advice: "Keep Thinking. Keep Speaking. Start Writing."

Dorothy is a woman of many talents. Writing is not among them. That's where I came in. The story that follows should be understood as a collaboration between historical subject and historian. It combines elements of and falls somewhere into the cracks between autobiography, oral history, biography, and documentary collection. Perhaps it should be called, for lack of a better term, a first-person biography.

This book is built upon a solid foundation laid by others. In an eighteen-month period between 1972 and 1974, Dorothy was interviewed by Joel Gardner, a staff member of the oral history department of the University of California at Los Angeles, with a total of forty-two hours of recorded conversation. The tapes were later transcribed and in 1982 bound in three volumes nearly fifteen hundred pages in length and made available to researchers. All of this had taken place before I had ever met Dorothy, though I had corresponded with her when I was doing research for my first book on the Communist Party. When we met for the first time in the spring of 1983 at her son's house in Boston, Dorothy asked if I would be interested in looking over her oral history and perhaps editing it with an eye toward publication. I quickly agreed because what I already knew of her past seemed to me a story of real human interest and historical significance, because I wanted to try my hand at oral history—and because I thought it would be a relatively simple task to undertake, something I could do in my spare time between teaching and other writing projects. That was an illusion I was soon forced to shed.

The UCLA oral history was recorded at the moment just before, during, and after Dorothy's decision to resign from the Communist Party. It provided a unique record of how she viewed her life at what was for her a moment of supreme crisis and decision. But it is not a complete record by any means, as no oral history can be. Reading through it, I kept coming across points I wanted elaborated or questions I felt had gone unasked. I also knew that Dorothy had changed her mind about a number of important issues in the years since she had been interviewed by Joel Gardner. So in the summer of 1985 I flew down to

Washington to conduct my own interviews with Dorothy in her new home, taping some thirty-five hours of conversation with her over two long weekends, which came to over three hundred single-spaced pages when transcribed. That, I hoped, combined with the original oral history, would suffice.

But the more I learned about Dorothy's life, the greedier I got for ever more information. The more I learned, the more gaping holes seem to appear in the story as represented in both the UCLA interviews and my own interviews. Sometimes I failed to ask the right questions; sometimes Dorothy failed to come up with much of an answer. Dorothy is no longer a young woman, and on many occasions she quite frankly acknowledged the limits of her own memory as I dredged up events from thirty, forty, and fifty years earlier and asked for her comments. Returning to hazily remembered territory in subsequent interviews yielded only marginally improved results and left us both feeling exhausted and frustrated. I needed to try another approach.

As I cast about for strategies in the months after our initial interviews were completed, my conception of the book gradually began to change. I got the idea of calling up some of Dorothy's old friends to see if they had any anecdotes or details about her early days that I could relay to her in the hopes of poking and prodding her memory. And then, finally, the real solution I was looking for came to me. Why not combine Dorothy's retelling of her life, as mediated through the questions posed to her by both myself and Joel Gardner, with the memories of others who knew her in her youth and in the years of her most active political involvement? And why not substantiate and enrich the memories of both Dorothy and those who knew her best by bringing in relevant pieces of the documentary record? The overall effect I wound up striving for was a combination of the "witness" device in Warren Beatty's film "Reds," with its chorus of John Reed's surviving friends and comrades, and the montage effect achieved through the "Newsreel" and "Camera Eye" sections in the trilogy *USA*, novels written by John Dos Passos in the 1920s and 1930s. The result may take a little getting used to by the reader of what follows, but will, I hope, prove more illuminating than intrusive.

Having at last discovered the book I wanted to write, I traveled to California in the summers of 1986 and 1987 and interviewed twenty people who had known Dorothy in her years in the movement. While I was there I burrowed into Dorothy's collected papers and her FBI files, both of which have been deposited at the California State University library at Long Beach. I also began to assemble contemporary sources, including newspapers and magazine articles, publications of the U.S. Department of Labor, and transcripts of the House Un-American Activities Committee hearings. The Federal Writers' Project guidebook for California proved particularly useful in helping me visualize and describe the places in which Dorothy won her spurs as an organizer in the 1930s.

Much of what follows is a nearly verbatim rendering of Dorothy's own reminiscences, edited only to the extent necessary to eliminate repetitions and clear up problems of syntax. I hope that those who know Dorothy well will recognize the characteristic flavor of her speech as they read these chapters. Dorothy is an accomplished storyteller who over the years has made good use of the examples provided by her own experiences as a political text. There was no need for me to "improve" upon stories that she has been polishing for so long. But linking together her stories did not produce a life history or an adequate explanation of the political milieu in which she worked. Even the stories she was most accustomed to telling relied too much on a fund of common knowledge and assumptions, or on the kinds of cues provided by facial expression and verbal emphasis, to be easily understood once reduced to the cold and distant medium of print. I was aware of this problem when I interviewed Dorothy and tried to get her to talk to me as if she were sitting down and writing a book, but with mixed success. Particularly after several hours of taping, we tended to lapse into a verbal shorthand, intelligible to the two of us but probably to few others. Whenever possible I tried to use Dorothy's own words and only her words, but when these would not suffice to make the narrative accessible and illuminating, I decided I would supply words of my own. To take an extreme example, consider the following exchange from the raw transcript of our interviews, in which Dorothy described a reception sponsored by "Friends of the Soviet Union" in San Francisco in 1929 for some Soviet pilots who had flown across the Arctic, a considerable achievement at the time. How, I asked her, had she felt about the event?

DOROTHY: It was just great pride that these fliers had shown in their flight [pause] advanced qualities of this new society.
MAURICE: Sputnik?
DOROTHY: Yeah, exactly.

What was I going to do with a passage like that? If I left it as it stood, would it present the true Dorothy to the reader? I think not. The true Dorothy, as I've come to know her, is sharp, articulate, and commanding. As I recall the moment of this exchange, it was recorded several hours into an interview on a day when both she and her interviewer were suffering from bad head colds. Had we both had an infinite amount of time and patience at our command, I suppose I could have gone back on a day when we were both feeling up to par and posed and reposed the question until I had in effect coaxed her into giving me the complete sentences and the logical unfolding of the idea the episode needed if it was to be understood by readers. But that alternative seemed impractical and the results contrived. What I chose to do instead was to rework the text myself, combining my own words with hers while retaining the form of the first-person narrative. In doing so, I sacrificed some of what oral historians would consider the purity of the unretouched transcript in the hope of creating a more accessible account. People rarely write the way they talk, and if Dorothy had been sitting down at the typewriter she would not have written the words she spoke to me that afternoon. The strategy I tried to follow was one of preserving as much as possible of Dorothy's colloquial style within the more formal constraints of written prose. Alex Haley described the process of creating *The Autobiography of Malcolm X* as one of writing "vicariously, as if I were Malcolm . . . putting onto paper . . . what hopefully would sound to a reader as if Malcolm X had just sat down and told that reader, from his memory, from earliest memory to the time he was talking." That is essentially what I was trying to do. When confronted with a passage in the transcript like the one about the Soviet fliers, I tried to write what I imagined Dorothy would have said had she enjoyed the luxury that writers enjoy and interviewees do not—that is, of polishing, rethinking, elaborating, and revising her own first approximation of her thoughts. In the end, this is what I wrote:

> These pilots were our Lindberghs. We saw their achievement as proof of the advanced qualities of the new society they represented—the same way a later generation of Communists would regard the Soviet launching of "Sputnik" in the 1950s.

Dorothy did not make either the Sputnik or the Lindbergh comparison. The former I suggested to her in the course of the interview; the latter occurred to me later as something she might have said had she been pressed to think of comparable events. Both seemed useful so I included both in the first draft I sent to Dorothy—and she agreed to their inclusion, as she did with every word that appears attributed to her in this book. While my fidelity to the spoken word was not absolute, I hope I've made up for that in fidelity to the spirit of Dorothy's story.

As I finished the first draft of each new chapter I sent it to Dorothy to read, and when I strayed too far from the model, my collaborator was always there to set me straight. Seeking to illustrate Dorothy's initial reluctance to join another radical organization after her resignation from the Communist Party, I had her saying to herself "No thanks—I've paid my dues." It's a phrase heard commonly enough on the Left that I assumed it would also be part of Dorothy's repertoire. Dorothy, however, swiftly set me straight: "Please take out 'No thanks—I've paid my dues.' It's a phrase I detest." In another instance, elaborating on Dorothy's account in her oral history of how her mother was converted to socialism while listening to a Socialist speaker by the name of J. Stitt Wilson, I introduced a familiar cliché to describe this conversion. Dorothy's critical response was soon in the mail: " 'Bolt of lightning' re J. Stitt Wilson. C'mon, I wouldn't say that!"

On questions of opinion, voice, feelings, intimate family relations, and so forth, Dorothy usually had the final word. I can't say I always took her suggestions with the best grace, particularly when I'd spent some hours or days polishing a particular passage and was told it would have to go. I was occasionally tempted, in the vanity of authorship, to think that I knew Dorothy's life better than she did herself. And I did not feel the responsibility to Dorothy's old friends that sometimes led her to omit stories she felt might hurt their feelings. But in the end, I reminded myself, this is the story of her life, not of mine, and the final say by rights should be hers.

When we turned to her public career and questions of historical accuracy arose, I felt myself on stronger ground in sometimes challenging and correcting Dorothy's memories. On occasions, however, even though the documentary record suggested otherwise, I still chose to go with Dorothy's initial memory. She says, for example, that the announcement of the Party's dissolution in June 1944 came as a shocking surprise to her. At the height of the wartime Grand Alliance against fascism, Party leader Earl Browder decided to replace the Communist Party with a "political association" as a symbol of his conviction that Communists could look forward to a postwar era of class peace and international harmony. Dorothy insists that the first she knew about these plans was when she read an article in the *Los Angeles Times* announcing that the Party had already been dissolved. But Browder had announced his plans in late January 1944; the proposal had been discussed repeatedly in the Party press in the intervening months. As an active Communist, who never let a day go by without reading the *Daily People's World*, how could she have missed it? She can't account for this seeming discrepancy; all she knows is that her memory is one of total shock and dismay. So be it. In this case I think the memory may be wrong, but it's more illuminating historically to let the mistake stand than for me to coax her into allowing me to correct her memory of the period. She *was* shocked; the foreshortened memory of her feelings about Browder's decision only emphasizes its impact. I sought to strike a balance between creating an accurate historical record and presenting Dorothy's way of remembering and reconstructing that record.

Let there be no mistake about it. The story that follows is that of Dorothy Ray Healey. Readers of *Which Side Were You On?* will notice, for example, that Dorothy's attitude toward Earl Browder's "Teheran policy" during the Second World War differs in significant ways from the interpretation I offered in my earlier book. There are a number of other questions of historical and political importance where Dorothy and I part company. This is not intended to be my life story or credo; it's hers. Of course inevitably my own interests, concerns, and blind spots—my "interpretive framework"—have intervened in ways subtle or not so subtle to shape her narrative. A different historian might have asked different questions, emphasized different points, and reworked the language of Dorothy's responses in different ways. The memories of someone who came of political age in the 1930s are here filtered through the sensibility of someone who came of political age in the 1960s. It's really not up to me to render the final judgment as to how small or great a liability that will prove to be. But as far as Dorothy and I are concerned, the message that comes through in this book is authentically her own. As she explained to Joel Gardner a few months after she had resigned from the Communist Party:

> If I were to write a book, I'd make the title of the book . . . a phrase out of the Communist song "The International." . . . The phrase goes, "No more tradition's chains shall bind us." Well, I would make the title of my book "Tradition's Chains Have Bound Us," because my argument would be that just as . . . capitalism operates through the false consciousness that it gives the majority of people who aren't able to perceive the reality of their own lives . . . , so the same thing happens with Marxists . . . . They, too, substitute a false consciousness for a real consciousness . . . . A real revo-

lutionary party [has] to be able to constantly keep alive that challenging, questioning and probing of the real scene around it . . . . Our theory never will quite match the reality, but at least one strives to approximate it, to see what is the substance, and not just the form.

In the end we decided on a different title for Dorothy's book, but we kept the same unifying theme. *Dorothy Healey Remembers* is the story of how Dorothy Healey first wrapped herself in the comforting illusions of "tradition's chains," and then finally cast them off.

1

Mama used to quote Shelley and other poets on freedom. "Strike to earth the chains that bind you/Ye are many, they are few." That was one of her favorites. These democratic, humanist ideals were the best part of what my mother had. She had her own ideas on many things, and she never changed them in all her years in the Party. I think Dorothy inherited that. At one time we used to have very bitter arguments about the Party, and the reason Dorothy stopped and thought about them later was because she was Mama's daughter. ■ Carol Jean Newman, Dorothy's younger sister.

According to _____ the Los Angeles County CP sums subject up as "the refutation of the theory that the children of party actives are never any good in the movement." ■ FBI report on Dorothy Healey, October 29, 1945 [name deleted by the FBI].

I was born in Denver on September 22, 1914, in St. Joseph's Hospital, and named Dorothy Harriet Rosenblum. My mother, Barbara, and my father, Joe, were born in the same year, 1884, in Hungary. They had been brought as children to the United States by their families, my mother arriving in 1888, my father in 1890. Both families independently made their way out to Denver, where my parents met.

I don't remember anything about Hungary. . . . Well, I'll tell you one thing I do remember. I remember that, on Easter, most of the Jews stayed inside the house. Because the peasants used to go around with buckets of water and, whenever they saw any Jew outside, they would throw the water on them. That I remember. . . . We were sitting in a wagon, and I remember that. And my grandparents had come to say good-bye. And both of them had walked for about a mile along in back of the wagon, crying very hard, saying they knew that they would never see us again. And I remember feeling very sad about that, that we would never see them again. But I hardly even remember them. ■ Barbara Nestor, Dorothy's mother. (This and subsequent quotations from Barbara Nestor are from an interview conducted by Sherna Gluck for the Feminist History Research Project in 1974, and are reprinted with permission.)

Papa's family, the Rosenblums, were very proud of their Hungarian background and thought of themselves as more Austro-Hungarian than Jewish. His father, Ignatz, spoke only Hungarian all the years he lived in America. He had been an actor in Hungary, and retained a self-defined "artistic temperment" which seemed primarily to be expressed in a disinclination to find a job. As a result his children all were forced to go to work at a very early age; my father got his first job when he was eleven years old. My father's mother, Marie, who I have only vague memories of, was a tiny woman, and rather feckless. Ignatz and Marie were warm people, but I have the sense that they were not very responsible people. The Rosenblums were a huge clan by the time I got to know them. My father had a brother and two sisters; each of the sisters had about ten children. I saw a lot of the cousins while I was growing up.

Mama's father, Kiva Herman, was what was called in the Jewish community a *shokhet*—someone who supervised the ritual slaughter of animals and poultry to make sure the food was kosher. Unlike my paternal grandparents, he and my grandmother Fanny were very orthodox Jews. The Hermans arrived in Denver very early on and Kiva was evidently the only Jew with any religious title. He was much respected in the Jewish community; people would come to him to settle arguments, and he was called "Rabbi." I remember my grandmother always wore a wig in Orthodox style. It sat on her head very awkwardly, and I used to watch it with fascination, wondering if it would fall off. For all the respect my grandfather enjoyed in the community, he never made much of a living, and so his children too had to go to work. The greatest bitterness of my mother's life, which I was to hear about all through my own childhood, was that she had had to drop out of school when she was in the fourth grade to take care of the younger children (she was the oldest in the family). My grandparents couldn't see the point of a girl going to school. She never forgave them for that.

> My father was an orthodox Jew. He was a great Talmudist, but he had never had any other kind of education, except the Talmud. . . . He was a patriarch and made life absolutely miserable for us, in all the things that "thou shalt not do." Women didn't need an education like men, you know. When I first heard the Jewish prayer that the man says, "I thank Thee, Lord, Thou has made me a man," and the woman says, "I Thank Thee, Lord, Thou made me what Thou sawest fit to make me" . . . it annoyed me, as young as I was. ■ Barbara Nestor.

I have been told that my grandfather Kiva and I were very close, that I looked very much like him, and that of all the grandchildren he was fondest of me. The Hermans used to live right across from the synagogue in Denver. My parents never took me there, so the only time I entered it was in my grandfather's company. Apparently I entered its doors with some trepidation; I once asked my grandfather if the people in the synagogue would know I was Jewish or whether they would try to stop me from entering. He smiled and said, "It's on your forehead. They'll know." Kiva died when I was two. I remember being awakened from my nap and being told that Grandpa was dying and being taken over to the house where Grandma and Grandpa lived on Tenth Street. For some reason his bed was in the kitchen, which was the center of the house. Suddenly this man whom I felt very close to became an object of terror to me. I had to go to the bathroom, which meant that I had to pass by his bed. I remember skirting around it as far from him as I could to go into the other room. It was the first time I had been in the presence of a dying human being.

I could never understand . . . when they said that God chose the Jews. I couldn't understand what he chose them for. They were driven from everywhere, you know, and disliked, and hated, and I knew about Jews. Some were very fine people, and some were just not worth the powder it would take to blow them to Hell. You know? So they were just people. ■ Barbara Nestor

My mother, like all her brothers and sisters, resented and rebelled against the orthodox atmosphere she was forced to grow up in. When she was twelve she decided to become a Christian. She read the Old and the New Testament and decided she like the latter better than the former. It wasn't that she was ashamed to be Jewish—later on Mama would quote approvingly something my older sister Frances once said: "I'm a Jew. I'm neither proud of it, nor ashamed of it." It was just a fact of life for her.

We never observed the sabbath, of course. Mama liked Jewish food, but that was the end of it. I was five years old before I'd ever heard a Jewish word because Mama absolutely refused to speak Yiddish. I never heard Mama speak Yiddish until she was old. All of a sudden when she's eighty-something she starts coming out with Yiddish. And she says to me, "You know what that means, don't you, Carol Jean?" And I say no. And she was so surprised. "You don't know any Yiddish?" "*No*, Mama, how would I know any Yiddish?" ■ Carol Jean Newman. Dorothy's younger sister.

After another two years Mama decided that the New Testament was filled with mythology, just like the Old Testament, and she became a militant atheist. She had long, terrible arguments with my grandfather, which left the man absolutely bewildered as to what to do with her. "How can you say this is a good God, a kind God, this God who creates an Adam and Eve, knows that they're going to sin, knows it ahead of time, and yet deliberately has them tempted in order to cast them out of Paradise?" These stories of disillusionment and rebellion were an important part of my background. I heard her recite them again and again all through my childhood.

I think I was really more questioning than rebellious. It was a long time until I became rebellious. What could you be rebellious against? There was nothing you could do about anything. There you were. But I would often wish that someday we'd find out that I didn't really belong to them, I wasn't really their child, that I had been left there by mistake, or something.
■ Barbara Nestor.

Although her formal education was limited, my mother loved reading. She could lose herself totally in books. She read everything and was a woman of considerable knowledge, if not erudition. People who had ideas, people who could talk knowledgeably about ideas, were the only people who mattered to her. All other aspects of life were secondary. That did not always make life pleasant for her children. As long as one had books, it supposedly didn't make any kind of difference what kind of clothes you wore or what neighborhood you lived in. But you had to have ideas. You had to read. That was the key to everything.

My parents were married in 1907. Mama had been working as a seamstress, an occupation she hated. After she was married she never worked again for money until after Papa died. Before their marriage Papa had been a railroad worker, and then a waiter. After his marriage and until his death in 1932 he worked as a traveling salesman. For a brief period, from 1918 until 1920, they owned a delicatessen in Fort Collins, but it was a total failure. Mama would give away the store to whomever would come in who couldn't afford to buy things. They finally had to give it up and move back to Denver. Papa then went back to work as a salesman; his longest stint was with the J.S. Hoffman Company selling cheese and smoked meat to grocery stores in a territory that stretched from Colorado west to California and north to Oregon and Washington. We moved around a lot because of his job. I went to nineteen schools all told by the time I reached high school. Although we never stayed long enough to establish roots in any one place, my father tried his best to provide us with a comfortable life. Unlike his own father he was a man with an enormous sense of responsibility, but he was never quite able to succeed at anything he tried. We never had enough money. I remember walking with my mother to the store to get a loaf of bread; some way or another she misplaced the bread, which had cost a nickel, and she sat down on the curb and cried, "Where will another loaf of bread come from to feed the family?"

My father loved music. When he was at home we would all gather around the piano. My sister and I both took piano lessons, my brother played the cornet, and Papa would play his mandolin, which was his great love. But he was a tragically unfulfilled man. And it couldn't have been easy for him to be married to my mother. The key to my mother's affections was being able to talk about ideas, and my father did not fall within that category. While growing up I felt love and compassion for my father, but not much respect. I don't think that my feelings about him are necessarily the same as my brother's or my sisters.' He was not the world's brightest man. I remember my mother having to correct his letters and his spoken English. But he was an extraordinarily kind man. I don't remember one time he ever raised his voice to any of us. His customers loved him. The train crews all knew him because he traveled so much and because he'd play the mandolin on his trips. After he died, particularly as she got older, my mother got very nostalgic about their marriage and forgot all the other things. But they were completely mismatched. Early on I remember thinking that they were probably going to get a divorce and speculating to myself which one I would live with. There were advantages both ways. If I went with Papa I would

18

get anything I wanted because he could never say "no." Mama would say "no" (although she only spanked me once in my childhood that I could remember, and she was distraught and in tears for the rest of the day as a result). If it came to it, I knew that I would go with Mama because she was the one who had by the far the greatest influence on me.

> They all said Papa was not very intelligent. I've told Dorothy, "You know, that isn't true. Read Papa's letters." Mama reduced Papa to that appearance, but it wasn't really him. ■ Carol Jean Newman.

Their marriage was tension-ridden for another reason: Mama was constantly getting pregnant. She bore six children. The eldest, Helen, died in 1908 at the age of six. When I was a young girl she had a baby boy who was born dead, strangled in the womb with the umbilical cord wrapped around his neck. My brother Bernard was the oldest surviving child; he was five years older than me; my sister Frances was three years older. Carol Jean, my mother's last child, was born nearly eleven years after I was. My brother Bernard was a very central figure in my childhood. He and my sister Frances got along very well, as did Frances and I. But in the frequent absence of my father, and because I was the baby in the family until Carol Jean came along, Bernard felt he had the responsibility to exert a paternal influence over me. I wouldn't stand for it, and we fought like cats and dogs. My relationship with Frances was as placid as my relationship with Bernard was stormy. We shared a bedroom, and she was always very loving and maternal toward me. Carol Jean's experience with the family, since she was so much younger than the rest of us, was very different than mine.

> I remember one heck of a fight when I was about three years old. Dorothy was a reader—Dorothy was *not* a dishwasher. The three older children took turns doing the kitchen work and she was supposed to do the dishes. My brother's outlook on life was one of extreme rectitude, and he knew that it was her turn and he said, "Get in there and do the dishes." And she said "Banana oil!" (That was a very common expression in the twenties.) And he got very angry, as he was wont to do, and he picked her up from the couch and dropped her. And she started to cry. I got very excited and upset and ran across the street to where my best friend lived, and yelled, "Bernard's killing Dorothy!" They didn't pay too much attention. Bernard did not kill Dorothy. I remember it so vividly because it was violent. She doesn't remember it at all. Isn't it funny how you remember things differently? ■ Carol Jean Newman.

My mother performed thirteen abortions on herself. I was out playing one day when I was six years old, on Montcrief Street in Denver where we lived, and I heard the ambulance come down the street. It stopped at our house, and Mama was taken off in the ambulance to the hospital. She'd gotten blood poisoning from her latest abortion, and almost died of it. I also remember waking up in the middle of the night once and hearing my mother saying "No, no, no, not again!" and running through the house to get away from Papa. He must have been terribly perplexed and wounded by this intense woman he found himself married to. Mama tended to blame herself for everything. She grieved for years for my sister Helen, blaming a "stupid doctor" for causing Helen's death, but blaming herself for taking Helen to him. Her sense of loss haunted my childhood.

When Helen died, something died. It affected my whole life. She was a remarkable little girl. She was in kindergarten, and the kindergarten teacher came to see her when she was so sick. She told me in all the years she had been teaching, she had never met a child so sensitive to others and so bright. As young as she was, she knew about socialism. ■ Barbara Nestor

Helen took on the role of angel in my mother's eyes. She told us Helen never did anything wrong. You can't really compete with a dead kid who's that perfect, though I tried. Dorothy just shut it out, I think. ■ Carol Jean Newman.

Mama also blamed herself for my aunt Esther's disability. She had been rocking Esther in the cradle when she was a baby and Mama a little girl, and as usual Mama was reading as she was doing it, and somehow Esther fell out of the cradle. When Esther grew up with a curvature of the spine, Mama felt it was her fault, though that was nonsense. Mama would be frantic if any of us ever used the word "cripple"; it was a forbidden word in our house. Mama's habitual self-reproach became a kind of family joke among our relatives, who gave her the nickname of "Regret and Remorse." She'd lock herself up in the bathroom and sob, or go storming out of the house weeping. We'd all be terrified that she was going to try and kill herself. If Mama went out by herself in one of her states, one of us would immediately get up and follow her to make sure she didn't try to commit suicide. My memories of Mama's moodiness were not as intense as Bernard's and Francis's, but even I was affected by them.

I say "even I" because I had a tendency from early childhood on of removing myself from unpleasant things in the family. I lived in a world of my own. Soon after my younger sister Carol was born, my aunt Esther came for a visit. I was sitting in the living room reading, and Mama and Esther were talking in the kitchen, and I heard Mama say, "Even Dorothy loves the baby." "Even Dorothy" became a stock family joke, because the idea that I would exhibit any normal emotions seemed so out of character. The fact that I was reading when Mama made the comment was also characteristic. Like Mama, and because of her influence, I became an omnivorous reader. When there was a family fight, or I was in a new place and likely to feel lonely, I could always find refuge in books. When we first moved to Oakland I was about eight years old. I didn't know any kids in the neighborhood yet, so I went to the barrel of books which was sitting unpacked on the front porch, dipped my hands in, and just kept going from one book to the next. When I didn't have friends, because I was new to a school, and had to eat lunch alone, I always found that books compensated. I don't know what I read, but they couldn't have been children's books because we really didn't have very many children's books. When I was twelve I picked up one of my mother's books, *Sons and Lovers*. When Mama discovered I was reading it she took it away and hid it. I couldn't understand why, until I reread it at sixteen and thought, "Oh, that's what she didn't want me to read." Anything that was the printed word was grist for my mill.

Early on Dorothy took on a demeanor that was not true to herself, a false front that protected her. She *appeared* to be very outgoing, but inside she was not like that. Dorothy is capable of real affection, but she's vulnerable, and so she puts on this. . . . She's acted this way long enough so that it's become her persona. She can't tell the difference any more. ■ Carol Jean Newman.

I had started what became the practice of a lifetime of not acknowledging what I really felt inside of me and fending off any inquiry. I didn't allow myself to think about things that bothered or upset me. As a result, it was always difficult for me to learn anything from what I did. I didn't draw many conclusions. I'd just keep going into things and not thinking about them afterward, tumbling from one experience to another. If I was wounded or rejected I didn't brood about it like Mama would have; I just started thinking about something else. Even though I read so much, I was never introspective. Nor was I shy. Once we were in a neighborhood long enough for me to get to know the other kids, I was very much a tomboy and an instigator of plays, and clubhouses, and gangs, and the like. In fact I usually would get to know the neighbors long before anyone else in the family did—which made the rest of the family shudder, because I was prone to discussing all our intimate secrets with whomever was willing to listen to me. And perhaps because I avoided thinking about my own problems, I was always intrigued by other people, finding out what made them tick, why they did what they did and thought what they thought. In some ways it turned out to be good preparation for life as an organizer.

When my father found out that I had gone to a Socialist meeting when I was sixteen and a half years old, he said, "What were you doing in a Socialist meeting?" And I said, "Papa, what do you really know about Socialism?" And he says, "Well, they say that Socialism doesn't really believe in God, and they don't believe in getting married or anything." I said, "Look, Papa, socialism has nothing to do with God or anything. Socialism is only that they believe that everybody should have the chance to develop whatever they have, that everybody is just as good as everybody else. No one is any better, no matter how high they are, or how low they are. They're all human beings. . . . " He says, "But that's what God wants." I said, "Then the socialists are trying to do what God wants because that's socialism." ■ Barbara Nestor.

Having given up two religions by her early teens, Mama was looking for something else to believe in. In 1900, when she was sixteen, she heard J. Stitt Wilson give a talk on socialism. This was the year that Eugene Debs made his first run for the presidency as a socialist candidate. Stitt was a minister and prominent socialist who in 1911 would be elected mayor of Berkeley. Stitt's talk had an enormous impact on Mama. This was the thing that she had been looking for, and she joined the Socialist Party soon afterward. Having decided that socialism was the answer, there was never a day thenceforth in her life when she wavered in her beliefs or in her commitment to activism.

Grandma never went out of the house without some kind of little shopping bag, something to carry literature, because you never knew who you were going to bump into, you never knew when you were going to make a convert. If at the end of the day you hadn't succeeded in selling it or giving it to somebody, you could leave it on the bus, you could leave it in a public rest room, you never know when you're going to make a friend. ■ Richard Healey, Dorothy's son.

When I was growing up our house was always filled with people coming and going, and talking, all with the settled conviction that socialism was the wave of the future. Papa was sympathetic, but never joined, and really did not like the fact that his wife became so involved in politics. But he'd never say, "You can't do these things." As far as the rest of the family was concerned, Mama's political views were looked upon as just another one of her vagaries.

The workers' flag is deepest red/It shrouded oft our martyred dead/And ere their limbs grew stiff and cold/Their life-blood dyed its every fold/Then raise the scarlet standard high/Beneath its folds we'll live and die/Though cowards flinch and traitors sneer/We'll keep the red flag flying here. ■ "The Red Flag," tune: "O Tannenbaum," lyrics by James Connell.

I attended my first socialist meetings when I was still in diapers. Of course there was no such thing as a baby-sitter in our house, so either the children would go into the meeting with her—I remember standing up on a table at one meeting and singing "The Red Flag"—or we were left out in the car. My brother made good use of those occasions; I would be asleep inside the car and he would stop passersby and ask if they would like to see the "frozen princess" inside. He'd charge them a penny to look in. I also remember a streetcar strike in Denver in 1918. My mother's brother Paul was one of the strikers. We followed around the streetcars that were operated by strikebreakers, shaking our fists and screaming names at them like "dirty scab."

My first-grade teacher mixed me up with another child who had the same name and blamed me for something she had done. I never did anything bad, I was such a good kid. So I got very upset and started to cry, and then said the worst thing I could think of to her, "You, you, you capitalist, you. . . ."She looked stricken and said, "Wouldn't you like to go lie down, dear?" I didn't know any swear words, and I thought I had said something terrible to her. ■ Carol Jean Newman.

Mama was a woman of great passion and expressed her beliefs with great vehemence. All her life she would go into tirades about capitalism every time she read a newspaper. Sometimes, in later years, I would come home and Mama would be all upset about something she had heard on the radio, and she would begin lecturing me once again on the evils of capitalism, waving her arms, and I would have to tell her, "But Mama, I'm *already* a Communist." Her hatred of war matched her hatred of captialism. I remember her taking us to the preparedness parades that were being held on the brink of American entry into the First World War. We were standing beside her and she sang out in a very loud voice: "I didn't raise my son to be a soldier! I raised him up to be my pride and joy!"

Sometime in her nineties, still a militant, still a fighter, Grandma was reminiscing about her life to me, and she said, "Ricky, do you know what I think was the greatest mistake I ever made?" And, you know, I waited with bated breath. What could it have been? She had a lot of years to make mistakes. What she identified was that when the Socialist Party split from the IWW in 1912, she went with the Socialists, and she said, "They were all right, but the IWW were the real fighters." ■ Richard Healey.

As a split began to develop within the Socialist Party in the years leading up to the war, my mother instinctively sided with the party's left wing. She thought very highly of the Industrial Workers of the World, who were then quite strong in the West. And she worked in support of the Ludlow, Colorado, miners, who went out on strike against a Rockefeller coal company, and whose families were gunned down by hired-gun thugs in their tent colony in April 1914, just a few months before I was born. Like a lot of socialists in the western states, Mama didn't need the Bolshevik revolution to teach her that the struggle for socialism was class war. But when the revolution came in Russia, she saw it as the affirmation of her own beliefs.

I put the ravages of that black orgy of April 20th, when a frail fluttering tent city in the meadow, the dwelling place of 120 women and 273 children, was riddled to shreds without a second's warning, and then fired by coal-oil torches with the bullets still raining and the victims screaming in their shallow holes of refuge. . . . I put that crime, not upon its perpetrators, who are savage, but upon the gentlemen of noble leisure who hired them to this service. . . . This is no local brawl in the Rockies. . . . What happened here is the most significant, as it is the most devastating human thing that has happened in America since Sherman marched to the sea. ■ Max Eastman, "Class War in Colorado," *The Masses*, June 1914.

Along with most of her Denver comrades, when the split came in 1919 Mama abandoned the Socialist Party and became a charter member of the new Communist Party. Of course at the time none of this was clear to me; all I remember is a blur of radical songs from the period. Soon after Mama joined the Communist Party it went underground. She lost contact with it when we left Denver and began moving around from city to city in California.

I was the cause for my parents' decision to move to California in 1921. I was a sickly child, and the doctors felt that the Colorado winters were too cold for me. We lived in Long Beach, Los Angeles, and Oakland (moving back and forth between Los Angeles and Oakland several times) before finally arriving in Berkeley, where I went to junior high and high school. On the train ride out to California Mama warned me that I mustn't tell anyone I was really seven. I was always very small for my age, and Mama didn't want to pay for a train ticket for me, and if you were under seven you could ride for free. But I was as always very sociable, so I immediately made friends with everybody and started visiting. I walked up the aisle talking to some stranger, saying that I was really seven years old but that Mama didn't have the money for the extra ticket. The conductor was walking right behind me at that very moment, and Mama was sitting across the aisle, looking stricken. The conductor smiled and patted me on the head as he walked by.

Junior high was the first time I was able to have a steady circle of friends. But like any other adolescent, I started feeling terrible self-conscious about all kinds of things about my appearance, especially my clothes. My mother, of course, thought that people should ignore such nonsensical bourgeois details as how you looked and what you wore. The important thing was what was in your mind. Besides, we didn't have much money. So she used to make our clothes, and she was a terrible seamstress. I remember in particular two dresses she made for me. Somebody must have given her the cloth. One was pink linen trimmed in brown, and the other was brown linen trimmed in pink. I wore those all through my junior high school days and hated them both. Intimidated by Mama's moral fervor, I never said to her how much I detested them. I imagine if I had said to her, "I hate those dresses, and I won't wear them," she would have found some way of getting me other clothes. She would have done anything for her children. But I was ashamed to say how much those dresses embarrassed me. I never learned the things that other girls were taught while growing up, how to fix your hair, or how to choose clothes.

Dorothy once said to someone, "How can anyone take a half hour to get dressed? I can always get dressed in five minutes." And the other person said, "Dear, you look it." She told me the story and laughed about it, but I'm sure it hurt her. ■ Carol Jean Newman.

At Garfield Junior High School in Berkeley most of my friends were the top students, which meant that they were also the most well-off kids, who lived up in the Berkeley hills, while we lived down in the lowlands. This was where I first met Kenneth May, who was the son of a professor at the university. We became friends, and he was the one who got me invited to parties up in the hills. (Years later we would reconnect when we were both members of the Communist Party.) When I was invited to my first party by these kids, I agonized over what I would wear. Part of the problem was that I was just beginning to develop physically. It was my fate to be quite buxom, and I was embarrassed and unhappy about my breasts. For years I didn't go to the beach so that I wouldn't have to wear a bathing suit. I had a party dress of sorts, and wound up putting a scarf over it that didn't match in order to hide the fact that I had breasts.

Those feelings of shame about my body were something else I got from my mother, who very clearly didn't like sex or sexuality. We once had a "mother-daughter" chat about sex, and the main thing I got from it was a sense of how distasteful she found the whole subject. This woman who was so emancipated in so many other things inculcated in me the idea that you didn't let a man kiss you unless you were in love with him. So, later on, if I kissed a man, I kidded myself into thinking that I loved him, which led to complications. As a teenager I was a complete sexual innocent, and would be a virgin on my wedding night.

I had three children in two years and seven months. . . . I read Margaret Sanger. And I did whatever Margaret Sanger did. But it didn't do me one bit of good. ■ Barbara Nestor.

I had my first serious boyfriend, Emile Rabin, when I was fifteen. Emmy and I went to Russian River together for a weekend once and slept in the same bed, but I kept my bathing suit on all night. The thought of doing anything else wouldn't have even crossed my mind. Emmy was involved in one famous family quarrel. In the summer of 1930, when I was fifteen, Mama and Carol Jean were visiting in Los Angeles with my grandmother and aunt Esther. Papa was on the road, so Bernard, Frances, and I were alone in the house in Berkeley. I decided I would hitchhike down to Los Angeles with Emmy, but Bernard told me I couldn't go and proceeded to lock me in my bedroom as a precaution. I wound up making a rope out of the bedsheets, sliding down out of my second-story window, and making my escape. Bernard telegrammed my mother to report on my misbehavior, but I arrived in L.A. before the wire did. Though I resented Bernard's authoritarianism, I respected his intelligence and learned a great deal from him, particularly about politics.

By the time I was twelve years old, there was absolutely no question in my mind what I was going to be when I grew up. Today I'd call it a "professional revolutionary." I didn't use such language then, but I knew by that time that when I grew up my life was going to be devoted to the revolution. Along with discussions with my mother, one of the greatest influences on me was reading Upton Sinclair's novels, books which no one remembers any more, like *King Coal, Oil,* and *Jimmy Higgins* (not *The Jungle,* which I found boring). I just throbbed with indignation over the unhappiness of the miners and the oil workers and the injustice and cruelty of the bosses.

And Mary found the magic word. "We'll have a union!" she shouted. "We'll get together and stay together! If they refuse us our rights, we'll know what to answer—we'll have a *strike*!" There was a roar like the crashing of thunder in the mountains. . . . The girl rushed on—exhorting with leaping words and passionate out-flung arms—a tall, swaying figure of furious rebellion. . . . And the crowd around her—they were sharing the wonderful rebirth; their waving arms, their swaying forms responded to Mary as an orchestra to the baton of a leader. ■ Upton Sinclair, *King Coal*, 1917.

My concept of what it meant to be a revolutionary was based on a montage of the organizers from the Sinclair novels, along with my childhood memories from Denver. I also began to read an enormous amount of history around this time. I was very taken with Charles Beard—at that point his writings seemed to me to represent great Marxist truths because he talked about the things that high school history never talked about, the underlying economic motives of history makers. I read everything he and his wife Mary Beard wrote. I had started reading Marx and Lenin, but at that point I think Walt Whitman and Henry David Thoreau had more effect on me. What I responded to in my readings were emotional rather than theoretical questions. I was developing a hatred of the brutality of the existing economic system, a hatred of the impersonal degradation of human beings. That's what moved me as a teenager, and stayed with me.

In 1928, my brother Bernard enrolled at the University of California in Berkeley and through him we reestablished contact with the Communist Party. He joined the Social Problems Club at the university, and there he came in contact with students who belonged to the Young Communist League (YCL). This was an election year, and the Communists were running William Z. Foster as their presidential candidate, and there was a lot of excitement about that among radical students. Our house was always filled with these students, some of whom were Communists. One person I remember meeting in particular was Meyer Baylin, who was then a Young Communist activist (in 1932 he would be arrested along with three others for jumping onto the track in the summer Olympics in Los Angeles, carrying a banner that read "Free Tom Mooney"); he would go on to be the CP section leader in San Pedro when I arrived there as a YCL organizer in the mid-1930s.

Mama formally rejoined the Communist Party in 1928, although she had considered herself a Communist all along. I was ready to join the YCL as soon as anyone asked me to. And so when my brother asked me to go to a YCL meeting with him, on December 1, 1928, I was beside myself with happiness. I joined the YCL that very night. Meyer Baylin handed me my YCL card. It turned out to be the most important decision in my life. I was fourteen.

2

The YOUNG COMMUNIST LEAGUE U.S.A. teaches and organizes the young workers to fight for the abolition of the capitalist government and the establishment of a workers' and farmers' government, like that of the Soviet Union. . . . The YOUNG COMMUNIST LEAGUE is the only youth organization that conduct [sic] its propaganda among the young workers in the shops, factories, within the army, navy, R.O.T.C. and C.M.T.C. and National Guards to fight against capitalist militarization, imperialist war, and for the defendse [sic] of the Soviet Union. ■ excerpt from "An Appeal to Young Workers," mimeographed pamphlet issued by the California YCL, 1930.

On February 25, 1931 subject was received at the Alameda County Detention Home, Oakland, California, under the name of DOROTHY RAY 1340 Josephine Street, Berkeley, from the Oakland Police Department. A petition, sworn to on February 26, 1931 alleges that on February 25, 1931, DOROTHY RAY did maliciously disturb the peace and quiet in the neighborhood of 11th and Broadway, Oakland, by loud and unusual noises and by tumultuous and offensive conduct and by then and there threatening, traducing, quarreling and challenging to fight certain police officers of Oakland. . . . [The record of the case] reveals further that she had passed out literature known as the "Daily Worker" on the streets of Oakland and caused the disturbance by inciting by-standers to unite against the police and act for the so-called "workers." The record disclosed that HEALEY felt she was doing right by helping the unfortunate unemployed, and that she was determined to continue her work. . . . ■ FBI memo, June 28, 1951.

I remember very clearly the first Young Communist League meeting I attended. It was held in Fraternity Hall on Peralta Street in Oakland. The Communist Party was in the middle of the last big factional fight of the 1920s, pitting the forces led by William Z. Foster against those led by Jay Lovestone. A Party leader by the name of Martin Young was there, representing Foster, and someone else was there representing Lovestone. They had a big debate that night, and afterward we all voted on whom we supported. Foster won by a large margin. I didn't understand a word of the debate. I just voted the way my brother and his friends voted, for Foster. Even now, if you go back and read through the polemics in that fight, they would be hard to understand, with both sides phrasing their arguments in absolutely ridiculous abstractions that had nothing to do with reality. Since that was my first YCL meeting I really had no business or right to vote, but Meyer Baylin, who was acting as the branch treasurer, and who was a Foster supporter, stamped my card "paid in full for the whole year" so that I could support his side.

Joining the YCL made a big difference in my life in all kinds of ways. I quickly lost interest in the friends I had made in junior high school. The parties I had started being invited to up in the hills had never really been fun for me anyway. I knew that they were important somehow and I was supposed to be enjoying myself, but I never really relaxed at them or felt a part of the group. They were rich—by my standards anyway—and I wasn't. And none of them talked about anything that I found very interesting or exciting. So I drifted apart from them, or maybe they cut me off as I got more involved in YCL activities. In any case the YCL provided a kind of ready-made alternative gang for me. Most of my YCL comrades were older, in their late teens and early twenties, and that also had a great appeal to me. I grew particularly close to Minnie Carson, who was Peggy Dennis's sister, and to Minnie's husband, Al Bock, who were both about ten years older than I was. They lived on Twin Peaks in San Francisco and I would go over there every moment I could to be with them. I don't know how they put up with me, but I was entranced, like any fourteen-year-old would be, by being accepted by these marvelous sophisticated adult friends. Of course they also made my former upper-middle-class friends in junior high seem much less glamorous by comparison.

My classes in school soon lost all their meaning for me. Good grades had always come easily to me, especially in English and history, and I had skipped a grade while in grammar school. But once I was in the YCL, school became only a sort of shadow existence that I had to get through. I don't remember attending a single extracurricular high school activity. My high school adviser was genuinely distressed by the increasing indifference I showed to my classes. She thought I was college bound, and called my mother in on two occasions to find out why I was not doing the work that I could do. Mama was furious, because she really believed in the value of education, and both my brother and older sister had been very good students. But I had nothing but contempt for "bourgeois education." The classes in school were for children, and were mostly brainwashing anyway. Why should I care? After all I was now a part of the people who really knew and understood what were the realities of our society. Being in the YCL, we were part of the chosen, the select. It gave you more than a sense of identity—it certified your superiority. Besides, YCL activities took up at least two or three evenings a week, which didn't leave me much time for my homework even if I had had the inclination to do it.

The only classes I felt I could learn anything from were those that the Party sponsored. These were held in Finn Hall at Berkeley. I remember hearing Sam Darcy, who was then the Party's District Organizer for what was known as District 13 (including California and Arizona), giving a class on philosophy and denouncing Schopenhauer as a "peanut philosopher." This was the real stuff. Nothing in high school could compare to it. I've completely forgotten why

Darcy thought Schopenhauer was a peanut philosopher, and of course never bothered reading him afterward to find out. I was too young to have much contact with Darcy in those days, but others have credited him with playing a significant role in getting the Party in California involved in labor struggles in agriculture and on the waterfront. I do remember his ability to stand up on a soapbox, holding the financial page from the daily newspaper, and make a fascinating speech about the social realities behind the dry statistics.

> The California Party was very fortunate that it had Darcy when it needed a man like Darcy, in the early 1930s, when there were the hard struggles in the Valley—flamboyant, dramatic, a hell of an agitator—and it had [Bill] Schneiderman for the Popular Front period in the later 1930s, when it was a question of tactics, relationships, and administration. ■ Al Richmond. [Richmond, who joined the YCL in New York the same year Dorothy joined in Berkeley, came to California in 1938 to help start a new Party newspaper, the *People's World*. He would serve as the paper's editor until 1968.]

It was action, not theory, that entranced me. I think I was very typical of young and even not-so-young Communists in my attitude. Offhand I would guess that the great majority of Communists, maybe 60 to 70 percent of the Party, never got around to reading much of Marx or Lenin. The Trotskyists were so good at theoretical debates because they had more time to read; they weren't doing the level of activity that we were. When I did get around to reading Lenin later in the 1930s, I read him strictly from my interest in history as history. I wasn't at all interested in nor did I understand the theoretical questions that were involved. It wasn't until the birth of my son in the 1940s, when I was at home for a time, that I reread Marx and Lenin, and the power of their ideas finally hit me. Then theory became exciting.

Of course the YCL always held—in theory—that theory was important. You were supposed to read either one hour before you went to bed at night or get up early and read one hour in the morning. You were even checked up on to make sure you were getting the reading done. But there was never any relationship between what the reading was and what went on in YCL meetings. It was all action, action, action. I would get annoyed with young Communists in the 1960s who never seemed to read anything, and I had to remind myself of my own experience in the 1930s. The one useful reading habit I picked up in the YCL, which stayed with me a lifetime, was the thoroughness with which you were expected to read the capitalist press. You never would dream of letting a day go by in which you hadn't read the newspaper, because you had to be able to speak about current events at street-corner meetings and sound like you knew what you were talking about. But the theoretical questions didn't mean much until you had some political background which they could help illuminate. You had to build up enough experience so that the theory mattered.

We took the discipline very seriously. Whatever assignments you had for the week you had to report on at the next week's YCL meeting. We always started with a checkup on last week's assignments. Had you carried out your assignment distributing leaflets or selling the newspaper or putting up posters? If you hadn't, you'd be the object of terrible criticism. For those of us who survived it, it was an invaluable training. An awful lot of people obviously didn't survive it, and it was quite understandable why. There was no such thing as a division between your personal and your political life. You were supposed to be totally selfless and dedicated to the revolution.

That was the ideal; in reality people could set their own limits. I once had a great fight with Archie Brown, who became one of the Communist leaders in the International Longshoremen's and Warehousemen's Union in San Francisco. Archie was a newsboy when he was recruited into the Young Communist League, a rough, tough, street kid. I remember riding on a streetcar with him from Berkeley to Oakland to go to a meeting. I was fourteen and he must have been sixteen. I had just read Krupskaya's *Memories of Lenin*, and the thing that impressed me was on the question of sex, how Lenin had decried promiscuity, using the example of the glass of water—that just as you wouldn't want your lips to be on a glass that was muddied by other people's lips, the same was true in a sexual relationship. Archie was having a lot of interesting sexual relationships at the time, and I told him this story very self-righteously. After all Lenin had said it, and anything Lenin said was supposed to be the final word on any question you wanted answered. I was absolutely appalled when Archie turned to me and said, "Look, I will follow anything that Lenin says on politics, but I understand that in Lenin's apartment there were two very narrow beds at opposite ends of the bedroom, one for Krupskaya and one for Lenin, and they didn't even sleep together. *That guy knew nuttin' about sex!* That's for sure! And I'm not taking my leadership from him!" I was very shocked at this.

In the event you ran afoul of authority in the YCL, the discipline was unevenly applied. I was called up for disciplinary action several times. Once I was sitting in the back of the truck that was taking us to the National Guard armory to distribute leaflets. (That was part of what we called "A.M." work, antimilitarism.) I fell asleep and the bundle fell off the truck, and I was brought up on charges of irresponsibility. I had to go across the bay to San Francisco to appear before a Party discipline commission. I was absolutely terrified. I felt like I was approaching the guillotine. I remember Harrison George, an old Wobbly who would go on to become the first executive editor of the *People's World*, was one of those sitting on the commission. They were all amused by having this fifteen-year-old child appearing before them, clearly scared to death. They just gently told me to stay awake in the future. The next time I was brought up on charges was for having hitchhiked down to Los Angeles with Emmy Rabin. I had neglected to get permission from the YCL to leave for the weekend. You weren't supposed to leave the city without permission. Again I got off with a warning, but it made a big impression on me. The most important thing you learned was to be able to do things you really didn't like to do—going house to house selling newspapers, ringing doorbells, walking miles to get where you were going (nobody ever rode anywhere in those days), learning to always come to meetings on time. I remember the lectures we were given about always being prompt: if you were five minutes late to a meeting it might cost your comrade his life. It's a habit that stayed with me all my life. I get frantic if I think I'm going to be five minutes late to an appointment. As a result I've wasted many hours getting to meetings on time and waiting for everyone else to show up. For those of us who wanted to become professional revolutionaries, such habits were expected to be as natural as breathing.

> To all workers of Oakland unemployed and employed:
> Every worker in Oakland is menaced by the threat of unemployment and starvation. . . . Unemployment is the result of the capitalist system, where a few own the factories and we millions must slave for them or die of starvation. When they can make profits out of us, they buy our labor power: when they cannot, we starve. ■ excerpt from a leaflet issued by the California Communist Party and Young Communist League, March 1930.

I joined the YCL at an auspicious moment. Less than a year after I joined, the stock market crashed, and within months millions of workers had lost their jobs. Capitalism was collapsing, just as we had predicted. Even before the depression started we had been going out to factory gates to distribute leaflets calling for workers to form unions and join the Party-organized Trade Union Unity League (TUUL).

There was one YCL branch that covered all of the East Bay. I was at first assigned to work in West Berkeley, which had a large Black community, where we put a lot of emphasis on questions of racial discrimination. But our main focus was on the need for unemployment relief. There was no government relief then, only private charities and an anemic county welfare system. At the start of the depression many of the unemployed blamed themselves for having lost their jobs, thinking it was all their own fault. Watching the changes in consciousness that took place over the next few years taught me lessons I never forgot, as we moved from agitation to organization and began to form neighborhood-based unemployed councils.

We would hold a meeting or a demonstration, people would be attracted and would join the unemployed council, and the next week they would be the ones leading the demonstration, while we'd be moving on to a new neighborhood to start the process over again. You'd keep doing that so that you were constantly developing new leaders. People grew with the organization and emerged with talents that they had always harbored but never been aware of before. It was an exciting thing to see and to participate in. Through the same process, individuals realized their potential to become leaders while the unemployed changed from being disembodied, fragmented, individuals into a collective force. People began to understand that their misfortunes were not their own fault and that they had rights which were being neglected. And we played an important role in that transformation.

By 1930 we were holding regular street meetings to protest unemployment. In Berkeley they were usually held at the corner of University and San Pablo Avenues, but we put most of our energy into the demonstrations in Oakland, which were held at the corner of Tenth and Broadway, in the center of Oakland's skid row. We started in early that year with small meetings designed to build toward a massive national protest on March 6 (which attracted huge numbers of the unemployed, perhaps as many as a million nationwide). In those street-corner meetings every YCL member was expected to take turns speaking. It didn't make any difference whether you were prepared or unprepared, a natural speaker or terrified by the very thought of it. Willy-nilly, most of us did acquire the ability to stand up in front of a crowd of people and hold their attention, even though very few of us enjoyed doing it. You had to fight to get the audience, and fight to keep the audience. The passersby weren't there to hear you; you had to grab their attention and keep it. You had to learn to speak naturally, as if it were all coming off the top of your head. You couldn't read a written speech at a street meeting. We didn't have loudspeakers in those days, so you had to learn to project your voice above the traffic noise and the street hubbub. And you had to learn to withstand heckling; there was a lot of heckling. My father happened to come by when I was speaking on a street corner some time in February 1930 before the big demonstrations took place, and he was just heart-broken to find his little daughter down there speaking to all those (as far as he was concerned) "bums." Later on I would do a lot of speaking on college cam-puses and people would sometimes compliment me for my ability to remain cool while being heckled. Once you've learned to hold your own on a soap box on skid row, it's no real challenge to stay calm behind a lectern in a comfortable UCLA auditorium.

> Keeping quiet gets us nowhere. We must organize. We must demonstrate. We must show our power—show our strength. Divided, we are weak. United, the working class is powerful. Let us demonstrate our power on March 6th—the day when all over the capitalist world, Demonstrations against Unemployment will take place. . . . The working class of San Fran-cisco must turn out in mass for the Demonstration on March 6th.
> ■ excerpt from leaflet issued by California Communist Party and Young Communist League, March 1930.

This was a formative moment for those of us in the YCL. We learned how to organize from the experience of putting together this big demonstration. Everybody was working very hard on small, practical tasks. All I thought I was learning was how to run the old mimeograph machine in the office. In fact I was absorbing the organizational habits that came to characterize my generation of radicals. We took the question of organization very seriously. In the 1960s New Leftists called a demonstration five days before they wanted it to take place, and they thought distributing one leaflet would produce it. In contrast, starting with that first big unemployed protest in 1930, we understood that you had to have a daily plan of building a demonstration, and that holding a dem-onstration could only be part of a larger strategy. You started with small dem-onstrations in relief offices, or in various neighborhoods around the city, and then built up to a big central demonstration. That's the way to turn out a mass following, so that you're not just bringing out your own militants each time. We didn't organize a demonstration just to express our own outrage at one or another injustice, or, worse, as an occasion for self-display. We brought new people to demonstrations as a way of increasing their knowledge of the power of collective endeavor. We learned that the consciousness of human beings is not a static thing. We learned to watch and measure the process of growth of the people participating. And we could see that organization gave them a power that they hadn't ever had before, and that perfecting that organization was our greatest, indeed our only, hope for success.

Not that we always made it easy for people to line up behind our banners. Our intense feelings of loyalty and devotion toward the Soviet Union proved both a strength and a weakness for us. On the one hand we were inspired by the Soviet example and felt that their success in building a new world was a token of our coming victory. In 1929 Soviet fliers had flown a plane called the *Land of the Soviets* across the Arctic, the first time it had been done. It was also the first time that a Soviet airplane landed in the United States. I went to a reception for them in San Francisco sponsored by a Party-organized group called the Friends of the Soviet Union. These pilots were our Lindberghs. We saw their achievement as proof of the advanced qualities of the new society they represented—the same way a later generation of Communists would regard the Soviet launching of sputnik in the 1950s. I don't remember much of what was said that night—the fliers spoke in Russian and somebody translated for them— but I do remember that they seemed ten feet tall to me.

I had my biggest thrill today. The U.R.S.S. came in at the Oakland Airport. There was an immense mob there. They raised the Soviet and the US flag together. That night James and I went to S.F. It too was wonderful. The first pilot, a representative of Amtorg, Lincoln Steffens, Mrs. Mooney, Clarence Toby, Y.P. [Young Pioneer] delegation, and Professor Kahn of U.C. all spoke. I shouted and waved the red flag. The fliers speak only Russian and Kahn had to translate everything. ■ entry in Dorothy's diary, dated October 19, 1929, with ferry tickets from Oakland to San Francisco pasted below.

That was the positive side of our feelings toward the Soviet Union. The negative side was our belief that the Bolshevik revolution had set the model for social transformation that all countries were destined to follow, and that was the main lesson we had to bring to the American working class. We had what we called "Red Sundays" where we'd all go to an industrial town to sell the *Western Worker* or to hand out leaflets. I would go out to Pittsburg, California, a little company town built around a steel mill. The company police and the city police were indistinguishable in a place like that, and any Communist they got hold of was beaten up. We worked out a system of clandestine leafleting, which worked pretty well. But having gone to all that risk and trouble, what did the leaflets have to say? I'll never forget one leaflet we distributed that was written by the man named Nick Daniels, who was then Party organizer in

Oakland, a Greek-born Communist later deported to Greece. It had a big headline across the top, "WAR, REVOLUTION, DEMONSTRATION," and then a line "Come to a movie about Soviet Russia to learn how to really live." I blush when I think of us distributing that leaflet house to house in Pittsburg. It was the most sectarian thing imaginable. What could it have meant to the workers there? It reminds me of the leaflets you'd see handed out by little radical sects in the 1960s with bold-print slogans like "Smash Imperialism!"

Lacking the imagination to conceive that any physical harm could befall me, and cherishing a romantic image of revolutionary self-sacrifice, I was never afraid to go into places like Pittsburg. I would walk from our house on Josephine Street to West Berkeley two or three times a week to sell the *Young Worker*, which was the paper of the Young Communist League, with absolutely no fear about being out at night in a Black community. And I would go across the bay to meetings in San Francisco and come home alone late at night. My mother would be worried as hell, but it didn't bother me. If I did get a little scared late at night coming home, I'd comfort myself with thoughts of Gorky's "mother," seeing myself crossing the frozen steppes to deliver literature, instructions, or whatever. When the police attacked our demonstrations I was horrified and enraged. But I never pictured anything bad happening to me personally. It was, from what I read, like being a soldier in a war. You don't really think that there is a bullet there that is meant for you. It's always meant for somebody else.

> Everything grew dark and began to whirl before the eyes of the mother. But overcoming her fatigue, she again shouted with the remnants of her power: "People, gather up your forces into one single force!"
> A large gendarme caught her collars with his red hand and shook her. "Keep quiet!"
> The nape of her neck struck the wall; her heart was enveloped for a second in the stifling smoke of terror; but it blazed forth again clearly, dispelling the smoke.
> "Go!" said the gendarme.
> "Fear nothing! There are no tortures worse than those which you endure all your lives!" ■ Maxim Gorky, *Mother*, 1906.

Before I turned sixteen I had been in a number of demonstrations that were violently broken up by the police. Although the FBI listed my first arrest as having taken place at a demonstration in February 1931, the event they described actually took place the previous spring when I was fifteen, on May Day 1930. I had gone down to Tenth and Broadway in Oakland that day, where the demonstration was scheduled to take place. The police had occupied all four corners and refused to allow us to hold a street meeting, so people were just milling around. Party headquarters was a block away. I took a big pile of *Daily Workers* and went back to Tenth and Broadway, and under the guise of selling the papers made a speech. I'd shout out a headline, and then I'd explain what it meant, and every once in a while I'd say, "Buy a *Daily Worker*!" The cops watched me for a few minutes, and then one of them gave a signal to the others, and they just picked me up in their arms and carried me off to a police wagon. It was a very ignominious way to leave the battlefield. They started to take me to the city jail and en route discovered how young I was, so they took me to the juvenile hall, where I was charged with disturbing the peace. This was the first time I used the name Dorothy Ray. I was afraid my father's job might be jeopardized if I was identified as his daughter, so as I faced the booking officer I thought, "What will I call myself?" I don't know why I decided on "Ray," but that became my name. Until 1943 it was the name I continued to use in both my personal and political life.

I stayed in the juvenile detention home about two weeks and proved the absolute despair of the custodians. At first they kept me in total isolation. I think they did it for my protection, fearing I'd be preyed upon by the older girls, since there was a great deal of lesbian activity going on. Despite my politics, they must have decided I was a "nice" girl. Of course I resented it. As soon as I was allowed into the common room with the rest of the girls I started agitating. Every time I was taken downstairs for an interview with the probation officers, I'd start in all over again. Finally there was a hearing with my attorney present. The probation officer stood up and said to the judge, "Your Honor, we'd just as soon be rid of her. All she does is agitate, agitate, agitate, day and night." At any rate, they released me and put me on probation. I was supposed to report to them every month until I was twenty-one. I reported twice because I was curious. I wanted to see what reporting to a probation officer was like. But that was enough to satisfy my curiosity. And it was clear that they were as uninterested as I was, so I never went back, and they never did anything about it.

> When I was about three years old Dorothy had the Young Pioneer group. She used to take me along. I was the youngest by a long shot. She was about fourteen. We'd play hide the thimble, and we'd sing the YCL song. ■ Carol Jean Newman.

In my last few years in high school I was involved in a whole range of Party-organized activities including the Young Pioneers. The Young Pioneers was our children's group. The group I was put in charge of was composed of fifteen or twenty Black kids from Oakland. They came each Saturday morning for the activities we sponsored, games and parties and singing and storytelling, always with a political moral. It was not at all unusual at the time for whites to go into the Black community and organize something like this. We never met any antagonism, although I don't think any of these kids had parents in the Party. Mostly there was a kind of good-natured tolerance for us. The parents didn't have any resources, and there weren't any other agencies providing them with the kind of services we had to offer. After a few months either the kids stopped coming, or I got assigned to something else, I don't know which it was. We made a more serious impact in the Black community by organizing around the Scottsboro case. We would go house to house, knocking on doors with a little tin can collecting money for their defense, and selling the International Labor Defense (ILD) newspaper *Labor Defender*.

In 1931 the Young Communist League made a decision that I should go to work in a cannery in San Jose. I already had been working in the summers in a cannery in Emeryville. But this was to be more than a summer job: this was industrial "colonization," and I was getting my first real experience as a union organizer. In order to take on the assignment I dropped out of high school a month before I would have finished my senior year. Mama was terribly disappointed because she wanted me to go to college. Both my brother and sister had gone to the university. Bernard would go on to become a doctor. In spite of her Communist loyalties, Mama considered the Young Communist League to have been a terrible influence on me. Here I was casually flinging away the chance for the education that she had been denied in her childhood. I could have refused the YCL assignment, of course, and nothing would have happened, but finishing school made no difference to me at the time.

I got a job in a peach cannery owned by the California Packing Corporation. It was a big cannery, with hundreds of workers, and even in the middle of the depression it was easy to get hired because the work was so bad and the pay so low. I was paid twenty-five cents an hour. As a minor, I wasn't even supposed to work there without a child labor permit, which I didn't have. One day the word was passed that the Deputy State Labor Commissioner was coming through, and I was sent to the bathroom and told to stay in the toilet until he left. The inspectors knew we were there, but it didn't make any difference. I was put to work pitting peaches. There were three boxes in front of you where you'd put the peaches depending on how ripe they were. The "pie box" was reserved for the fruit that was the most decayed, rotten and dirty, including the fruit that had fallen on the ground. I wouldn't eat fruit pies for years after that because I knew what went into them.

I couldn't have been on the job more than six weeks when the strike began in the cannery where I was working in response to a 20 percent wage cut. The strike was called by the Cannery and Agricultural Workers Industrial Union, which was part of the Trade Union Unity League. The workers in two other canneries walked out the same day we did, and the strike soon spread up and down the Santa Clara Valley. I was the only organizer the union had working on the inside of my cannery. The workers in my cannery were mostly Anglo women. But in the other canneries there were large numbers of Mexican women. I tried to talk to each worker on the line. They were very receptive, perhaps a little amused by the spectacle of this child doing all this agitating. They knew I was a Communist, and it didn't seem to make any difference to them. I didn't have to get them to sign a union membership card, I just tried to get them to identify with the common cause. I was learning how to listen to workers to discover what it was they considered wrong with their conditions. Lots of times on the outside what you considered the terrible things about a job were not the things that would have the greatest effect on those actually doing the job. On another occasion at a Los Angeles walnut plant, I had been trying to organize a strike around the issue of wages and had not met with much success. What finally brought about a spontaneous walkout on the part of the workers was the fact that as they stood at the tables sorting the nuts, splinters from the legs of the tables would tear their stockings. They were just infuriated by this. It was not the kind of issue that I would have thought up to organize around. In order to be successful as an organizer you first had to acquire the ability to listen to what the workers had on their minds, and then you had to learn to articulate coherently back to them what they already felt in a disconnected or fragmented way.

When the strike began, the employers saw to it that we could not find a hall to rent in all of San Jose. Nor were we allowed the use of any public spaces. Whenever we would hold strike meetings in St. James Square in San Jose, the police would come and break them up. My good friend from San Francisco, Minnie Carson, was one of the most effective strike organizers. On one of the first days of the strike the police threw tear gas canisters at us while she was giving a speech in the park, and one of them hit Minnie and cut her cheek wide open. She had a scar there for the rest of her life. Alex Noral, another strike leader, and I rushed her to the hospital. Whenever we were attacked by the police I would become absolutely hysterical with anger and fury. When the kids in the 1960s started calling the police "pigs," many of the older people in the Party were offended by it. I never was. We had yelled other names at the police in the 1930s, like "cossack," but we meant the same thing. In the end, of course, they succeeded in breaking the strike. We were unable to hold it together for more than a week, since we could never have a meeting without being attacked.

> The strikers were faced with intimidation and suppression from local authorities, provoked in part by the aggressive tactics of the union. Open mass meetings and parades were broken up by police. Large numbers of special deputies were reported sworn in, riots occurred, and numerous strikers were arrested. The strike was lost and none of the union demands were met by the employers. The rank and file was disillusioned with the C&AWIU, and for the remainder of its career the union had little or no influence in the canning industry in California. ■ "Cannery Worker's Strike, Santa Clara County, July 1931," U.S. Department of Labor, *Labor Unionism in American Agriculture*, Bulletin No. 836, 1945, p. 85.

Until the founding of the CIO in the mid-1930s, the Party's attitude was that strikes like the one in San Jose had an importance in themselves, regardless of the outcome. You never really lost a strike because each strike was, supposedly, a revolutionary training experience in which the workers' hatred of capitalism would harden. Such notions had a bad effect. We didn't understand the need for consolidating our gains, to make our unions serve the workers as a union, to provide leadership and continuity. We had the same illusion that had done so much harm to the IWW in its heyday. We had to learn that you cannot keep workers in an interminable state of emotion and upheaval. There has to be a breathing space, a time to consolidate. Those unions in the Trade Union Unity League with more experienced leadership, like the marine workers and the needle trades, understood that to an extent. In unorganized industries, like the canneries and agriculture, we had to learn those lessons for ourselves. In San

Jose when the strike was broken we were left with nothing, no organized supporters or experienced leaders to provide the basis for future organizing attempts. The CIO later did organize that cannery, but as far as I known it had no connection with our earlier effort.

When I returned to the Bay Area late that summer of 1931 I decided to marry Lou Sherman. I was not yet seventeen. Lou was a twenty-one year-old YCL member. "Sherman" was his Party name. He was the brother of Bill Schneiderman, who later became chairman of the Communist Party in California. Lou was a good-natured man. We never fought, but we did not have a lot in common. There were two factors in my wanting to get married: one was to be married for the sake of being married (you didn't feel that you had made it if you didn't either have a boyfriend or were married); the other thing was to get away from home. I really don't know why I had this feverish desire to get away from home, because my mother didn't really interfere with my life. She tried occasionally, but in the end I always ended up doing what I wanted.

> My mother firmly believed that no woman could be happy without a man. She really believed that. She would say, over and over, "No matter what they say, every woman wants a husband." Perhaps that influenced Dorothy, that she really didn't have it until she had a husband. I remember the day she got married to Lou. She was 16. She bought a blue organdy dress at a thrift shop that morning. I remember thinking there was something funny about buying your wedding dress at a thrift shop the day you were getting married. There was something poignant about it. I was very young, but I still felt that way. ■ Carol Jean Newman.

I got pregnant almost immediately after I married Lou. Minnie had discovered a new birth control method, a kind of foam device, which did not work well at all. She and I and another friend all got pregnant while using it. Her husband Al went to see Inez Williams, who was to become famous as the abortion queen of northern California, to negotiate abortions for the three of us. First he asked the price of one abortion, which turned out to be fifty dollars. Al said, "Well, what if I bring in a second woman?" Inez said, "Well, then the price would go down five dollars, forty-five dollars each for two." And then he says, "Well, what if I bring in a third?" And she replied, "My God, I'll put you on the payroll!" Of all my abortions—I would have two others—it was the most scientifically done. Inez had a very good establishment. It was a big building in San Francisco. There were doctors and nurses, and it was all very efficient. I went home to my mother, stayed in bed a day, and that was it. It was just taken for granted we would have the abortions. Who could think of a revolutionary having a child? We couldn't take time off, it was unthinkable.

Soon after Lou and I got married we moved to East Oakland, where for a short time I served as YCL organizer. One of the reasons we were able to do so much in those days was because nobody had a job. That meant the Party gained the use of dozens of full-time organizers who would otherwise have found paying jobs. "Moscow gold" wasn't much in evidence. People scraped by in various ways. We lived in the absolute worst slums of Oakland. My brother, who was then in college and struggling to get by himself, came to visit me one time. He was horrified by the place we lived in. When he left I found a ten-dollar bill that he'd left under the vase on the table. My sister Frances, who had a job in Los Angeles with Sears Roebuck, making all of sixteen dollars a week, would also pitch in. Things would get a little easier later on with onset of the New Deal programs. Then it became possible to get a job, as for example I would in San Francisco in 1935 with the National Youth Administration, which gave you enough to live on and left you plenty of time for organizing. Until then, we really scrounged. There was some kind of food stamp program operating in Oakland in the early 1930s, and on Saturday nights my great indulgence was to go across the street to the grocery store and use my food stamps to get a package of cigarettes and the *Ladies Home Journal*, and go back up to my dinky apartment and have the whole evening to myself, just reading, and feeling so decadent. (Of course, you weren't supposed to use food stamps for nonfood purchases, but the grocer didn't seem to care.) Years later, Louise Todd and Oleta O'Connor Yates and I were reminiscing about the old days, and they both said that was also their great indulgence whenever they were exhausted and were free for a rare evening. They would get the same kind of magazines— never anything serious—and sit home and read.

Later that fall of 1931 Lou and I moved to East Los Angeles on assignment for the YCL. I served as the YCL organizer in Boyle Heights, which was at that point a mostly Jewish immigrant neighborhood and the center of Communist strength in Los Angeles. We lived on Soto Street, across the street from Hollenbeck Park. It was there that I first met Ben Dobbs, a young radical (not yet a member of the YCL; he would join the following year), who many years later become one of my closest associates in the leadership of the Los Angeles CP. Ben was then involved with the local John Reed Club and with a group called the Blue Blouses, who performed agitprop skits on street corners and off the back of trucks around the city. Ben and his then wife Lollie came over every weekend for wild sessions of a card game called Long Beach rummy with Lou and me. Most of my memories of the marriage are not as pleasant. It turned out that I had gotten scabies from that filthy place in Oakland where we had lived, and I wound up giving it to the entire Schneiderman family. They were furious at me. This was just not a marriage made in heaven. Lou and I separated soon afterward, though we did not formally get divorced until 1935.

In Los Angeles the unbelievably sadistic Red Squad goes ahead merrily cracking skulls. It is aided by many squads of private shock troops, who use everything from whips to pick handles upon their victims. Concerts, lectures, plays, even a track meet for children have been broken up.
■ "California Casualty," *The Nation*, August 29, 1934.

The Communist movement in the early 1930s, like the civil rights movement in the South in the early 1960s, enjoyed only the most tenuous constitutional rights. And outside of the South, California had one of the worst records of civil liberties violations in the 1930s. The police and various right-wing and employer-sponsored vigilante groups were in open collaboration. We were constantly attacked in those days. It didn't matter whether we were meeting in a hall or on a street corner or a private home, and it didn't make any difference how quiet and disciplined we were. The police would raid the meetings, beat everybody up, and arrest people. If you were a Communist,. you simply did not have a right to free speech. When William Z. Foster, the Communist Party's presidential candidate, came to speak in Los Angeles in 1932, he was grabbed by the police, stuck on a train, and "deported" from the city.

It wasn't just Communists who were treated this way. Everything was "Communist" as far as Captain William "Red" Hynes, the head of the police red squad, was concerned: the unemployed councils, student groups, even the American Federation of Labor. Hynes got his start as an agent provocateur in the Industrial Workers of the World in the 1920s. When he was exposed he came out openly as a cop and made it to the heights (or the depths) as head of the red squad. He became a power in himself in the city; like J. Edgar Hoover on a national level, he was untouchable. The red squad police had a catchall list of crimes that people could be arrested for: unlawful assembly, disturbing the peace, inciting to riot, or vagrancy. People were also charged with violation of California's criminal syndicalism law, which dated back to the red scare days of 1919. Hundreds of people, including Anita Whitney, founder of the California Communist Labor Party, were arrested on criminal syndicalism charges in the early 1920s. (Whitney was sentenced to five years in San Quentin, though she was pardoned before she had to serve her term.)

> If ever a revolution was due, it was due in California. Nowhere else has the battle between labor and capital been so widespread and bitter, and the casualties so large; nowhere else has there been such a flagrant denial of the personal liberties guaranteed by the Bill of Rights; nowhere else has authority been so lawless and brazen; nowhere else has the brute force of capitalism been so openly used and displayed; nowhere else has labor been so oppressed; nowhere else has there been a falser or more poisoned and poisoning press. ■ "Upton Sinclair's Victory," *The Nation*, September 12, 1934.

In some ways the red scare had never ended in California—the authorities had simply run out of reds in the mid-1920s. With the start of the depression they got a fresh supply. My main activity once I got to Los Angeles was organizing unemployed councils. By 1933 I moved to the south side of Los Angeles, around Slauson and Main. Every week we would take a new delegation of unemployed down to the metropolitan welfare office to demand higher relief payments or jobs. Every week "Red" Hynes and the red squad would be there, and people would be beaten up. But every week we'd go back again. We were determined we would outlast them.

The Communist Party was growing, but it was still quite small in the early years of the depression. By 1933 there were fewer than 25,000 members nationally, and only about 700 in Los Angeles. Unlike the Bay Area, which always had more of an ethnic mixture, the Party in Los Angeles was predominantly Jewish, mostly needle trades workers and house painters from Boyle Heights, mixed in with some professionals and a few Hollywood people. We were also beginning to develop a core of Black members, thanks largely to the efforts of Sadie Goldstein, a middle-aged immigrant with a thick Russian accent who went into the ghetto on Central Avenue, the little Harlem of Los Angeles, and recruited new members through the Scottsboro and Angelo Herndon cases. One of the members she recruited was Pettis Perry, who became a national leader of the CP. Sadie was a totally selfless and remarkably effective organizer and was accepted without hostility in the Black community.

In 1933 the emphasis of our organizing efforts began to change. Until that time we had been primarily concerned with organizing the unemployed around issues like increasing relief payments and stopping evictions. Now we began to concern ourselves more with workers who had jobs. At the beginning, in terms of our daily activity, the new emphasis mostly meant that we spent more time leafleting in front of factory gates. We didn't have much of a foothold in the union movement, and we didn't have many people with jobs. The shift to an industrial focus had been decided at the highest levels of Party leadership and was announced in the form of an open letter to the Party from Earl Browder. It didn't seem to me at the time that we were going through any momentous change in our strategy. Changes which seem so dramatic in retrospect or from the outside were less earth-shaking to those of us who actually lived through them. Of course, I was quite young and not very reflective about such things. Still, there had never been any great line of demarcation between one organization or another. In their weekly activities, Communists would float from one organization and emphasis to another, from the Trade Union Unity League to the International Labor Defense to the unemployed council. You would do one thing one day and the other the next day. Now we just seemed to be devoting more of our days to working for TUUL. What began as just a shift in emphasis in our daily routine would soon have dramatic consequences in my own life.

3

Mac lowered his voice. He moved close and put his hand on London's knee. "Listen," he said. "I guess we're goin' to lose this strike. . . . But we're getting the stiffs used to working together; getting bigger and bigger bunches working together all the time, see? It doesn't make any difference if we lose. Here's nearly a thousand men who've learned how to strike. When we get a whole slough of men working together, maybe—maybe Torgas Valley, most of it, won't be owned by three men. Maybe a guy can get an apple for himself without going to jail for it, see? Maybe they won't dump apples in the river to keep up the price. When guys like you and me need an apple to keep our God damn bowels open, see? you've got to look at the whole thing, London, not just this little strike."

London was staring painfully at Mac's mouth, as though he tried to see the words as they came out. "That's kind of reva—revolution, ain't it?"
■ John Steinbeck, *In Dubious Battle*, 1936, p. 290.

RAY: Dorothy (true name believed to be Ross). H—dk. brn; E—blue; wears glasses; W—110; A—20–34; H—5–1; Photo 28063; Imperial County. C&AWIU agitator. Said to be close friend of _____ ; now serving time in the Imperial Valley County Jail. ■ caption on Dorothy's mug shot, 1934.

On New Year's Eve, 1933, I left Los Angeles for the Imperial Valley and arrived in the town of Brawley the next day. A delegation of Mexican farm workers had come to Party headquarters in L.A. and asked for organizational help. There had been a one-day strike the previous November by a local union called the Mexican Mutual Aid Association. The association had negotiated a modest wage increase, but many of the growers were ignoring it. And when they met to renegotiate at the start of January, the growers were unwilling to meet their demands. Facing this impasse, they turned to the Communists for help. Our TUUL union, the Cannery and Agricultural Workers Industrial Union, could draw on resources outside the Imperial Valley to aid a strike, it had established a good record of winning strikes over the last year, and perhaps the workers felt that by bringing in the Communists they would scare the growers into a more cooperative attitude. Because of the short notice, the Party wasn't able to send the most experienced CAWIU organizers into the Imperial Valley. Instead they gave the assignment to Stanley Hancock, who was then the Party organizer in San Diego. Stanley had worked in the circulation department of a San Diego newspaper. He didn't have much of a background in union organizing, but did have the qualification of actually having been born in the Imperial Valley. Later on he would work for the *People's World* in San Francisco before breaking with the Party in 1940. (He wound up testifying before HUAC and at one of Harry Bridges's deportation hearings; I have a hunch that the FBI had some hold on him and blackmailed him into turning informer.) It was a policy at the time that when you sent a Party member into a situation like this you would try to send along a YCLer for training. A few days before New Year's I was called into the CP office and told that Stanley was going to work on the strike and they needed someone from the YCL to go with him, and "You're it, kid." Ordinarily I would have had no objection, but I happened to be pregnant again. I told them, "It's impossible, I can't go, I'm pregnant. I have to get an abortion." But they just said, "Oh, you'll have time, we'll get you back in plenty of time." So I went. My previous experience with agricultural strikes had been in the El Monte berry strike of June 1933, which had pitted Mexican berry pickers under CAWIU leadership against Japanese growers, but I had only given a couple of speeches. Stanley and I both had a lot to learn when we set off for the Imperial Valley.

Only fanatics are willing to live in shacks or tents and get their heads broken in the interests of migratory workers. ■ Paul Scharrenberg, California AFL spokesman, quoted in Carey McWilliams, *Factories in the Fields*, 1939, p. 212.

There had been a long history of radical involvement in agricultural organizing in California, going back to the days of the Industrial Workers of the World. The IWW's efforts had been broken up during the red scare, and the Wobblies never managed to reestablish themselves in the fields. The Communist Party began its own involvement in agricultural organizing in the late 1920s. The Communist-organized Agricultural Workers Industrial League, a predecessor to CAWIU, had made a pioneering foray into the Imperial Valley in 1930. Eugene Dennis, then known by his given name Francis Waldron, had gone to the Imperial Valley with other Communists that year to organize strikes among the lettuce and cantaloupe workers. But their efforts were quickly suppressed; thirteen of them were arrested on charges of criminal syndicalism and wound up serving long sentences in San Quentin. Dennis went underground to escape the dragnet and eventually made his way to the Soviet Union, returning in 1935 to become the district organizer in Wisconsin. For awhile, after the first Imperial Valley strike, the Party concentrated its efforts on canneries, but with the failure of the San Jose strike of 1931 the CAWIU shifted its emphasis back to field workers.

In 1933 a new wave of agricultural strikes broke out in California; CAWIU led twenty-five strikes that year involving tens of thousands of workers, most of which won at least small wage increases for the strikers. That was very noteworthy—until the mid-1930s even most industrial strikes were going down to defeat, and agricultural strikes were notoriously hard to win. Only the Communists were seriously interested in organizing this low-paid, migratory, and largely foreign-born work force. (In 1933 AFL unions led only two strikes of California farm workers.) The San Joaquin cotton strike the previous fall was a kind of watershed. It involved some eighteen thousand workers under CAWIU leadership who held out for twenty-two days. It attracted a lot of attention because of the violence used against the strikers. Three strikers were killed, and three thousand workers marched in their funeral procession. The strikers set up a camp on a forty-acre farm they had rented outside of Corcoran, and five thousand people lived there for the duration of the strike. In the end the union won a partial victory, gaining a smaller wage increase than the original demands. Two Party members, Pat Chambers and Carolyn Decker, were the main leaders of the strike. Carolyn was only a few years older than I was and already a very accomplished organizer. Pat was a small, quiet, older man, very capable and very respected for his organizing abilities and his commitment. When he went in to organize the cotton workers, he was still recovering from having his jaw broken by vigilantes in a cherry pickers' strike that spring. CAWIU's successes excited the fears of the big growers, who were determined to stamp out the movement before it spread any further.

Despite charges by the growers that the Communists were conspiring to destroy California's agricultural economy, we were rarely the instigators of these strikes. They usually broke out spontaneously and then the workers would come and find us. Most of the workers we encountered in the early 1930s were Mexican, with some Filipinos, and only a scattering of Blacks and Anglos. The Dust Bowl refugees were just beginning to arrive in the state. Over the next few years the labor force in the fields changed considerably, partly because of the mass deportations of Mexican workers. The Mexicans had a history of radicalism and were quite willing to cooperate with Communists. The growers thought that the "Okies" would be more docile, but to their dismay they would soon discover that their new work force was just as obstreperous as the old one. Once they came to that realization, their opinion of the virtues of sturdy, all-American labor underwent a dramatic change. I found it interesting to read the newspaper stories and editorials during the Kern County cotton strike in 1937. The same kind of propaganda that had been used against the Mexicans in the early 1930s— it was no use giving these people clean quarters, they liked to live like pigs, and so forth—was now being used to describe native-born Anglo-Saxon citizens.

I drove down to Brawley with Stanley Hancock and with a Mexican-American labor organizer named Frank Nieto. (Frank had led the workers' delegation to Los Angeles to ask for the Party's aid. He was one of the warmest, most intelligent people I'd ever known; the word "selfless" is much overused, but it really described him. He had lost his left hand somehow and the stump was always covered with a glove. He would later join the Party and work as a CIO organizer.) The Imperial Valley was a self-enclosed feudally run barony, surrounded by desert. The workers lived a miserable existence and were treated like virtual serfs. Those who lived there year round lived in little shanties with dirt floors. Others lived in tents. It was usually brutally hot. Even in January when we arrived the temperature was in the eighties or nineties, and in the summer it was always well over a hundred. The growers provided no drinking water for the workers except for that in the irrigation ditches, and those ditches were used for everything, including washing and toilets. Driving into the Valley you had the feeling of leaving the United States behind you. The ordinary legal rules and protections, imperfect as they were, no longer applied. The most horrendous things could go on, and did go on, and all you could expect was that perhaps months later the news would gradually leak out to the people who read the *Nation* and kept up with such things.

When we got to Brawley we met with the local leaders and then called a meeting for January 4 of all those who were interested in a strike. (It was a measure of our inexperience that we didn't know that starting on January 1, the very day we arrived, California had initiated a marketing control scheme, limiting the amount of lettuce shipped out of state to raise its price. The shippers actually welcomed the prospect of a strike for that reason—and because they were confident that once a strike began they could quickly smash it.) Brawley was the largest town in the Imperial Valley, with a population of about ten thousand. It had more Mexican workers concentrated in one place than anywhere else in the Valley, and the area just below it was one of most fertile growing areas in the state for lettuce. Brawley served as the center of the strike, drawing supporters from all the other little towns in the region, like Holtville, and Calexico, and from El Centro, the county seat.

Azteca Hall in Brawley served as strike headquarters. The meetings were large and enthusiastic. At the first meeting that was held, there were several thousand workers (some seven or eight thousand all told would go on strike), and we set up rank-and-file committees of workers to run the strike. For us a strike was always an education for revolution, and you couldn't educate for revolution if people didn't run their own affairs. We set a strike date of January 8 and began to make preparations. There was a negotiating committee, an educational committee, a picketing committee, a committee to run the strike kitchen, and so on. The Workers International Relief committee began sending in truckloads of food—that was the kind of outside support that the Party could mobilize. (The best fictional description, by the way, of a Communist-led agricultural strike that I've ever read is John Steinbeck's *In Dubious Battle*, which I think is a better book than *The Grapes of Wrath*, at least as far as the description it offers of the momentum of that kind of struggle.)

At that first meeting we announced that we were Communists, and we later held a meeting for those interested in joining the Party. That was a dramatic occasion. I drove out to one of the worker's homes in the desert. It was after dark and the only light was a flickering lamp. We were gathered in this tiny room. I spoke in English about Communism and someone translated my words for the two dozen or so workers crammed into this tiny room. The response of the Mexican workers was essentially, "Of course we're for the revolution. When the barricades are ready, we'll be there with you, but don't bother us with meetings all the time. We know what to do, we know who the enemy is!" They were part of the generation of Mexican workers who had come out of the Mexican

---

Revolution: very anticlerical, very sophisticated politically, and very anarcho-syndicalist in orientation. "Just tell us when the revolution is ready. We'll be there."

> MR. TAVENNER: How many cells or units in the Communist Party were set up in Imperial Valley during the period you have described?
>
> MR. HANCOCK: I do not have it in my mind, but I am inclined to say a couple, and probably confined to Brawley. We probably had 20 or 25 party members recruited from the Imperial Valley. It had no whole significance in the activity of the Communist Party because these were in the main uneducated laborers of Mexican extraction, many of whom spoke no English. They read a Mexican weekly newspaper issued by the party, named Lucha Obrera, L-u-c-h-a O-b-r-e-r-a. Some party literature came across the Mexican border into Imperial Valley. I remember magazines like Hoy, and El Machete, the daily organ of the Communist Party of Mexico. . . . At the most we had 20 to 25 people who signed a card, and they never actually became our conception of the Communist Party member. They drifted away, and we lost track of them. ■ Stanley Hancock, testimony before the House Committee on UnAmerican Activities, March 1, 1954.

We held meetings twice a day, in the afternoon and at night inside Azteca Hall. We started every day around five o'clock in the morning getting our picketers assembled and dispatched. One of the problems in a strike like this was that you couldn't just go and set up a picket line in the same place every day, as you would in a strike in a factory or on the waterfront. The farms were spread out all over God's green acre. You couldn't set foot on the farm itself, because that was trespassing. You had to reach the workers on the road leading up to the different farms, head them off before they arrived at work, and let them know about the strike. The picketing committee always had the hardest job. Everybody took their turn at it. Beginning the second day of the strike, January 9, there were police attacks, mostly by the state highway patrol. They didn't wait for us to get in position in our picket lines; they would throw tear gas at us even before we even left Brawley.

By our second day in Brawley there was a warrant out for our arrest. We had to sleep in a different home every night so that the police couldn't find us. Once I was in a little room, stretching out on the floor to go to sleep, and about twenty minutes later the door opened and in came two or three Filipino men. I said hello, and they said hello, and they lay down, and about a half hour later another few came in. This kept on for a while, until there were probably twenty men there. There was no self-consciousness on anybody's part that I was the only woman among them. Everybody just stretched out and went to sleep, and in the morning we woke up and greeted each other, "How are you, comrades, fellow workers?" I don't remember then or in any organizing drive in the CIO where I found sexist attitudes among the workers (I found plenty among CIO leaders, and even in the Party itself, but that's another story). If you seemed to know what you were doing, then the workers had respect for you, even if you were young and female. The relations between the Filipinos, the Chicanos, and the few Anglos involved in the strike was also a remarkable thing to watch. All of them, in their own way, were initially afflicted with feelings of mutual racial animosity, and yet within a few days the suspicions and the prejudices just evaporated through the comradeship that came from sharing common experiences and hardships, especially the police attacks.

Pop Hanoff and Pat Chambers both came down to the Imperial Valley after a few days to provide underground leadership for the strike. The underground leaders were the older and supposedly wiser leaders. They stayed in El Centro, and Stanley and I would go up two or three times a week to meet with them and discuss strategy. Pop, whose real name was Elmer Hanoff, was a state leader of the Party. I had already seen him in action during the San Jose strike, and while he was a nice enough man I was not impressed by his knowledge or intelligence. Chambers was a skillful strike leader, but our meetings with them were a big waste of time. No matter what they told us to do or not to do, the initiative was in the hands of the growers and the police, not in our hands. We usually wound up ignoring most of the advice they gave us. Pat's experience wasn't of much use because every agricultural situation was so different. Knowledge gained in one area of California wouldn't necessarily equip you to deal with a situation in another part. We were facing a more violent situation than the San Joaquin strike, as violent as that had been. And workers in the Imperial Valley were far more vulnerable than those in the earlier strike because they were so spread out. This cumbersome dual leadership did nothing but complicate our already busy schedules.

> MR. WALTER: In most instances where a situation of this sort existed, there was somebody present at State headquarters to give the proper national guidance?
> MR. HANCOCK: That is correct. I think I can go a bit further. It is my very strong belief, based on my experience in that period of time in the labor group, that there was a C.I. [Comintern] representative. . . .
> MR. WALTER: In other words, to some degree, the entire activity of a local strike was controlled by a representative of the Russian Cominform [sic]?
> MR. HANCOCK: At least in policy, general strategy; that would be correct.
> ■ Stanley Hancock, testimony before the House Committee on UnAmerican Activities, February 24, 1954.

1934 was the year when the Associated Farmers began to be very active in breaking strikes in California. Whenever I see the name of that group I think the word "farmers" should be placed in quotation marks, because very few of the instigators were ever farmers of any sort. The group was bankrolled and run by the railroads, the bankers, the utilities, as well as cannery owners and big growers, as the La Follette Committee hearings later revealed. The use of vigilantes wasn't restricted to the Imperial Valley or even to the agricultural strikes; it was characteristic of all strikes in the early to mid1930s, including the big waterfront strikes. The Associated Farmers would mobilize what they would call citizens' committees to break the strikes. They controlled much of the press, where each strike would be depicted as the prelude to the red terror. To strike against "farmers" was to strike against private property, a threat to every bank teller and Woolworth's clerk's dream of owning their own home or small business. Thousands of them, recruited through the local Kiwanis club or American Legion post, enlisted in the Associated Farmers and similar groups, dressed up in their overseas caps, and armed themselves with ax handles and rifles. They would never admit that agriculture was a big business run by huge corporations; their propaganda always pictured this little farmer who could not pay one cent more to his already-overpaid workers. We saw them as the advance guard of American fascism; they were certainly one of the reasons why California racked up so bloody a record of labor violence in the 1930s.

> Armed with bright new pick-handles, their faces grim, eyes shining with steady purpose a large band of "vigilantes" composed of irate citizens, including many war veterans, smashed their way into three Communist "hotspots" here last night, seized a mass of red literature and severely beat nine asserted radicals. ■ *San Jose Mercury-Herald*, July 20, 1934, quoted in McWilliams, *Factories in the Fields*, p. 227.

We'd hardly set off in the morning before we'd get attacked. When the American Civil Liberties Union sent a lawyer, Al Wirin, down to act as an observer of the strike in late January, he was kidnapped by vigilantes in El Centro, beaten up and robbed, his car was wrecked, and he was driven miles out into the desert and abandoned. The vigilantes told him that if he ever came back they'd kill him. The ACLU played a very courageous and militant role in these years. It organized a mass meeting to test the right of people to gather together in the Imperial Valley, having first gotten a federal injunction against the police coming in to break it up. They were able to hold the meeting, but as soon as it was over, many of the Mexican workers who attended were arrested, beaten up, and deported.

On January 12, the local authorities decided that things had gone far enough, and they were going to end the strike in one great raid. A policeman came into Azteca Hall in plainclothes and asked for Dorothy Ray. I thought he might be one of the vigilantes and said, 'What do you want her for?" He said, "I have a warrant for her arrest." I was down in the office offstage; I immediately ran up onto the stage—there were hundreds of people in the hall, preparing food, getting ready for the mass meetings, having committee meetings—and I shouted that the police were there. The cops and the vigilantes outside barricaded the doors to prevent anyone from leaving. There were no windows in the lower portion of the hall, but there were little windows higher up, and they began lobbing tear gas through the windows. A worker by the name of Murietta, a huge man, picked me up, took me to the back of the hall, and pushed me through an open skylight. He dropped me down to some other strikers already on the ground waiting to catch me. Then he did the same thing with Stanley, and they took us off to hide us at their homes. Here we were, supposedly the experienced organizers, but they had been prepared for the attack, and we hadn't. Back at one of the houses they dug up the dirt floor under the beds and hid us there. The police broke into fifty other houses that day searching for us, but they never found the right house. Meanwhile a mob of police and vigilantes had virtually demolished Azteca Hall, smashing furniture and typewriters, and to top if off the fire department showed up and flooded the hall with their fire hoses. Over the next few days one hundred and fifty strikers were arrested and hundreds more were beaten up. They didn't have enough room in the jail to hold all the prisoners, so they put up stockades to hold the overflow.

The next day we decided we had to show ourselves to the workers to keep them from thinking the strike was over. We agreed that I should be the one to speak, because Stanley was more important to keep on the outside as a strategist. We got out some leaflets saying there would be a strike meeting at six o'clock across the street from Azteca Hall—we weren't going to get caught inside again. At ten to six I walked to the hall. Hundreds of workers had already gathered. I stood on the shoulders of two men and started speaking, and almost immediately the state police pulled up in their cars, with lights flashing, and jumped out with dogs. A group of workers formed a semicircle, as if they were shielding someone, and the cops and the dogs set out after them in hot pursuit. Meanwhile another worker took me by the hand, and we got away by running down a dry irrigation ditch in the field.

We managed to hide out for another week. A ten-thousand-dollar reward was posted for our apprehension, but none of the strikers would betray us. But without any way to meet with the workers, the strike was rapidly falling apart. Stanley and I finally decided to take a risk and met with a reporter in a bar on January 18 hoping to get word out about what was happening. He was very obliging and said it was a great story. He must have followed us back to the place where we were staying, because he turned us in. Whether he was a police agent all along or did it for the reward, I have no idea. The next morning the young boy at the home where were staying shouted to his mother that the police were coming. We looked out, and we could see about ten or fifteen men with submachine guns, going from house to house in the Mexican colony searching for us. We didn't want to be found in this house because the family would be arrested and deported, so we ran outside. Stanley, with longer legs, ran a lot faster and made it down to a tent at the end of the lane. I made it as far as the privy and ducked in there. After about two minutes. I was getting ill from the smell, so I made a dash for the tent where Stanley was hiding. When we could see them getting closer all the time through a little hole in the canvas, we rolled out under the far side of the tent. We might have gotten away, except for a high barbed-wire fence along the back of the colony. So we just stretched out in a ditch and lay quietly, hoping they wouldn't find us. The next thing we know we hear a trembling voice saying, "Stand up, stand up, or I'll shoot!" We stood up and there was a state highway patrolman pointing his gun at us and shaking uncontrollably. He was terrified. We were the terrible Bolsheviks. Here we were, the two of us, neither of us very imposing physically and me all of nineteen years old. These big armed men were far more scared than we were, except I was getting pretty nervous about those shaky hands holding machine guns.

We were taken first to the Brawley jail and then to the county jail in El Centro and booked on four charges: unlawful assembly, inciting to riot, vagrancy, and a law known as "rout." Rout was a nineteenth-century ordinance that said that if two or more people get together to discuss an act which, if consummated, could result in a riot, then a crime has been committed. When I was arrested I remembered that I had a piece of paper in my pocket with the address where Pat Chambers, Pop Hanoff, and two or three other Party and union leaders were staying in El Centro. We were handcuffed when they put is in the patrol car, so I couldn't do anything about it. Fortunately, when we got to jail they immediately searched Stanley, but they didn't have a woman jailer present to search me. I was put in a cell by myself and as soon as I was alone, just like in the movies, I chewed up and swallowed the address.

The first question we had to deal with was that of bail. We had a rule in CAWIU that the first ones to be bailed out were the workers themselves, and that the union organizers were to be the last. But I had a special problem: I was pregnant, and the time in which I could have an abortion was running out. After consultation with the other strikers, we decided I would be the first one bailed out. I returned to Los Angeles and had the abortion. As usual, when I needed to recuperate, I stayed with my mother. She regarded my arrest and jailing as just part of the class struggle, part of life. She wasn't afraid of my going to jail—she figured that the class struggle takes care of its own.

Stanley and the others soon got out on bail. Back in Los Angeles we had very intensive joint meetings of the Young Communist League and the Communist Party to discuss the lessons of the strike. This was very typical. Always our main concern after any action was "What did we do wrong? What could we have done better?" This was another of those pressures which, if you survived it, toughened and developed greater capacities in people. I can't remember any time after a major strike or campaign when people were complimented for their work. We always looked for what was weak, what was inadequate. Many of the criticisms of our role in the Imperial Valley centered on the inadequate provisions we had made for what would happen after a police attack. How could we ensure that the strike would go on without us? We should have anticipated the attack and arrests. We knew what the Imperial Valley was like. We did too little to develop a local leadership: we should have been there to consult with the workers, rather than attempting to run things to the extent that we did.

I can now see other weaknesses in our conduct of the strike, which only became obvious to me years later. One sad memory, which illustrates both our inexperience and the ultraradical character of the Party line at the time, is of the day one small farmer from the area came in and said he wanted to discuss a contract. I looked at him in amazement. Sign a contract and end a strike? You didn't end strikes like that. We wanted all the growers to capitulate; to sign a contract with just this one small grower would encourage reformist illusions, make it seem like there were good growers and bad growers, and thus dull the workers' hatred of capitalism. When this grower came in ready to sign, which would have given us a small victory and divided our enemy, all I said was, "We'll discuss it, come back some other time."

> After more than 2 months of observation and investigation in Imperial Valley, it is my conviction that a group of growers have exploited a "communist" hysteria for the advancement of their own interests; that they have welcomed labor agitation, which they could brand as "Red," as a means of sustaining supremacy by mob rule, thereby preserving what is so essential to their profits, cheap labor; that they have succeeded in drawing into their conspiracy certain county officials who have become the principal tools of their machine. ■ General Pelham D. Glassford, "Report to the Board of Supervisors of Imperial County," June 1934, quoted in La Follette Committee hearings, Part 55, p. 20148.

We made another mistake after the strike, when government mediators and commissions came in to investigate what had taken place. We regarded the state apparatus as one undifferentiated reactionary instrument of the ruling class. One of the investigations was headed by General Pelham D. Glassford, a retired army brigadier general, who was sent to the Imperial Valley by the U.S. Labor Department as a federal conciliator. He wasn't any friend of ours, but the final report he issued was very critical of the conduct of the growers and the local authorities. When his mission in the Valley was announced, the governor of California denounced it as a violation of states rights. Our situation was in some ways comparable to that of the southern civil rights movement in the 1960s; if we could have enlisted the power of the federal government on our side, we could have used it as a wedge against the hostile forces at the state and local level. But we wouldn't have anything to do with Glassford; we were sure that if we said a good word for him, we'd only be encouraging reformist illusions about "the state." (The quotation that was always attributed to Marx, that the state was merely the "executive committee of the ruling class," does not appear in his writings. What Marx actually said in the *Communist Manifesto* was that "the executive of the modern state is but a committee for managing the common affairs of the bourgeoisie." That is a much more flexible concept, which opens up the possibility of conflict within the state and between different classes for influence or control of the state.) It was typical of Communists in this period to take ideas that had some validity and stretch them into rigid laws that allowed for no exceptions. We ignored the tensions within the state, the ebb and flow of interests that made it possible to win a useful legislative victory here and a useful court decision there. We did not understand how to use the contradictions that were present within the system for the benefit of our cause, or how to use limited victories as stepping stones to winning greater victories.

There was also a problem in our basic organizing strategy, with its focus on migratory field workers. Of course, we had only inherited a situation that had already begun. It's not like we could just pick and choose which workers to organize. But we were facing an almost impossible challenge in trying to organize an inherently unstable work force. When CIO organizers arrived later in the decade they had the advantage of working with an already existing local of fruit and vegetable pickers. We hadn't reached these shedworkers in 1934. They were highly skilled and were key to the functioning of the industry, because when the crop is picked it has to be packed and sent out immediately. By building an organization around this stable nucleus of shed workers, the CIO was able to achieve far greater successes than CAWIU had ever been able to. In the 1960s I was very impressed with Cesar Chavez's grasp of organizing strategy. He started organizing around small fruit to start with, where there was a semiper-manent work force. That gave the union continuity. These workers didn't move around to follow the different crops. You didn't start fresh every time there was a strike. With us, each time we had to start from scratch. It was a heartbreaker because you'd spend four, five, six weeks in the most intense struggle and didn't have anything to show for it afterward unless, purely by chance, you'd run into some of those same workers later in another location.

Pat Chambers, who was still underground in El Centro, had gotten arrested while we were up in Los Angeles. The district attorney in the Imperial Valley offered to make a deal, which would encompass all the people who had been arrested who didn't live in the Imperial Valley. Now that the strike was broken, he wanted to clear the books of us. If we would plead quilty to the charges against us, we would all be given suspended sentences. We wouldn't have to spend any time in jail if we would agree to take what was called a "floater," that is, to leave the area and not come back for the period of the jail time. Pat accepted the offer, and when we heard about it we were absolutely indignant, because to us this represented a violation of what we called a class approach to the legal system. We would never plead guilty. We would never make deals with the prosecution. Having agreed to the D.A.'s conditions, Pat had already left. We had a discussion and decided that he had to come back to the Imperial Valley to show that we would not give into these kinds of pressures. Naturally he was arrested as soon as he came back to the area. (Pat was destined to spend a lot of time in jail. He and Caroline Decker and sixteen others were arrested in July on charges of criminal syndicalism, picked up in the wave of hysteria provoked across the state by the San Francisco general strike. Pat and Caroline and six others were convicted, and their arrests destroyed the CAWIU. They didn't get out of prison until their convictions were reversed on appeal in 1936.) Our decision about Pat was another example of self-destructive rigidity. In any case, Stanley and I told the district attorney that we would not consider such a deal, and we returned to the Imperial Valley in February.

A new strike started in early February, this time of pea pickers, centered in Calipatria. One of the unusual things about this strike was that many of the workers were Anglos, the first time I had encountered them in any significant number in the fields. They contacted us and didn't care that we were Com-munists any more than the Mexicans or Fillipinos did. We used to drive out into the desert every night about midnight to meet with them. They had devised a new technique to reach other workers, a roving picket line in auto caravans. They would shout to the workers still working who didn't know about the strike.

It was a well organized affair, but it too was broken when the police and vigilantes attacked the strikers' camp in mid-February, and drove them out.

Our trial began in March in the Brawley courthouse. We decided to act as our own lawyers. A lawyer named Grover Johnson had come down in January to defend us. He was an interesting man who had been a law partner of Senator Burton Wheeler and a district attorney in Butte, Montana. In the late twenties he moved to San Bernadino. Out of a simple commitment to justice rather than out of any political sympathy (he was actually rather conservative at the time), he began to handle cases where workers had been attacked for organizing, and became radicalized as a result of what he had seen. He went into the court in Brawley arguing on a writ of habeas corpus for Pat Chambers. As he was coming down the courthouse steps, he was accosted by a group of vigilantes with guns, who started to beat him. His wife, Gladys, ran to their car—they kept a gun in the car to protect themselves—and as soon as she came out of the car she was arrested on a charge of disturbing the peace and jailed for defending her husband. Another sympathetic lawyer, Wilbur Breeden, was jailed on a vagrancy charge. Since the lawyers were as vulnerable to attack as we were, Stanley and I decided to defend ourselves.

The trial was a farce. The justice of the peace who heard the case had never had any legal training. When any question of legal procedure came up, he would turn to the district attorney and say "Mr. Heald, what do I do?" And Mr. Heald would tell him. There was enormous local interest in our trial. They put a loudspeaker outside the courtroom to broadcast the proceedings to the hundreds of people who gathered every day (inside, most of the seats were reserved for supporters of the Associated Farmers). There's not much to do in Brawley, and the trial had some of the atmosphere of a county fair, with these two wild Bolshevik agitators as the star attraction. One of the highlights of the trial came when I was on the stand and Stanley, acting as my lawyer, was asking me questions. We were trying to demonstrate the terrible working and living conditions that the Mexicans faced in the Imperial Valley. Stanley asked me about the food the workers ate, and I was saying how they mostly lived on beans, they couldn't afford anything else, and wasn't it ironic that in this center of vegetable production, they couldn't afford to eat a fresh salad. The foreman of the jury stood up and said, "Your Honor, do we really have to listen to any more of this Red agitation? I was in the war, and the soldiers had to eat plenty of beans, and if it was good enough for American soldiers, it's good enough for these dirty Mexicans!" The district attorney was very upset and said, "No, no, no! Now sit down, you're not supposed to do that!"

Q. According to information by authorities there, you testified at that time—I am not saying this is true, but we are informed that you testified that you had no respect for officers of the law and judges and some people should be eliminated and liquidated or something of that sort. Do you happen to know whether the transcript of your trial would show that you gave such testimony?

A. First of all, there is no transcript of the trial tried in the Justice of the Peace Court. Unfortunately for us it was not taken down. . . . However, I could give a very categorical denial of such a statement. ■ excerpt from the transcript of Dorothy's interview before the State Personnel Board when she was being considered for the position of deputy labor commissioner, February 10, 1940.

It was no great surprise when the jury returned at the conclusion of the trial, after about ten minutes' deliberation, with a verdict of guilty. Stanley and I were both sentenced to 180 days in jail, the maximum for disturbing the peace. We appealed, but because it was a misdemeanor we could only take the case as far as the county superior court, which of course rejected our appeal.

We began serving our jail sentences on May 14. Neither at that time nor during any subsequent jailings did I terribly mind the experience. It was a lot worse for the men—they were sent out to a work camp, and the vigilantes harassed them, digging a grave nearby, burning a cross beside it, and leaving a cat-o'-nine-tails along with a note saying "If you reds come back, this is what you are going to get." But for me, jail was a time in which I could do two things which I always loved to do anyway: read and talk. It was a funny thing about that Imperial Valley jail. The food was horrible: bread (no butter), black coffee, mush, salt pork, beans, potatoes, and that was about it. I don't think I saw a bit of fresh vegetable or a piece of fruit for six months. And though the other women could bring in food from the outside, I wasn't allowed to. But they did allow me to bring in all the books I wanted. I had crateloads of books. I guess they thought food was more important for my morale than books, but for me it was just the opposite. I didn't give a damn what I was eating. I ate a lot of onion sandwiches there: the other women had a lot of onions and didn't mind sharing them.

Among other subjects, I spent a lot of time reading books on psychology. I'd never had the chance to do it before. So I had books by Freud and Watson and others. While I was reading, the matron of the jail, a woman in her thirties named Mildred Cox, used to come up to talk to me. Most of the other prisoners were Mexican women, arrested for prostitution, who were being deported or given floaters to get out of town and not come back. They were rarely in jail for more than a few days. So Mildred would come and tell me about her life. Her stories were quite interesting, though a little repetitive, because it turned out she was an incredible nymphomaniac. Every morning she'd come in to tell me the previous night's exploits, because she had to have somebody to talk to about it, and she figured I was safe enough. I wasn't in a position to tell any of her neighbors about what I'd heard. But I was keeping a diary, and there wasn't much else to write about, so I started writing down what she described, including the names of the men involved, and trying to analyze it as a kind of amateur psychologist, drawing on the books I was reading. What would a behaviorist make of her? What would the Freudians say? On the day I was scheduled to get out of jail, one of the other women inmates with whom I'd become friendly warned me, "Look, you better hide that diary of yours. If you think you're going to get it out, you're not, because I've heard them talking, and they're going to take it away form you." I said, very naively, "Oh, they can't do that," and didn't hide it. But when Mildred came in she asked me for the diary. I said, "That's my property. I won't give it to you." She said, "You're not leaving here with it. If you want to stay in jail, you can stay in jail." So I thought, "The hell with it, what do I care?" and gave it to her. She just put it in her desk unopened and forgot all about it. I found out what happened next from Emma Cutler, who had come to the Imperial Valley as an ILD representative and been arrested and who served her time after I did. She told me that one day some of the deputy sheriffs were rearranging the furniture in the jail office and found the diary in Mildred's desk and asked her, "What's this?" She said, "Oh, that's the diary of that little red bitch we had upstairs." So they opened it and started to read it. Emma warned me, "You'd better never go back to the Imperial Valley, because if Mildred Cox ever gets hold of you she's going to kill you."

I loved talking with the other women prisoners. Most of them were prostitutes, and I was fascinated by their lives. We'd play a lot of cards together, and just talk, talk, talk. Once I tried to explain to a group of them why I was in jail. I was describing what a strike was and why it was so important that other workers didn't act as strikebreakers. They couldn't quite grasp the idea of scabbing and why we regarded them so negatively. Finally one of the women spoke up, "Oh, don't you understand what she's talking about? It's the same thing as chippies." A chippy was their slang word for a woman who had sexual relations without being paid. A woman named Helen was in jail with me for awhile. She had tried to set up a whorehouse in the Imperial Valley without paying protection money to the cops, and they'd arrested her. Every Sunday a group of society ladies would come to the jail to visit us, feeling they were performing some kind of Christian duty, but they were so condescending that every woman in the jail hated them. One Sunday Helen was locked up in her cell for some minor infraction instead of being allowed into the common runway between the cells, and when the society ladies came through one of them came over to Helen and said, "Oh, my good woman, what are you in here for?" Helen replied, "Why, you dirty bitch, I'm in here for selling what you give away." We were spared any further visits from the society ladies.

One Sunday afternoon, some months after Dorothy had gotten back from the Imperial Valley, she and Bernard and his wife Marion were over at Mama's for Sunday dinner. I was playing outside when this woman came down the street with a lorgnette and a tight black suit. Her name was Norma. She turned out to be a prostitute and exotic dancer Dorothy had met in jail and given Mama's address to. All the kids in the neighborhood dashed over to see her as she walked into the house. My brother was a very handsome man. he was also a very stuffy man. And Norma made a play for him, to his vast embarrassment. She also offered to do one of her dances. I was just enraptured. I thought it was a wonderful idea. But Bernard got up and said, "Come on Marion, we're going home." I was stunned that he could be so rude to this woman. Afterward Bernard said to Dorothy "How could you invite a common whore to our mother's house?" Dorothy was just being friendly. I think I still have a postcard of Norma doing a fan dance or something. ■ Carol Jean Newman.

While I was in jail the International Labor Defense ran a big campaign to support us. Like all "class war prisoners," I would get a few dollars from them every month to buy cigarettes or toothpaste. There were threats from the vigilantes that they were going to break into the jail and lynch us, or attack us when we were let out, and the ILD publicized the threats in an attempt to protect us; they even named a branch of the ILD in Huntington Park the Dorothy Ray club. When I finally got out of jail in November, Bernard and Frances drove down to pick me up. We had a motorcycle police escort all the way to the county border—for my protection, and also to make sure I really left. As I was driving away from jail the women prisoners who remained behind stood at one of the upstairs windows and sang a song I had taught them, "The Red Flag."

The six months I was in jail turned out to have been very important ones in reshaping the Party's political outlook. In California these were the months of both the San Francisco general strike and Upton Sinclair's EPIC campaign. In San Francisco the Marine Workers Industrial Union, which was a TUUL organization, joined forces with a rank-and-file group led by Harry Bridges in the International Longshoremen's Association, an AFL organization. Together they launched a strike that united longshoremen up and down the Pacific Coast and, for a time, united all the unions in the city in solidarity. We learned that you couldn't just reject the AFL as we had done in the past, as an outmoded reactionary body incapable of being reformed.

Upton Sinclair's victory is astounding. It bears him out in his early assurance of success and his insistence from the beginning that he sensed a ground swell of revolt against the present order. It is the more remarkable because of the widespread belief that the red scare following the general strike had so aroused California that there was a reaction against the radicalism of Mr. Sinclair. . . . He [will] win others to his belief that the economic and political jungle we live in today is no more necessary and inevitable than were the foul horrors of that human cesspool of the stockyards which he—to his everlasting honor—revealed in his most famous book, "The Jungle." ■ "Upton Sinclair's Victory," *The Nation*, September 12, 1934.

We also learned an important lesson from Sinclair's campaign. Sinclair had been a socialist ever since the Debs era. He had run for office on the Socialist ticket many times without much success. In 1934, to the dismay of his comrades in the Socialist Party, and to our contempt, he decided to run for the Democratic nomination for governor in California. He put together a ticket called End Poverty in California, or EPIC, which took as its slogan "production for use, not profit," and advocated state-sponsored cooperative enterprises. The EPIC movement swept the Democratic Party, gained Sinclair the Democratic nomination (if not, ultimately, the governorship), and roused enormous popular enthusiasm. We would have nothing to do with the Democratic Party, and so we were left on the outside, denouncing the movement. We called him a "social fascist," which was terrible nonsense. (Lest it be thought that such sectarianism was solely a CP attribute, it's worth remembering that the Socialist Party expelled Sinclair for his act of heresy.) Our position was that you could not reform a capitalist party, that nothing could be gained through the two-party system. But we learned something from Sinclair's success. What happened had not fit our definition of what was possible or not possible. Here was a Democratic Party struggle that did have a progressive social content. Slowly we began to change our ideas about the potential role of progressives in the Democratic Party and started to work within the EPIC movement.

Meanwhile the Soviet Union and the International Communist movement had begun a reevaluation of the threat posed by Nazi Germany. In the early 1930s Communists had attacked the socialists in Germany and elsewhere as the main political danger, because they competed with us for the leadership of the working class. They would deceive the workers and prevent them from fighting for their true interests. So at the same time that we were calling for a united front against fascism, we were denouncing the socialist leaders as people who could not be relied upon to stand up to fascism, which, understandably, made real antifascist unity difficult to achieve. Hitler's triumph made terribly clear the danger of our earlier notions, as well as the very stark differences between a fascist regime and "bourgeois democracy" as represented by someone like Franklin Delano Roosevelt. By the mid-1930s the issue of anti-fascism permeated all our mass work. In countries like France and Spain where big socialist movements existed, Communists sought to unite the Left into antifascist united fronts. In the United States we sought to work with the socialists, and we also began to reevaluate our earlier, highly critical assessment of the New Deal.

Gradually we were recognizing that we had been wrong on some large questions. Critics at the time and some historians since have maintained that we American Communists changed our ideas about the labor movement, the New Deal, and the threat of fascism only because we were told to do so by the Communist International and the Soviet Union. They forget that the YCL began to initiate policies that could be termed "premature People's Frontism" in the American Youth Congress and other organizations two years before the Seventh World Congress of the Comintern officially ushered in the new line. Of course what Soviet leaders like Stalin and Comintern leaders like Dimitrov had to say was enormously important to us. As for our own national leadership in New York, I had at the time a naive and all too typical impression that it was made up of human beings of extraordinary foresight and abilities. Whatever they had to say, they obviously knew what they were talking about. I can't remember ever critically reading any Party document that outlined the policies of the period and asking, "Now, is this right? Does it reflect what I know is taking place? Is it accurate in its analysis?" I read those documents with the presumption that of course whatever they contained was right, and to the extent that it was possible tried immediately to apply what I had read to my daily activities. There was often fierce debate among top Party leaders on policy, but by the time the line came down to us it was presented as if nothing but unanimity had prevailed at the top. No minority positions were ever presented, no alternatives to present policies were ever considered by the rank and file in open debate.

Having said all that, I still think it leaves a false impression to say that we changed directions only because of orders from Moscow. The United States was a long way from the Soviet Union, California was a long way from national Party headquarters in New York, and I—a very young, very obscure, and rather unreflective member—was a long way from state Party headquarters in San Francisco. When I began to hear about the new political policies and ideas that have come to be known as the Popular Front (we never called it that, by the way; for us it was the People's Front), they made sense to me on an intuitive level—as I think they made sense to many other rank-and-file Communists—because they seemed to fit in with my own sense of the kinds of corrections that needed to be made in our approach. Perhaps "corrections" is too strong a word. It wasn't so much that I fully understood what was *wrong* with our old policies as I understood what was *right* about our new policies.

There was, as I've noted, a lack of genuine theoretical understanding in the Party, for all our talk about theory. We were so busy with day-to-day organizing that we could rarely consider the larger questions facing our movement; in the midst of the Party crisis in 1956 the charge that was made over and over again was that we had been deliberately kept so busy that nobody had time to think. Whether it was deliberate policy or not, it was certainly true that the Party lacked the kind of internal political structures that might have encouraged us to ask substantive questions about the meaning of our own experience. That led to the enshrining of the Party leadership, contributing to their aura of infallibility, and making the likelihood of anyone's challenging what came from them negligible. The fact that by the mid-1930s the international leaders of the Communist movement were advocating changes that made sense in practical terms for American domestic politics only enhanced their authority among us and increased the likelihood that in the future we would continue to accept their leadership—even when they were wrong, as was all too often the case.

4

For twenty years, our Party has been actuated by a vision of a cleaner, greater, and more progressive Los Angeles. For twenty years, the Party has fought against the vested interests and forces of corruption within our city, often bearing the brunt of their attack upon the people's rights. Many planks of the program which the Party has championed from its very founding are today accepted by the vast majority of the people. No longer are the Communists alone in fighting for Old Age Security, Unemployment Relief, Labor Unity, Government Aid for Farmers, Equal Rights for the Negro People, and the other slogans that have marked the history of our Party in the United States and in Los Angeles. ■ excerpt from *2 Decades of Progress, Communist Party, LA County, 1919–1939*, p. 17.

Ah, the Popular Front. I'm not going to get wound up in that because I'm still sorting out my thoughts. However, I think I once told you about an incident that sticks in my mind. It was an election night party in San Francisco in 1938. As the returns came in and it was clear that [Culbert] Olson made it, a young woman dashed over to Bill [Schneiderman] and gushed. "We won, we won." Very coldly, very precisely, Bill replied, "We did not win, comrade. The Democratic party won." I believe the incident sticks in my mind because I was caught up in the young woman's elation. Why? ■ letter from Al Richmond to Dorothy, June 30, 1971.

The second half of the 1930s, the years of the People's Front, was a time of enormous excitement and sizable expansion for the Party. Nationally, the Party grew from 25,000 members in 1934 to twice that in 1936 to 75,000 by 1938. In Los Angeles, where I had settled at the end of the decade, the Party had nearly three thousand members, making it one of the most important centers of Party strength outside of New York City. Of course, that still left us a small party in a large country, but because we were organized so that we could move as one, our practical influence was much greater than membership figures alone would suggest. In California the growing influence of the Party could be seen in the organization of the new CIO unions, in the growth of popular movements opposing both domestic reaction and the spread of fascism abroad, and in electoral politics, where—if we still were not able to win victories for avowed Communists—we contributed in significant ways to the victories of other progressive candidates. We had a feeling that history was on our side and that we were making history every day. But for all our sense of elan, the fact remains that the Left's influence was distinctly limited. We had a large and immediate impact on a whole range of practical questions, where the workers and others we were trying to reach could see for themselves that we had something to offer. We had much less impact on the country's overall ideological outlook than we liked to think.

In the political sense the mid-1930s was upbeat as all get out. We felt we were making real advances, that the system was falling apart. We felt we were heading towards a socialist America. A period when everything that came out of the Soviet Union sounded wonderful. A period when we began to make some inroads in organizing the workers. And the whole political atmosphere then made it easier for us to function. We felt that the world was moving very, very fast. People joked about expecting the revolution in two or three years, but there was a feeling that this *was* a revolutionary period. No question that in our lifetime we'd see socialism. ■ Jack Olsen, YCL district organizer in California.

Shortly after I was released from jail in the fall of 1934 I was sent to New York City to attend a plenum of the Young Communist League (a "plenum," in the jargon of the movement, was an enlarged meeting of the National Committee or some other authoritative body). The YCL leaders in California, Jack Olsen and Archie Brown, did not want to attend this meeting and insisted I should go because, they said, I had been a big strike leader and would be able to report on my experiences. The real reason they didn't want to go had more to do with some dispute they had going with the national office, and they chose to remain a safe distance away. I was not the right person to send, as I tried to tell them, because I had been in jail during the San Francisco general strike and the EPIC campaign, and was less well informed than many others. Just the same, I soon found myself on a bus heading across country.

All we had been able to scrape together for the trip was money enough for a bus ticket and fourteen dollars to live on. I wasn't halfway across the country when my money ran out. When we got to Pennsylvania we hit a snowstorm, and the heating system on the bus broke down. By the time I reached my destination, seven days after leaving California, I was half-starved and half-frozen and completely penniless. I had never been East before, and I was incredibly naive. I was standing on a street corner in New York asking people how to get to the headquarters of the Young Communist League when a cab driver pulled up and said, "You're all alone in the city. You just arrived?" I said yes. He said, "Do you have any friends or family here?" I said no. He said, "Well, get in and I'll take you." "I haven't any money," I said. "That's all right. Get in the cab." When I did he turned to me and said, "Now, let me tell you the first lesson you better learn. You never tell anybody in New York City that you don't have family or friends here, that you don't know where you're going, and that you're lost. Don't you understand what can happen to a young girl in

New York?" But my luck held, and the cab driver took me straight to Communist Party headquarters down on West 12th Street.

There for the first time I met the national leaders of the Young Communist League. Without any chance to eat, sleep, or change clothes I walked right into the national plenum meeting. Gil Green, Mac Weiss, and other national YCL leaders were giving reports. I didn't understand a word of what they were saying. It all seemed so eloquent and was couched in very esoteric inner-Party language. Eventually it was my turn to give a report on the situation in California. It is not a happy memory. I had no idea what they wanted from me. I got up and started stammering out a very disjointed account of the past year's struggles in California. And what made it all the worse is that some guy in the back of the room kept interrupting me every two minutes: "What about this? What about that?" I was getting angrier and more unhappy and even less coherent with each interruption. Finally I was able to finish and sat down in total misery. Then the guy in the back of the room called me over and introduced himself as "Max." I said to him, "I don't want to talk to you. You're a rude person. Even if I had known what to say you made it impossible for me to think." I turned around and started to walk away. One of the other YCL members came over and said. "Hey, don't you know who that is?" "No, who is it?" "He's the representative of the Young Communist International." A representative of the Young Communist International, someone who came from the Soviet Union, was God incarnate, full of all the wisdom of the world. I stood there petrified, ashamed of how I had insulted the representative from Mecca. He came over and patted me on the shoulder and said, "That's all right, don't feel bad. It's your comrades who are at fault for letting you come without having any discussions with you about what is needed to report on."

I met Max soon afterward in California, at a state Party meeting in a farmhouse in Ontario. I was assigned to give a report on behalf of the Young Communist League. This time he got hold of me before I was scheduled to speak, and said, "I will work with you, so you'll know what kind of report to give." What "working with me" meant was that he dictated the entire speech to me. I was even more uncomfortable delivering this speech than I had been in New York. It was very polished, but none of it came from me. Afterward Celeste Strack, who was a national YCL leader and a brilliant student at UCLA, and Louise Todd, one of the younger state Party leaders, came up to congratulate me. I told them, "That's not my speech. Max wrote it. I had nothing to do with it." It wasn't that I disagreed with what he had given me to say, but I didn't like pretending that I had written this "advanced" speech on my own.

We had a lot of people in the Young Communist League who had found the truth and, by God, they expounded it and would brook no opposition. Dorothy was different. She used to glory in discussions with people who disagreed with her. She is one of the few people I knew who actually relished having political arguments with the Lovestoneites and the Trotskyites. ■ Jack Olsen.

While in California, Max taught classes for the YCL leaders at my mother's house. My brother Bernard by then was in medical school at USC and at the same time was reading a lot of Trotskyist literature. He never joined the Trotskyist movement, but he was very impressed by Trotsky's intellectual capacities; he even got me to read some of his books, though I remained very critical of them. Trotsky was regarded by the Communist movement as a counterrevolutionary and imperialist agent. Bernard and I would have wild shouting arguments about it. When Max heard about my brother's reading habits, he said to my mother, "Do you mean you allow your son to come into this house when he reads Trotsky?" My mother said, "Of course I allow my son. What are you talking about 'allow'? I'm delighted when he comes!" Max said, "Well, comrade, then you must choose between your son and me. I will not come into a house where a person who is impressed by Trotsky is allowed to come." Many other Communists would have said, "You're absolutely right." Families were broken up over this kind of issue. But my mother, although a very dedicated Party member who had absolutely no sympathy for Trotskyism, was also a very independent woman and would not capitulate to that kind of pressure. She replied, "My dear comrade, while I have great esteem for you as a representative of the Soviet Union and of the Young Communist International, if it comes to choosing between my son and you, there is no problem in my mind. You don't ever have to come back again." I learned a lesson from her. You could have very sharp disagreements with people, but you didn't have to break with them over those questions.

After my return from New York I was sent to San Pedro to organize a branch of the Young Communist League. San Pedro lies just to the south of Los Angeles, opening onto a protected bay, and serves as the city's major port. It was a very important center of Communist activity, the base for our local organizing among sailors and longshoremen. There had been a Communist Party unit in San Pedro for many years, but never a YCL unit.

> There were ups and downs in agricultural organizing in the 1930s. After the general strike in 1934 it was suddenly much easier and much more fruitful to build unions in the factories and warehouses and on the waterfront, so there was a lot less attention paid to agriculture. I know in the YCL we were so damn busy trying to build our base among longshoremen that when we had a person like Dorothy, instead of sending her someplace like the Imperial Valley we'd send her to San Pedro. ■ Jack Olsen.

In some places the YCL was primarily a student organization, but that was not the case in San Pedro. Most of the members we attracted were young sailors and longshoremen, and most of our political efforts went into building the union movement. We started with about five YCL members and ended up a year later with fifty. The YCL worked very effectively in the rank and file caucus in the International Longshoremen's Association, which was an AFL union, and helped lay the groundwork for the organization of its successor the International Longshoremen's and Warehousemen's Union (ILWU), which became a mainstay of the CIO in California. The ILWU was led by Harry Bridges, who was very close to the Communist Party, but the union was far form being an ideologically closed shop. The San Pedro local was always led by men who were politically opposed to Bridges and who frequently ignored International policies. One of the workers I met on the San Pedro waterfront, who later became a leader in the ILWU, was a longshoreman named L. B. Thomas. He was regarded with suspicion by many Communists as a right-winger. There was this great tendency in the Party to dismiss people who weren't with us 100 percent as "phonies." Sometimes they were, but sometimes they were people like L. B. who just had different approaches and ideas. I learned not to pay much attention to the labels that were put on people, if they were competent and willing to work hard. We became very good friends and edited a rank-and-file bulletin together. This was a transitional moment for the Party's strategy in the labor movement. We were moving away from independent organizing back into the mainstream of the labor movement. The TUUL union on the waterfront, the Marine Workers Industrial Union, was still around when I got to San Jose. Within another year it would dissolve, along with the other TUUL unions, and its members would join the AFL. I became an honorary member of the MWIU because I helped them organize the marches on the Sailors Snug Harbor, which was a private relief agency for sailors on the beach in San Pedro.

I was enchanted with the sailors I met in San Pedro. They were already veterans of great labor struggles, very courageous, militant, and politically sophisticated. I can remember sitting in the headquarters listening spellbound to the yarns they would spin of life aboard ship and in the ports they visited. The YCL also helped organize the Cannery Workers Industrial Union in the fish canneries on Terminal Island in San Pedro harbor. We got a federal charter from the AFL for the cannery union, which was what they gave you when they didn't have a union with jurisdiction over an industry. That allowed us to take all the workers of all the different crafts within the cannery into one industrial union. Our main organizer there was a brilliant young Communist named Jack Moore, who led a very successful organizing drive and won a contract from the employers. By this time we had learned the significance of signing that contract.

While I was in San Pedro I shared a house with a group of young Communists. I suppose it was what would later be called a "commune," but we didn't think in those terms. It was just a question of getting by with little or no money. As the local YCL organizer I was supposed to get paid five dollars a week, but it was part of my job to get that five dollars donated by sympathizers in San Pedro, which meant I often didn't get paid. Every night I'd go eat with a different family. It was like being a schoolteacher or a minister in a nineteenth-century village, it was considered part of your upkeep. For the first time in my life I started to gain weight because I always ate a lot of bread so that I wouldn't have to eat the meat—I didn't want to take the more expensive food out of the mouths of the people I was sharing with.

The waterfront was a tough place to organize, and we faced a lot of violence in San Pedro. One incident turned into both a political and a family tragedy. A seaman named Britt Webster lived in our house in San Pedro. He had come originally from a very wealthy family in Boston, became radicalized in college after he visited a New York City slum, and went to sea. He was involved in a tanker strike in the harbor, and at the time was part of rank-and-file caucus trying to take over the local AFL sailors' union. A goon squad from the union attacked our house and in the ensuing fistfight one of the goons was knocked to the sidewalk, where he struck his head and died. Two years later Britt, who by that time had married my sister Frances, was arrested with some others on a charge of murder. It was a frame-up. Britt had been part of the group that had been attacked, after all, and he was eventually released. But he could not handle the pressures of the arrest and trial and lost his sanity. He eventually wound up confined in a seamen's hospital in San Francisco, where he committed suicide.

> Once you reached eighteen you had your choice. You could join either the Party or the YCL. The Party always said that work among young people was important, so there had to be a youth organization. But the Party itself usually took priority. It was a battle where you were going to put people. It depended in part on the inclinations of the individuals involved, and in part on whether YCL leaders were able to win the battle to get sufficient forces to build the organization. ■ Jack Olsen.

The leadership of the YCL decided that because I had done such a good job in San Pedro I should go to San Francisco to be a YCL organizer. Actually, I wasn't a good YCL organizer. If I was good at anything, it was what we called "mass organization." What you were supposed to do with the YCL as an organization unto itself, apart from the popular struggles it helped support, was something I never quite understood. In San Francisco I tried to involve myself in the same kind of mass organizing that I had done in San Pedro. I got a job working for the Alaska Cannery Workers Union office. This was a seasonal industry, and most of the workers would be recruited either in San Francisco or Seattle. Their office was in a big building on the waterfront, and the YCL ran a union recreation center out of the same building to attract young longshoremen and seamen. Seamen would come on the beach and have no place else to go except the gin mills. Like the IWW halls in the lumber towns in the Northwest in the old days, the center served as an alternative place for them to hang out. I had long had a horror of alcohol, and the time I spend around the waterfront did nothing to change my opinion. I later got a job working as a waitress on the waterfront; I had to open up the restaurant at six in the morning and step over the drunken bodies of longshoremen or seamen in order to get inside. I was a very unsatisfactory waitress and never held a job very long. I didn't mind counter work, bringing workers their coffee or sandwiches, because I loved to talk with them, ask them about what was happening on the ships or on the docks. When there weren't any meals to be served, I'd sit there talking over the counter to all the workers who came in instead of tending to the side work of polishing the napkin holders and the coffee maker.

I wasn't happy in San Francisco. In 1936 and 1937 industrial unionism was finally beginning to take off nationally. John L. Lewis led his mine workers and a number of other important unions out of the AFL and formed the CIO. In Michigan workers were sitting in at GM plants to demand recognition of the United Auto Workers, and sit-down strikes were spreading across the country in other industries as well. Everywhere Communists were in the thick of the action and reaping the rewards of their involvement. My future husband Philip "Slim" Connelly, for example, was a Newspaper Guild organizer who became secretary of the Los Angeles CIO Council and chairman of the California CIO Council. I didn't care about titles and power, but I wanted in on the action instead of being stuck in San Francisco, an incompetent waitress and an even worse YCL organizer.

In the summer of 1937 I went to talk to Frank Carlson, who was state chairman of the YCL, and asked to be reassigned to union work. Frank absolutely refused to hear about it. "It's true," he said, "you are a failure. But you've got to be disciplined and learn how to do it. You should become the organizer for one little club in North Beach instead of continuing as the city organizer, and that way maybe you'll learn how to do it right." His response reduced me to tears. He left me crying in the YCL office when the state chairman of the Communist Party, Bill Schneiderman, came walking in. "What's the matter, Dorothy?" I told him that I was miserable as a YCL organizer and that Frank refused to let me go to become a CIO organizer. He said, "Well, that's preposterous. Of course you should do it. There is no comparison of the importance of it. We don't have so many people with your kind of experience that we can just throw them away." So he called a meeting of the Party and the YCL leadership, and they passed a resolution that I be released from my YCL assignment. Only Frank voted against it.

I had already been offered an organizing job in Los Angeles with a new union led by Donald Henderson. Henderson was a former economics professor who became involved in organizing agricultural workers after he was fired from his academic position because of his radicalism. He organized a union first under the auspices of TUUL, brought it into the AFL in 1935, and finally in 1937 took it into the CIO. By that time it was known as the United Cannery, Agricultural, Packing and Allied Workers of America (UCAPAWA), with its acronym spoken as a word that sounded like "Yucca-pow-uh." It was never a very big union, but for a time it had a very diverse following, including cannery and packing workers in New Jersey, sharecroppers in Alabama, beet field workers in Colorado, and citrus workers in Florida. In California, the Party's efforts to organize field workers had just about come to a halt with the arrests in 1934; the organization of UCAPAWA led to a rebirth of agricultural organizing. This time around we were much more effective because of the lessons we had learned from the setbacks of the early 1930s. Henderson was a very bright, energetic man, but I was never one of his big fans, because he wasn't a very good administrator. UCAPAWA internally was a very slack organization. Since Henderson was mostly involved with UCAPAWA's east coast organizing, we didn't see much of him out in California in any case.

Henderson had a brilliant idea, which was to organize the food processing industry as a base for organizing agriculture, and in agriculture to organize the people who weren't migrants, who stayed in the towns year-round, and use them as a nucleus to build locals of UCAPAWA. And for awhile it worked. I remember we built seven locals strung down through the San Joaquin Valley. We found some marvelous people who became the leaders of those locals. ■ Elizabeth Eudey, UCAPAWA organizer 1938–1940.

Many of UCAPAWA's organizers were Communists. Nobody else wanted to work in this field. For that same reason, many of the organizers, and some of the union officers, were women. I was elected as an international vice president at a UCAPAWA convention in 1938. I wasn't too happy about the circumstances of my election, because when I was nominated for the position the speaker kept stressing the fact that I was a woman. I was resentful and thought, "What the hell difference does it make that I'm a woman? Am I qualified or not?" I suppose you could say I was not very advanced in my thinking on the "woman question" in those days. Actually the fact that I was a woman was a very legitimate consideration; the work force UCAPAWA was trying to organize included many women, and the union needed women officers. Despite my own backwardness, the Left-led unions as a whole did much better on issues of sexual equality than most of the rest of the labor movement, which remained utterly male-dominated, even in industries with primarily female work forces.

Even though I was not in any conscious sense a feminist in the 1930s, I was still somewhat nonplussed when the women's liberation movement came along in the sixties and spoke as if it had invented the "liberated woman." I didn't see anything all that new in what they were advocating. That's how many of us had lived our lives all along. It would never have occurred to me in the 1930s or afterward to subordinate what I was doing to what any male companion wanted. Like many single women in the Party I took it for granted that I would have my own "career"—although that is not the term I would have used to describe what I was doing—and that I would get involved with men or not as I chose.

Healthy sport, swimming, racing, walking, bodily exercises of every kind, and many-sided intellectual interests. . . . that will give young people more than eternal theories and discussions about sexual problems and the so-called "living life to the full." Healthy bodies, healthy minds! . . . And I wouldn't bet on the reliability, the endurance in struggle of those women who confuse their personal romances with politics. . . . No, no! that does not square with the revolution. ■ Clara Zetkin, "Lenin on the Woman Question," International Publishers, 1934, p. 12.

After Lou and I separated, I was involved with a number of men. If I had been asked at the time, I would have said I was very happy with the life I was living. I had none of my mother's "regret and remorse." I didn't spend any time thinking about might-have-beens and should-have-dones, and I had this somewhat mystical belief that whatever turned up was for the best. I wasn't very self-analytical. In retrospect, in personal life as in politics, I became aware of patterns that I could not see at the time. My relationships with men were not as uncomplicated as I thought. My "liberation" from conventional standards of female behavior did not consist so much of getting what I wanted in my private life as in not attaching a great deal of importance to what I was missing. There was one guy I'll call "Dutch" who I met in San Pedro and with whom I lived for about two years. He was a seaman on steam schooners on the west coast. I stayed involved with Dutch for so long—this is a dreadful confession—because I felt it was my Party duty to do it. We needed to have a seaman stay on the beach. And he was lonely and he was one of our best members and if that's what he wanted, and it's what he did want, then it was my Party duty to give him what he wanted. Later I started thinking of this as my "Salvation Army" approach to love and marriage. You're bestowing yourself because that's what somebody else wants and what do you care? It shouldn't matter one way or the other.

I got involved with Don Healey in 1939. Don had been a professional dancer in the early 1930s and had moved to Los Angeles to try to get into the movies. He wound up instead as the business agent in the painter's union and in 1936 joined the party. He became the L.A. director of Labor's Non-Partisan League. He was an excellent public speaker, and very influential in city and state politics. He was extremely bright but learned totally from experiences rather than from reading. As far as I could tell, he absorbed his politics through his fingertips. When I married Don in 1940 he was considered the big catch of all the guys around the Party in Los Angeles, very popular and very handsome.

I had often slept with men not because I gave a damn about them but because it was the easiest way to establish friendships and because it reassured me of my attractiveness. Shortly after Don and I got married I had plastic surgery on my nose. Since my brother was a doctor by then I could get the operation done for practically nothing. Here I was, raised by Mama to be indifferent to appearances, and yet I'd always carried this vague discontent about the way I looked. I had not been an attractive child. I remember when I was eleven living in Oakland and some neighbor said to me, "My, what a shame your looks are spoiled by your nose." That stayed with me. After the surgery, I discovered that I held my head in a new way; until then I had always unconsciously tried to keep people from looking at my profile. I would always face them directly, so that my nose would not be as noticeable. I was much more comfortable with my appearance afterward, though also vaguely ashamed at having given in to what Mama deemed bourgeois standards.

In the 1930s, as in the 1960s, sexual freedom was not quite as "free" for women as it was for men. That was brought home to me by an incident during the Kern County cotton strike in 1938. When the strike broke out I was pregnant for the third time. I had known about my condition for some time and had gone to a chiropractor who supposedly had a new technique for performing abortions. But it was a racket; all she had actually done was to paint my uterus with iodine. Still, I was able to set off for Kern County assuming everything was taken care of, because when the iodine started coming out I thought I had aborted. Life during a strike under the best of circumstances is physically and emotionally exhausting. I was out every day on picket lines that had to cover all of Kern County—Delano, Buttonwillow, Shafter, Bakersfield, Arvin—from six in the morning until two o'clock the next morning. Like every strike, it involved constant movement, constant meetings, constant speaking, and constant worry about the state of organization and morale.

Midway through the strike I went to a function sponsored by a strike support group. I was sitting on the floor talking to an official from the Farm Security Administration, when all of a sudden I started feeling very uncomfortable. I ran to the bathroom and barely closed the door before I realized I was miscarrying. I was angry that I had been fooled by the chiropractor, but relieved that in any case I was no longer pregnant. I went back to the meeting as if nothing had happened, when all of a sudden I started having terrible pains. I went over to a fellow UCAPAWA organizer, Pat Callahan, and said, "You've got to get me back to the hotel. I'm sick."

Pat drove me back to the flop-house where La Rue McCormick, from the International Labor Defense, and I were sharing a room. She was asleep when I got there, and I didn't want to wake her so I just crawled into bed. But the pains continued to get worse, and finally I crawled down the hall to the toilet, vomiting and hemorrhaging all the way. I got to the bathroom and passed out over the toilet bowl. La Rue woke up with the vague feeling that I'd been there. Luckily she decided to turn on the light and saw the trail of vomit and blood. She called an ambulance, and I was taken to the closest hospital, which happened to be a Catholic hospital. By that time I had lost a lot of blood; according to the ambulance attendant in another twenty minutes I would have died.

LaRue had me booked in the hospital under a false name because she was afraid that if I was registered as "Dorothy Ray" the growers and the newspapers might find out about my condition, and it would be used somehow to discredit the union. But the next day she couldn't remember the name that she had used and didn't know how to find me. She couldn't very well go up to the sisters in charge and say she'd forgotten my name. So, thinking fast, she went to a ten-cent store around the corner and bought a dollar's worth of trinkets and went up to the sisters and said she wanted to give away free toys to the children. That way she got to go from room to room until she discovered me. My brother and sister once again came to rescue me and brought me back to L.A. to recover, a lengthier than usual process became of the infection and complications.

> Back to the 1930s, I question Richard's judgment that you are fascinated by the 1930–1935 period solely because those were your formative years. The class-against-class line had the beauty and attractiveness of utter simplicity. It corresponded to our own age of innocence. Later life became more complicated, and in every complication there tends to be some loss of certainty; by definition something is complicated because the alternatives are not simple. ■ excerpt from letter from Al Richmond to Dorothy, November 9, 1971.

In reading labor histories dealing with the Party's activities in the 1930s, especially those written by younger historians, I find a certain amount of romanticization, manifested in a tendency to celebrate the Party's promotion of class struggle in the early part of the decade, and a tendency to criticize the Party's "sell-out" in the late 1930s. It is true that the early 1930s have a certain charm that the latter 1930s lacked. It was so much simpler, us against them, and everybody but us were scoundrels. The early days were times of great militancy and pioneering efforts, but there is no question in my mind that the Party played a far more important and commanding role in the rise and development of the CIO. That was the time of our greatest involvement in the class struggle, a time when lasting gains were made. If there was ever a moment when we came close to being what we always said we were, a party of the working class, that was it. The years between 1937 and 1940 were so jam-packed with organizing drives and strikes that I felt like a whirling dervish. There were field workers' strikes all over California: in Fullerton, Modesto, Salinas, and Bakersfield, to name just a few. These were bitter struggles, with arrests and violence, as in the early 1930s. But they differed from those early strikes in that each of them we managed to gain something for the workers involved.

I moved back to Los Angeles at the beginning of 1937 as a UCAPAWA international representative. Because of the deportation of Mexicans from California and the great influx of Okies and Arkies, most of the field workers we dealt with now were Anglos. One exception was a strike of orange pickers in Orange County, centered in Santa Ana, where once again I lived in a Mexican colony. The small growers, who were mostly Japanese, wanted to settle with us, but the big Anglo growers, who controlled the shipping and the bank loans, wouldn't let them. I was arrested again in that strike, generating big headlines about "Dorothy Ray, Outside Agitator," but I didn't spend much time in jail. And by this time, thanks to the investigations of the La Follette committee and people like Carey McWilliams, the growers weren't able to use vigilantes with the impunity they had in the Imperial Valley Strikes.

> We used to say that when Culbert Olson was elected governor, socialism came to California. It was a joke, of course, but it did make a big difference. . . . Carey McWilliams was the head of the state division of immigration and housing, which had under its aegis, for reasons best known to the California bureaucracy, agricultural labor. He had a very left-wing staff. In the cotton strike Carey would hold hearings for us to establish a "prevailing wage." . . . His findings weren't binding, but we found we could use them to carry on the strike, and we'd settle with individual growers if they'd put this wage into effect. It was a very different atmosphere from before. It was a Culbert Olson atmosphere. It was a Carey McWilliams atmosphere. ■ Elizabeth Eudey.

One of the most successful organizing drives I was involved in was at the California Sanitary Canning Company, which was located on Long Beach Boulevard in Los Angeles. It led to a strike in the summer of 1939. The cannery was owned by two brothers, George and Joseph Shapiro. They absolutely refused to recognize the union. Most of their workers were women: some Jewish, some Russian, and most of them Mexicans. I learned a lot from that strike. First of all, I absorbed some notions that I suppose could be called feminist, although as I've said, we didn't use that term at the time. When I met Mexican women who worked in the fields, in the countryside, they were almost always part of a family unit. Their concerns and demands were those they shared with other workers, male and female. But in the city, where some of the women were by now the second generation to be working outside the home, the women were more independent and vocal. The contract demands the union was fighting for, equal pay for equal work and maternity leave, came directly out of their work experience. For many of them, the union became the channel through which they found their voices. They wouldn't have called themselves feminists either, but they were fighting for their interests as women as well as their interests as workers.

I also learned a lot about Mexican culture in that strike. The proximity of Los Angeles to Mexico and the constant influx of new migrants gave these workers a vibrant sense of national identity. The cultural ties were very strong. Songs that were popular in Mexico were soon being sung in Los Angeles; and there were dozens of Los Angeles social clubs based on Mexican birthplace. A strong sense of national identity held these workers together, but did not prevent them from making common cause with others, like their Jewish and Russian fellow-workers. Some years later there would be a big inner-Party battle over whether Mexican-Americans should be considered an oppressed national minority, the same way that we had traditionally regarded Blacks. Delfino Varela, a gifted young social worker who moved to Los Angeles in the 1950s was a leader in the battle to gain this recognition for his fellow Mexican-Americans. National CP leaders were very resistant, but remembering my experience with the California Sanitary strike, I gave Delfino my full support.

We wore down the Shapiro brothers' resistance by organizing picket lines in front of their homes. They were big poohbahs in Jewish organizations in L.A., so we got all kinds of Jewish organizations to adopt resolutions condemning their refusal to bargain. Finally they agreed to meet with us, and at a dramatic midnight bargaining session they gave in and recognized the union. We didn't win much beyond union recognition in that first contract, but having opened the door for collective bargaining, in subsequent years the contracts got much better.

I was also involved in a campaign to organize walnut workers in Los Angeles, who were mostly women (this is where I discovered the importance of the torn stocking issue). Sam Yorty proved very helpful to us in that struggle. He was then a state assemblyman and he and Jack Tenney were considered the two "Red assemblymen"—a little ironic, considering their subsequent careers. Yorty would come to our union meetings and tell the workers why they should join the union. He was a great orator with a fondness for alliterative phrases. He'd build his speeches around the repetition of phrases like "We must fight the masters of monopoly and the princes of plenty." The women just adored him. I even went out with him a couple of times. In just a few years he was making a name for himself and carving out a bright political future by becoming the scourge of the supposed Communist plot to take over the States Relief Agency.

A few nights ago I spoke to 1,500 women—women who work picking walnuts out of shells. It was one of the most amazing meetings I've ever attended. The remarks of the speakers were translated into five different languages. There were Russians, Armenians, Slavs, Mexicans, etc. All ages of women, from young girls to old women. A whole row of old Russian women who couldn't speak a word of English, dressed in their shawls and scarfs. . . . This was the first meeting these people had ever attended—that is, their first union meeting. You should have been there to *feel* the thing: the excitement, the tension. And you should have watched some of these women as they got up to their feet and tried to tell about their experiences. They had to struggle with themselves to get a word or words. But the profound meaning they conveyed! ■ Letter from Carey McWilliams to Louis Adamic, October 3, 1937, reprinted from Vicki Ruiz, *Cannery Women, Cannery Lives*, p. 135.

We filed charges of unfair bargaining practices with the National Labor Relations Board against the walnut growers. They had been firing union organizers and had set up a company union in violation of the Wagner Act. It took three years, because the growers fought it every step of the way through the courts, but we finally won. This was the first time I had ever dealt with the NLRB; their attorneys and trial examiners were sympathetic to the union, and they did everything they could to help us out. One of the special problems we faced in UCAPAWA was that agricultural field workers were specifically excluded from the benefits of the Wagner Act. When we were organizing cannery workers or shed workers in the field, we could petition for representation elections, or file charges as we did in the case of the walnut growers. But that was not the case when we were organizing the workers who were actually out harvesting the fruit or cotton or vegetables.

"Are you Mrs. Joad?"

"Yes."

"Well, I'm Jim Rawley. I'm camp manager. Just dropped by to see if everything's all right. Got everything you need?"

Ma studied him suspiciously. "Yes," she said.

Rawley said, "I was asleep when you came last night. Lucky we had a place for you." His voice was warm.

Ma said simply, "It's nice. 'Specially them wash tubs."

"You wait till the women get to washing. Pretty soon now. You never heard such a fuss. Like a meeting. Know what they did yesterday, Mrs. Joad? They had a chorus. Singing a hymn tune and rubbing the clothes all in time. That was something to hear, I tell you."

The suspicion was going out of Ma's face. "Must a been nice. You're the boss?"

"No," he said. "The people here worked me out of a job. They keep the camp clean, they keep order, they do everything. I never saw such people. . . . ■ John Steinbeck, *The Grapes of Wrath*.

There was one New Deal agency that proved helpful to us in the fields, and that was the Farm Security Administration. The FSA administered a system of migrant labor camps in California. When I read about the Joads arriving at the temporary safe haven of the "government camp" in *The Grapes of Wrath*, I knew exactly what they felt like. Those FSA camps were heaven, not just for the workers but for UCAPAWA as well. In the San Joaquin Valley, where I was organizing, FSA camps like Weed Patch and Buttonwillow had meeting rooms and elected camp councils. If you went to the council and asked permission to speak, they would usually set up a meeting for you. There was a relative degree of stability and continuity in the camps; when you went back, you could find the same workers you talked to the previous time and sign them up.

The camps were clean, which made it possible for the workers to enjoy a decent standard of living. Outside the camps, life for migrant workers was a constant scrabble for the meanest kind of existence. It was a struggle just to get enough water to wash your clothes or to take a bath once a month. Everything was so hard, so terrible, so awkward. I stayed in one migrant shack with a family that had five children. I shared one big iron bed with all five of them, just lying on the bed springs, covered with a grimy sheet. There was no sanitation except for a privy out back, where the only way you could tolerate the stink was to hold your breath until you came out. Those kinds of conditions, rather than making workers more likely to join the union, left them exhausted and demoralized. Those showers and flush toilets at the FSA camps did half of our organizing for us. The mood of the workers was different. They were clean, and as a result they were confident, independent, and able.

> The FSA camps were centers of organizing. Of course, it varied: some camp directors were liberals, some weren't. The regional office of the Farm Security was very friendly, very protective of organizing agricultural workers. We were the ones who did it, we were a bunch of hard-working kids who worked our tails off, so they liked us. ■ Elizabeth Eudey.

Our relationships with both the federal government, represented by the NLRB and the FSA, and the state government, once Governor Olson came into office, were very warm and helpful. I began to appreciate two things which I had not understood before: first, that the fact that someone works for the government doesn't mean that they've been co-opted and sold out; and second, that it can make an enormous difference what administration is in power and what kind of appointments they make. The contrast between our experience as organizers at the start of the decade and at the end was incredible. I didn't draw any kind of grand theoretical conclusions from this contrast, but it planted a seed, a doubt about the way we had previously interpreted Marx's comments about the state. I began to understands that the "political superstructure" of society could enjoy a measure of independence from the economic base because of the clash of interests between classes and even within the bourgeoisie itself.

> Governor Olson . . . incurred the resentment of growers by appointing a Cotton Wage Hearing Board to air the issues under dispute and to seek

terms for settlement of the strike. . . . Growers held a mass meeting of protest in Madera on October 25, 1939. Speakers served . . . an ultimatum to the effect that if the strike leaders were not imprisoned and picketing prevented, the growers would take the law into their own hands. . . . They planned to break up by force a forthcoming strike meeting in Madera County Park. Some 300 growers armed with clubs and rubber hoses invaded the park the following day and forcefully disrupted the gathering. The State highway patrol fired tear-gas bombs into the crowd to quiet the melee. . . . The publicity attending the Cotton Wage Hearing Board rendered both groups more willing to compromise. . . . One grower after another broke away from the standards of the Associated Farmers and the Agricultural Labor Bureau and accepted the union compromise wage offer. . . . ■ "Cotton Strike, San Joaquin", *Labor Unionism in American Agriculture*, Bulletin No. 836, 1945, p. 178.

Even though I was now working as an organizer in the CIO, rather than the Communist-organized TUUL, I remained completely open about the fact of my membership in the Party. Everyone knew me as a "dues-paying" Communist. I have always been amused by that phrase. I never regularly paid dues to the Party until 1946. When you moved around a great deal, the way I did, the bookkeeping never kept up with you. But you could still be a Communist accepted by others as Communists, whether you paid dues or not. There is this myth that the Party ran like some kind of well-oiled machine, but it was never that well organized internally. There was a standing joke in the Party that if you wanted to have a leave of absence you didn't need to ask for it, you just moved across the street. The inefficiency was so enormous that your transfer to the new club would take years coming through. If you wanted to be active you still were active and nobody cared about the rest. But that inefficiency also meant that an enormous number of people fell through the cracks. The FBI did a much better job of keeping track of our members than we did, unfortunately.

A review of the indexes of the Los Angeles Field Division was made for the purpose of bringing together in one Subject file all the pertinent information relative to this individual. . . .

3-19-38 Now active in Walnut Growers plants. One of the main organizers for Agricultural Workers under which heading come the Walnut Pickers. Is C.P. organizer.

8-5-38 As an International Organizer of the UCAPAWA in Los Angeles is very much in evidence at the Industrial Union Council (CIO).

9-1-38 With Pat CALAHAN and LORETTA ADAMS, appeared in the San Fernando Valley and in Orange County to agitate strike activities just after the speech of HARRY BRIDGES at the CIO State Convention in Los Angeles in August, 1938. . . .

12-22-38 One of the nine vice-presidents elected to International Executive Board of UCAPAWA conclave held in San Francisco in December 1938. . . .

2-17-39 Organizer of the United Cannery Agricultural, Packing and Allied Workers of America. On 2-16-39, appeared before the assembly interim committee investigating unemployment and relief and hurled the charge that the Associated Farmers were responsible for bringing migrant workers to California. . . . ■ excerpts from FBI report, April 17, 1941.

I was beginning to be active in the L.A. CIO Council, and there were huge internal struggles taking place between Left and Right on the Council. When I spoke in these debates at Council meetings, I was regarded by everyone present as a Party spokesman. I tried to maintain good personal relations with our opponents. The ILWU local in San Pedro was considered under "right-wing," which is to say anti–Harry Bridges, leadership. But the leaders of the local were old friends of mine like L. B. Thomas and Bill Lawrence who remembered me from the YCL days. I'd fight them on the floor of the Council, but when we left the meeting we were on friendly terms. Whenever I was involved in a strike, I could call the leaders of the San Pedro ILWU local, and they would do everything they could to help. That to me was the most important question, the "class question"—when you needed solidarity, could you count on people? I could count on them. The fact that I was a publicly known Communist helped a great deal in my relations with the CIO Right, because they had no reason to be suspicious of me. They knew what I was up to. I made no bones about who and what I was. They liked that.

In a Left-led union like UCAPAWA, which did not have a strong internal opposition faction, I enjoyed certain liberties that Communists in other unions did not always share. I wasn't going to lose my job for being open about my politics. Questions about how open to be about our politics, and how best to organize our own members within a given union or workplace, were complicated ones for the Party. Up through the mid-1930s the Party would have meetings of Communists within various unions or workplaces, and some of our closest allies were very unhappy about it. They would say, "You people meet privately to arrive at your conclusions, and then you arrive in a body at a union meeting and that's what you fight for. You've already made up your mind before the debate takes place." We couldn't just shrug those objections off. There were also more opportunistic reasons why the Party began to reexamine the way it organized its members within the labor movement. For the first time we had close ties with top national labor people like John L. Lewis. Earl Browder, the Party's general secretary, was particularly concerned with keeping them happy. By 1938 the Party was abandoning its "fraction" meetings and shutting down its shop newspapers. That made it easier for us to get along with non-Communists, both locally and nationally, but it left a larger question unanswered, which was how to combine a commitment to trade unionism, and serving the day-to-day interests of workers, with a long-term struggle to convince workers that capitalism and reform struggles were not sufficient, that socialism was the ultimate goal for which we were fighting.

Although Browder supervised the behind-closed-doors contacts with top CIO leaders, most of us in the unions assumed that the Party's chairman, William Z. Foster, was an equal spokesman when it came to trade union questions.

It was Foster, after all, not Browder, who had an impressive background in the labor movement, as organizer of the packinghouse workers' drive in 1917 and the steelworkers' strike in 1919. Publicly Foster always spoke of the need for maintaining CIO unity, but his emphasis tended to be slightly less conciliatory than Browder's. We had no idea that there was a fierce private battle going on between the two. Foster had nearly died from a heart attack at the beginning of the decade. But by the mid-1930s he was writing again for the Party press and turning out pamphlets. He was always a very prolific writer. I remember a collection of his pamphlets that was very influential among us called *Organizing the Mass Production Industries*, published in 1936. He didn't make many national tours or public appearances outside of New York the way he once had, but we just assumed that was as a result of his heart condition. In our eyes he remained the authoritative public spokesman on issues confronting the labor movement. It is an oversimplification to assume that just because Browder was general secretary and he said or did something, that's what filtered down to us in the rank and file as the last word on Party policy.

The growth of the labor movement in the late 1930s was part and parcel of the whole change in the political atmosphere that had taken place since the start of the 1930s. That became very evident during that cotton strike in Kern County in the fall of 1938. By then the John Steinbeck Committee had come into existence to aid agricultural organization. Despite its name, the committee was initiated by the actress Helen Gahagan Douglass, who was its prime mover. (Helen was also a major figure in such Popular Front organizations as the Hollywood Anti-Nazi League—involvements which would come back to haunt her in her political battle with Richard Nixon.) The Steinbeck committee mobilized broad public support for agricultural organizing, not just among Hollywood people, but throughout the state. One real contribution the committee made was writing articles and publishing pamphlets to counter the growers' propaganda in the newspapers (the *Los Angeles Times*, for example, owned about eight thousand acres in the Imperial Valley and was not exactly a totally disinterested observer of the agricultural strikes). During the Kern County cotton strike the Steinbeck committee sponsored a statewide conference of academics, union people, workers, and Hollywood personalities to help drum up public support for us. The public response to such appeals was yet another measure of how much had changed since the early 1930s. Just as in the early days of the depression, the right wing was setting up its so-called citizens' committees to drum up hysteria and opposition to the strikes. But those groups were now being effectively countered by groups and campaigns on the Left, which raised funds, sponsored meetings, published pamphlets, turned out supporters on the picket line, and so on. This was all of great importance to our successes in that period.

UCAPAWA still faced serious problems. We could sign up a lot of people, and we began winning strikes, but we never developed a really stable membership or a system of regular dues collection. The seasonal nature of the work and the migratory nature of the work force made things very difficult. And we never had the resources we needed to sustain our organizing campaigns. John L. Lewis had given UCAPAWA fifty thousand dollars of CIO money to begin organizing, which sounds like a lot of money, but it wasn't anything compared with the hundreds of thousands of dollars pumped into the Steel Workers Organizing Committee. Agricultural organizing was very important to us in California, but it wasn't a priority for either the national CIO or the Party.

When the 1938 recession hit and hundreds of thousands of union members were laid off in the auto, steel, and rubber industries, the CIO cut back its subsidy to UCAPAWA. That meant that we had to lay off a lot of organizers, particularly in the fields where you knew you weren't going to collect enough dues to pay back the money you laid out on an organizer's salary. This was a poor union. UCAPAWA organizers had to pay for their organizing materials, application cards, union buttons, and leaflets out of their own salaries. We got forty dollars a week, and many of us took only half of that so that we could put another person on the organizing staff.

> The organization of the democratic front for victory in the elections is not an easy and simple task, due to . . . the many factors which still stand in the way of the unification of the democratic forces. We Communists are keenly aware of the responsibility we bear to bring about this unity. . . . Today this movement is gathering around the support of Senator Olson, the leading progressive candidate for the Democratic nomination for Governor in the August primaries. ■ William Schneiderman, "The Democratic Front in California," *The Communist*, October 1938, p. 663.

Because of the financial crisis in UCAPAWA, I lost my job in 1939 . I then went to work as the Los Angeles county organizer for Labor's Non-Partisan League. LNPL had been established by the CIO in 1936 as its political action arm, its first task to work for Franklin Roosevelt's reelection. Despite the opposition of the national AFL leadership, in California the LNPL drew support from both CIO and AFL unions. I've never understood why historians of the 1930s have paid so little attention to the LNPL. In Pennsylvania, Michigan, California, and other industrial states, it played a key role in mobilizing labor's new political power. It proved a very effective organization in registering voters, getting union members to the polls, and making sure that politicians responded to the labor movement's concerns.

In fact, the LNPL really embodied what we thought the People's Front meant. In addition to having unions affiliate directly to LNPL, in Los Angeles we set up chapters in the assembly and congressional districts where rank-and-file union members could join with community activists from churches, PTAs, and other groups in a new kind of organized alliance, working within but also maintaining their independence from the two-party system. LNPL's chapters raised issues—like the fight against racial discrimination—which were not part of electoral politics-as-usual in the United States in those years. Another significant People's Front coalition created around the same time in Los Angeles was the Congress of Spanish Speaking People, which united the diverse Latino population. Ramon Welch and Tony Salgado were important leaders of the group. The Congress only lasted two years, but its example and influence lingered on in successive Latino movements in southern California.

By this later 1930s the Communist Party had become an enthusiastic supporter of President Roosevelt and the New Deal. California got its own state New Deal late in the decade. Upton Sinclair's 1934 campaign had brought hundreds of thousands of newly registered voters into the Democratic Party and really transformed it. After Sinclair's defeat the EPIC clubs became Democratic Party clubs, and many Communists joined up. We also ran our own candidates for office form time to time; in one election for state controller the Communist candidate Anita Whitney attracted over one hundred thousand votes. Although our focus, in California as well as nationally, was on finding ways to be effective within the two-party system, we knew that whatever political clout we developed depended on our ability to keep up the pressure for signficant reform from outside the realm of electoral politics through the CIO, the LNPL, and other groups. Culbert Olson's successful campaign for the governor's seat in 1938 was a great triumph for this new kind of politics. It would be an exaggeration to say that Olson triumphed only because of our support, but he certainly would have had a much harder time without us. Olson got his start in California politics in his successful run for the state senate in 1934 as an EPIC supporter. Communists helped form the Federation for Political Unity, which brought together our own forces with those of the EPIC people, independent progressives like Robert Kenny, and union leaders, and served as one of the main sources of support for Olson in 1938. When he took office in January 1939, he was the state's first Democratic governor in forty years.

> What the Communists had that nobody else had was national and international connections with a point of view. There's nothing more powerful than a point of view. Among the things that Communists brought with them into the movement was a knowledge of organization. . . . I saw what intelligent direction, what organizational experience, what single-minded purpose can do. Even though their numbers were not very large, they had already had a lot of experience. It was fascinating to see how these people moved into the Democratic clubs, gave them real structure, it was really something. ■ Ellenore [Bogigian] Hittelman, an EPIC activist who would join the Party in Los Angeles in the mid-1930s.

Olson's triumph was short-lived; he would only serve one term. Soon after he became governor he found himself hamstrung by attacks from conservative opponents in the legislature; our own relations with him crumbled under the impact of the Nazi-Soviet pact and the Party's subsequent break with Roosevelt. But for a moment, in the early days of his administration, we had the highest hopes, particularly since one of his first acts as governor was of great symbolic importance to the Left and the labor movement. That was the pardoning of Tom Mooney, who had been in prison since 1916 on a framed-up bombing charge. It was a rare demonstration in the 1930s where you didn't see placards or hear chants demanding "Free Tom Mooney." Some 35,000 people turned out to greet Mooney when he spoke at the Los Angeles Coliseum in January 1939 (tragically, Mooney did not have long to enjoy his freedom and vindication;

he would die before another year passed). We had other victories to celebrate that year. LNPL played an important role in the successful recall campaign against L.A. Mayor Frank L. Shaw in the fall of 1938. It was a successful collaboration of the good-government people, who were primarily concerned with the corruption of Shaw's administration, and the LNPL, which had its own concerns. (It was during this campaign that Sam Yorty broke with the Left. He had wanted to run for mayor but was rejected as a candidate by others in the anti-Shaw coalition. Yorty decided that it was Don Healey and the CP who were responsible for Fletcher Bowron's getting the coalition's endorsement for mayor. He was wrong. It was the good-government people, led by Clifford Clinton, who refused to accept Yorty. But Sam never forgave us.) One of the first official acts of Shaw's Republican successor, Mayor Bowron, was to abolish the L.A. police department's Intelligence Bureau—the red squad—a source of great satisfaction to those of us who had been on the wrong end of Red Hynes's billy clubs in earlier years.

> A formal request was placed before the Fair Board of Imperial County . . . for the use of the auditorium on Memorial Day. . . . Lt. Gov. Ellis Pat-terson and Dr. Towne Nylander were scheduled as the principal speakers of the evening. This entirely reasonable request was flatly refused on the grounds that these men were antagonistic to the principles of Democracy, and the board was swayed by the resolution read by G. G. Bennett of the Associated Farmers in making their decision. . . . The Fair Board saw fit to let the use of this auditorium on one occasion this month to a group known as the Bachelors Bazaar Club for the purpose of staging a spectacle titled "Parisian Nights" which proved to be nothing more than a "men only" hoochee coochee leg show of the lowest moral status. . . . In the minds of the Fair Board, is this kind of entertainment of more educational value to the people of Imperial Valley than an open forum meeting with discussion of vital subjects? We leave this question to the people to pass judgment. . . . ■ broadside distributed by Fresh Fruit and Vegetable Workers Union, Local 78, UCAPAWA, CIO.

For me, the best illustration of how much had changed in a few years, and how much we thought was going to change in coming years, was a mass meeting held at the Imperial Valley fairgrounds in 1939. It could never have taken place before Olson's election—just as Olson's election would have been unlikely without the upsurge of labor organization in mid-1930s. The use of the fairgrounds was controlled by a board representing both the county and the state, but dominated in reality by members of Associated Farmers. Local 78 of the Fresh Fruit and Vegetable Workers, which was affiliated with UCAPAWA, decided to hold a rally there and along with Labor's Non-Partisan League applied for a permit. Their application was turned down by the county commissioners. LNPL launched a statewide campaign to reverse the decision, and Olson personally intervened to pressure the board to reverse the decision. Finally Local 78 got is permit. Hundreds of us drove down for the rally from Los Angeles.

It was the first time I had been back in the Imperial Valley since being released from jail in 1934. The fairground was jammed with fifteen hundred workers and supporters. It was the first legal rally ever held by organized labor in the Imperial Valley. Workers wearing CIO buttons paraded into the fairgrounds, ignoring the Associated Farmers vigilantes who were posted at entrances trying to intimidate them. The lieutenant governor of California, Ellis Patterson (who had started the decade as a Republican, converted to the Democratic Party after the EPIC campaign, and who was close to the Party), flew down from Sacramento in a small plane which landed right on the fairgrounds. In his speech he called for a third term for Roosevelt and condemned red-baiting. There was a tremendous emotional response from the crowd. Unionism was now legal in the Imperial Valley. It wasn't the revolution, to be sure, and it certainly didn't guarantee us smooth political sailing in the years to come, but it was no mean achievement for a decade's work.

5

MR. TAVENNER: You say your activity in the party continued until September 1939. What was the reason for its termination?

MR. KIMPLE: At that time I was informed that I was under suspicion of being a police spy. . . .

MR. TAVENNER: Was the suspicion of your connection with the police department made known to the rank and file members of the Communist Party?

MR. KIMPLE: No, sir; not at that time.

MR. TAVENNER: Can you give the committee a reason for it?

MR. KIMPLE: Yes, sir. Because of the position which I held, it would have been very demoralizing to the membership of the Communist Party if they knew that the man who had all of their membership records was in fact one of the Hines Red Squad. ■ testimony of William Ward Kimple before the House Committee on Un-American Activities, June 30, 1955 [Kimple joined the Communist Party in 1928 as an informer for the Los Angeles police, and rose in the Party hierarchy to the highly sensitive position of assistant to the County membership department.]

"Isn't it a fact," pursued Mr. Tenney, "that a lot of Communists get state jobs by claiming they've quit the Party?"

Miss Ray answered this with: "Frankly, Mr. Tenney, I know if I were to indulge in red baiting it would please this committee very much. But I am not a renegade. I do not betray those whom I have worked with. Furthermore I believe that at a time like this anyone who attacks the Communists in this country is a traitor. The Communists today are our greatest bulwark against the Nazi menace. If the Nazis conquer Soviet Russia they will be within rowboat distance of the United States."

But Mr. Tenney interrupted: "I want to ask you a direct question: Do you think the state should employ Communists?"

"Mr. Tenney," said Miss Ray, "I was brought up in the Jeffersonian ideal: The devil take a man's politics if he is an able worker." ■ *San Francisco News*, December 4, 1941.

The 1930s were not an "isolationist" decade for those of us on the Left. As engrossed as we were in domestic battles, we never lost sight of international developments. The world was heading toward another war, fascism was on the march, and we felt we were in a race with time to alert the rest of the country to its dangers. In particular, Communists developed an intense emotional involvement with the outcome of the Spanish Civil War. From 1936, when the fascist uprising began, through 1939, when the Loyalist government in Madrid fell, we had a feeling that the essence of what we were fighting for and fighting against was concentrated in that war. Here was a beleaguered popular front government fighting for its survival against not only internal reactionary forces but also against the combined forces of Italian and German fascism. Many men I had met in the YCL and the union movement went to Spain to fight as volunteers in the Abraham Lincoln Battalion, and many of them never came back. The names are too many to remember them all. I was asked by a young New Yorker who was going to mail letters to his mother every month while he was in Spain. He'd left behind a whole number of letters to be mailed because she didn't know he was going and he wanted her to believe that he was alive and well in California. I don't know whether he survived or not. There were constant rallies and meetings to build public support and raise funds for the cause of the Spanish Republic. The collection speeches at these meetings would always end with a reference to the Lincoln Battalion volunteers, "They are giving their lives, we are asking you simply to give money." Everyone knew the songs of the Republican cause and would sing them at these rallies. Up until the last moment we didn't think it was possible that the Republic would lose, because its cause was so just and so many had given so much for its victory. I still shudder sometimes when I'm at a demonstration and hear people chanting that slogan, "The people united can never be defeated." Unfortunately, history has proved that to be untrue, time and again.

On August 23, 1939, the Soviet Union and Nazi Germany signed a non-aggression pact. A week later the Nazis invaded Poland, and the Second World War began. With the signing of the Pact and the start of the war, the Communist Party adopted a new slogan, "The Yanks Are Not Coming." During the years of the People's Front we had been the most consistent advocates of collective security against the spread of fascism. Now, we argued, the Second World War was in essence a repetition of the war of 1914–1918, an "imperialist conflict" to divide up the world, and none of the belligerents deserved the support of the international working class.

Our abrupt change of line had a tragic impact on our work in the mass organizations. Lenin once used a phrase that gained currency among American Communists after the pact, that "the train of history makes sharp turns and those who are not skilled riders fall off the train." That train could make zigzags and detours and reversals, but we were determined to stay on board. Whatever the relative merits or defects of our new policies, there is no question that they suddenly made the Party much more vulnerable to attack than it had been for a number of years.

The outbreak of the Second Imperialist War . . . fundamentally changes the situation hitherto existing. . . . The previous alignment into democratic

and fascist camps loses its former meaning. The democratic camp today consists, first of all, of those who fight against the imperialist war. . . .
■ "Keep America Out of The Imperialist War!", declaration of the National Committee of the Communist Party, USA, September 19, 1939.

We immediately lost some Party members in Los Angeles, particularly in the needle trades and in the Jewish community. The most important losses were on our periphery, where groups like the Hollywood Anti-Nazi League collapsed. Until August 1939 we felt we had been swimming with the tide of history and public sentiment; now we were once more swimming against the tide. Despite the myths later propagated about the "Red Decade," the Communists had never enjoyed full political acceptance in the 1930s; what we had won was a kind of grudging tolerance. The Party's change of line, by cutting us off from the allies we had made during the People's Front, weakened us significantly.

It was my opinion in 1939 and remains so today that the Soviet Union was justified in signing the Pact. England and France and, indirectly, the United States had proved at Munich and elsewhere that they could not be relied upon as anti-Nazi allies. They wanted to make a deal with Hitler, and if it had to be at the expense of the Czechs, so be it. And if they were willing to sacrifice Czechoslovakia, they certainly weren't going to spring to the aid of the Soviet Union in the event of a Nazi invasion. Even in the last months of peace the Western allies made no serious effort to establish a common front with the Soviet Union against Germany. Considered in terms of diplomatic necessity, Stalin and Molotov were doing what the leaders of any state would do in similar circumstances, taking those steps which would best protect the interests of their own country.

But whatever justification the pact had as realpolitik, there were other aspects of our policies and of Soviet policies in that period which were simply indefensible. First of all, Communists in the United States and elsewhere translated a diplomatic document into a political directive (and not for the last time by any means). Just because the Soviet Union was forced by circumstances to sign a pact with Germany did not mean that we should have in any way downplayed our own opposition to the Nazi regime—certainly not to the extent that we argued that there was no essential difference between Nazi Germany and British imperialism, and that a victory for either camp in the new world war would be equally undesirable.

Secondly, Soviet leaders erred in accepting the pact at face value instead of as the temporary and fragile expedient it really was. When the Nazis finally did invade in June 1941, the Soviet Union was utterly unprepared to meet the attack even though Stalin had ample warning that it was coming. Finally, there were aspects of Nazi-Soviet "cooperation" between August 1939 and June 1941 which were unjustified by any standard. In 1967 I traveled to the German Democratic Republic for the East German Communist Party Congress. I met a man named John Peet, an English journalist who had lived for years in East Berlin, where he edited a publication called the *East German Report*. His wife, a Bulgarian woman, was a survivor of a Nazi concentration camp. She and Peet had served as advisers for the film "Judgment at Nuremberg." One of the stories they told me during my visit concerned the fate of German Communists, many of them Jewish, who had been in exile in the Soviet Union in the late 1930s. As a sort of perverse good-will gesture, Stalin handed these German Communists over to the Gestapo after the signing of the Nazi-Soviet Pact. They were, of course, immediately sent to concentration camps. The only way to survive in the camps was to be taken under the protection of some organized group among the inmates. If you were on your own, you died. Because Communists had been the first ones arrested, they had the longest "training" in how to survive. They were more likely to know how to scavenge food and medicine and how to avoid the most grueling work assignments. When the newcomers arrived in 1939 there was a big debate among the old German Communists in the camps as to what attitude to take toward them. It was in essence a question of life and death: take them in and they had some chance of survival, ignore them and they had none. But the fact that the exiles had been deported by Stalin tipped the balance against them; it meant that they must be "enemies"—surely the Soviet Union would never hand over good Communists to Hitler. So the old-timers refused to have anything to do with them, and as a result they all died long before liberation came.

MR. CHOPSON: You were credited with having expressed an opinion on some occasion that our present form of society should be dramatically changed. Now, did you believe that at one time? I mean the basic organization.

A: I believe just the process of evolution; I believe society will change. . . .

MR. CHOPSON: Just a moment. I said that it should be basically and immediately changed; in other words in what might commonly be called revolutionary fashion. I don't like to use that term. In other words, immediate and complete revision of our social organization is necessary.

A: I think that a revision of our social order would be a good thing and a necessary thing. I don't think it is in the order of the day something that one could even discuss at the present time. I think society changed since I made the statement. Since the Roosevelt administration we have certainly seen a revolutionary change, using the word you don't like, I think in the last four years. I know in my union, the things that have happened in our industry have been almost revolutionary. ■ excerpt from the transcript of Dorothy's interview before the California State Personnel Board, February 10, 1940.

While much of the world descended into horror in 1939, our lives in the United States went on much as before. I took a civil service examination for a position as state deputy labor commissioner, more as a lark than anything else. My friends derided the idea that as a publicly known Communist I could ever be appointed to such a position. But I studied the labor code backward and forward and on the written exam I received one of the top scores in the state. I also had to go through an oral exam, and later, when it became a matter of public record, I found out what my interviewers thought of me. Mostly their assessments were very positive, although it was also clear they were not quite sure what to make of me. One comment I particularly enjoyed ran as follows: "The most forceful woman I have seen of that type. It is certainly not force of good looks!" Good looks or not, in the end I was offered the position. I remember Jack Moore, then the Party's educational director in Los Angeles, said to me after I took the exam, "Water will flow upstream before you get that job." When I got the news, I sent him a telegram saying "Water has flowed upstream today."

I moved back to San Francisco in August 1940 to take up my new duties. I was officially entrusted with the authority to enforce the state's quite progressive labor code. I was given a huge police badge, with the authority to arrest employers—they were the only people I could arrest, which of course delighted me. This was the first time I had ever enjoyed the luxury of a regular and substantial paycheck, making $240 a month, three times what I had made working for UCAPAWA. And, at least in the beginning, I found it all quite intriguing. The codes covered many aspects of what today would be occupational health and safety as well as questions of wages and hours and the regulation of child labor. Workers would come to us and file claims that they had been deprived of their vacation pay or they were required to work seven days a week or whatever, and we would hold hearings and decide whether or not the labor code had been violated.

I was surprised to discover that only the AFL unions really knew how to use the labor code. The CIO seemed oblivious to our existence. I kept calling them and saying "Hey fellas, when you're organizing a plant we can be of great help to you." But they never took me up on the offer. It was the reverse of what one would expect, since the AFL was supposed to be absolutely voluntarist in philosophy and suspicious of state intervention, while the CIO had put the Wagner Act to such good use. But the AFL had always had a close connection with municipal and state politics. They had helped set up agencies like the one I was working for, knew how they worked, and made good use of them. I sometimes felt in those years as if I was working as an AFL business agent.

As deputy commissioner I divided my time between office hearings and going out to do field examinations, checking for code violations. I remember going along on inspections of Chinatown sweatshops with the federal wage and hour administration inspectors. That turned out to be a useless exercise. The garment employers in Chinatown would be cited for every conceivable violation of state and federal codes, but there was no follow-through. The inspections we did on our own were much more effective, because the individual deputy had the latitude to keep following up on a case if he or she wanted to, going back to make sure that conditions were improved.

After the first year or so, I started feeling bored. I was helping a few individual workers, but nothing I could do in that job was contributing to any larger good. It was really no place for a revolutionary. I might have resigned of my own volition in 1941 if I hadn't come under attack that year from the Tenney

Committee in the California State legislature. Along with Sam Yorty, Jack Tenney had once been one of the Party's closest allies in the state legislature. He had been president of the American Federation of Musicians local in Los Angeles, and chairman of Labor's Non-Partisan League for Southern California. Like Yorty, he broke with his left-wing allies in 1939. In a power struggle within the musicians' union he was voted out of office, and as a result he swung completely to the Right politically, turning on his former friends with a vengeance. He decided to launch an investigation of "Communist infiltration" of the Culbert Olson administration. Tenney's investigations were part of the revived red scare atmosphere that prevailed in the early years of the war. They also reflected local political considerations. The growers and the newspapers were eager to divert attention from California's social ills, particularly since the near-simultaneous publication in 1939 of Steinbeck's novel *The Grapes of Wrath* and Carey Mc-Williams's indictment of agricultural labor relations, *Factories in the Field*. The Republicans were searching for a means to guarantee that the aberration of Democratic control of the governorship would be brought to an end; Tenney and other conservative Democrats wanted to regain control of the Democratic Party from its progressive wing. All of their interests were thus served by an attack on Olson as a coddler of Communists. The State Relief Administration was an obvious target and the opening wedge of a campaign that spread to other state agencies, including the one that employed me.

> The attractive young brunette, demonstrating assurance that ranged far beyond the bounds of self-confidence, batted her long lashes, rolled her large eyes, and gestured prettily as she informed the committee she was appointed to her state job in 1940, despite the following circumstances: She was a member of the Young Communist League from the time she was 14 years old, and—to the best of her belief, a member of the Communist Party—until she "disaffiliated" in 1939. . . . She said she never knew that UCAPAWA was a Communist front organization—but admitted she always told workers she was attempting to organize that she, herself, was a Communist. "I never did try to hide it," she said, defiantly. ■ "State Deputy Admits Strike Work as Red," *San Francisco Examiner*, December 5, 1941.

In November 1941, Tenney got around to me. Everything I had been involved in since 1930 was dug up and sensationalized. But there was nothing they could prove about my current involvement with the Communist movement. I told them, truthfully, that I was no longer a member of the Young Communist League; I was not so forthcoming about the status of my Party membership (I had been a Party member since 1932; technically I had been on leave from the Party since August 1940). When I felt that people I was working with had a legitimate right to know about my political allegiance, I always told them I was a Communist; I had no qualms about denying membership when my inquisitors were only asking to serve their own partisan motives. I needled Tenney about his earlier involvement with Labor's Non-Partisan League, when he himself had worked with Communists without any apparent worries. In general, I gave the committee such voluminous and irrelevant answers to their questions that by the time I had finished they no longer remembered what they initially asked me.

After my appearance, the state labor commissioner's main assistant called me into his office and said that the governor demanded my resignation. I told him to go to hell. I hadn't done anything wrong. I'd been a good deputy. If they had left me alone, I would have quit out of sheer boredom. Instead, out of principle and stubbornness, I held on to the job for another year and a half. Had this been the 1950s I undoubtedly would have been fired as soon as I was called before the committee; had Tenney gotten around to me a few months earlier, the same thing might have happened. But his timing was off. By the time I was called to testify, the Red Army was fighting a tremendous battle a few miles from Moscow to turn back the Nazi invaders, which did a lot to deflate would-be red-hunters. And before another week had passed, the Japanese had bombed Pearl Harbor. The country suddenly had more important things to worry about than the presence of a couple of suspected Communists in the state bureaucracy.

> When the Nazis attacked Russia, I was standing on a street corner in San Francisco with Dorothy and Mama. We heard the news and Mama turned to Dorothy and said, "What does this mean?" Dorothy said, "I don't know, but everything's changed now." I remember Don Healey haranguing a crowd, "The yanks are not coming," it's an unjust war, and then switcheroo, boom, there we were. It was, of course, a wonderful feeling being on the majority side for a change. ■ Carol Jean Newman.

Starting in June 1941, I followed the war news very closely, and like many other people, Communists and non-Communists alike, held my breath as the Germans approached Moscow. When the Japanese attacked Pearl Harbor and Roosevelt made his "day of infamy" speech, Communists immediately pledged our all-out support for the war effort. Hundreds of Communist men in San Francisco and elsewhere rushed to enlist in the armed forces. We had always said that if the United States was ever attacked, we would defend our country. With the Soviet Union and the United States as allies, we felt no conflict at all between our patriotic sentiments and our political beliefs. So unquestioning was our support for the war that a few months later we raised no objection when Japanese-American citizens, including some of our own comrades like Karl Yoneda, along with his non-Japanese wife, Elaine Black, were sent to relocation camps in the western desert. The *People's World* fired its sole Japanese-American employee in those early months of the war. (Al Richmond reminded me a few years ago that my ex-husband Lou was one of the few Communists who publicly criticized the Japanese relocation policy.) It was yet another example of our inability to find or even conceive of a way to be simultaneously supportive and critical in our judgments, the flaw that was the basis of the "pendulum" appearance of our policies.

With the Soviet Union as America's military ally, a new "popular front" was reborn on an even broader basis than in the 1930s. Nationally organized groups like Russian War Relief and locally organized groups like the Hollywood Writers Mobilization drew support from all kinds of people, virtually across the political spectrum. We were naturally heartened by this. Our attitude was that at last people were seeing the truth of what we had been saying all along. What we didn't understand at the time was just how shallow the roots of the Soviet Union's current popularity would prove. It was a remarkable thing to see how the Soviet Union was first transformed into "our gallant Soviet allies" in government propaganda and the media, and then how just as easily it could revert back to the hated enemy. Here was *Time* magazine coming out with its front cover devoted to a stern but kindly looking portrait of Uncle Joe as "man of the year"; here was General Douglas MacArthur sending cables to the Red Army saying that "on your gallant banners hang the future of civilization"; here was Mayor Bowron of Los Angeles declaring June 22nd, 1943, a day of tribute to the USSR and speaking at a Hollywood Bowl concert sponsored by Russian War Relief. In 1943, in the aftermath of the battle of Stalingrad, I wouldn't have believed it would have been possible to dispel all that goodwill so easily.

With the war on, and the Tenney committee temporarily in the doldrums, I began to look for ways to get politically active again. As long as I kept my job as a state labor commissioner, I couldn't take part in open Party activities. One of the activities I did become involved with was the formation of the Tom Mooney Labor School in San Francisco. Frank Carlson was its main initiator, but many non-Communists also pitched in, and it initially had very broad support and participation from the labor movement, including the Central Labor Council. The school attracted hundreds of students every term to classes in labor relations, politics, and a wide range of other subjects. I taught a class in labor history there during its first term. Later in Los Angeles I was involved with organizing a similar effort called the People's Educational Association school, which also attracted a broad range of support and students.

In 1943 I got pregnant for the fourth and final time. Don Healey and I had now been married for two years. On the surface it seemed like a happy marriage. We never fought. My sister Frances lived with us for a while in San Francisco and she was just horrified by my marriage, because she thought Don totally dominated me. Don would always decide if we would go out in the evening, what we'd do, what time we'd come home, all those kind of questions. But I didn't care in the least. On questions that were important to me, I'd make up my own mind. Don was a very kind and good man, and even though our marriage had serious problems, we remained close friends until his death.

> I don't think Dorothy's husbands impinged much on her. She didn't care much if they were unfaithful because she didn't care much about them. Don was a notorious womanizer, and it just didn't affect her much.
> ■ Carol Jean Newman.

From almost the beginning of our marriage Don had been involved with other women. He said to me when we had gotten married, "If you object to my sleeping with other women, just tell me and I'll never do it." And in my stupidity and my arrogance I told him "When you reach the point of maturity that you no longer want to sleep with other women, you'll do it. I don't want you to do it for me. You've got to do it for yourself." He not only slept with a great number of women, he always proceeded to tell me about each one. I acted as though I didn't care, and if anyone had asked me, I would have shrugged it off: "He's free to do what he wants. What difference does it make?" I really only appreciated how much I did care when he came back from the army and I started having nightmares in which I kept trying to follow him around from party to party trying to find him, without success.

Don was drafted in 1943. He loved the army. He was promoted to sergeant and was repeatedly nominated by his commanding officer to go to Officers Candidate School. As with many Communists during the war, his nomination was blocked because of his politics. And because he was a Communist, he wasn't sent overseas and spent the entire war stationed in Alabama. Nevertheless he thoroughly enjoyed the service. It was so structured and organized and defined. There was nothing abstract about it. Don hated abstractions. That's why he eventually left the Party in the 1950s, a time when every club meeting was consumed with debates over the big questions of strategy and theory, but with very few practical outlets and results. Don was just bored to death in that situation. He was a very practical man and a very good organizer, and would go on to be the main organizer of the huge anti-Vietnam war demonstration when Lyndon Johnson came to Los Angeles in 1967.

Before I got pregnant, I met with Louise Todd, who was the CP's state secretary, and Oleta O'Connor Yates, who was the county organizer in San Francisco. I told them I was getting on in years—I was twenty-nine—and I thought it was time I had a child. They said, "Sure, of course"—but I'm sure that if they had said otherwise, I would have heeded Party discipline and forgone the pregnancy. About a month before the baby was due I left San Francisco to stay with my mother in Los Angeles; Don was in the army by then. I went through the motions of asking for a transfer in my state job from San Francisco to Los Angeles, knowing full well they wouldn't give it to me and not really caring. At first I took a leave of absence, but eventually I resigned, no doubt to their great delight and certainly to my own relief. I must say that it's remarkable to me how naturally and un-selfconsciously I went back home to Mama to have my child. It never occurred to me to stay in San Francisco where I was already living, even though I had been away from home since I was sixteen.

When I arrived in Los Angeles, I immediately went down to the Party office to volunteer my services. Carl Winter was the L.A. county Party chairman. He didn't know me and didn't seem very impressed by what I had to offer. Finally he decided I could clip the newspapers for the office files. I would clip five newspapers a day and then take them down to the Party office. It was a very good habit to get into, and to this day I still do it for my own use. I remember being in the CIO office one day, about a month after my return to Los Angeles, and everyone there saying, "Please, Dorothy, go home. You're going to have the baby right here in the building." I gave birth to Richard the next day, June 18, 1943.

Dorothy has a tremendous feeling for children. If there was a child around, especially an abused child, she would manage to "interfere." I learned how to do it from her, the indirect way. I learned that if a mother is scolding a crying child, if I could get close and say, "My that's a pretty child" or "My, that child really looks like you," something like that could defuse the situation. It always worked. You were showing a side of the child that they wanted to see. Dorothy has done that all her life. ■ Carol Jean Newman.

I turned out to be one of the most typically doting mothers anyone's ever seen. As far as I was concerned everything revolved around my son. Who would have thought motherhood could be so exciting, so much fun? I was determined that he would not grow up as a "Party orphan." That phrase was used to describe the children of some Communists, where the parents were so involved in politics that they hardly ever saw them. Those children grew up resenting and hating this outside intrusion into their lives, and not surprisingly very few of them would be politically active themselves when they became adults. By the time I moved into Party leadership after the war, Richard was in a nursery school. I had a very strict rule that at three-thirty every afternoon I left the Party office, no matter what was happening or who was in town from the national office, and picked him up. And every evening from five to seven o'clock was his time and I wouldn't even answer the phone. If I had a meeting to go to on a Sunday, then all day Saturday was his day with me. When meetings were held at my house in the evening, as they quite often were so that I didn't have to leave Richard, I would leave the meeting if he called to me from the bedroom, regardless of what was being discussed or who was speaking. I discovered that he was most open to talking about what was really on his mind in the half hour or so after he had been put to bed and before he fell asleep. So when I put him to bed, I would sit by his bed and just talk, and that's when he would share confidences with me. Richard also had the considerable benefit of his grandmother's presence and care. In 1945 we bought a couple of ramshackle houses on a lot on Eighty-Fourth Street. Mama lived in one of the houses with Fedya Nestor, the man she married in 1936, while Richard and Don and I lived in the other.

When Don got back from the army in 1945 and found me established as a new Party leader, he was very unhappy about it. Unlike me he had never been an open Communist. With his wife a Party functionary, there was no longer any question about his own affiliations, and that seemed to make a big difference to him. He felt inhibited by it and made no effort to go back into the kind of mass work he had been doing before the war, which was the only kind of political work he was really interested in doing. Soon after he returned from the army we stopped having anything to do with one another sexually because he physically could not enter me. I thought there was something wrong with me, and I even went to a doctor, who told me, "No, nothing wrong with you. You're normal." I did not understand it at the time, but in retrospect I can see how unhappy I was and how I was reacting against a challenge to my integrity and my uncertainty as to whether or not I was attractive enough to keep a man. And, as had been true in my first marriage, we did not have that much in common. In 1946 he fell in love with Shevy Wallace, a woman who worked with me in the Party office. Don and I were still living together, and she came to me and asked if I objected to her going out with him. I said, "No, not at all." I encouraged them, in fact, because I knew by then I wanted to get out of the marriage. We separated later that year and were divorced in 1947.

About six months after Richard's birth, Maurice Travis, a leader of the International Union of Mine, Mill and Smelter Workers, came to see me and implored me to come help them as a union organizer. Mine-Mill was a CIO union, with Left leadership and a distinguished radical past, the direct descendant of Big Bill Haywood's Western Federation of Miners, which had been one of the original IWW unions. I would have jumped at the chance a year earlier, but now because of Richard I was very reluctant. But the union kept pressuring me, because all their experienced male organizers were in the army and there were few experienced women organizers to take their place. So, despite my qualms, I took the job. My responsibilities included organizing new plants and servicing contracts where Mine-Mill already had been recognized. Most of my work was in aluminum plants, including two big plants across the street from one another in Torrance, Bohn Aluminum and Alcoa Aluminum. (The designation Mine, Mill and Smelter workers was not taken literally in determining our jurisdiction; we also organized a lot of metal fabrication plants.) I soon discovered that unlike UCAPAWA, Mine-Mill was a very structured union. The local met and the executive met, and there were clear lines of authority and responsibility within the union.

It was when I went to work for Mine-Mill that I first became known as Dorothy Ray Healey. Ever since I was a teenager in the YCL I had been Dorothy Ray. The international secretary of the union was a conservative Catholic by the name of Leary. When I applied for the job, Travis suggest I used "Healey" because it sounded like a good Irish-Catholic name. Afterward it was just too much trouble to change it back.

> Although the reactionary forces backing the [John L.] Lewis conspiracy succeeded in creating some temporary confusion in the ranks of the labor movement, labor's patriotism. . . . headed off all attempts to provoke a strike movement. . . . A UAW conference in Los Angeles voted to condemn Lewis' policies. . . . The convention of the International Longshoremen's and Warehousemen's Union, on the recommendation of Harry Bridges and other international officers, voted to condemn Lewis as a traitor, and reaffirmed its support to President Roosevelt and his win-the-war policies.
> ■ William Schneiderman, "California and the Coming Elections," *The Communist*, July 1943, p. 651.

When I returned to the union movement, the California CIO appointed me as an alternate member to the regional War Labor Board. The board set up panels with representatives from labor, business, and "the public" to hear grievances and head off strikes through arbitration. I think I was the only woman in the country appointed to a board. Both the AFL and the CIO had pledged that they would not engage in strikes for the duration of the war, and the Communist Party, of course, was gung-ho for the no-strike pledge. I also began to get involved again in the internal battles in the Los Angeles CIO Council. We battled over a range of issues, some of them consequential and some less so. Slim Connelly was secretary of the council, and many of the issues that came before the council were exacerbated by Slim's bad-tempered response to anything he regarded as a challenge to his personal authority.

> _____describes HEALEY as one of the most able leaders in the Los Angeles area. As an indication of this, _____points out that subject is the only person who has to date been successful in working with _____of the Los Angeles Industrial Union Council. She states that she can get what she wants from _____without any opposition. ■ FBI report on Dorothy, October 29, 1945. [The last blanked-out name is probably that of Slim Connelly.]

I served as floor leader for the Left in many of the fights in the CIO council because I was a known Communist and had nothing to lose by being out front on issues. We gave a great deal of emphasis to the fight for Black and Chicano rights. We were deeply involved, for example, in the Sleepy Lagoon case, defending young Chicano men who were being framed in a local murder case. The CIO Council also took the lead in organizing against "restrictive covenants," which prevented Blacks from buying houses in many neighborhoods in L.A. We also organized defense committees for Black families when white vigilantes tried to drive them out of their homes.

In this same period, I became part of what was sometimes derisively referred to in the Party as "God's committee," a group of Communists in the CIO leadership who met together regularly for classes and discussion. The classes were taught by a woman named Eva Shafran, who was a wonderful teacher, one of the few I've met who could take a current question and relate it back to the Marxist classics without making the process seem forced or artificial. For the first time I really immersed myself in Lenin's writings.

This was the period of the "Teheran line," when the Party's general secretary, Earl Browder, argued that the spirit of wartime unity evinced at the first meeting of Roosevelt, Churchill, and Stalin at Teheran in December 1943 was going to carry over into the postwar era. I could not accept the conclusion that Browder drew from it, that the wartime cooperation of management and labor in preventing strikes and maximizing production should continue after the war was over. Browder was in effect declaring class peace for the forseeable future. And in order to further this spirit of international and domestic harmony, he argued the Communist Party should dissolve itself and become a "political association."

> We are not prepared to give any broad theoretical generalizations for this period. But we know, as we go into it boldly, without the slightest hesitation, that we are firmly guided by the theoretical heritage of Marxism

and that the Teheran Declaration which was signed by Churchill, Roosevelt and the great Marxist Stalin represents the only program in the interest of the toiling masses of the whole world in the next period. ■ Earl Browder, *The Communist*, February 1944, p. 104.

In a way what Browder was doing with the "Teheran line" was very similar to what we had done in August 1939, taking a diplomatic document and turning it into a blueprint for our domestic political line. The Nazi-Soviet Pact had led us overboard in one direction; the Teheran declaration was leading us overboard in the completely opposite direction. Even before Browder dropped the bombshell about dissolving the Party, there were problems in our wartime perspective. We were subordinating everything to the one goal of winning the war—a perfectly valid goal which led to absurd excesses. So, for example, the United Electrical, Radio and Machine Workers Union (UE), one of the most progressive unions in the CIO, had actually come up with incentive pay plans that depended on the individual speedup of workers. The bosses were getting away with murder because *they* weren't going to subordinate anything to win the war—they were already getting all kinds of incentives like cost-plus contracts that guaranteed them huge profits. All the sacrifices were being placed on the backs of workers, and the Party was losing its own identity as an independent revolutionary movement as it subordinated itself to a "don't-rock-the-boat" and "support the commander-in-chief" approach.

> Some liberal critics of Communist policy have accused Earl Browder of "betraying" the interests of labor because he does not call on the trade unions to prepare for battle against the capitalists, as do John L. Lewis, Dubinsky, Reuther, Norman Thomas, and the Trotskyites. Browder rejects the defeatist view that there must be a major class conflict, and points to the growing evidence that both labor and capital can agree on a common post-war program in the national interest. ■ William Schneiderman, review of Browder's *Teheran—Our Path in Peace and War* in *The Communist*, July 1944, p. 653.

The actual dissolution of the Party at a national convention in New York in June 1944 came as a shock to me. When I saw the story in the paper—in the *Los Angeles Times* of all places—I called a close friend in the Party and started crying on the phone: "They've taken the party away from us. How can they do that?" I then got very angry and for the first time I started complaining openly, or at least openly to other Communists, particularly those in the CIO, about the decisions being made in New York by our national leaders. Nobody paid much attention to me. People just said, "Oh, well, that's Dorothy letting off steam!"

> Even as he promulgated Americanization and democratization, the Earl of Kansas certainly exploited centralism to the hilt, and took maximum advantage of the "cult of the individual." If pre-1935, there was a certain unity between political content and organizational practice, post-1935 there

was increasing dichotomy and contradiction. It was one of the supreme paradoxes of CP history that the metamorphosis into the CPA [Communist Political Association] was effected with organizational practices that, on their face, were a negation of the political rationale for the CPA. ■ letter from Al Richmond to Dorothy, May 11, 1974.

I suppose if I'd brought up my criticisms of the Teheran policy in a formal way at a Party meeting I might have been kicked out. In any case, I was loud enough in my complaints so that even though no one took me very seriously, everyone knew what my position was. That turned out to have important consequences for my future. In May 1945 the French Communist leader Jacques Duclos published an article criticizing Browder's Teheran line, and very soon thereafter Browder was kicked out of the leadership and then the following year out of the Party, and all those most closely identified with the Teheran line were operating under a cloud.

I know there were many Communists who had felt exactly the way I did during the war and still more who would later claim to have felt that way, but because of "democratic centralism" they had mostly kept silent. The Duclos article had an electrifying impact on the Party, and an unprecedented wave of antileadership sentiment swept through its ranks. The membership felt betrayed, and wanted to throw the rascals out, as it were. With old leaders discredited, new leaders had to be found, and I was asked to join the county leadership. That should have made me happy, but it didn't. I enjoyed what I was doing in the CIO and didn't want to move into formal Party leadership. And I was contemptuous of the response of many Communists to the Duclos article. They wanted scapegoats and ignored their own responsibility for having gone along with the Teheran line in the first place.

MR. WEREB: This meeting went on for a day, full day, and a night. . . . Different people approached microphones located at strategic positions on the convention floor. . . . As these members would come up, they would come up with a prepared text praising the Duclos letter and damning Browder but darn good.

The very first speaker that I recall was William Schneiderman. . . . He stood there before these 400 delegates and said he was very sorry that he had cooperated with the Browder revisionism and that if the party would elect him or appoint him as the head of the State Communist group, he would try to be more militant and lead the party to a more militant role.

Next came, I believe, Dorothy Healy [sic]. She was always revolutionary. She just went on down the line staying with the rest. . . . ■ testimony of Stephen A. Wereb before the House Committee on Un-American Activities, July 1, 1955. [Wereb was an FBI undercover agent in the Los Angeles Communist Party from 1943 through 1948; he was describing a state convention of the Communist Political Association in June 1945].

All over the country the Communist Political Association held emergency local and state conventions to debate the issues raised by the Teheran line and the Duclos article and select delegates for a national convention to undo the decisions taken the previous year. I was chosen as a delegate, along with a few others from Los Angeles, because I was known as a pre-Duclos opponent of Teheran. One of the consequences of this decision was that I lost my job with Mine-Mill. They felt that having one of their organizers seen at a national convention of the Communist Party was not going to do them any good, and so they gave me an ultimatum: don't go, or don't come back. But I figured there were plenty of organizing jobs around, so that didn't deter me. Besides, the Party was my patrimony, my heritage, my family, and I was outraged at what had happened to it. I was determined to go to New York. This would be my first time at a national Party meeting. Unlike my first trip, by bus with fourteen dollars in my pocket, this time I traveled by Pullman coach: times had changed.

There were many things about that national convention which left me feeling distressed. First of all, a lot of those in the leadership were using a rationale that Celeste Strack had proposed in a preconvention article, that the whole Teheran line was an example of the corrupting pressures of the capitalist environment we lived in, the seductive appeal of bourgeois ideology. I thought, "Poor little Communists, unable to withstand the capitalist pressures." Marxist ideology must be very fragile if it is so easily subverted by bourgeois ideology. It was a rationale that let the leaders off the hook and that left the Party itself off the hook. If all the blame could be placed on bourgeois ideology, then we didn't need to examine the mechanisms within the Party which allowed the Teheran line to be accepted so uncritically.

I was also unhappy with the role that I found myself playing at the convention. I gave a speech describing the effects of the Teheran line on my work at Bohn and Alcoa Aluminum. Of course I was very critical, and I had good reason to be. But Browder was sitting right in front of me as I spoke, and I remember thinking, "I don't like what's happening here." It reminded me of what happens in a chicken yard when a hen gets hurt and all the other chickens start pecking at it. Everybody was singling out Browder for attack, because he had been the leader, and because he wouldn't perform a mea culpa. It was too easy to make Browder the enemy who had to be destroyed, to put all the blame on him and pretend that his destruction would leave the rest of us pure again. I was disturbed by the adulation of William Z. Foster at the convention. It was true that he had disagreed with the Teheran line. But the fact that he had kept his dissent private and then communicated it abroad didn't make him any kind of principled hero. Nonetheless, it was Foster who was the inevitable choice as chairman of the reconstituted Party. The post of general secretary went to Eugene Dennis the following year, but he had very little independent power. Foster, Bob Thompson, the new leader of the New York District, and Ben Davis, the top Black leader and a New York City Councilman, were the three controlling influences on Party decision making in the next few years. (This was the first time I had seen Dennis since he went underground in 1930 when he was still known as Francis Waldron; until then I had not known that the "Eugene Dennis" who had emerged in the late 1930s as a Party leader was the same person I had known in California.)

For all my misgivings, once the convention was over I immediately began to retreat into the mythic concept of the Party leadership as all-seeing, all-knowing people who were very different from ordinary mortals like myself. As late as 1952, when Carl Marzani came to Los Angeles on a tour to promote one of his book clubs, I remember his sitting in my living room and saying, "You know, Dorothy, Party leaders don't know any more than you know." And I refused to believe him, because I knew how little I knew, and I still thought they just had to know more.

When I returned to Los Angeles another county convention was held, this time to ratify the decision taken at the National convention to reconstitute the Party and to elect new county officers. There was also a state convention which went through with the same procedure. (It was one of the curious things about the way the Party was set up in California that the bulk of the Party's members had always lived in Southern California, but the Party headquarters was always located in San Francisco. For reasons of both pride and convenience this had always rankled the Communists in L.A. county, and would continue to do so until 1957, when southern California finally became a separate district organization.) At that 1945 county convention, Nemmy Sparks was elected as county chairman.

There were a couple of other important posts to be filled in the county leadership, including those of organizational secretary (or "org sec" as it was known in Party jargon), and trade union secretary. The county committee wanted me to take over the position as org sec so they could show the members that there had been a shake-up of leaders, and it wasn't going to be just the same old faces. I was the mostly likely new face, because I fell into all kinds of useful categories as a pre-Duclos opponent of the Teheran line, as a trade unionist, and as a woman. I didn't want the job, and for two days I held out. I told them, "Number one, I don't know anything about what an org sec is or what one is supposed to do, and doesn't anyone remember how bad I was as YCL organizer in San Francisco? Number two, I'm a known Communist in the CIO Council, generally accepted by the non-Communists, and it's not like we have so many people who fit that description that I should so cavalierly be taken out of there. And third, all right, if I have to join the Party leadership, then let me be the labor secretary, the person in charge of coordinating the Party's trade union work, because that's something I know about." I just met a blank wall. "You have to be org sec, you can't be labor secretary, and that's all there is to it." I didn't understand their obstinancy at the time, but when I look back I think it was probably a question of sexism, because in Party custom the org sec was often a women's job, while women rarely if ever became trade union secretary. They gave that post first to a man by the name of Morgan Hull, who was one of the initial organizers of the American Newspaper Guild. When he got sick the following year they brought in an old friend of mine from the YCL, Ben Dobbs, who would become one of my closest allies in the internal battles to come. In October 1945 I walked into the Party headquarters in Los Angeles to assume my new duties as org sec.

6

DOROTHY HEALEY is one of the most capable, articulate and theoretically developed Communist Party members in Los Angeles.

DOROTHY's own description of her being advanced in the Communism [sic] movement is an interesting one. She says that the reason she has been pushed into leadership is because "of my glib tongue." That is true to a degree, but she not only talks fluently, she thinks decisively and logically. Subject works well with other people and has a great deal of ability in leadership in that she can get people to take the action she wants taken. . . . HEALEY has a sound and workable knowledge of organizational forms and is possessed of initiative and ingenuity in developing new forms where necessary. She is flexible in methods and thought, never deviates politically from a basic line. She is fond of cutting corners as far as legalism is concerned and would rather take a chance than lag in action. . . . She forms deep and unswerving loyalties to friends and will fight any opposition to win a point. She can discuss things calmly and unemotionally but has a furious temper if she feels comrades are either unfair or stupid on any political points. ■ FBI report, October 10, 1945.

The first thing I did upon being appointed organizational secretary of the Los Angeles County Communist Party was to meet with my predecessor in the post, Max Silver. Silver was very bitter that he was no longer in the leadership (he would soon quit the Party and appear as a friendly witness before HUAC), and he obviously wasn't pleased to have this young interloper coming around to ask him questions about his job. I said, "Max, what does an org sec do?" And he replied, "Well, Dorothy, it all depends on who you are as to what the job is. If you know what you're doing, it's one kind of job, and if you don't know what you're doing, as you don't, then it is a very technical kind of job." I sat there for a second looking at him, then stood up and said, "Oh, go to hell, you pompous ass," and walked out. I decided I'd just have to teach myself the job.

I shut myself up in the Party library (which was mammoth and marvelous at that point) for two weeks to read through back issues of the *Party Organizer*. This was a Party journal that came out all through the 1930s and discussed organizational problems, and it was the closest thing I had to a textbook. I was trying to get the hang of something that I had not until then really known much about, and that was the daily internal life of the Communist Party. The Party may have believed in the revolutionary overturn of existing social relations, but it was as bound as any other organization, perhaps more so, by unspoken but powerful customs, habits, and etiquette. I was always running into problems with things which were taken for granted by the functionaries who grew up politically immersed in the inner life of the party. I didn't even understand the language at first. When you are an inner functionary you learn to speak in party jargon that is immediately understandable to your immediate constituency but not to anyone outside. In my previous political work, I had always spoken primarily to non-Communists in the labor movement, so I had rarely used the Party language.

In some ways the Party in the 1930s and 1940s had been really two separate, or rather overlapping, parties. There were those who functioned only within the internal life of the Party, and then there were those who either functioned on the outside, or who somehow managed to combine the mass work with involvement in the internal life of the Party. Those of us who conducted our political work primarily on the outside, in the labor movement or in mass political or protest movements, had to be able to defend the policies of the Party not only to those who already accepted it, but to all those non-Communists and anti-Communists we encountered every day. You had to debate issues and explain things in terms that others would understand. Among Communists active in the CIO I remember a kind of general attitude that the Party's leaders were there to be in charge of the big abstractions but that we were the ones who were actually leading the workers. I found it annoying that "hothouse Communists," people who never had to defend the policies of the Party to outsiders, somehow considered themselves the better, truer Communists for their isolation.

I think my background made a difference in the way I functioned once I did move into Party leadership. I retained the habit I acquired in the labor movement of trying to think through why we were advocating a particular policy—I had to, if I was going to be able to convince others outside the Party of its validity. That made my life as a Party official a stormy one. I never accepted the definition of democratic centralism that was so common in the Party, that no matter what experience showed after a given policy was decided on, the fact that the policy had been set meant that you never again questioned or challenged it. Without drawing any systematic conclusions from what I was thinking and doing, from the mid-1940s on I was in an almost constant state of challenging this or that aspect of party approach. What I was doing wrong, in retrospect, was failing to generalize from my criticisms. I'll never forget how in 1951, Viv Weinstein, who was the Party's division organizer for the Nineteenth Congressional District, saying to me, "Dorothy, you're challenging the line of the party." And I replying, in all sincerity, "Me? I wouldn't think of challenging the line of the party. It's this, that and the other policy I disagree with. But the line of the party I would never think of challenging." (As if the line of the party was something apart from its constiuent parts.)

Dorothy was a great down-the-liner. Much better than most down-the-liners because she had her innate charm and good nature and her love of people. So she wasn't a mean person. But down-the-line. She had great confidence in her leaders. ■ Ellenore Hittelman.

The organizational secretary was the person who had the responsibility for what I suppose could be called the housekeeping chores of the Party, overseeing the collection of dues, membership activities, distribution of literature, political education, and in general seeing to it that the various levels of Party organizations functioned smoothly together. I soon found that despite my initial qualms, I enjoyed the job as much as the kind of political work I had been accustomed to in the labor movement. There was a greater range of questions to confront every day.

The first thing I had to learn was how Party clubs functioned and who the people were who belonged to them. I made it a practice every week to go to one or two club meetings and sit there quietly listening to the members, making notes as to who impressed me the most in initiative, understanding, and ties with the broader community, and especially who knew anything outside of the inner life of the Party. The club was the basic unit of organization in the Party. Clubs were organized on various levels. In the late 1940s we mostly had community clubs based in a particular neighborhood. Whenever possible these would be located within a single political unit, like an assembly district or Congressional district. There were also shop clubs, which would involve all Communists in a given work place, and industrial clubs, which would bring together workers from many shops in an industry where we didn't have enough members in any particular shop or, as in the building trades, where it didn't make sense to organize on a shop basis. There were also professional clubs for lawyers, doctors, the Hollywood people, and so forth. The size of the clubs varied over the years, depending on circumstances and the organizational fads that periodically swept the Party. They could range anywhere from ten to fifty or so members.

> MR. TAVENNER: Can you take each of the sections represented by congressional districts and tell us the type of organizational work in the particular district starting with the eleventh?
>
> MR. SILVER: The eleventh district comprised the San Fernando Valley, taking in Burbank, Glendale, North Hollywood, and I believe part of Pasadena. The bulk of the organization was around Van Nuys, and the bulk of the membership were a carry-over from the unemployment days. . . . The twelfth district took in Pomona into Los Angeles, the various towns and City Terrace. . . . In Pomona and San Gabriel Valley, et cetera, there were just small groups of people with very little activity. . . . The thirteenth district took in part of Boyle Heights territory, and, I would say roughly, the section in town north of Sunset and east of Vermont. This was a strong section with quite a number of branches and people active in the community proper, and a place where the membership could go out on a Sunday for solicitation for the People's World or the sale of literature and come back with good

_results. The Fourteenth Congressional District took in the downtown area and the Central Avenue section. That is the Negro community. The party always paid attention to the work among the Negro people. . . . The major concentration of that section, of the fourteenth, was in the sixty-second assembly district in the Negro community. The fifteenth district took in Hollywood, and the central part of the town as far south as Slauson or east of La Brea, I believe. That was, in the main, a composition of middle-class people or higher-skilled laborers or workers, rather. The party was quite active, especially in the fifty-seventh assembly district, which was in the Hollywood territory. In the sixteenth district, which is in the western part of the town and went through as far as, I believe, Beverly Hills, Santa Monica, Venice, and the Adams territory, we had a few very active spots. In the West Adam territory as well as in the fifty-ninth assembly district we had a very large branch, and some organization in Santa Monica and Venice. ■ testimony of Max Silver before the House Committee on Un-American Activities, January 21, 1952. [Silver served as L.A. county organizational secretary from 1938 until succeeded by Dorothy in October 1945.]

I discovered that how well the clubs functioned usually depended on one pivotal person. If you had a club leader who knew the neighborhood or the industry, who kept up on local and national issues, who knew how to run a meeting efficiently, and knew how to inspire other members, then you had a well-functioning club. These club leaders were not on the Party payroll. They were volunteers who were willing to take on a tedious and thankless job. Larger clubs would have an executive committee, with a chairman, an educational secretary, a membership director, and maybe a press and literature agent. They would meet separately from the rest of the club to plan the agenda for the regular meeting, often just before the regular meeting in order to cut down the number of "inner party" meetings people had to go to.

The political activity of individual members was supposed to be discussed at Party meetings, though it was often skipped or rushed through. That was a problem for us, because if an individual club member was working in a particular union or mass organization, it was likely that from week to week not much would have happened, and there were only so many times you'd want to listen to the same report over again. And yet if you didn't have that discussion, then that member might start to feel, "What's the point in coming to club meetings?" I think it was a good thing when the club meetings were used to check up on members' activities, because it helped instill a sense of individual and collective responsibility. "Comrade, you were going to sponsor a resolution at your union meeting condemning the Taft-Hartley bill. How did it go?" It gave people the sense that we weren't just talking for the sake of talking. Club decisions were not to be lightly made and immediately forgotten.

Club meetings were also fund-raising events. You could be sure in any given week that either the Party or the *People's World* was going to be in the middle of a fund campaign, particularly in the McCarthy years when our legal expenses skyrocketed. We passed resolutions that people were not supposed to bring their mass organization fund raisers into the party. "Go ask for money from non-Communists for a change." But in practice it was often a case of you take in my wash and I'll take in yours; you buy my ticket to a raffle and I'll buy yours. Club meetings were also used as occasions to sell pamphlets. All during the 1930s and 1940s the Party was publishing dozens—hundreds—of pamphlets every year, on current issues as well as history and theory. Those historians who say that the Party never had anything to say about socialism obviously haven't paid much attention to that vast pamphlet literature. Party pamphlets were usually relatively inexpensive, a nickel or a dime, but you didn't just buy one for yourself. Everybody would buy five or ten pamphlets to sell or give to others. Along with all the fund drives and raffle tickets, not to mention your regular dues, it started to add up before too long.

In theory each club had two tasks to accomplish. When the Party decided on a national level to launch a particular campaign, the clubs were supposed to find a way to help out. Suppose, for example, the Party decided to protest the selling of scrap iron to Japan, as we did in the late 1930s. Club members would be assigned articles or pamphlets to read about the issue, would discuss it in a meeting, and then would try to figure out how they could be most effective in drawing others into the campaign. Comrade X might be a member of a trade union local that was meeting next week. Would they be willing to pass a resolution on the issue? Comrade Y knows the minister in a church down the street. Could we involve a church group in the campaign? It became a red thread that ran through everybody's activities for the next few weeks or months. When it worked well, which it did on occasion, within a few weeks you could watch a ripple effect begin to take place, as people and groups farther and farther away from the Party's periphery began to talk about the scrap iron issue, or whatever, and join the campaign. It gave our members a real sense of the power of disciplined collective activity.

The other task of the club was to watch for and participate in appropriate local campaigns. This was a far more difficult task, because you really had to get to know a neighborhood or an industry. What were people in the community concerned about? Was it housing? Schools? Police protection or police brutality? How could the Party get involved? What could be learned? You were supposed to know which were the most important organizations, the churches, unions, and fraternal groups. Who were the important leaders and how much weight could they swing in an election, or in changing people's minds on a given issue?

The party, oi. It is, in my mother tongue, an "eidele zach" (literally, a delicate thing). . . . Why did [the CP] get that way? Certainly the mechanical rigid imitation of the what-is-to-be-done model led to excessive reliance on "professional revolutionaries" and extreme centralism. . . . A tragic irony was that even the mechanical selection of an organizational model was loused up, it being a combination of 1902 and post-1921, and not the party that actually led the revolution in 1917. . . . All the evils inherent in the situation were accentuated by the restrictions on openness. Once a veil of secrecy is interposed between the party and the masses, it becomes very easy to drop another curtain between leadership and membership. In this connection, Lenin was on the nail when he said talk of inner-party democracy is empty rhetoric when the life of the party and its personalities is not public. Anyway, the cult of confidentiality at the top, coupled with at best a half-hearted fight to win the legality and legitimacy that would make CP membership open, helped to create the deplorable political and ideological level of the clubs. This was constantly bemoaned, sincerely bemoaned; the problem became like Mark Twain's weather, and indeed nobody could *do* anything about it without demystifying the organizational system that, by and large, excluded the clubs from the decision-making process. ■ letter from Al Richmond to Dorothy, May 11, 1974.

Just as the Party's concerns were supposed to filter down from the center to the broader community through the activities of club members, so the concerns of the broader community were supposed to filter back up and, at least to some extent, shape the Party's outlook. That rarely happened. The Party was just not prepared to be that flexible or that open. There was one beneficial effect of this emphasis on local activity by club members, and it could be seen in operation at Party meetings and conventions. No matter what political subject was under discussion, people could stand up to speak about their own experiences in a union or in their community. They didn't feel like they had to be experts on national politics or political theory. It sometimes got tedious, sometimes it was strictly a publicity job for that individual. But occasionally it could be enlightening, and it meant that people felt like they were a part of what was going on in the world and had something to say about it.

Until the late 1940s when the political climate grew too hostile, clubs were encouraged to hold occasional open meetings where members could invite people in from the neighborhood or the work place. You'd have a speaker or refreshments, something out of the ordinary. When someone new walked into a meeting, immediately somebody would go up to talk to them, to make a personal contact and to make sure they felt welcome. This was particularly true if the newcomer was Black or Chicano. Club leaders also tried to keep tabs on existing members. If someone missed one or two meetings, an alarm was supposed to go off in the club leader's head, and they would go and visit the person to find out what was the matter.

I have to say that most of the club meetings I sat in on were very boring. We lost a lot of members as a result. The thing that saved us is that people didn't always judge the party by what their own club was like. There were a lot of other organizations and activities that Party members could, and indeed were expected to, get involved in. Above the clubs in our organizational chart we had what was known as sections, drawing together all the clubs in a particular area, and above the sections were divisions, pulling together two or more sections. Finally, there was the county organization. And at each level there were commissions, groups that oversaw the Party's work in particular fields or among particular groups, like the Mexican commission, the trade union commission, the cultural commission, and so forth. Everyone was encouraged to participate in one of these commissions, so the club was rarely the sole contact members had with the party. In Los Angeles in the late 1940s the average Communist might devote three nights a week to Party activities: one night to the regular club meeting, one to a mass organization or trade union, and one to a Party commission. This very intricate infrastructure was enormously important to the functioning of the Party. It trained people in political work and gave them a sense of participation in something real and on-going. Our politics were not abstract: they had the very tangible quality of a hundred evenings or more each year devoted to working with other Communists for common goals. With all its problems, and there were many, the internal structure of the Party provided an education for our members in the nuts and bolts of political activism that could not be obtained anywhere else.

Another thing I discovered when I became a Party leader was what it meant to live a life permanently "on call." People would come by or call you up at all hours with every imaginable problem. This was what being a professional revolutionary had always meant to me, that I would be of service and available whenever and for however long was necessary. But, as busy as I had been all through the 1930s, I had never been in a situation where so much was expected of me. To function effectively, a Party leader had to be constantly attentive to what people wanted and to respond as well as possible to meeting those needs. It was a little bit like reading a different novel every day, being exposed to other people's problems and expectations, trying to fathom their motives, understanding what made them happy or despairing. Unlike reading a novel, you could never just put it down and return your attention to your own life. Other than the times I reserved for Richard, it would never have occurred to me that there was any such thing as "office hours" in my job. You were never through. I think one of the reasons I gradually became disinclined to do a lot of socializing was because even going to parties turned into work for me. People would use the opportunity of a social gathering to talk about Party business. Not only that, but I could never really relax at those affairs. I had to be very careful about what kind of language I used or what jokes I repeated because I found that if I said something casually at a party, the next day it made the rounds of the movement. Increasingly I decided I would rather stay home evenings if I had the chance.

> Dorothy could have been more effective if she had adopted a few of the habits of people who weren't as dedicated as she was. You can be dedicated and still be part of a social milieu. She wasn't. It was almost as if she shied away from it. She was a totally political person. I wish I had a dollar for every dinner invitation she turned down. ■ Jack Berman. [Berman got to know Dorothy in the late 1940s when she was active in California's Independent Progressive Party.]

Although there was no such thing as a typical day in the life of a Party organizer, there was a kind of rhythm I soon fell into. I might start the morning with a meeting of the staff to hear reports on what people had been doing for the last few days and what they were going to be doing for the next few days. I'd want to know what meetings they were planning to attend, because we tried to spread ourselves as widely as possible, and rarely would more than one of the county leaders go to any single Party meeting. After that, each day held something different. A section organizer might come in and talk about a big political or personal crisis in some particular section. A trade union organizer might come in just to shoot the breeze. (Until 1948 it might just as likely be a non-Party as a Party trade unionist. They'd want to know, "What's going on? What do you people think? Here's what we're thinking. . . .") Each week I would encounter literally hundreds of people, each of whom knew exactly who I was and what we had said to each other the last time we were together. One of the greatest challenges I faced was being able to fit together names, faces, and political estimates in the first few seconds after someone walked through my door. Because of my previous organizing experience, I was pretty good at it. And I was, as always, curious about finding out what made people tick. After a few meetings I would have worked out a theory about most of the people I dealt with, which may or may not have been a good theory but that did help me keep track of who was who.

One of the people I had to figure out right in the beginning was the county organizer, Nemmy Sparks. Nemmy was a very cultured man, a chemist by training, about fifteen years my elder. He had a wide range of political experience, having served as Party organizer in Pittsburgh, Boston, and Wisconsin, until finally being sent to Los Angeles to replace Carl Winter. We had a complicated relationship, because while I respected him I also found him a difficult man to work with, bureaucratic and short-tempered. He was far too accustomed to simply pounding the table and saying "This is the decision and this must be done." We had some terrible fights. At first he tended to treat me the way he treated his wife Alice, which was very badly. Alice was an intelligent woman who had somehow been convinced that she didn't know anything. In Party work, she was always consigned to the financial department or to handling administrative work, or to running a bookstore. Her real Party work, in her own conception, was serving as a sort of comrade-mother to her husband, protecting and caring for him. Nemmy expected and demanded no less. He was very much the male chauvinist, and I think he expected me to treat him with the same respect and submission that his wife offered. I put up with it for a while but finally walked out of the office one day and refused to come back. He came to me pleading for me to return, and after two weeks I finally did come back. After that we got along without any real problems.

> People like Nemmy Sparks and Carl Winter were very rigid characters. In an organization like the Party, with its excessive centralization, one individual can make a big difference, in the spirit in which they lead, in the tone that they set. Nemmy would bring in people who behaved as he did, or as he taught them to behave. Very autocratic person. ■ Al Richmond.

I have to give Nemmy credit for putting up with my violations of Party etiquette. There was a political commission where the top Party people in politics and some sympathetic non-Communists would meet to discuss tactics. I just took for granted that I should go to such meetings, when in fact, the org secretary wouldn't ordinarily do that. He raised no objections to my participation. And, toward the end of his stay in Los Angeles, he became very good about allowing me to speak out at board meetings on the policies I didn't agree with. I later understood from him and from my own experience how important it was for him to have me play that role. Usually you're surrounded by people who agree with whatever you say, which can be very frustrating. You don't have anyone to bounce stuff off. When I became county chairman myself, I was horrified at first when people came to me with every conceivable kind of question, as if I were now suddenly omniscient. Whether it was a personal matter involving the relationship of husband and wife, or a theoretical question of the relationship of "base and superstructure," or a practical political question of what to do in the auto workers union, it all came across my desk. Those who brought the question to me took for granted that what I had to say would be the last word in wisdom. In the beginning I thought, "Oh my God, what am I supposed to say?" But it is amazing how fast in that atmosphere you start to think that maybe you really do know all the answers.

In the few years that we worked together in the late 1940s, I discovered that even though Nemmy had held responsible Party posts around the country and had done his job as effectively as anybody else, he was not part of what he bitterly referred to as the "old school tie" group among the leadership. He didn't have any more idea than I did about the ins and outs of the big battles that were going on behind the scenes in New York over such issues as the Progressive Party, and he resented his exclusion. I started to feel more sympathetically disposed to him as a result, and I wasn't at all happy to see him go when in 1948 he left Los Angeles, with secret orders to set up a nationwide underground organization for the Party. During the next few years he lived in Mexico. Later he returned to New York and acted as the clandestine editor of *Political Affairs* while Herbert Aptheker was its "open" editor.

As Los Angeles' No. 1 Red, [Dorothy Healey] cracks the whip over 4000 Communists and perhaps thousands more undercover Reds. . . . DID YOU KNOW THAT YOUR HOME LIES IN A CLEARLY DEFINED COMMUNIST OPERATING DIVISION? ■ "Communism in L.A.—How It Works," Los Angeles *Mirror*, August 22, 1950.

When I became organizational secretary in 1945, the Party in Los Angeles had about 3200 members. Four years later the Party had grown to almost 5000, which was the high point of its history. California was the second largest district in the country after New York, and the bulk of the California Party's membership was in Los Angeles. Nationally the Party held its membership steady at about 50,000—which meant that as our membership grew we came to account for about a tenth of the total Party membership in the country. Often historians present the history of the Party as if the thirties were our single great moment, "the heyday of American Communism," as the title of one recent book put it,

The Herman family: Fanny and Kiva (Dorothy's grandparents) and their children Rose, Paul, Sam, Esther, and *far right with her hand on Esther's shoulder*, Barbara, 1895. Dorothy Healey collection.

Joe and Barbara Rosenblum, Dorothy's parents, 1903. Dorothy Healey collection.

Bernard, Barbara, Frances, and, *center*, Dorothy Rosenblum, age 7, 1921. Dorothy Healey collection.

Dorothy with Lou Sherman, 1932.
Dorothy Healey collection.

Dorothy, 1941. Dorothy Healey collection.

Don Healey with Dorothy's sister Carol Jean and her mother, 1943. Dorothy Healey collection.

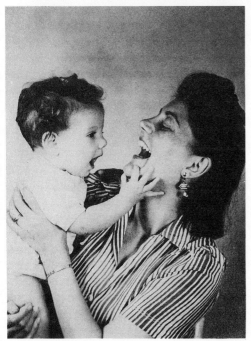

Dorothy and Richard Healey, 1943. Dorothy Healey collection.

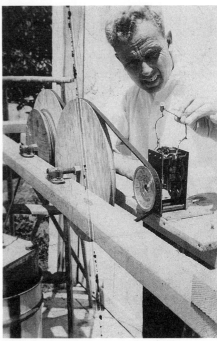

Dorothy's stepfather, Fedya Nestor, with "perpetual motion machine." Dorothy Healey collection.

Ben Davis and Dorothy Healey presenting food donations to Eugene Judd, president of UAW Local 216, during the General Motors strike, 1946. Courtesy California State University, Long Beach, Archives.

William Z. Foster and Robert Thompson, 1946. Dorothy Healey collection.

Picket line in Los Angeles protesting first Smith Act trial, 1949—Dorothy and Frank Spector in the first row. Courtesy California State University, Long Beach, Archives.

Dorothy jailed in grand jury investigation, June 1949. Courtesy, Los Angeles Times

Dorothy, 1949. Dorothy Healey collection

Los Angeles Smith Act defendants on their way to the courthouse, July 26, 1951: (left to right) FBI agent, Henry Steinberg, Slim Connelly, Dorothy Healey, FBI stenographer, Rose Chernin. Department of Special Collections, University Research Library, UCLA

American Communist Party delegates in Volgograd, USSR, June 1961. From left, Mike Davidow, Sam Davis, Anne Burlak Timmons, Soviet guide, Jake Holms, Dorothy Healey, Arnold Johnson, Jack Kling, Ellen Davis, Soviet guides. Dorothy Healey collection

Dorothy Healey, breaking the ban on Communist speakers at UCLA, 1963.
Courtesy California State University, Long Beach Archives

Communist party officials, February 1976. From left to right: Henry Winston, national chairman; Gus Hall, presidential nominee; Angela Davis; and Jarvis Tyner, vice-presidential nominee. UPI/Bettmann Newsphotos

Angela Davis gives the clenched fist salute in court appearance to face charges of conspiracy, kidnap, and murder, Fall 1970. UPI/Bettmann Newsphotos

Richard and Dorothy Healey, 1980. Dorothy Healey collection

Dorothy, 1983. From the film "Seeing Red"

with the implication that everything that followed was just a sort of trailing penumbra. In fact, the immediate postwar years were actually our most productive years in southern California. I think there's a miscalculation in many historical accounts as to just how quickly and uniformly the cold war hysteria grabbed hold. We recruited a lot of new members in that period: young people, trade unionists, Blacks, all kinds of people. In the labor movement, in Hollywood, and among the ranks of liberal activists, the effects of the "grand alliance" days had not completely worn off. From 1945 through 1948 we continued to play an important role in Los Angeles politics. We may have been increasingly fighting with our back to the wall, but at least we *were* fighting.

> Most of the questioning of Mrs. Healey centered about the People's Educational Center and the American Youth for Democracy [AYD], with [Tenney committee counsel Richard] Coombs attempting to show that these organizations are Communist-dominated, and therefore un-American. . . .
> Coombs questioned her at length about a recent A.Y.D. banquet at the Ambassador.
> The witness said the meeting was for the purpose of presenting awards to young Americans who had distinguished themselves.
> One of the awards, she said, was presented by Col. Evans Carlson to Bill Mauldin, the cartoonist. Atty. Gen. Robert W. Kenny and Ingrid Bergman were among those who made the presentation, she said, and another recipient was crooner Frank Sinatra. Dorothy Parker was master of ceremonies. ■ "16 called to testify in Fascist—Communist quiz," Los Angeles *Daily News*, January 3, 1946.

The Red Scare of 1919–1920 was part of the folk memory of every Communist. We knew what it was like to face this kind of postwar reaction, and at first it seemed we were infinitely better equipped to cope with it than our predecessors had been twenty-five years earlier. The labor movement was much stronger, and we were a much stronger factor within it. The administration in Washington was moving in a very reactionary direction in both domestic and foreign policy, but Harry Truman was at first regarded by many people as a kind of interloper in the camp of the New Deal, someone who did not deserve to wear FDR's mantle. There were thus many people in the Democratic Party and the labor movement who would not have agreed with us on everything, but who we at least expected would remain our allies on the most pressing domestic political questions. It was not until 1948–1949 that those illusions were dispelled. We then realized that we were facing a much more dangerous situation than even that of 1919–1920.

> LACCP has total membership of 4,332 as of 6/1/49 according to county records, and 4,546 according to division records. Has 829 AFL members and 546 CIO members. Twenty-one percent, or 935 LACCP members are employed in industry, and concentrated efforts being made to increase this figure. ■ FBI report on Los Angeles Communist Party, July 15, 1949.

Though I was not chosen as labor secretary in 1945, I was still a delegate to the CIO council from Local 700 of Mine-Mill and would remain one until 1949. I took part in all the battles in the CIO council in its last, most contentious years. Every Friday night there would be fiery debates at the meeting of the CIO Council. It was the best show in town, and people came flocking to it to sit and watch. I was also given special responsibility by the Party to work with our members and allies in the UAW.

I think that the single most important development that took place in the union movement in the year after the war had to be Walter Reuther's election as UAW president. In the UAW we made the defeat of Reuther our major priority. Communists like Wyndham Mortimer and Bob Travis had played a major role in the organization of the UAW in the 1930s, most notably in the Flint sit-down strike of 1937. We still had a lot of members and friends in the union after the war. The UAW was not only important in itself as the largest industrial union in the country; it also represented the balance of power within the CIO. After the war the Left held power in eleven CIO unions, including such important ones as the UE and the ILWU. A very tenuous alliance existed between the Left union leaders and the people who represented the center in the CIO, like CIO and Steelworkers' Union president Philip Murray. There were a lot of pressures pushing leaders like Murray to the Right, but as long as we could stay a factor in UAW internal politics and at least guarantee its neutrality in any internal CIO battle, then it was unlikely that Murray would go along with a sharp break with the Left.

We had a long tradition of working closely with non-Communist leaders of the UAW in Los Angeles, people like John Allard and Bill Goldman, and in 1946 we agreed that we would cooperate in every way we could to ensure that an anti-Reuther delegation be sent to the national UAW convention. That meant we had to support Cy O'Halloran, who was UAW regional director, for reelection. O'Halloran was a drunken stumblebum and totally incompetent. But he had good people on his staff, and it didn't seem too high a price to pay. In a situation like this, you're not always presented with an ideal choice. We were able to send a 100 percent anti-Reuther delegation to the UAW convention, the only region in the country to do so. In other important UAW centers, particularly in Detroit where Carl Winter had gone to be head of the Party, the results were much less favorable—I think because of the sectarian line Communists followed there. In the aftermath of the repudiation of the Teheran line, Communists often went overboard to emphasize the Party's "independent stand," without paying sufficient attention to the concerns of those who had been our allies in the past in the trade union movement. There was a price to be paid for indulging in that kind of ideological luxury at a moment like that, and part of it was Reuther's election.

It is difficult to overestimate the meaning of Walter Reuther's overwhelming victory at the UAW convention in Atlantic City this week. For the Communists have lost their last chance to dominate or deeply influence an important segment of the American labor movement. . . . In doing so they have lost their last chance to dominate or deeply influence the whole American political left. ■ Stewart Alsop, November 6, 1947.

In Los Angeles I sat in on these meetings of anti-Reuther UAW people and met with emissaries from the national UAW, from R. J. Thomas, who was then UAW president and Reuther's rival. There was a completely matter-of-fact acceptance of my being there and playing that kind of role. And that says something about the climate of the time: at least in some places and in some circles, the Party was still considered a legitimate force in the union movement. We still enjoyed our "citizenship." Reuther's election, though, was the turning point in the balance of power in the CIO. Had he gone down to defeat in 1946, had he been unable to secure a sympathetic majority on the UAW's executive board in 1947, I don't think there would have been the expulsions of the eleven Left-led unions three years later. And if those unions had not been expelled from the CIO and we had retained our base in the labor movement, the history of the 1950s might have been very different, not only in terms of what happened to the Communist Party but what happened to American unions. Stewart Alsop was one of the few people at the time who understood the meaning of Reuther's triumph. It shifted the balance of power within the CIO from the left center to the center right. And Reuther knew what to do with power, which was not something we always understood, for all of our "Bolshevik" hard headedness. We could have taken lessons from a socialist like Reuther, who was quite ruthless. He just barely won in 1946, but a year later he was able to totally shape the character of the leadership of that union and its policies. That's something that the candidate we supported, R. J. Thomas, had not been able to accomplish in six years in office. To be fair, I should add that Reuther played a more progressive role in the 1960s, in support of the civil rights movement and in opposition to the war in Vietnam. But I don't think there has been enough attention paid to the damage he wreaked in an earlier stage in his career.

[Los Angeles] is a Henry Wallace stronghold. That's true whether he is running for President or talking against war or just talking. He can fill any auditorium or stadium in town and has filled them. ■ *The Progressive*, February 1948,

By 1946 people in the mainstream of the labor movement were giving serious consideration to the possibility of launching a third party. The massive strikes of 1945–1946 among auto, steel, and electrical workers convinced many observers that there was a new wave of militancy in the working class, which was true, hence a higher degree of political class consciousness, which was questionable. Truman had seized the mines when the miners went on strike and had threatened to draft the railroad workers when they wanted to go on strike, and though he vetoed the Taft-Hartley Act the following year, he didn't put his heart into the fight in Congress to sustain the veto. With the exception of a few years during the war, Communists had believed that the breakup of the existing two-party system and the emergence of a new independent party representing the labor movement, Blacks, and other groups was a necessary and long overdue step. Just as "organize the unorganized" had been the central slogan of the 1930s and had largely been accomplished in the course of the decade, we now felt that it was possible that the historical moment had arrived for the emergence of the new third party. And Henry Wallace, Roosevelt's vice-president during most of the war, was an obvious choice to lead such an effort. For all those people who opposed Truman from the Left and saw him as leading the country away from the policies Roosevelt had stood for, Wallace was a symbol of continuity with both the spirit of the New Deal of the 1930s and of the Grand Alliance days of the Second World War.

> Here's Henry Wallace, dispossessed, and he wants to be the President of the United States. And here are the people in Los Angeles who are mad for Henry Wallace, and it's natural that they should be. He was made to order for Los Angeles. He was a very peculiar man. ■ Ellenore Hittelman.

There were two schools of thought, each of which had adherents within and without the Party, on the proper strategy to follow. One held that the best strategy was for Wallace to fight within the Democratic Party, enter the primaries in 1948, and try to wrest the nomination away from Truman. That was the position taken by Bob Kenny, the former California attorney general and an important figure in progressive politics in the state. Bob was vehemently opposed to the idea of organizing an independent party, but he was just as passionate an organizer nationally within the Democratic Party to dump Truman. Kenny had a big impact on my life. For the first time I came to respect the politics of someone who was not in any way sympathetic to Communism but who was genuinely devoted to what we used to call "bourgeois democratic" concepts. That is to say, he believed in the democratic process, civil liberties, and equality before the law without the slightest compromise or equivocation. He had been a judge, a state senator, and finally California attorney general, a post he held until his unsuccessful run for governor in 1946. He was always willing to work with Communists around issues of common concern. That was not so unusual among Democratic politicians in the later 1930s and early 1940s— what was unusual was that he never tried to keep his contacts with us hidden. He wouldn't even *allow* us to keep them hidden. Once, at the height of the McCarthy period, I said to him, "Bob, when I want to call you in the future, I'll leave my office and go to a pay phone, and I won't give my name." That way we could have been reasonably sure that the FBI or whoever else was tapping his phone and mine wouldn't know he was talking to me. He replied, "That's ridiculous. You call me from the Party office. I never have relationships under subterfuge. We're friends and that's all there is to it." His example taught me that the categories the Party developed to describe people outside its ranks could be very misleading: the term "bourgeois democratic," for example, carried with it the implication that it described someone who might make a useful short-term ally, but who was ultimately going to prove weak and unreliable. The use of such abstract terms fed an unjustified sense of our own superiority while leaving us contemptuous of some of our best friends.

Kenny wanted the Wallace fight to be conducted within the Democratic Party. Maybe Wallace could win the nomination for himself, or if not, maybe he could at least block Truman's renomination in favor of someone more palatable. We weren't opposed to that strategy on principle, although we didn't think it had much chance of actually succeeding. But already in 1946–1947 our feeling was that if it was possible to launch a third party *with significant support from within the labor movement*, that would be our preferred strategy. Until the middle of 1947 it wasn't necessary to make any hard and fast choice between the two, so we worked within the labor movement to encourage an independent political initiative while still trying to keep up our contacts within the Democratic Party. We didn't want to break any alliances prematurely or unnecessarily.

In August 1947 the first step was taken toward the creation of a third party in California. Hugh Bryson, who was the left-wing president of a west coast CIO union known as the Marine Cooks and Stewards Union, played a major role at this conference, which set up a provisional committee to organize what became known as the Independent Progressive Party. The new group's most pressing and immediate goal was to begin collecting the several hundred thousand valid signatures we would need to get it on the ballot in 1948. We couldn't wait until after the 1948 primaries to launch this effort, because by law all our signatures had to be on file by March, and the California primaries were not held until June. (All of this, by the way, took place six weeks before the famous founding conference of the Cominform in October 1947, which Joseph Starobin has argued was the deciding factor in the Party's decision to go ahead with the Progressive Party campaign. There were all too many occasions on which we shaped our approach to domestic politics in response to some Soviet diplomatic declaration or policy, but this was not one of them.)

> In connection with the development of the Wallace peace campaign and the third party movement, our generally correct political orientation and line was considerably weakened for a time by our failure to wage an adequate and sharp enough struggle against a host of sectarian and opportunist tendencies. We were much too slow in combating the erroneous views of certain party leaders and district organizations, as well as many of our trade union cadres who, up until the announcement of Wallace's candidacy, expressed doubts as to the advisability of an independent Presidential ticket and confused the maneuverings and treacherous position of most of labor's top officials with the position being taken by the rank and file. ■ Eugene Dennis, report to the February 1948 meeting of the CP National Committee.

The problem was that these kinds of campaigns have a self-reinforcing dynamic. When you gear up for this kind of campaign, with one set of assumptions, you tend to lose track of developments that, if you'd been paying attention, might have undermined those assumptions. In every union, in every mass organization, in every area where the Party had influence, support for the Progressive Party became the top priority. The all-important detail we ignored in the critical year before the election campaign began was that the leaders of the CIO and the Truman administration were drawing closer together, not further apart, for reasons having to do with both national politics and internal CIO politics. CIO leaders figured that given the political mood of the time, Truman was the best they could hope for. Moreover, after Reuther's victory in the UAW, they began to look for an issue which they could use to break the power of the Left in the CIO. Loyalty to the Democratic presidential candidate in 1948 could be just such an issue. Having set off on the crusade for a new third party, we lost sight of the fact that we were abandoning one of the preconditions we had set for its organization, which was a solid base within the labor movement. Our isolation from the working class in later years was not the product of our "right-wing opportunism" during the Browder period. Our wartime enthusiasm for the no-strike pledge didn't always work to our advantage, but we survived its fallout. In this country, unfortunately, you don't lose contact with the working class by moving to the right. It's when you move to the left that you risk everything. That's what we decided to do in 1948, and it was a gamble we were destined to lose.

> So here we go with the Progressive Citizens of America, and a roster of new alphabet groups that came out of all this, each time losing a couple of members. The times were bad, no question about that. But at the very moment when you should be trying to keep every connection that's possible to keep, to go around chopping off those connections. . . . We started Democrats for Wallace with a conference in Fresno. But already I could see there were people around there and that wasn't what they wanted. They wanted an independent candidacy for Wallace. It finally got down to just Bob Kenny and me arguing against it. Relationships *are* politics. If you're going to play in the game of electoral politics, then you have to play by those rules. Don't kid yourself that you can get absolution from broken relationships like you can from your own disciplined members, where you can just walk in and say, "Sorry, but this is the decision," and then there's grumbling and stuff, but people go along. In the outside world you can't expect that kind of reaction. ■ Ellenore Hittelman.

Had Henry Wallace received anywhere near the five million votes expected by his supporters, the fallout from the Party's single-minded emphasis on his campaign would not have been as serious—would not, that is, have left the Communists stripped of allies and vulnerable before the Right's vengeful counterattack. Like everyone else I was misled by the size and the enthusiasm of the crowds that Wallace was attracting across the country. In Los Angeles ten thousand Chicanos came to hear Wallace speak in Lincoln Park under the banner of "Amigos de Wallace," and twenty-five hundred blacks came to hear him speak in Watts. We filled Gilmore Stadium, with its 32,000 seats, on three occasions. Charlie Chaplin endorsed him; Katharine Hepburn spoke at the first of those

Gilmore Stadium meetings and made a very powerful speech supporting Wallace and attacking red-baiting. The Students for Wallace movement was very strong at UCLA, and we recruited many young people into the Party as a result. In Berkeley, Wallace was banned from speaking on campus but managed to attract eight thousand students to hear him speak from a sidewalk adjoining the campus. In the California primaries in June, about a half million people cast ballots for candidates who had filed or cross-filed as Progressives, one fifth of the total primary vote. It was a very energizing campaign, and no one in the Party thought that Wallace could possibly end up with less than five million votes nationwide.

But even while I was swept up in the enthusiasm of the campaign, I still argued at meetings of the political commission that we shouldn't put all our eggs in one basket. I was just frantic at the possibility of abandoning all our long-term alliances in the labor movement and the Democratic Party. Because the IPP was running as a separate party, it was required to offer a full slate on the ballot, which meant running Congressional candidates as well as a presidential candidate. If it had left some positions empty, that meant that anybody who wanted to could file as the Independent Progressive Party Candidate for that office, and the IPP would be stuck with them in November. That created a real problem, because in some Congressional districts there were very progressive candidates running on the Democratic ticket, like Helen Gahagan Douglas, who was running for reelection from the Fourteenth Congressional District, and Chet Holifield, running for reelection in the Nineteenth District. We asked Douglas and Holifield to file nominating petitions in the Progressive primary (in California candidates could run in as many separate party primaries as they chose), but they declined. So we felt we had to nominate candidates in those districts, and chose Sidney Moore, a Black leader in the CIO public workers union, for the Fourteenth District, and Jack Berman for the Nineteenth District. Despite the fact that neither of them actually did any real campaigning, the decision to put them on the ballot in the first place led to the severing of a lot of alliances. Instead of fighting reactionaries, it seemed to some former friends that we were now playing a spoiler role, undercutting the strength of some of the best left-liberals in the Democratic Party.

> My candidacy was a mistake. We couldn't even explain it to our own people, let alone to the community at large. ■ Jack Berman.

In retrospect it's clear that we should not have filed anyone against Douglas or Holifield, and just taken the chance of some outsider grabbing those ballot lines. A similar issue arose two years later, when Douglas had given up her Congressional seat to run against Richard Nixon for the U.S. Senate seat. By this time the Korean War had broken out and Douglas had endorsed American involvement. There was a great fight within the leadership of the Communist Party as to what our attitude should be towards Douglas's candidacy. In L.A. we felt that our priority had to be the defeat of Nixon, because of his role on HUAC, particularly in the Hiss case, and his sponsorship of the Mundt-Nixon bill, which would have outlawed the Party. We didn't agree with Douglas's support of the war, obviously, but we also recognized that there was no way a credible candidate for the Senate could take any other position at that time. But Archie Brown and Bill Schneiderman argued in a meeting of the state board that, quoting Lenin, there were times when Communists had to swim against the stream, and this was one of them. The state leadership decided that international issues were of paramount importance, and here Douglas was merely the "lesser of two evils" because she too supported the Korean War.' So they decided that the position of Communists within the IPP should be one that favored having the party run its own senatorial candidate to oppose both Nixon and Douglas. Ben Dobbs and I were forbidden to tell either the L.A. County Committee or the L.A. membership of the Party of our disagreement with the decision to oppose Douglas. If anything, the resulting campaign left us treating Douglas as if she was the worst of the two evils: while Nixon was an open reactionary, she was a perfidious liberal and thus more likely to sow illusions among the voters. The votes we took away from her were hardly decisive in the final outcome, but knowing that we made only a small contribution to a Nixon victory is cold comfort.

In the national campaign that fall Truman outmaneuvered both his Republican and Progressive opponents, adopting some of the liberal positions of the Progressive Party like support for civil rights, while continually red-baiting the Wallace campaign. The pro–cold war liberals in the Americans for Democratic Action, the Socialists, and the Trotskyists all joined in a chorus condemning Wallace as a Soviet dupe or worse. (Whatever their intentions, Norman Thomas and other "Anti-Stalinists" were helping to prepare the ground for McCarthyism through the hysterical character of their attacks on Communists in those years.) The Progressive Party lent ammunition to its critics with the defeat of the "Vermont resolution" at its national convention. That resolution declared, "Although we are critical of the present foreign policy of the United States, it is not our intention to give blanket endorsement to the foreign policy of any nation." That was to say, simply, that neither the Soviet Union nor the United States were above criticism. There was no reason why the Progressive Party should not have adopted such a position; the Communists could have maintained an independent position on the question if they chose to do so.

In the end, Wallace got just over a million votes instead of the five million we had predicted, or even the two million his opponents had conceded him. Close to 200,000 of Wallace's votes were cast in California; Wallace's percentage of the total vote in the state was just under 5 percent, roughly double the national average. In Los Angeles he actually managed to carry five precincts, part of a total of thirty he won nationwide. But we had little cause to celebrate our relatively better showing here. The Wallace campaign split the state and Los Angeles CIO councils; neither council formally endorsed Wallace, but they also refused to follow national CIO directives to condemn his candidacy, and as a result the right and center forces walked out. After the election the national CIO lifted the charters of both the California and Los Angeles councils. That was a blow we never recovered from. I can't emphasize enough how great a defeat that represented. Since the 1930s the CIO councils in places like Los

Angeles and New York had been the backbone of Popular Front politics: they had the resources and the legitimacy to rally labor, liberals, Blacks, and others in the community around a progressive agenda. There was nothing comparable to take the place of the councils once they were gone. The expulsion of Left-led unions from the CIO and raids on their membership by newly chartered rivals followed soon after the councils' charters were lifted.

The November vote confirmed just how vulnerable and divided the progressive camp was. Our opponents now felt they could attack us with impunity. We were entering a period of sustained legal assault which would continue, in one form or another, until the mid-1960s.

7

6/11/49 Subject arranged to consult with her attorney prior to appearance in Federal Court. Disclosed to a relative that the Communist Party maintains no membership records for security reasons. . . .

6/25/49 Subject confers at length with William Taylor regarding articles in Daily People's World which she terms "chauvinistic" and composes letter of criticism to Al Richmond and William Schneiderman. Proposes "charges" be brought if situation not improved immediately. . . .

7/6/49 Subject conferred with Sid Burke of the People's World regarding possibility of having "Wedding Party" for Philip Connelly and herself in order to raise funds for the paper. . . .

10/13/49 Communist Party paid $800 for leaflet printing and instructed by subject, through local apparatus, to mobilize for citywide distribution when verdict of New York trial announced. . . .

11/5/49 Subject scheduled to address a Morning Freiheit Mass Meeting in honor of Abe Olkin; due to family illness of her son, Richard, instructs Henry Steinberg to substitute for her. . . . ■ FBI summary of results of "technical surveillance" of Dorothy's home telephone, December 8, 1949. [The telephone tap was maintained continually from 1946 until the date of this memorandum—and no doubt for some years thereafter.]

Henry Wallace was denied one vote in Los Angeles that he should have gotten. In late October 1948 I went "underground" to avoid a subpoena issued by a federal grand jury investigating alleged subversive activities among government employees. The timing was not coincidental. Part of Truman's strategy for discrediting the Wallace campaign was to have the Justice Department launch a series of headline-generating investigations, like that of the Los Angeles grand jury, while at the same time indicting the Communist Party's national leaders for violation of the Smith Act.

Those indictments also served other and larger purposes. The Smith Act, passed by Congress during the "little Red Scare" of 1940, made it a crime to conspire to advocate the overthrow of the government by force or violence. It was first used against the Trotskyists in Minnesota during the war, and the Communists, to our discredit, not only refused to come to their support but actually organized to prevent other people from supporting them. It was a position which would all too soon be thrown back in our faces as we attempted to gather support for our own leaders on trial.

On the face of it, the Smith Act indictments were ludicrous. In a saner political climate, it would have been impossible for the government to convict Communist leaders on such charges. We had no illusions about the United States teetering at the brink of revolution. We weren't either so foolish or so "adventurist" as to be storing dynamite in the basement in preparation for the big day, no matter what the Hearst press charged. We made no bones about our commitment to Marxism-Leninism, but our understanding of that tradition allowed us to be advocates of a peaceful transition to socialism in the United States—though we also warned that if the ruling class were to disregard a popular majority for socialism and unleash violence against the people, then the people would have the right to respond accordingly. The distinctions which seemed so clear to us were to prove impossible to convey to a jury in a time of anti-Communist hysteria like the late 1940s and early 1950s. In any case, the Smith Act indictments should not be taken at face value. We weren't being punished for any "clear and present danger" we posed to the government of the United States; rather, we paid the price for holding unpopular ideas at a time when men in power in Washington were imposing a new cold war conformity on the American public.

> The net of justice which today snared four top Los Angeles Communists was first woven in New York's Foley Square Courthouse beginning in January 1949.
>
> There the Communist Party's 11 highest ranking members went on trial before a jury in Federal Judge Harold R. Medina's court charged with conspiring to teach the overthrow of the U.S. government by force.
>
> That charge—constituting a violation of the Smith Act enacted during World War II—was climaxed by a verdict of guilty brought on Oct. 14, 1949, at the end of a stormy, historic nine-month trial. ■ "Justice Began Closing Trap on Reds in 1949," Los Angeles *Mirror*, July 26, 1951.

Eleven Communists, including the Party's general secretary Eugene Dennis, Henry Winston, Ben Davis, John Gates, Gil Green, Robert Thompson, and other top leaders, were brought to trial in 1949, in what became known as the Foley Square trial. It was not so much a trial of the defendants as of one of the books they had read. The prosecutor would read aloud passages from Marx or Lenin that seemed to call for the use of "force and violence" to overthrow capitalism, then would show that the Party published those books or used them in its classes. This "proved" that the leaders of the Party were guilty of conspiracy. No overt acts of violence or even preparation for violence on their part were required to be shown as evidence. The defendants tried to argue that their understanding of the meaning of those passages was quite different from that imputed to them by the prosecution, but to no avail. Louis Budenz, a former Communist turned professional anti-Communist witness, charged that the

Communists habitually made use of "Aesopian language"—which meant that whenever we talked about peaceful change, it was intended as a kind of code or double-talk to confuse outsiders. This was a very convenient concept for the prosecution, because it meant that if the defendants openly advocated violence they were guilty, and if they openly opposed violence, they were still guilty—and deceitful hypocrites to boot. All of this made the Foley Square trial into an Alice-in-Wonderland trial, and after many months of testimony all eleven Communist leaders were found guilty. The following year, with the Korean War just beginning, the circuit court upheld the convictions, and it began to dawn on me that the convictions were actually going to stand. A year later the Supreme Court upheld the convictions, and the defendants were ordered to report to jail.

One of the most depressing aspects of the trial was that unlike the great political cases of the twenties and thirties, like that of Sacco and Vanzetti or of the Scottsboro Boys, or even the hearings involving the Hollywood Ten in 1947, there was almost no public outcry. Liberals were divided, demoralized, or worse yet, in some instances enlisting on the side of our persecutors. That wasn't, as I will argue later, universally the case, certainly not in Los Angeles. But as the 1950s began, it seemed to us that we were on our own. And that sense of isolation exacerbated the Party's worst political deficiencies.

> With Dorothy and Slim, that was a no good thing going on there. They were in this tiny little house, where the walls were made of paper. My then husband and I had used to go over there occasionally because Slim was his patient, and Dorothy and I were by then old friends. We would go over there, and sooner or later Slim would just start yelling at her. It was awful. I really don't know how Richard survived. ■ Ellenore Hittelman.

And as if all that wasn't enough to contend with, my own personal life was in turmoil for the better part of a decade because of my marriage to Slim Connelly. I married Slim in 1947, and as was true of all my marriages, did so for all the wrong reasons. I knew almost immediately that it was a mistake but was stupid enough to let it drag on for almost a decade. Even after I realized Slim was not the husband for me, I continued to hope that he could provide a "father figure" for Richard. Here was a boy being raised by his mother and grandmother, and I didn't think that was a good thing at all. But Slim was no better a father than a husband. He was really a tragic figure. The Party had done a terrible thing to him by taking him out of the newspaper industry, the one thing he knew and loved. Turning him into a "leader" in the CIO just brought out his most egocentric and self-destructive side. And it was only made worse when he subsequently lost his power because of the anti-Communist purges in the CIO, while I kept rising in Party leadership.

> There were cycles of some kind with Slim. He could be very sweet, but he could also be just nuts. You could see this man growing with power, to the point where he became positively authoritarian. I had an office next door to his in the CIO building. I once saw him pick up the telephone and

call a man named Van Griffith (whose father had given Los Angeles Griffith Park); Griffith was at this point chairman of the police commission, appointed by Bowron. Slim called him up and said, with a horrible grin on his face, "Well Van, I understand the mayor intends to blah, blah, blah. . . . If he does that, I will blow this whole place sky high. . . . "And I'm thinking, "My God, is this the way to keep friends?" But Slim just loved this kind of thing. . . . ■ Ellenore Hittelman.

In 1948 Slim was forced out of his position as executive secretary of the California CIO, and then the national CIO yanked the charter of the Los Angeles Council, which he had led for a decade. He became Los Angeles editor of the *People's World*, but obviously that was a step down for him, because he had been used to and enjoyed exercising real power. He always had a problem with drinking, and when all of these props to his ego were removed, it got worse. People would come to our living room for a meeting and just address themselves to me and ignore him. Or we'd go out to some function, and someone we didn't know well would come up and address him as "Mr. Healey." It was very humiliating for him. If I had to go to New York for a meeting, it was a major production to placate him.

My mother and grandmother were really quite extraordinary in their ability to be loving and supporting. On the other hand, their marriages were pretty terrible. . . . I detested my stepfather, who lived with us until 1957. . . . I do have one memory of walking with Slim, a complete drunkard at this point in his life, but walking on a picket line protesting the Rosenberg's death sentence in 1953, with people throwing things at us and screaming things like "Let's have fried Rosenberger." It was bloodcurdling. Well, walking with him there to protect me was quite wonderful, and for the first and only time I could see him as a hero. ■ Richard Healey.

It was Richard, finally, who freed me from my dilemma. Part of my responsibility to him, I thought, was to spare him the pain of losing another father. And then I learned that there were some confidences Richard hadn't shared with me in those evening sessions at his bedside. One day in 1957 while making his bed I came across his diary. And of course like any good mother I read it. And then I discovered how he hated and feared Slim. Not that Slim had ever mistreated Richard. He never hit him or yelled at him. But there are other ways in which children can be hurt. When Slim would get drunk, which was frequent, he would stand in the doorway of Richard's bedroom and scream the most outrageous invective at me, all of his anger coming out uncontrollably. He knew that the only place that I was vulnerable was where Richard was concerned. Richard, of course, would wake up. Slim was a huge man who at that point weighed close to three hundred pounds. This giant in the doorway screaming at his mother must have seemed like a nightmare figure to him. When I read Richard's diary and learned just how terribly this affected him, I finally shed that misplaced sense of responsibility to stay in the marriage any longer. We were divorced in 1958. I helped him get a job in New York with the World Federation of Trade Unions. He later came back to Los Angeles, where he lived until his death in 1981. He remained in the Party for most of that time, and as I got into more and more trouble with the leadership he unfailingly took my side.

> This is a story of political persecution and developing Fascism in the United States. It's a story of events in Los Angeles, California, U.S.A., but events just like it have occurred in Denver, in Cleveland, and elsewhere in this country in the past twelve months. It is a story that should wake up millions of Americans, and make them realize what is happening to the liberty we fought for in 1776, and from 1860 to 1864 [sic]—from 1941 to 1945, the liberty we talk about every year on the Fourth of July. ■ "It's YOU They're After," pamphlet published in defense of the Los Angeles twenty-one by the Civil Rights Congress, 1949. [The Civil Rights Congress was the Communist-organized successor to the International Labor Defense and the National Negro Congress.]

I had already tangled with California-based inquisitors, like the Tenney Committee, on several occasions. Those were pretty freewheeling affairs, with lots of accusations and lots of headlines but no serious legal consequences. But when we got word from a friend on a federal grand jury in October 1948 that the Department of Justice had sent a special prosecutor to Los Angeles and that there was going to be a large number of subpoenas issued for Communists, we knew we were facing a more serious challenge.

> The government was trying to find ways of putting Communist Party officials into jail as quickly as possible. For this purpose they set up a grand jury to investigate the Communist Party. The problem that the people who were subpoenaed before the grand jury had was that they were perfectly willing to speak about themselves and their own activities, but they were unwilling to give the names of anyone else who was not publicly known. There were many people in the Party whose jobs or professional life depended upon keeping that a secret. So when people were subpoenaed they came to John McTernan and me for advice as to what they should do. We advised them that once they spoke about themselves they would probably have given up their Fifth Amendment rights and have no basis for refusing to give the names of anyone else. If they wanted to have the best shot at staying out of jail and yet not disclosing the names, they should refuse to answer any questions beyond their names and addresses. They followed our advice and were cited for contempt. It wasn't until later, in an appeal from another case, that the Supreme Court ruled that there was a Fifth Amendment right to refuse to disclose membership in the Communist Party. ■ Ben Margolis [Margolis, along with his law partner John McTernan, are National Lawyers Guild activists who played a central role in legal cases involving civil liberties in Los Angeles in the 1940s and 1950s.]

The government's strategy was to use the grand jury to force us to choose between naming other people as members of the Communist Party or refusing to testify, which would mean being cited for contempt and sent to jail. We decided that in order to prevent the government from closing down the Party in L.A. by jailing all of its leaders for contempt, some of us would make ourselves unavailable to the subpoena servers. I was one of those chosen to go underground. If I hadn't, I would have shared the fate of ten other Communists who received subpoenas on October 25. They were taken before the grand jury and promptly thrown in jail for refusing to answer the prosecutor's questions when directed to do so in a federal trial court. It was a remarkably efficient way of putting away political dissidents without having to bother with indictments or lengthy trials. Most of that original group received sentences of six months in prison. Ultimately subpoenas were served on twenty-one people, the "Los Angeles 21," as we became known.

> Those subpoenas were served before 7 o'clock in the morning and called for an appearance at 10 o'clock the same day. We went to the court and asked for a delay, saying we'd had no time to prepare for this thing. That request was denied. People were taken before the grand jury, questions were put to them, they refused to answer, they went back to the court, there was a government motion to compel them to answer. We argued that the [Fifth Amendment] privilege applied, the court decided against us, and they were all ordered to answer. Back to the grand jury, where the questions were put to them a second time. Now their refusal to answer was contempt of court. They were brought back before the court and a hearing was held as to whether or not they were guilty of contempt. That process took all day and continued after dinner until nearly midnight. At every stage of the matter we were asking for continuance [postponement]. At two minutes before midnight, when the court had held them in contempt, I remember this vividly, I stood and said to the court, "We are appealing your judgment, we ask that you set bail pending appeal," and his response was, "Your wish for continuance is granted." *That* was something he was willing to hold over for another day. Which meant that the people would go to jail that night. And they stayed in jail for several days while we got a release from the court of appeals. When they were released on bail they walked out of the jail house and were handed new subpoenas to appear the following morning. Then they went through the whole process again, and this time they were held in criminal contempt and sentenced to a period in jail.
> ■ John McTernan.

I stayed underground for six months, living in Los Angeles in the homes of various Party members. I found it a much more trying experience than the six months I had spent in prison in the Imperial Valley. It was an imposition on the people I stayed with and difficult for me. In jail, you can just be yourself. In someone else's home, I always had to be concerned about whether I was fitting in with the rhythm of their household, trying not to disrupt their lives too much. And I couldn't just relax and read. I was still operating all this time as a Party leader. In fact, it was while I was underground that I became the top Party leader in Los Angeles.

When Nemmy Sparks was summoned back to New York and given the assignment to organize the Party's national underground apparatus, Ben Dobbs and I had to make a recommendation to the County Committee as to who should be Nemmy's successor as county chairman. When Ben was appointed to the post as county labor secretary in 1946 we quickly became close friends and developed total confidence in each other. I think Ben would have made an excellent Chairman. I liked being organization secretary because I was free to make the job whatever I wanted it to be. In terms of skills and background, Ben and I were pretty much interchangeable. So in the end we simply flipped a coin, and as it turned out I became chairman and he took over my post as org secretary. Ben had absolutely no hesitation about an arrangement that made me his superior in the organizational hierarchy. When the state chairman, Bill Schneiderman, heard about my new office, he was beside himself. He could understand a woman being org secretary, but not chairman: that just wasn't right. But Ben and I stuck with the decision, and Bill eventually came around.

> I don't recall flipping any coin. She was so much smarter than me that there was never a question in my mind. It came up at a state board meeting that I should be the county chairman, but I thought that was just nonsense. ■ Ben Dobbs.

I was still operating from the underground, and that made it very difficult to meet with others to discuss Party business and strategy. I would have to be smuggled into a car, lie down on the floor of the back seat, be driven to a rendezvous point and transferred to another car, go through the whole procedure again to get into a third car, and only then be taken to the place where the meeting was going to be. After awhile I began to think it wasn't worth all the trouble. What finally decided the issue for me was when I learned that Richard, who was then six years old, had caught the mumps. Being separated from him for so many months was a terrible pressure. I had this great desire just to be able to touch him. And even though he had my mother and my stepfather and his own father and stepmother, who were then living nearby, to care for him, he still suffered from my absence. How do you explain a grand jury investigation to a child? When I heard that Richard was sick I immediately called Ben and said, "This is nonsense. The grand jury will stay in session until they get me. I'm the one they want. It's stupid politically, and it's killing me personally because of Richard. I'm coming home." I got back to my house on a Saturday night in late April, spent all day Sunday with Richard, and first thing Monday morning a federal marshall came to the door and handed me my subpoena.

> Dear Richard:
> Well, just as we expected, Mommy finally went to jail. I'm sorry I didn't have a chance to tell you myself, but I was surprised when it happened too.

It is very nice here, and if only I am sure that you are O.K. and not being *too* sad, then I won't mind it at all.

Shall I describe the jail to you? We get up at 5:30 a.m., make our beds, and sit around for awhile. At 6:30 we go for our breakfast. This morning I had mush (just like I make for you), coffee, and a hard-boiled egg. About 11, I had some soup. Tonight, the other girls tell me, we'll have some very good stew.

To pass the time, we sit and talk, play cards, and read. So, you see, it really isn't so bad.

But oh honey-baby, Mommy does want to know that you're happy and having a good time. Next time you see Terry, you and he can talk about your mommies. Have Terry tell you about the jail game he plays.

Lots of love,
Mommy

■ letter to Richard [June 29, 1949].

Everything that followed proceeded according to script. They'd served me with a *subpoena duces tecum*, which meant that I had to produce the books of the Party. I claimed that I didn't have any knowledge of where the books were. They then asked me a string of questions about other people, and each time I took the Fifth Amendment. I was ordered to appear before Judge Pierson Hall, refused once again to answer the same questions, and after some weeks of legal maneuvers, I was sentenced to a year and a half in jail for contempt of court. I was initially refused bail, but Ben Margolis got the U.S. Court of Appeals to issue a bail order, and I got out after a day and a half. For the next year the Los Angeles cases wound their way through the appeal system, along with some similar cases from a Colorado federal grand jury, until in February 1951 the Circuit Court of Appeals reversed our sentences. And in a separate case the Supreme Court validated the use of the Fifth Amendement. It was a legal victory but in some ways a political defeat, because when we took the Fifth it made it seem to many people as if we had something to hide, as if the Fifth Amendment were tantamount to an admission of guilt. That is not how we saw it at all. As I came out of the grand jury room I told the newspapermen waiting there, "I'll answer any question that you want to ask about myself or about the Party. But I will not answer any of their questions."

You refuse to produce any books and records, you refuse to answer any questions, you refuse to give any information and, finally, after you are found guilty after a very considerable deliberation you stand there and make a defiant statement which to me can be construed as nothing else but a defiance to the whole system and structure of government. ■ Judge Pierson M. Hall, U.S. District Court, Southern District of California, June 28, 1949, remarks upon pronouncing sentence on Dorothy.

One of the most effective repressive instruments used against the Party in the McCarthy era was the threat of deportation of foreign-born Communists. In the end, only a relatively small number of people were deported, but thousands were threatened by the Immigration Service. Frank Carlson was one of the California Party leaders caught up in the deportation scare; he spent many months on Terminal Island before lawyers from the Committee for the Protection of the Foreign Born were able to win his release.

My own family was victimized by the Immigration Service, although we don't show up in the statistics of deportations. In 1955 my mother's second husband, Fedya Nestor, was deported to Bulgaria. Technically he left voluntarily, but this was after a long internment by immigration officials during which he had been worn down. Fedya had lived in the United States for many years, but he had never been naturalized, much to my mother's disgust. In her own way, Mama could be quite patriotic, and she would have big arguments with him, saying how can you live here and not become a citizen? "I am a citizen of the world," he would reply loftily. Such idealism didn't do him much good in the long run. He had joined the Party sometime in the 1930s, but he wasn't much of a Communist. He was basically a dreamer, and his notions about politics were a mixture of anarchism and, of all things, DeLeonism (the Socialist Labor Party, for some reason, had always attracted a large number of Bulgarians).

> Mama kept saying she wanted a real man, someone she could look up to, who could tell her what to do, but she did the same thing with Papa and Fedya, which was the minute she saw any signs of independence out of them, she'd clip their wings fast. ■ Carol Jean Newman.

Fedya was a sweet, amiable man, without much sense. He could never hold a job long enough to earn much money, so Mama basically supported him. He was an amateur inventor and would spend his time tinkering with a "perpetual motion" device he was building in our backyard—in fact it was still there when I sold our house in Los Angeles in 1980. One of the reasons why he agreed to accept deportation was because he had some notion of taking his invention to the Soviet Union and donating it to the government. Actually, it was no easy matter to get him into Bulgaria. In order to prevent the U.S. government from engaging in a wholesale deportation of foreign-born Communists, the Soviet Union and the eastern European governments had a standing policy of refusing to accept deportees. I had to use my Party connections to get the rule waived for Fedya. When the poor man got to Bulgaria he found that no one was interested in his invention. Not only that, but he was under a great deal of suspicion, as an American. Neither Bulgaria nor the United States treated Fedya very well. After his deportation, the government ruled that he was not entitled to Social Security payments, which was particularly unjust because the system is after all in part funded by employee contributions. He lost everything he had put into it. (It wasn't until after he died that the Social Security system decided to award a widow's allotment to Mama. That surprised her no end. Here she was receiving a regular check, thanks to Fedya, whom she hadn't seen in twenty years, when he had never been able to bring any money into the household in the years they lived together.)

In June 1951 the Supreme Court upheld the Foley Square convictions. It was a moment that both the Party and the government had long awaited. For the Party, it was taken as the definitive signal that it was "five minutes to midnight," that fascism was on the verge of triumph, and that the only way the Party could avoid total destruction was to adopt a form of underground organization modeled on that used by the resistance movements in Nazi-occupied Europe. For the government, it was the go-ahead signal for further Smith Act prosecutions—which of course lent credence to the "five minutes to midnight" analysis.

Our experience hiding out from the grand jury was a foretaste of what the real Party underground would be like. We tried, without much success, to pass on some of the lessons we had learned to the national office. I had gone back to New York in 1950 on Party business, and one of the things I told them was that under no circumstance should they ask mothers with young children to go underground. It just wouldn't work and would cause too much suffering. Later that year we got a request from the national office to send someone down to Mexico to see if it could serve as a safe hiding place for people in the underground. We sent someone down, and he came back and said that Mexico was out. Any "gringo" was going to stick out like a sore thumb, and if they were looking for a nearby country to use as a haven, they would probably do a lot better in Canada. I reported this assessment to a meeting of the national secretariat, which included Gus Hall, who was acting General Secretary while Gene Dennis served a one-year sentence for contempt of Congress. In the fall of 1951, in the midst of our own Smith Act case, I picked up a newspaper and read that Gus Hall had been arrested in Mexico. Hall, along with Gil Green, Henry Winston, and Robert Thompson, had all vanished just before they would have had to go to prison to serve their Smith Act sentences. Ben and I just looked at each other and shook our heads, as if to say, "So much for our advice."

Ben and I were in charge of choosing people in Los Angeles to go underground. I hated doing it. We would go to each person, one by one, and tell them what was in store for them—and we also told each of them that they were free to turn down the assignment. If they accepted, it meant they had to disappear, change their names, move to a new city, and have no contact with their family or friends for no one could say how long a time. As it turned out, some of those we sent into the underground had to endure it until 1955. I was astonished how many people were willing to do it. They shared this intense feeling that terrible things were in store for the country and that this was the only way of guaranteeing the survival of the Party. It was inspiring to see how much they were willing to sacrifice, but it was awful that we had to ask them.

My sister was a Party activist and I was not a citizen. So between the two of us, our home was constantly under surveillance. When I was asked by Dorothy, I don't remember her very vehemently urging me to go into the underground. But I knew my troubles. I knew I wasn't a citizen. And the Party was under severe attack. I wasn't unhappy to go underground. But I found out after I was in the underground that it was a disastrous mistake.

I lost contact with everybody that I had built up a relationship with [as a rank-and-file ILGWU activist] after sweating it out in these shops and taking abuse I wouldn't ordinarily take from the bosses. Since going to work in Los Angeles I had built up a list of two hundred names, addresses, and phone numbers, pretty near all Blacks and Chicanos. When I went underground I had to destroy the list. There was no one else to turn it over to. All those contacts lost. And what did we gain by going underground? Okay, I caught up on my reading. I read Aptheker on the Negro Question, I read *Huckleberry Finn*. But the basic link between the [Party] leadership and the masses of people was removed and buried for four or five years. And the FBI had me in their net from the very beginning. ■ Ethel Shapiro-Bertolini. [Ethel Shapiro came to the United States from the Ukraine as a child in 1922, joined the YCL and the CP in the late 1920s, and worked for years as a union organizer in Chicago, Buffalo, Gary, Indiana, and Brooklyn before moving to Los Angeles in 1949, where she worked as a garment worker until joining the underground. She remained in the Party until 1974.]

In Los Angeles, as elsewhere, the idea was that we would have both an open above-ground leadership and an "unavailable but operative" underground leadership. The real decisions would be made underground and conveyed to the open leaders by a courier system. That way, even if the open leaders were picked off through arrests, the Party could continue to function. There would also be a "deep freeze" level of underground leaders, people who would have no ongoing role to play in Party decision making but would simply try to keep out of sight of the FBI until they might be needed. Ben Dobbs briefly played that role. We also collected a lot of money and put it in the care of some trusted individuals. We bought dozens of mimeograph machines and thousands of reams of paper and cached them away in people's houses. I don't know what happened to the money; I presume most of it was spent to maintain the underground. But no one could remember where we had hidden all the duplicating equipment, and for years afterward I would get calls from people saying, "Hey, you want this mimeograph machine that's been rusting in my basement since 1951?"

We ate up every resource we had. Every friend, every car, every meeting place to maintain the underground. It was just a horror. . . . Dorothy and I had a conversation and she said, "I think you ought to go." Take no part in the movement, have no contact with the leadership, but be ready to take over the Party. That was the deep freeze. For six months I was still in L.A. and didn't leave the house of a guy I knew as a youth, a very wealthy guy, who was willing to take me in. Then I went to San Bernadino, and then to Portland. This went on about a year or so. I think I saw my wife twice. Then it was decided that Ada could join me with the children. The little girl was three and the boy was six. A month later it was obvious that I was being followed. We separated immediately. I traveled around the country for awhile, but finally I said to hell with it and went home. I made that decision on my own. ■ Ben Dobbs.

From the beginning the underground was a disaster. It was like a bad spy movie, with all of these secret messages and meeting places. We were turning ourselves into a caricature of the conspiracy that the Hearst papers and the Tenney committee had always accused us of being. The courier system was clumsy and time-consuming, and the FBI swiftly penetrated much of the operation, as they proved when they picked up Gus Hall in Mexico and later arrested Bob Thompson in a cabin in the Sierra Mountains near Sonora.

The main difference between the way the underground was set up in Los Angeles and in the rest of the country was that the other districts sent many more people underground. I think we sent only seven or eight people all told. We were determined to preserve as much of open, above-ground, and legal activity as possible, and throughout the early fifties we continued to hold public meetings in the name of the *People's World*. This was very important as far as the morale of Party members was concerned, because they could see that the Party was still there.

> John Gates came to L.A. and said, "We're undoubtedly facing fascism if we're convicted. We have to change the Party. We have to make sure it's made up of people who are absolutely committed. Those you feel who are on the fringe or any danger at all, get rid of them." That started a terrible situation. How do you make those kinds of judgments? I think maybe we lopped off a thousand members before Dorothy said, "This bullshit has got to stop." ■ Ben Dobbs.

The great irony of the McCarthy period is that we did almost as much damage to ourselves, in the name of purifying our ranks, as Joe McCarthy and J. Edgar Hoover and all the other witch-hunters combined were able to do. One of the most catastrophically stupid things we ever did was to choose this moment to launch an internal campaign against white chauvinisim. (In the Party we tended to use the term "white chauvinism" instead of racism.) The campaign was initiated by Pettis Perry and Betty Gannett in 1949. They were then functioning as the main figures in the above-ground national leadership. I had first met both of them in California: Perry, who was Black, had joined the Party in Los Angeles through the Scottsboro Boys campaign in the early 1930, and had served for awhile as chairman of the L.A. county organization; and Betty Gannett, who had come to the United States from Poland as a child, had moved to California in the 1930s and was one of the founders of the *People's World* and served as the state educational secretary before returning east.

Starting in the 1920s the Party had emphasized the importance of combatting racism, both in the broader society and in its own ranks. We were justifiably proud of the fact that, almost alone among American political parties (or for that matter virtually any institution in American life at that time), we were a working model of racial integration. Blacks took their place in the Party's ranks and leadership in roughly the same proportion as they were represented in the population as a whole. In the late 1940s, we had between four and five hundred Black members in the Los Angeles CP, just under 10 percent of our total membership. We had a strong base in Black communities like Compton, Willowbrook, Watts, and the neighborhood I lived in, South L.A. We attracted Black members because we were always involved in campaigns for full equality: in the late 1940s the Party led campaigns against housing discrimination and for equal employment opportunities. We were also involved in many defense cases, like one involving Bucky Walker, a young Black serviceman framed up in San Bernardino. In the labor movement we pushed for equal treatment of Blacks by employers and the unions, even the AFL unions, where it was a particularly tough fight. Frank Alexander, a carpenter, a veteran of the Abraham Lincoln Brigade, one of the "L.A. twenty-one," and one of our more important Black members, was the first Black ever elected as a delegate to the Los Angeles Building Trades Council. We held on to many of the Black members we recruited by paying special attention to all the conscious and unconscious ways in which whites in a racially divided society, even whites who think of themselves as revolutionaries, can display attitudes of racial superiority. I think it was to the Party's lasting credit that it was never complacent about those issues, and as a result came closer than anyone else on the Left before or since to building a genuinely interracial movement.

However, with the white chauvinism campaign of 1949–1953, what had been a legitimate concern turned into an obsession, a ritual act of self-purification that did nothing to strengthen the Party in its fight against racism and was manipulated by some Communist leaders for ends which had nothing to do with the ostensible purpose of the whole campaign. Once an accusation of white chauvinism was thrown against a white Communist, there was no defense. Debate was over. By the very act of denying the validity of the charge, you only proved your own guilt. Thousands of people were caught up in this campaign—not only in the Party itself, but within the Progressive Party and some of the Left unions as well. In Los Angeles alone we must have expelled two hundred people on charges of white chauvinism, usually on the most trivial of pretexts. People would be expelled for serving coffee in a chipped coffee cup to a Black or serving watermelon at the end of dinner.

> On September 2, 1949, the Section Council of the Central Section, LACCP, met at 4201 South Main Street. _____served as Chairman and introduced HEALEY as the principal speaker on white chauvinism in the Communist Party. HEALEY stated that the principal task of the Communist Party in eliminating white chauvinism is to develop an intense struggle for jobs and security for the negro people, seeing to it that they secure jobs in banks and chain stores, by struggling for a permanent FEPC in California, and by raising the question of renting to negroes in all areas. She stated that Party members must rent to negroes or be expelled. She stated that chauvinism in the Communist Party would not be tolerated and any white comrade found guilty of chauvinism would be expelled. ■ FBI report, June 28, 1951.

I had a personal run-in with one Black leader in the midst of this campaign which I long had reason to regret. Bill Taylor came to Los Angeles in 1949 to head the Party's county Negro Commission. He was from a West Indian background and had been in the Party since the late 1920s, serving as District Organizer in Washington, D.C., before coming to Los Angeles. He was a close friend of Henry Winston, one of the leading Blacks in the national leadership, and I think Winnie and Pettis Perry expected that Bill would soon replace me as chairman of the county organization. But Bill was not a good Party leader. First of all, he was inefficient. Los Angeles had a hard-working Party, and most of its leaders drove themselves. Bill didn't. He'd take on assignments, and they'd never get done. He was also in the habit of taking gifts from Party members. Being on the Party payroll was never particularly lucrative, but in many Party districts, members would provide Party leaders with a suit of clothes, or a car, or some household gadget. There was one wealthy building contractor in Los Angeles, a Party member, who was always trying to ingratiate himself with the leaders by giving them gifts. It was all justified as representing the gratitude of the working class to its leaders, but it was really a subtle form of corruption, like the perquisites available to Party leaders in the Soviet Union, only on a much less grand scale. In time we developed a rule that Party leaders could never accept gifts for themselves. You could take donations for the Party, but nothing for yourself. Bill violated that rule constantly.

So very early on it became apparent that Bill was going to be a problem for the Party, and the first criticisms of him actually came from Black comrades who, after all, had to deal with him frequently because of his position on the Negro Commission. Eventually we decided we wanted him out of the leadership and out of Los Angeles. It was not the most propitious time to make such a request about a Black leader. In the fall of 1950 Pettis Perry and Betty Gannett came out to Los Angeles from the National Office to investigate the situation— not to investigate Bill but the rest of us for having criticized Bill.

> When some of the leading Negro comrades expressed criticism of Comrade Taylor, their criticism was used by [Dorothy Healey] as an all-around authoritative analysis of his work. . . . What was present in this case was the desire to hide behind the criticisms of the Negro comrades, because it could not be said that the Negro comrades were guilty of white chauvinism in criticizing another Negro comrade. This tended to conceal the atmosphere of white chauvinism, and further tended to widen the gap between the Negro comrades. ■ "On Vigilance in the Struggle Against White Chauvinism, A Self-Critical Analysis by the LA County Board," *The Party Review*, November 1, 1950.

What they expected of us was that we would confess to being white chauvinists. For a long time we held out. Those day-long meetings, which went on day after day, were just terrible. At one of them I said something to the effect that Taylor's failure to carry out his responsibilities had enhanced whatever problems of chauvinism existed in the Party. Betty screamed at me that my use of the word "enhance" was in itself a chauvinist remark, because it was putting the blame on the victim rather than on the oppressor. Whites were the oppressor, and nothing Blacks could do could "enhance" the atmosphere of racism. Finally, in a weak moment, I looked over at Taylor and saw he was very unhappy.

Personally, he was a very charming man. Most white comrades were very fond of him because he was so warm and friendly and made them all feel that he loved them all. And there he was feeling so crushed. And I thought to myself "Oh Christ, this is ridiculous, so what difference does it make? I'll say it was white chauvinism and get the whole thing over with." If I'd had more sophistication about the way things worked in the Party, I would never have done that. Once you give in on something like that, you've just opened yourself up for another demand. As soon as we had "admitted" to being guilty of white chauvinism, the demand came that we had to formalize our admission in a written public statement. So I wrote a silly document about white chauvinism which was published in a preconvention discussion bulletin in 1950. I did not have enough imagination to see how Bill and others would use my "confession" from then on as a red flag to discredit everything else we were trying to do in the district. Bill stuck around for all the years I was in the Party and became a kind of rallying symbol in every party fight around whom the dogmatists could gather. But he never improved his own style of work. Years later, after I stepped down from the leadership, my successors would start by having the same warm relationship with him, but within a few months they had exactly the same problems. They'd go absolutely out of their mind, just as we had, because the guy never would do anything.

Because it was almost impossible to criticize a Black leader, the Party suffered and I think the Black leaders themselves suffered. I always felt that the sharp criticisms I got in the YCL and in the Party really benefited me a great deal. Even when they were unjust, you could learn from them. It was a steeling process. And a lot of times you gained information and an awareness of things you did that you weren't aware of. In ordinary life, one is always fortified by the consciousness of one's own good intentions. One rarely sees the impact of what one does upon other people. And so the sharp give and take in the Party was tremendously important for people's development and maturation as leaders. When Blacks were spared that, it wasn't doing them any favor. It is true that there has always been a reluctance on the part of whites on the Left to follow Black leadership. On the other hand, when you overextend that, as we did in the Party at that time and as sections of the New Left did later on, when you have the notion that only Blacks can lead or that you must uncritically accept Black leadership without any standards, then you get reverse application of what you're trying to fight for. (I should add that some Black leaders, like Abner Berry and Doxie Wilkerson, had no hesitation in accepting criticism from their comrades, white or Black.) One of the great ironies of the white chauvinism campaign is that we lost a large number of Black members because of it. They were just contemptuous of the whole thing because it had so little to do with fighting racism in the real world outside the Party's ranks. And the FBI later made effective use of the "white chauvinism" issue as part of its own repertoire of dirty tricks.

On February 23, 1961, the Los Angeles [FBI] Office advised that it had completed the anonymous mailing of 85 copies of a second "green sheet" which repeated the charges of "white chauvinism" against the Southern California District white leadership to the same individuals who had received the previous "green sheet" mailing. The second mailing brought back into sharp focus the division between the white and Negro comrades. . . . These mailings were concentrated in the Compton and the Moranda Smith Sections of the Southern California District. The Los Angeles Office letter of June 8, 1961, advised that through the efforts of Los Angeles informants who kept dissension alive and because of the mailings of the "green sheets," membership in the Compton Section dropped to such a point where the section was disbanded and merged with the Moranda Smith Section. This latter section, which was once the largest and most active in the district, thereafter spent so much time fighting the district leadership that recruiting and fund raising practically ceased. ■ J. Edgar Hoover to New York FBI headquarters, September 8, 1961.

The struggle against white chauvinism only ended in 1953 when Foster stepped in and put a stop to it with an article in *Political Affairs*. It was, unfortunately, only one example of the kinds of wounds we were inflicting on ourselves at the time. When I went to New York in 1950 to consult with the national office about setting up the underground, I was told that Party leaders had consulted with the French Communist Party about how they protected their organization during World War II. The French CP grew enormously in the last year of the war because of its leading role in the resistance, but earlier it had pared down its ranks to about 10 percent of prewar membership (I don't know if this is what actually happened; this is what we were told.) This was the model we were given to shape our own perspective. It was not a time to recruit new members or even to be concerned with holding on to our existing members. We had to trim down to fighting shape. People were not leaving the Party because of McCarthyite attacks. They developed a bunker mentality and dug in for the duration. Where our losses came in the early 1950s, they came by and large as the product of our own decisions.

The Party ordinarily carried out an annual registration of its members. This registration never took place at Party meetings. It was the rule that the Party organizer would go around to members' homes, so that there would be no collective pressure on anyone. If members had any criticisms of the Party they could tell the organizer about them then. Now, we were told, we were simply to ask the question, "Do you want to be in the Party?" If they had any reservations or questions at all, we were to say, "Well, why don't you drop out and remain a friend of the Party?" We were not to encourage them in any way to stay. As a result, over the next year our membership in Los Angeles dropped from about 5000 to 4000. One-fifth of our membership was just thrown away.

Another example of a self-inflicted wound was our new policy on homosexuals. Until 1948 the Party had no official policy regarding homosexuals. This was a long time before the gay liberation movement appeared, and many Communists shared the prejudices of the general society, but you could be a homosexual in the Party and nobody was going to bother you about it. In 1948 we were told that all homosexuals had to be dropped from membership. They were considered too great a security risk, being vulnerable to blackmail from the FBI. This wasn't just paranoia on the Party's part, since in some instances gays were forced to become informers by the threat of having their sexual habits revealed. It was a stupid policy nonetheless. After all, we had a number of Communists in Los Angeles who became informers because they worked for the post office and their jobs were at risk if they refused, but no one ever proposed that all government employees be dropped from our membership. I personally met with Harry Hay to tell him that we were going to have to drop him from the Party rolls. It was a very amicable discussion: I made it clear to him that this was not a moralistic judgment by the Party, and he could see the logic of the security argument. The Party's loss would prove, in the long run, to be the gay movement's gain. Harry went on to found the Mattachine Society, which was the forerunner of the gay liberation movement of the 1960s.

Around this same time, we also decided that people going to psychiatrists or psychoanalysts had to drop out of the Party. One of the most distasteful tasks I performed as org secretary in the name of security was to meet with Phil Cohen, a therapist who figures significantly in *Naming Names*, Victor Navasky's account of the red scare in Hollywood. Cohen had ties with the Party, and a large number of Party members went to him for psychological treatment. I was told to meet with him every week and get a rundown on the people he was seeing: What was bothering them? Were they likely to have a breakdown? Should we regard them as security risks? The irony here was that Cohen later turned out to be working hand-in-glove with the House Un-American Activities Committee, persuading his Hollywood clients to turn informer. I did it for about three or four weeks, and then I told Nemmy that the whole thing was demeaning to our members, and I wouldn't do it any more.

The Party's mania with security issues coincided with and was influenced by the postwar eastern European purge trials. In the 1930s I had had big arguments with my brother about the Moscow trials because he rightly considered them outrageous frame-ups. In all honesty I have to say that I didn't go through any great process of soul-searching about the trials. It all seemed very remote to me, and I was preoccupied with political events in the United States. In 1950 I was summoned to a meeting in Alexander Trachtenberg's apartment in New York. There were about seven or eight of us there, all organizers from important Party districts. It was the middle of the afternoon, and the shades were drawn. It was very melodramatic. I've forgotten who was running the meeting, but he had a slide projector and a screen set up, and after we sat down, he flashed on the screen hundreds of names of former U.S. servicemen who had been stationed in the southern Italian seaport of Bari during the Second World War, which after the invasion of Italy had become a center of American intelligence operations in the Mediterranean during the war. Evidently the Soviet Union had supplied these names to the Party. We were supposed to see if we recognized any of them from among our own district membership, because they would then be dropped as government agents.

That was crazy. The Party itself had recruited many agents for the Office of Strategic Services (OSS) in the early days of the war, from among our foreign-born members and veterans of the Abraham Lincoln Battalion who had the contacts or skills necessary for aiding partisan operations behind the Nazi lines. I personally helped recruit a few people for the OSS. We had never regarded service in the OSS in the same light as radicals today would regard someone with a history of CIA employment. We were as proud of our members who had gone into OSS as we were of those who had fought the Nazis on any front. But as the purge trials in eastern Europe unfolded, part of the evidence being presented against the accused Communist leaders was the accusation that they had had wartime contacts with American intelligence and had then allegedly been recruited as agents. Some of the OSS operations run out of Bari had been in support of Tito's Partisans in Yugoslavia, and Tito was now anathema in the Communist movement from breaking with Stalin. So if we accepted the bizarre logic being presented to us, we would assume that anyone with an OSS background was probably a secret Titoist, which meant he was an imperialist agent and had to be purged. I went back to Los Angeles and told Ben Dobbs how preposterous I thought the whole thing was.

Events in eastern Europe did lead indirectly to the expulsion of one California Communist. Roy Hudson was a sailor who had been in charge of the Party's trade union work in the Popular Front years and during the war. He had been in disgrace since the Duclos article because of his close ties with Browder; he made the mistake of abstaining on the initial vote in the National Board endorsing Duclos's charges against Browder. He was exiled from New York, first to Pittsburgh and then to San Francisco. In San Francisco he proved quite popular as an organizer on the waterfront. The longshoremen and the seamen both looked on him as one of their own. That got him into trouble with other Party leaders in San Francisco, particularly Archie Brown and Bill Schneiderman, who were jealous of his influence. With the purge trials, Hudson came under suspicion because he was married to a woman who had been born into the Hungarian royalty; as a former aristocrat she was by definition to be suspected of harboring counterrevolutionary sympathies. When Roy refused to disassociate himself from his wife, he was brought up on charges before the state board and was eventually expelled. I remember sitting quietly through that state board meeting on Roy Hudson, knowing that it was all nonsense, knowing that Roy was not only being victimized because of the national Party's security mania but also because of Archie and Bill's resentment of his role on the waterfront. And yet I didn't say anything.

The Bureau desires to point out to you that at this time the case of the eleven national leaders of the Communist Party, who were convicted under the Smith Act, is presently on appeal before the U.S. Supreme Court. If the decision of that tribunal is favorable to the Government, the way will be clear for the prosecution of other Party leaders.

Dorothy Healey is one of the individuals against whom the Department may desire to take prosecutive action. This makes it incumbent upon you to give her investigation continuous and detailed attention. It is particularly

important that her whereabouts is known at all times. ■ J. Edgar Hoover
to Los Angeles FBI headquarters, April 26, 1951.

By 1951 the FBI was following my every move. There was always three
carloads of FBI men sitting in front of my house. I'd drive Richard to school,
three blocks away, and these three cars would follow in a convoy behind me.
I'd go shopping at a market nearby and the agents would come into the market
with me while I did my shopping. The morning I learned of the Court decision
in the Foley Square case, I went down to the Party office on Sixth and Spring
Streets and as usual took a coffee break about ten-thirty. There was a restaurant
right under the office, and I was sitting at the counter reading the *Daily Worker*,
which had a complete description of the latest developments in the Smith Act
case. One of the FBI agents came in and said, "Do you mind if I sit down here?",
pointing to the stool beside me. I knew who he was, so I just said as coldly as
I could, "Public place," and kept on reading. He looked over my shoulder at
what I was reading and said, "Well, you know what that decision does for us.
We now have total power in terms of what's going to happen to you and your
family. If you'll cooperate with us, as Elizabeth Bentley did, then we can promise you that neither you, nor your mother, nor your son will go to a concentration
camp. Otherwise you'll join the rest." I stood up, and put my hand over my
breast, and starting shouting. "This man is trying to attack me, this man is
attacking me!" Everybody came running, and he was utterly mortified and said,
"I haven't touched her! I haven't touched her!" While he tried to explain himself
to the angry crowd, I got up and walked upstairs. It felt very good to put the
FBI on the defensive for once. It would be many long years before I knew that
kind of satisfaction again.

8

Communism is running wide open here in Los Angeles, right under our noses.

Its "dictator" is a tough-talking, poker-playing woman, only 4 feet 10 inches tall and four times married.

Under her leadership the Communist Party of Los Angeles County is pouring out a line of hatred against the United States government. . . .

TOP DOG IN THE LOS ANGELES COMMUNIST SETUP IS A TINY FIREBALL NAMED DOROTHY RAY HEALEY. . . .

Dorothy Healey is a bitter women in her 40s, hard as nails and with the vocabulary of a longshoreman. She is known as "the Little Dictator," with good reason.

But if the occasion demands, she can turn on the charm. She plays an excellent game of poker when friends gather at her home, 1735 W. 84th St. . . . ■ "Communism in L.A.—How It Works," Los Angeles *Mirror*, August 21, 1950.

The Supreme Court handed down its decision in the Foley Square case on June 4, 1951. Just over two weeks later FBI agents in New York rounded up such "second string" leaders as Elizabeth Gurley Flynn, Pettis Perry, and Claudia Jones. After that we knew it couldn't be long before the arrests came in other places. On July 26, I was still in bed at about eight in the morning when I heard pounding on the door. I was alone; Slim had already left the house to go to work, and they arrested him three blocks away. I knew instantly who was at the door and why they were there, and I thought, "Oh, hell, it's too early. I'm not going to let them in. I'm tired." But they kept pounding and then came around to the back, and I heard them starting to come in the back door. I got up and demanded, "What the hell do you think you're doing?" They said, "We have a warrant for your arrest." I said, "Oh dear, all right, let me see the warrant." They showed it to me, and I said, "Well, do you care if I call my attorney?" They said no, so I called Ben Margolis and told him I was being arrested.

Then they said, "Look, do you mind, there has to be a woman with you constantly from now on. We have a stenographer out in the car. Do you mind if she goes in with you to the bathroom while you take your shower?" I said, "No, if that's what you have to do, that's what you have to do." So she came in, and I showered and dressed. Then I was still not quite ready to face the rest of the day, so I said, "Do you mind if I make coffee?" "No." It was all so polite, on both sides, as though they and I had been rehearsing for this moment for years and years and wanted to make sure it came off without any unpleasantness. I made the coffee and said, "You must forgive me. I've very uncomfortable drinking coffee in front of you and not offering you any, but I simply can't serve coffee to FBI agents. It's against my principles." They laughed. "We understand your principles. Go ahead."

> Four top Los Angeles Reds and seven other California Communist Party leaders were arrested today in a series of simultaneous raids here, in New York and San Francisco as part of a government crackdown on the party's "second-string" national committee. . . . Each is accused of conspiring from 1945 to the present to bring about the violent overthrow of the U.S. government. ■ "Four Top L.A. Reds Jailed, G-Men Nab Seven Other State Commie Bosses," Los Angeles *Mirror*, July 26, 1951.

Eleven of us were arrested that day: Slim and I, Rose Chernin and Henry Steinberg in Los Angeles, and Bernadette Doyle, Ernie Fox, Rude Lambert, Mickey Lima, Al Richmond, Loretta Stack, and Oleta O'Connor Yates in San Francisco. Bill Schneiderman was arrested that same day in New York; Frank Carlson, Ben Dobbs, and Frank Spector were arrested about a month later. The government eventually dropped Bernadette Doyle from the case because of her poor health. Not all the arrests had proceeded with the decorum that marked mine. Rose Chernin had been doing housework when they came, and they wouldn't let her change her clothes. Ben Dobbs was arrested when he was sitting in a movie theater with his young son watching a Disney cartoon, scaring the kid half to death. There were also arrests that summer and the year that followed of Communist leaders from Hawaii to Puerto Rico and everywhere in between: over a hundred "second string" leaders all told were indicted for violation of the Smith Act.

The government planned to try all the California defendants in Los Angeles. They could not have gathered a more representative group of Communists together, and our collective experiences reflected the history of both the American and European Communist movements. I had known and worked with most of them for years. Slim was my husband, Ben Dobbs my closest associate in the L.A. Party leadership. Frank Carlson, with whom I had fought for the right to go to work for UCAPAWA back in 1937, held the post of educational director of the Los Angeles CP when he was arrested. He was a gifted organizer and theoretician. My ex-brother-in-law Bill Schneiderman was the Party chairman in California, a post he had held since the mid-1930s. A naturalized citizen, he was the appellant in a landmark Supreme Court case. The Court ruled in *Schneiderman* that just because someone joined the Communist Party he was not necessarily an advocate of the use of force and violence to overthrow the government and so could not be stripped of citizenship solely on the basis of Party membership. That decision was handed down at the height of Soviet-American wartime cooperation; the fact that eight years later he was back in court because of another Supreme Court decision, this time in the "Dennis case" (as the Foley Square case was officially known), says a great deal about the political character of the law.

Al Richmond, who I had not known well until the trial but who afterwards became a very close friend, was born in London where his mother, a Russian revolutionary, was then living in exile. She brought him to the United States when he was still an infant and then took him back to Russia after the Czar was overthrown and before the Bolsheviks seized power. They returned to the U.S. in the 1920s, where Al grew up and joined the YCL. He was a reporter for the *Daily Worker* before he arrived in San Francisco in 1937 to help found the *People's World*. Although Al had only a high school education, he was an enormously well-read and cultured man, considered around the *People's World* office as a kind of walking encyclopedia. Rose Chernin Kusnitz was a close friend of my mother's. She was serving as the executive secretary of the Los Angeles Committee for the Protection of the Foreign-Born when she was arrested. She had been born in Russia, before the Revolution, and came to the U.S. as a child. She joined the Communist Party in the late 1920s and ran for alderman on the CP ticket in the Bronx. She had returned to the Soviet Union in the early 1930s, when her husband helped build the Moscow subway system. Since the mid-1930s she had lived in Boyle Heights. Ernie Fox, also brought as a child to the United States from Germany, had been a coal miner and a seaman, an organizer for TUUL and AFL maritime unions, and later for UCAPAWA. Carl Rude Lambert had helped lead the "Bonus Army" veterans in Washington in 1932 and later became an ILD organizer. He was in charge of Party security, which meant that he tried to ferret out FBI and police spies. He was also a renowned fund raiser, with innumerable useful contacts. Albert Jason "Mickey" Lima had been a commercial fisherman and then a member of the Lumber and Sawmill Workers Union in Eureka and was one of the state leaders of the Party. Frank Spector was a genuine Old Bolshevik, what we called a "1905er," that is, someone whose political involvement in Russia dated back to the abortive 1905 revolution against the Czar. He had been deported to Siberia and came to the United States in time to become one of the founding members of the American Communist Party. He was one of those arrested for criminal syndicalism in the 1929 Imperial Valley strikes and served a couple of years in San Quentin as a result. Loretta Starvis Stack became politically active as a teenager in Boston through the American Youth Congress, where she was recruited into the YCL. I first met her when she was working as a UE organizer in L.A. during the war. At the time of her arrest she was serving as the state org secretary for the California CP.

Henry Steinberg was one of the better-known Communist community leaders in East Los Angeles, and when he ran for the board of education in 1951 he received almost forty thousand votes. At this time the East Side was beginning to change from a Jewish to a predominantly Chicano population. Henry had helped organize the Community Service Organization, the first organization to fight for Chicano representation in city government. The CSO had been instrumental in securing the election of Ed Roybal, the first Chicano on the city council, who would go on to become a U.S. Congressman. At the time he was arrested, Henry was serving as the county legislative director for the Party. Oleta O'Connor Yates was the only one of us who qualified as "old Californian," her great-grandparents having come to the territory in the 1850s. She had a typical "south of Mission" Irish-Catholic working-class upbringing and attended the University of California at Berkeley. She joined the CP in 1933 and was a frequent candidate for public office on the Party ticket, winning forty thousand votes in a San Francisco mayoral race. She had held the post of chairman of the San Francisco Party since World War II. Because she was the only defendant in our trial who actually took the stand, when our case came before the Supreme Court years later it would be known as the "Yates case."

At first, Rose Chernin and I were alone in the women's section of the jail. The northern California defendants were not brought down to join us until the beginning of August; the trial would be in Los Angeles. Rose had never been in jail before and was very unhappy; I had to persuade her that there was nothing to be frightened of, that the jailers were not singling us out for mistreatment (she had been particularly disturbed by the initial body search, in which all of your orifices are poked and peered into in a search for contraband), and that the other prisoners were not going to harm us. By the time Oleta and the others arrived, Rose was an old-timer, and this time she helped me assure them that nothing terrible was going to happen to them in jail.

In many places, indicted Communists had a difficult time trying to find lawyers to represent them. We were much luckier in Los Angeles, where we enjoyed the luxury of being able to choose among a large number of lawyers eager to take our case—though some of them would suffer for their decision. Our chief counsel was Ben Margolis, with whom I already had a long legal and political association. Al Wirin, chief counsel of the southern California ACLU, came into the case early on; I had known him since the early days of the 1930s. Leo Branton, a young black lawyer who had just finished trying his first important case, that of the black G.I. Bucky Walker, was soon recruited; he would later go on to defend Angela Davis. Our other lawyers were Norman Leonard, from northern California, and Alex Schulman, an attorney for the local AFL council. (Schulman lost his job with the AFL for coming to our aid; another lawyer, Dan Marshall, who was an old friend of Slim's and lawyer for the Catholic diocese in Los Angeles, lost the diocese as a client because he represented Slim in his bail appeal.)

Our first big battle, which lasted for nearly five months, was to be released on bail. The prosecutor, Ernest Tolin, demanded bail be set at $75,000 for most of us, $100,000 for Bill Schneiderman, telling the newspapers that our crime was "akin to treason." Judge William Mathes, before whom the case was being tried, did everything in his power to keep us in jail on a hardly more reasonable $50,000 bail. Every time a higher court up to and including the Supreme Court would direct that bail be lowered, he'd find a new technicality to justify continuing such high bail. It wasn't until December, with bail reduced to $5,000 for some defendants and $10,000 for the rest, that we were once again able to enjoy a limited freedom.

The one thing that made those five months tolerable is that every day, Monday through Friday, we defendants were brought together into a federal marshall's holding cell to allow us to prepare our defense. And since there were no facilities for feeding us, we were allowed to make our own arrangements for having food brought in. A group of about forty or fifty of our comrades undertook to provide two meals a day for the fifteen of us plus our lawyers and whoever else was lucky enough to be there with us, five days a week for five months. These were the most wonderful meals I have eaten in my lifetime, both because they were culinary masterpieces, true labors of love, and because they represented the commitment of the unsung heroes and heroines of our defense campaign. We all gained weight. The trial itself was the occasion for another display of dedication by our supporters. While we raised a considerable amount of money to pay the lawyers, we knew we could not possibly afford the trial transcripts that were necessary if we were to mount an appeal. Ben organized a volunteer service of stenographers and typists who transcribed, typed, and mimeographed each day's testimony for our lawyers' use in preparing the next day's cross-examination and for the court record we would use in our appeal to the appellate court. Twenty people participated in this project, coming from their jobs after work to the defense office and working long into the night to have the material ready for the next day—and this went on for over five months.

> The California case had preceded ours, and I remember how impressed I was with the testimony of Oleta O'Connor Yates, the only defense witness. It was a magnificent summation, and it was clear that the California people had independently resolved to point their case in a new direction and give emphasis to the issue of civil liberties while setting forth the program and the political aspirations of the party. . . . They just had a different view of life and politics—whether it was due to the maverick history of the state, the sunny climate, distance from New York, I know not. They were the "Yugoslav" branch of the American party and as such aroused the ire of Foster, but I secretly admired their gumption. ■ George Charney, *A Long Journey*, p. 215 [Charney was convicted as one of the "second string" leaders in the second New York Smith Act case.]

Those of us who were on the Party's state board—myself, Al Richmond, Oleta O'Connor Yates, Bill Schneiderman, and Mickey Lima—constituted ourselves for the duration of the trial as what we called the trial committee. We conferred over the legal strategy to follow and how it should fit in with the Party's overall political strategy. That meant that we had to sit down and actually analyze the Party's current line, something which our normal round of political activities ordinarily left us little time to do. It was now several months since the Party had decided it was "five minutes to midnight," that an all-out war with the Soviet Union and the onset of domestic fascism was all but inevitable, and that as a consequence we had to shift to an underground existence to have any hope of surviving. Remarkably, at our very first session, the trial committee came to the unanimous conclusion that the Party's estimate was mistaken. While it was true that the Party was under attack (we could hardly forget that, given the circumstances under which we were meeting), that did not add up to a convincing parallel with Germany in 1933 or Italy in the early 1920s. To speak about the onset of "fascism"—when our Party offices were still open, when our Party press was still publishing, when the labor movement was able to function legally, and there were the first stirrings of what would become the civil rights movement—seemed a perverse and inaccurate characterization. This was a time of hysteria when civil liberties were at risk, but we had lived through such times before. The reality was that for most people in the country life was proceeding pretty much as usual. It was not the apocalypse.

> The lawyers in the case were aware of and took part in the discussion among the defendants over the "five minutes to midnight" line. We felt there was still room to fight. There had been periods of repression previously in American history when it would have been easy to say that doomsday was around the corner, and in each instance it had been overcome over a period of time. Among the basic historical trends in the United States was a trend that protected civil liberties. The lawyers in California had been under attack, but we had won some notable victories. The bar, for example, refused to "excommunicate" or disbar lawyers who were allegedly Communists. We agreed with the decision that the defendants made that this was not the end of the world. ■ Ben Margolis.

The trial committee decided to write a letter to the national underground leadership of the Party and lay out our disagreements with the "five minutes to midnight" line. We urged that the underground be dissolved and the Party resume as much of an open and above-ground existence as possible. Through the circuitous channels those kinds of messages had to travel, we got back a message essentially telling us to mind our own business. We were simply responsible for legal defense decisions in our own case; they were the ones who would make the operative policy decisions for the Party. We felt it was impossible to separate the legal and political questions. Herschel Alexander, who was the underground party chair for L.A., was continually criticizing the trial committee for its "bourgeois legalistic illusions," and he was backed up in this by the national underground leadership, who should have known better. When we got out of jail on bail in December, the underground leaders predicted we would be back in jail in two or thee months. In fact, we were out of jail until the end of our trial, the following August, and then released again on bail after a month to await the outcome of our appeals. They thought we were too enamored of our lawyers (and we did have great respect for them, particularly Ben Margolis), made too many legal rather than political motions in the courtroom, and in general acted as if we expected to beat the rap. Actually we didn't expect quite that much. We thought we'd be convicted, and for the five years that our case worked its way through the appeals process we lived in constant expectation of having to serve our sentences. But our trial and possible imprisonment still didn't add up to fascism, however unjust and disruptive they proved in terms of our own lives.

When we were still awaiting the outcome of our appeal for bail reduction, the underground leadership instructed us to raise the full bail for Bill Schneiderman. Once he was out of jail, he was supposed to skip the country. We discussed the idea with Bill, and he and the rest of us rejected it. The decision to have four of the Foley Square defendants jump bail after the Supreme Court ruled against them already had had a devastating effect on other Smith Act defendants. Their bail jumping was the main justification the government offered for setting such high bail for the rest of us in the first place. If Bill skipped now, we would never have been released on bail, and we would have found it next to impossible to raise any more bail money among our supporters. Who would be willing to mortgage their house to provide us with bail money if they suspected the money was just going to be thrown away? It was yet another example of how, in response to the government's attack, we were being pressured to turn ourselves into the very sorts of conspirators they accused of us being. We sent a message back to the underground saying, in effect, "nuts." (One other problem we had with raising bail was that the newspapers printed the names and addresses of those who provided bail bonds or money for us. My brother Bernard, who had little sympathy for my political views, put up the money for my bail in August 1952; his name appeared in the Los Angeles *Times* the next day, and as a result he was passed over for a promised promotion to chief of the anesthesia department at Cedars of Lebanon hospital.)

Our trial began on February 1, 1952. Early on we organized a group called the California Emergency Defense Committee to mobilize public support. The committee was originally headed by Dorothy Forrest, who later became a defendant herself in the St. Louis Smith Act trial. My dear friend Helen Travis was also involved in its leadership. The committee published pamphlets and sent out speakers to unions, churches, and community organizations to tell our side of the case. It circulated petitions asking people to sign as *amicus curiae*, individuals challenging the legitimacy of the indictment. One of the most successful of its activities was to organize groups to come down and observe the trial, so that we never had to face an empty courtroom. Every day there were lines of people waiting outside for the start of the trial, to come in and observe. The Defense Committee spoke of the observers as a "people's jury" and encouraged representatives from the Quakers, ACLU chapters, the unions, and Black and Chicano groups to report back to their organizations what they had seen. We couldn't sway the jury or the court's decision in the case, but at least we could see to it that in areas of public opinion important to us the government's case would be understood for the frame-up it was.

[Healey] was observed at the Party's State offices in San Francisco many times between June and December 1945 and thereafter. . . . In 1945 she attended the National Convention at which the Communist Party was reconstituted. . . . Later in 1945 she spoke at a Los Angeles meeting in support of a report on labor which urged that at the end of the war the unions should 'reclaim their right to strike.'. . . [In 1948] she urged Party members to join Independent Progressive Party clubs and to get non-Party people to join also. . . . ■ Brief for Petitioners, United States Supreme Court, October Term, 1956, *Yates* v. *United States*.

The government's charges against us were based on a series of actions on our part which, in themselves, were innocuous and perfectly legal. The indictment said that we had conspired "unlawfully, willfully, and knowingly to advocate and teach the duty and necessity of overthrowing the Government of the United States by force and violence." The marvel of the Smith Act was that all the prosecution had to prove was that we did these perfectly legal things in furtherance of an ultimately illegal end: we were not involved in overthrowing the government or even advocating the overthrow of the government, we were simply conspiring to so advocate at some unspecified time in the future. Even many of our own supporters never quite grasped the fine distinctions drawn by the Smith Act, which allowed perfectly legal acts to be criminalized. As in the Foley Square case, it was a trial of books. The prosecutor would have witnesses read big chunks of violent-sounding passages from Marx, Engels, and Lenin. This kind of trial could not have been conducted in any other advanced capitalist country—France or England or Italy—because the basic concepts of Marxism were so well known, studied in every university, and familiar to every active trade unionist, that people would have laughed at the outrageous simplifications offered up so solemnly at our trial. That was a peculiarly American phenomenon.

The prosecution presented some twenty-odd witnesses against us. Most of them were FBI informers, but the saddest characters were people who had started off as committed Communists but through one or another form of blackmail were persuaded to testify. One of the witnesses was a merchant seaman who had been a close family friend in the 1930s; he was told he could only get Coast Guard clearance to go to sea again if he testified. A former Party leader named John Lautner was a key witness against us, as he was against many Smith Act defendants across the country. He had been unjustly expelled by the Party as a government agent in the late 1940s and was so embittered by his treatment that he turned around and became what he had been so unfairly accused of earlier. As Al Richmond recounts in his autobiography, Lautner made the mistake of claiming on six separate occasions in his testimony that he had seen Al attending the Communist Party national convention in New York in July 1945. Since Richmond was at that time stationed in an army unit in England, our lawyers had no trouble refuting Lautner on that point—not that it made much difference in the jury's willingness to accept his testimony.

Q: Were you directed to secure any other printing apparatus by Bob Thompson at this meeting?

THE COURT: Were you?

THE WITNESS: Yes.

Q. BY MR. BAILEY: Will you state what his directions were?

A: His directions were to increase the order on flat mimeograph machines to supply the whole structure, every group of three in the structure, to supply with one of those hand machines from the third level down, and to increase the order and to expedite the production of these machines, because they were so slow in coming. . . .

Q. BY MR. BAILEY: Specifically, did you talk to Dorothy Healey about any of these mimeograph machines?

A: Yes. . . .

THE COURT: What did she say and what did you say?

THE WITNESS: She told me that [Jack] Kling sent her down, that I should show her that machine, how it works, and that I should give her a sample I had took. . . .

Q: What do you mean when you say you gave her a sample?

A: I gave her a machine as a sample.

■ John Lautner testimony in the California Smith Act trial.

In my case, Lautner told the jury a story about having met with me in party headquarters in New York in 1949, shortly before his explusion, where he was supposed to have instructed me in the use of some kind of folding mimeograph machine. For many years I thought that Lautner had simply made up the existence of this device: how do you fold a mimeograph machine? But Junius Scales, who Lautner later testified against in a North Carolina Smith Act case recently wrote that he had seen such a machine, which could in fact be disguised to look like a tea tray. Of course there's never been a law against the possession of mimeograph machines of any description. In any case, I had never been shown any such thing. But how could I prove it? It really didn't make any difference. All such testimony was introduced simply for atmospherics: given the logic of the Smith Act and the prevailing political climate, no jury was going to free us regardless of how many times we proved Lautner a liar.

> One of the prize exhibits in the government's case was a book turned over to the FBI by Mrs. [Daisy] Van Dorn, which she identified as a super-secret outline of a coming revolution smuggled into the United States by Russian sailors. Defense attorney Leo Branton, Jr., led her through testimony that she won the book, "History of the Civil War in the U.S.S.R.," at a Communist party raffle, and had been cautioned by at least two of the defendants, William Schneiderman and Oleta O'Connor Yates, to keep its contents secret. Branton then astonished the courtroom by producing three copies of the book from the Los Angeles public library, together with documents attesting that they had been purchased from an American publishing concern in New York which distributes the book and that they had been available to the public since 1947, when Mrs. Van Dorn turned her copy over to the FBI. ■ Los Angeles *Daily News*, May 14, 1952. [Daisy Van Dorn joined the Communist Party in 1945 as an FBI informant. She also testified that she had seen Ben Dobbs "at least 20 times" at CP headquarters in San Francisco in 1945; Dobbs did not return from his military service in Europe until February 1946.]

There were important ways in which our trial differed from the earlier Foley Square case. First of all, we offered a vigorous cross-examination of government witnesses. There was not a single witness who appeared whose testimony our attorneys did not challenge, and we often got them to make substantial concessions: that we had been fighting on behalf of the rights of ordinary people, that there was nothing covert about our activities, and that "force and violence" had little to do with our actual day-to-day activities or even our theoretical positions. One prosecution witness, Nate Honig, got us in trouble with the national Party leadership by conceding under cross-examination by our lawyers that we believed there was a 70 percent chance that the revolution would take place peacefully in the United States, and only 30 percent odds that the ruling class would not peacefully yield to majority will and thus precipitate a violent conflict. As far as the underground leadership was concerned, to solicit such a concession from a witness verged on revisionism, and they were very critical of us.

> We had some basic disagreements with the manner in which the Dennis case had been tried. In their defense the Communist Party in effect said, "Yes, we're a single party, we all believe the same thing, we're either all innocent or all guilty." It turned it into a trial of the Party instead of a trial of people. Our position, which was taken over the objection of the Party in the east, was that they had to prove separately the guilt or innocence of each person. Under American law you couldn't have guilt by association. We also took the position, factually, that the New York defendants in both the first and second Smith Act trials were unwilling to take, and that is that members of the Communist Party did not agree on everything. There were differences of opinion, there were arguments. The way that the Party actually functioned was that differences were ironed out, and once a decision was made, then a Party member was bound by that decision but always had the right to try to change that decision. That was our position in the case, and that was what won the case for us [before the Supreme Court]. Of course, I don't think *any* kind of defense would have won for the Dennis case. It was the height of the McCarthy period. Our case was brought up when things were beginning to improve. ■ Ben Margolis.

Midway through the trial, over the long Memorial Day recess, Bill Schneiderman and I went back East to argue out some of the tactical and policy questions that had emerged since the start of the trial. We went up to Croton, New York, where Party chairman William Z. Foster lived, to see if we couldn't get him to see things our way. Our discussion centered around two main issues. The first was the question of cross-examining witnesses. Foster felt that the tactic only lent legitimacy to their testimony and that we should have simply ignored them, as if to say that their testimony was of such inconsequential value that we would not dignify it with a reply. There was a certain logic to that approach, but only if one shared his assumption that the case would never get a fair hearing at any stage in the appeal process and that we were only speaking to History, as it were, through our courtroom tactics. We did not share that assumption. The second issue we debated with Foster was whether the individual defendants should take the stand in their own behalf. In the Foley Square trial most of the defendants had taken the stand and as a result had been tossed back in prison for contempt of court when they had refused to give names of other Communists. We couldn't see the point of needlessly inflicting more punishment on the defendants without serving any particularly useful political or legal ends. As far as Foster was concerned, this was evidence of both our misguided faith in "bourgeois legalism" and of personal cowardice, a view shared by the underground leadership. We were not persuaded by the argument or the accusation. We stuck to our decision that we would only put a single defendant through the ordeal of cross-examination.

> We had a terrible judge who would have thrown away the key on everybody. We knew that you couldn't get up there and testify and choose not to give names. Yates on direct testimony went beautifully. On the cross-examination it was names, names, names. She refused to answer. Legally at that point she really had no defense. She was stuck. So if we had put on everybody, they all would have been cited for contempt. ■ Ben Margolis.

Oleta had volunteered to take the stand and play that role, and after much discussion we decided that because of her old California background and her articulateness, she would be the best choice. When she took the stand in June she gave a remarkable presentation on the witness stand of the real nature of our theory and practical activities: we reprinted her testimony and circulated it widely. The assistant prosecuting attorney, Norman Neukom, was a vulgar, ignorant man. He was so astonished when one of the defendants was quoted on the need for Communists to engage in continual study. "Imagine," he told the jury, "grown-up people feeling the need to continue to study history and economics and philosophy after they've left school." For him, somehow, this was further evidence of the evil nature of our conspiracy, grown-ups discussing books they had read. In his cross-examination he wasn't interested in or capable of refuting any of the substantive points Oleta made about Party theory and activities; all he wanted to do was to try to force her to name the names of other Communists. Oleta kept refusing to answer, saying it had no relevance to her testimony, knowing full well the consequences of her refusal. At the end of her first day of cross-examination, Judge Mathes remanded her bail because of "contempt of court," and she went back to jail. He sentenced her first to a year and later to an additional three years in jail for contempt. (On appeal, the contempt charges were overturned, and Oleta was finally released.)

> On the night that Dorothy and Slim are released from jail on bail we go over to their house. I say to Dorothy, "what was jail like?" (At this point I'm afraid myself of going to jail.) She says, "It wasn't half-bad." Typical Dorothy response. Well, I'm glad to hear that. So I start asking her a lot of other questions: What was the food like, how did they treat you, what about the other prisoners? She's delighted, she's now been sprung, she can just really expand. Slim had walked out of the room by this point, but he could still hear everything she had to say. And she was talking about how she would save up her soda crackers every day, because she loved to have

tea and soda crackers before she went to sleep. And I was saying, "Oh really? You could get tea any time you wanted?" And she says, "Of course, there's always hot water from the tap, and you have a mug." Typical Dorothy, making the best of everything. "I would save the tea bags from lunch, and if I couldn't get to sleep I would just brew a little tea and have some soda crackers." Finally Slim can't stand it any more, and he comes out of the bedroom screaming and yelling like he's going to tear the house apart. "How dare you talk like that? There I was trying to fall asleep night after night with those lights shining in my face, and you're talking like it was a rest cure!" That marriage was no good from the beginning, but by the time they got out of jail . . . ■ Ellenore Hittelman.

At the end of our Smith Act trial in 1952, while the jury was out deliberating its verdict, I got a call from a comrade who I will call Daniel, whose wife worked in the *People's World* office. He called me at home and said that he and his wife would like to come over to our house, and that they wanted to see both myself and Slim. I was so glad that he asked for Slim to be there because I was always worried by the fact that people would come over and just ignore him. I turned to Slim and said, "Daniel just called and he wants to be sure you'll be here." Slim didn't look happy to hear that. They arrived and sat down. And the first thing Daniel said was "Do you know that your husband and my wife have been having an affair all during the trial?" I was utterly taken aback. This was the wrong time to be hearing about this, because I was already stretched as tight as a wire waiting to hear the jury's verdict. But my first obligation as Party leader was to make sure that nothing untoward happened to those two. So I spent the entire time convincing Daniel that this was not significant, that these things happened, it shouldn't break up their marriage, we could certainly keep it among ourselves. All the time I'm just sick inside. When they left I was too furious even to talk to Slim and just ran into my mother's house.

The next day we started in. And what was terrible was that I had such a dog-in-the-manger attitude. I didn't love this man and he was finding comfort somewhere else. Why should it bother me? But I was outraged. I didn't want him, but I didn't want anyone else to have him. It seemed all too familiar because of what had happened with Don, and it revived all my old feelings of inadequacy. The worst thing that came out of it was that Slim was convinced by my reaction that we really did still have something going in our marriage. Why would I care so intensely about his unfaithfulness if I didn't care about him? All I knew was that somehow I had to find a way to get out of this marriage without destroying him. After all, I am the Party leader. He is a Party member. I am responsible for him. I know how ridiculous an attitude that must seem, but the other side of it is that it was only this same sense of responsibility that kept me going during that period. How else could I manage to keep juggling all the different expectations I had to meet, from the Party, from Slim, from my son?

Richard and I used to talk about what would happen if and when I had to go back to jail. I told him he had so many parents to choose among; he could be either with grandma or with Don and Shevy, and life would go on without any strain for him. I assumed, stupidly, that that was sufficient. It was a shock for me to discover that, on the contrary, he had enormous fears about what it would mean for his mother to be taken away to jail. When he told me one day that there was not a night he went to sleep without his last thought being "Will my mother be there when I wake up?" I finally realized how obtuse I'd been.

When my mother was in trouble, I understood it as a bad society attacking a good person. I do remember crying and asking, when I was six or seven, why did she have to be a Communist, why did she always have to go to meetings? I cried horribly when she was jailed the first time on the grand jury charges. But I gradually grew resigned to it: it was a fact of life, there it was, she wasn't going to change, she was a Communist and I was going to have a hard time. There was no way to question it, any more than there was to question why my mother was married to this terrible man. They were just things that adults did and you had to live with them. Around eighth or ninth grade was a particularly painful time for me, in fact I was skipped a half grade by the school in the hope that if I was put in with a new group of kids things would calm down. The school counselor was quite conscious that I was being persecuted. Persecuted is too strong. Isolated, ostracized. I remember some kids chasing me into the house and my grand-mother coming out swinging a broom at them. That was extremely satis-fying. I also remember, when things were at their worst, my mother saying to me in her optimistic Communist style, "Just say hello to a new person every day and you'll find friends." And my utter rage and fury that she didn't understand how scary even that was. ■ Richard Healey.

After Oleta's testimony ended and the defense and prosecution made their final presentations to the jury, the jurors went out to consider their verdict. They began their deliberations on Thursday, July 31, and they did not return until the following Wednesday. This was very unusual in a Smith Act case, and I allowed myself the tiniest bit of hope for an acquittal. When they finally came in and the foreman read the verdict of guilty fourteen times, once for each defendant, I could see some of the jurors crying. I've often wondered what the debates must have been like inside, though I never found out. Each of us gave our speech to the court, and each of us received the same sentence of five years in prison and a $10,000 fine. Our bail was ordered eliminated and we were immediately remanded back into custody, which started yet another round of appeals until our release on $20,000 bail each a month later. Then we began what turned into a nearly five-year wait for our case to reach all the way up on appeal to be decided by the Supreme Court.

The eventual Supreme Court decision had a number of bases. First of all, the entire case was reversed on the ground that the instructions to the jury had been erroneous. . . . The Court, without overruling its earlier decision in the Dennis case (although using some language that was really difficult to reconcile with Dennis), held that those instructions were erroneous. If that had been the only ground for the ruling it would have gone back for a new trial for everyone. But the important part of the decision was that they had evaluated, as we had argued, the evidence against each individual. [In the prosecution's case] the question had been "does the Communist Party advocate this?" not "did the individual defendant advocate this?" Now the Court held that the evidence was insufficient to sustain a conviction against any one defendant. That as to five defendants the evidence was so sparse that they could not be tried again; that as to nine defendants they could be tried again, but the evidence would have to be stronger and more conclusive. The government came in a couple of months later and moved for a dismissal on the grounds that they couldn't meet the burden of proof that the Supreme Court had set. ■ Ben Margolis.

The end of the trial did not mark an end to our disagreements with Party leaders over strategy. We immediately quarreled with them over the basis of our appeal. They wanted us to focus on large political questions, like First Amendment guarantees of the freedom of speech. We wanted to include such appeals, naturally, but because of the nature of the case we had presented we also felt that we could fight on narrower legal (or as our critics would say "legalistic") grounds. Through their vigorous cross-examination of government witnesses, our lawyers had laid the basis for an appeal based on the question of the sufficiency of evidence: did the evidence presented by the government prove enough about the individual defendant's intent and knowledge to serve as the basis for conviction? And it was on that question, just short of five years later, on June 17, 1957, that the Supreme Court ruled in a six-to-one decision in *Yates* v. *United States* that it was not enough for the government to conjure up this kind of general conspiratorial atmosphere: that some unnamed person had said XYZ, which was inflammatory, and that we were part of the same Party, so we were guilty of the same thing. Rather, the evidence had to show, as it did not, that we ourselves had each knowingly participated in illegal activities which were not covered by the First Amendment. As Justice Harlan, who wrote the majority decision, declared: "Those to whom the advocacy is addressed must be urged to *do* something, now or in the future, rather than merely to *believe* in something." It wasn't enough, in other words, for the government to prove that Dorothy Healey was a Communist leader and a believer in the (wildly misrepresented) doctrines of Marx and Lenin: they would have had to prove instead that I personally had participated in advocating that people go out and, say, buy guns and ammunition in preparation for the revolution. And that, of course, I had never done. The *Yates* decision was narrowly written, so that it did not directly confront the question of the Smith Act's constitutionality, but it virtually gutted the law. The Court dismissed the cases against Slim, Rose Chernin, Frank Spector, Henry Steinberg, and Al Richmond. I and eight other California defendants were still technically subject to a retrial, but the nature of the Court's decision made it all but impossible for the government to consider continued prosecution of the case, and before the year was out our indictments were dropped. In a final grotesque act of vindictiveness, the Justice Department retried a single Smith Act case, involving Junius Scales in North Carolina, and managed to obtain a conviction. That Scales had resigned from Party the previous year made no difference, and he wound up serving more than a year in prison until his sentence was commuted by the Kennedy administration. Equally grotesque was the fact that the Party refused to come to his aid since he had quit; I was reprimanded by the national office for sending along a two-hundred-dollar contribution from the Southern California CP to his defense committee.

The impression that younger radicals in the 1960s had that *all* liberals capitulated to McCarthyism in the 1950s was not borne out by our experiences in Los Angeles. While there were all too many liberals willing to throw us to the McCarthyite wolves if it would help them save their own hides, others proved more principled. The Los Angeles branch of the ACLU played an important role in challenging McCarthyism. It was a very different organization from the national ACLU, where someone like Morris Ernst was actually informing on other ACLU members to his great friend J. Edgar Hoover. The leaders of the Los Angeles ACLU were probably the kind of people that Ernst was informing on. We'd had close ties with Al Wirin from the Imperial Valley days right down to our Smith Act case. During our trial, the local chapter of the ACLU got a new leader, Eason Munroe, who had led the fight against a state law requiring teachers to take loyalty oaths and who had been fired from his own teaching position as a result. Eason was not only a thoroughgoing civil libertarian but also very politically sophisticated. He initiated a new stategy of building the ACLU as a mass membership organization rather than just something you joined and got an occasional newsletter from. He did a very remarkable job organizing new chapters.

The American Friends Service Committee also refused to treat us as pariahs. Shortly after our trial the AFSC sponsored an encampment for a weekend at a resort on Lake Arrowhead and invited me to participate. What stands out in my memory is the genuine human warmth displayed toward me by these people who refused to be intimidated by labels and hysteria. This was the weekend I first met Bob Vogel, who was in charge of the AFSC's peace activities in Los Angeles. He would later move to New York, where I reencountered him in the 1960s, when he was very helpful in our campaign against the McCarran Act. At a time when every other hall in Los Angeles was denied us, the Unitarians always made their facilities available. Steve Fritchman, pastor of the First Unitarian Church, was like the rock of Gibraltar when it came to defending our rights to our beliefs. He led the fight against proposed state legislation that would have compelled churches to sign loyalty oaths in order to preserve their tax exemption. He and his wife Frances were both old-line New Englanders, true descendants of the abolitionists, with an intense passion for democracy and hatred for racism. As a result, he was dragged before HUAC on several occasions, where he was an unfailingly polite but unfriendly witness. Other liberals who came to our defense included A. A. Heist, a minister who formed the Bill of Rights Committee; Dan and Dorothy Marshall, two devout Catholic supporters of the Bill of Rights Committee; and Phil Kirby, who later went on to become the main editorial writer for the Los Angeles *Times*, who was then working for a magazine called *Frontier*.

Working with and getting to know such people had a big impact on me. It made me more willing to continue trying to reach out to a broader, non-Party public. In Los Angeles, bad as things were, we never felt as isolated as Communists did in other cities, and it had an impact on our political estimates. It was all part of a continuing process through which I was learning the important differences between the labels we'd give people and the reality of the human beings beneath those labels. Phil Kirby, for example, would accept any invitation to speak to anyone on the Left, including meetings sponsored by the *People's World*. Phil was not a Marxist, not part of the organized Left, but simply a faithful small "d" democrat. Knowing such people not only influenced my estimate of our immediate political prospects but gave me another little shove down the road toward reevaluating our larger theoretical understanding of American society. The Party's traditional analysis of "the limits of bourgeois democracy" often made it impossible for us to really understand what was happening in the United States. That became apparent when we had to come up with an explanation in 1954 for the Supreme Court's decision in *Brown* v. *Board of Education*, which overturned the "separate but equal" justification for racial segregation. The only way we could explain it was in terms of the growing strength of anticolonial struggles around the world and the need for the State Department to be able to counteract the anti-American propaganda. We simply could not comprehend the historic struggle that has always gone on in this country between reactionary and democratic forces, a struggle that could not simply be reduced to a clash of economic interests, as we tended to. Only gradually did it dawn on us that there was far more subtlety and richness involved in these questions and debates than we had always assumed.

Beginning in 1955 I took part in a series of meetings in Los Angeles organized by Dave McReynolds. At that time Dave was a student at UCLA and a member of the Socialist Party; he went on to become an important figure in the pacifist movement as a leader of the War Resisters League in New York. Dave thought it would be a good idea if people from groups on the Left that ordinarily had nothing to do with each other got together for discussions that might help break down the stereotypes we all held of one another. This was an anticipation of the "American Forum" discussions that A. J. Muste organized on a national basis in 1957. Dave told me later that I was the first "Stalinist" he had ever met, and he was somewhat taken aback to discover that I was more open on many questions than he had expected. Bob Vogel of the AFSC was one of the participants. Another was Ted Yudicoff, who was a member of the Independent Socialist League, the group led by Max Shachtman; I believe it was at one of these meetings that I first met Michael Harrington, who was then one of the leading young Shachtmanites. We had very freewheeling discussions. I found that I could not always answer the questions they posed to me about how, as a Marxist, I could justify the things going on in the Soviet Union with regard to democracy, freedom of speech, and access to information. I admitted as much to them. These meetings were a big influence on me, because they gave me an opportunity to think seriously about the Soviet Union and its problems.

I remember how we cried when Stalin died. He was my greatest hero. The whole family cried. It was a major, scary thing. For me as a little kid, he was more than just a hero, he was a protector. I remember going to the foreign language movies with Grandma and Grandpa, movies from eastern Europe and the Soviet Union, and I don't remember much about the movies except that the beginning or the end usually had a big, full-color picture of Stalin. It was wonderful, heart-warming. He was the source of stability, truth. . . . I remember one Christmas in 1950 or 1951, my mother took me to a toy store, and there was a little shooting arcade in which the bull's-eye was Stalin's head. My mother got into a huge argument with the toy store owner. I felt completely outraged and upset that here was wonderful Stalin with his head in a bull's-eye. ■ Richard Healey.

By the time Stalin died, Ben Dobbs and I were starting to question a lot of what we read in Soviet sources. The Cominform (Communist Information Bureau, formed in 1947 by the Communist Parties of the Soviet Union, the eastern European nations, France, and Italy) put out a publication with the glorious title *For a Lasting Peace, For a People's Democracy*, and we would moan over many of the items it published. We were unhappy, for one thing, with the way in which charges of "Zionism" were being used in the purge trials. We had always been politically opposed to Zionism for denying that there were class questions which divided Jews and for arguing that only in a Jewish state could Jews be free. We believed instead that only under socialism could Jews be guaranteed their freedom. But we had always tried to differentiate among trends within Zionism, because there were Socialist Zionist groups with whom we felt we could form united fronts on various issues. And we insisted that Zionism be treated as a political movement, not as a synonym for Judaism as a religion or Jews as a people. These distinctions were being blurred in what we were reading and it disturbed us. I also remember a particular editorial in the newspaper that made us furious: it singled out the Russian people from among all the people of the Soviet Union as the greatest, the most courageous, the most revolutionary, and so forth. Ben and I both felt that this was just a continuation of the Great Russian nationalism that Lenin had scathingly condemned in his own time.

Starting shortly after Stalin's death, *For a Lasting Peace* began to make somewhat murky comments condemning "the cult of the individual." We didn't quite know what that meant, but we tried to read between the lines. We decided that some kind of reconsideration was going on in the Soviet Union. This was something that Ben and I only discussed between the two of us. It may have duplicated conversations that other close friends or small groups in the Party were beginning to have, but it was in no sense a general or open discussion. That would soon change.

9

The fact that the Party has tried in the past year to be sharply critical of its work, should not blind us to the contribution which we made. . . . Wasted years? Nonsense! They have been full and vital years. Today, we must be determined that the lessons of this past year, full of shock and pain, will be translated into an increasing ability to root our Party in the American scene, by overcoming the long-standing disease of infantile leftism. ■ Dorothy Healey, "Report to the Southern California District Convention," April 12, 1957.

I was at a meeting with Dorothy and five or six others early in 1958. One by one, each of us said, "That's it, I'm getting out." Dorothy said to me, "You can't do that, you're a stalwart." "No," I said, "I'm leaving and you should too." And she said, "I'm not going to let those bastards have the Party." ■ Paul Jarrico. [Jarrico, a blacklisted Hollywood screenwriter, was producer of the independent film classic *Salt of the Earth*, released in 1954.]

Considering what we had just gone through, the Party survived McCarthyism in Los Angeles with remarkably few losses. Our local membership, which had stood at an all-time high of close to five thousand in 1949, was reduced to about three thousand eight hundred at end of 1955. If that proportion of members had remained in the Party nationwide, we would have had more than thirty thousand members left of the fifty thousand or so that had been in our ranks in the late 1940s. Because attrition was so much heavier elsewhere than in Los Angeles, we were reduced nationally to under twenty thousand. It would take a blind optimist indeed to be cheerful about the Party's immediate prospects in the mid-1950s, but neither was it the case that we were ready only for the "dust heap of history." Though greatly reduced, the Party's membership was not insignificant by previous standards: In 1955 it stood at about the same size it had been in 1933. And we had survived the worst that the U.S. government, with all the resources at its command for making life difficult, had been able to dish out. With McCarthyism on the wane, with Soviet and American leaders making tentative steps toward resolving some of the differences between the two countries, and with our leaders beginning to emerge from prison after the completion of their Smith Act sentences, the Party seemed to be shaking off the torpor of previous years.

In 1955 Gene Dennis sent Fred Fine, a veteran of the Party underground, on a tour of the Party districts. Gene had just been released from prison with a conditional release that kept him from playing an open political role until the end of the year. Fred told us that Gene honestly wanted to know, with no holds barred, just what the district leaders had thought about Party policy over the past decade. I was flabbergasted. Having been in the Communist movement for the better part of three decades, I had never seen anything like this happen before. The national leaders were there to tell us what we were doing wrong out in the districts; it was not their habit to solicit any kind of reciprocal criticism.

Something even more astonishing happened in January 1956 at a meeting sponsored by the Party in Carnegie Hall in New York City, the kind of large public gathering of Communists that had not been seen in years. Dennis, now able to act openly, made a speech declaring that the Party was guilty of having made serious misjudgments since the late 1940s, and promised a "new look" at past policies and assumptions. Here was the general secretary of the Communist Party coming right out in public and saying for all to hear that he and his coleaders had made mistakes. In April at a meeting of the national committee, Dennis fulfilled his promise in a report that was soon published and given to our members, in which he excoriated the "left sectarianism" of the past decade. I was delighted. For the first time in the history of the Party, the national leaders weren't blaming the districts or our members for what had gone wrong. The fault, Dennis was saying, was not in the way that Party policies had been carried out, but rather in the policies themselves as conceived and initiated by Party leaders.

When Communist leaders from all over the country assembled in the Jefferson School auditorium in New York City on April 28, it was the first open National Committee meeting in five years. The Party had stopped holding such meetings, fearing that they were an invitation to the government to just swoop down and arrest all our leaders at once. I had never formally been elected a member of the National Committee; as country chairman in Los Angeles, though, it was assumed that I held equivalent rank in the hierarchy. This meeting in April 1956 was in Party parlance a "plenum" or enlarged meeting of the National Committee. Bill Schneiderman, Louise Todd, and I were there representing California. In some ways it felt like a reunion. There were about a hundred people attending, including the national leaders, the leaders in all the districts, and some prominent trade unionists. I knew most of them, but hadn't seen many for a long time: some had been underground or in jail, and almost all of them had had to face Smith Act trials. The only people who weren't there were those who were still in jail for their Smith Act convictions, like Gus Hall, Bob Thompson, Gil Green, Henry Winston, and Elizabeth Gurley Flynn.

The National Committee meeting opened, as was customary, with the general secretary's report. But it was not the usual exercise in institutional self-congratulation. Dennis denounced the "left sectarian" cast of the Party's policies since the later 1940s. He singled out the overestimation of the danger of war between the United States and the Soviet Union as the main error that the Party had made in the years since 1945. Because we believed war all but inevitable, we subordinated everything else to foreign policy questions. In the CIO, for instance, the fight around the Truman Doctrine and then the Marshall Plan became our main concern; and it was primarily because of our estimate of the war danger that we had encouraged the launching of the Progressive Party. Dennis was not saying that we were wrong to be concerned with the possibility of war breaking out or that we were wrong to have opposed the Truman doctrine and the Marshall Plan; our error lay in subordinating everything else to those concerns. Equally damaging had been the belief in the early 1950s that domestic fascism was about to overcome all democratic resistance and that the Party had to shift to an underground existence. William Z. Foster was openly angered by Dennis's report; it was my first inkling of how deep the divisions ran within the national leadership. But he was alone in his criticisms that day and cast the sole vote against the report's official acceptance (three other national committee members, Ben Davis, Ed Strong, and Carl Winter, abstained on the vote).

Dennis's report would have been enough to make the day memorable. But after dinner we returned to the Jefferson School for what we had been told would be a special session. We didn't have the slightest idea what was planned. We were warned that no one could take notes on what we were about to hear or speak about it to anyone who was not in attendance. Leon Wofsy, Dennis's political secretary, then started to read the text of Khrushchev's "secret speech" to the Twentieth Party Congress the previous February. We were told at the time that this copy of the speech had been provided to us by the British Communist Party, but that was a polite fiction. I'm sure it came directly from the Soviet Union. (Morris Childs acted as the regular courier between the Soviet Union and Party headquarters. Years later it was revealed that Childs had been an FBI informer all during this period.)

> It became apparent that many Party, Soviet and economic activists, who were branded in 1937–1939 as "enemies," were actually never enemies, spies, wreckers, etc., but were always honest Communists; they were only so stigmatized and often, no longer able to bear barbaric tortures, they charged themselves (at the order of the investigative judges—falsifiers) with all kinds of grave and unlikely crimes. . . . It was determined that of the 139 members and candidates of the Party's Central Committee who were elected at the XVIIth Congress, 98 persons, i.e., 70 percent, were arrested and shot (mostly in 1937–1938). (Indignation in the hall.) ∎ from the transcript of Khrushchev's "Secret Speech."

Leon started to read the speech, and it must have taken him three or four hours to complete the reading. Within a half an hour I was convulsed with tears. It was unbearable. Just this voice going on, piling up facts upon facts, horrible facts about what had happened in the Soviet Union during the years of Stalin's leadership. At one point in his report, Khrushchev read to the delegates letters written to Stalin by the some of the old Bolsheviks he had imprisoned, who described to Stalin the tortures they were undergoing and told him that he was surrounded by enemies who were destroying the human beings who were the capital of a socialist society. It was like the old days of czarism, when the cossacks charged into the crowds in the streets with sabers flashing, and no one would believe that the czar himself, that good and pious man, could possibly know what his subordinates were doing. Suddenly all the pieces fell into place; all those little doubts that Ben Dobbs and I had discussed over the last few years were not only confirmed but magnified a thousand times.

> We felt that we were alone, abandoned by everybody: by the Party, our friends and comrades. We knew that for everyone outside—even for our own families—we were probably guilty, since the Party had decided on our arrest. I knew all that from experience. I had myself reacted like that during the trials in Moscow, Budapest, and Sofia. For what sincere and honest communist—even a relative of the man whom the Party had arrested—could avoid doubt? How could he conceive that the Party—which he had always placed above everything—could resort to illegal procedures, to monstrous acts intended to make innocent men confess? ■ Artur London. [London, one of the defendants in the 1952 Slansky purge trial in Czechoslovakia, described his reaction to his own arrest in his memoir *The Confession*.]

Nothing had prepared me for the magnitude of what we were hearing. We had marched for so many years with the purity of the Soviet Union as our banner. We had believed it completely. We had read so many lies about our own Party in the capitalist press that we felt we could dismiss reports of cruelty and repression in the Soviet Union as just so much propaganda. The Trotskyists and others who attacked the Soviet Union from the Left had their own ideological fish to fry, so we could dismiss them just as easily. And here we were, after all these years, sitting in a meeting of the Party's leaders and being told by no less an authority than the First Secretary of the Soviet Communist Party that it was not all capitalist and Trotskyist propaganda after all; that wretched, bloody crimes had been committed in the name of defending socialism. It was hard to avoid thinking that we bore a significant measure of responsibility for them because we had denied the very possibility that such a thing could happen. If we had been more cynical over the years, if we had had some idea in the back of our mind that "well, yes, things *are* pretty bad in the Soviet Union, but for politics' sake we can't admit it," then we would have been much better prepared for what we learned that evening.

> At the time of the Khrushchev report it was very handy to be able to say: well, we didn't know what was going on and we had very plausible reasons for disbelieving those who said some evil things were happening. Anna Louise [Strong]'s outcry to you poses a question that the rest of us could and did avoid: suppose we had known? The clear implication of "but we didn't know" was that if we had known we would not have kept silent as

she did. I'm not so sure, and here I do not presume to speak for anyone but myself. In this context I am reminded of Paulie Robeson's disclosure of his father's regret at having kept silent after Itzik Feffer gave him some inkling of what was likely to happen to Jewish cultural figures. ■ letter from Al Richmond to Dorothy, May 16, 1984.

What was devastating—and at the same time liberating—about listening to the Khrushchev speech was that it severed the bonds that kept us in subordination to the Soviet communist leaders for all those years. Just as rank-and-file members of our own Party looked to American Communist leaders as perfect beings incapable of error, we had taken the same attitude to the Soviet leaders. They knew what they were doing in the Soviet Union and by extension must know what was best for us to do in the United States. We had surrendered our capacity to think independently, to look at reality and say this is what's happening and this isn't. Thinking back, there is no question that this was the most significant day of my life since I had joined the YCL nearly three decades earlier. For the first time I began to understand the meaning of my own years of political guerilla warfare against particular aspects of Party policy. Now I could see that what I had been reacting to was not just this or that tactic or nuance of policy. What I had been resisting, however imperfectly and at an instinctive level, went beyond tactical questions. What was involved was the decisive strategic question of the absolute necessity for a revolutionary party to be independent of the foreign or domestic needs of another country. Lenin had said that the test of internationalism was the ability to fight your own ruling class, and it now seemed obvious to me that one couldn't do that if one was acting as the voice of another country.

> You had an organization that was the only really important organization on the Left. It did a lot of fine things. It produced, it really did. It had strength, it had a following, it was proved right in many instances. And also you developed an intellectual vested interest in a position. If you can in any way rationalize that vested interest, there's a tendency to maintain it. I suppose Dorothy was for a long period of time as responsible as anybody else for that. But then she started carrying on this fight with the Party, and it took a great deal of courage, because the Communist Party was her life. ■ Ben Margolis.

It was around eleven o'clock in the evening when the reading of the report finally ended. I had been crying for several hours. I made a dash for the door because I didn't want to talk with anyone. Ben Davis came over, and I will always remember his kindness. He didn't say a word but put his arm around me as we walked downstairs and got me into a taxi. I went back to the hotel where I was staying. About half past twelve the phone rang and it was Bill Schneiderman, who wanted to talk to me. Word had gotten around about how upset I was. I just said, "No, I don't want to talk to you. I don't want to talk to anybody. I just want to think. Just leave me alone."

The next day there was another session. The thing I remember most about it was a comment by Jim Jackson, an up-and-coming Black leader. He said, "I don't understand what all this emotional reaction is to that speech, all this great political to-do. Why, comrades, everybody knows you can't make an omelet without breaking eggs." I felt chilled by the repetition of that all-too-familiar cliché. Yes, we had always understood that in a revolutionary situation unfortunate things were bound to happen, people might be killed or be imprisoned unjustly. In the heat of battle many decisions might be made that in retrospect would not always seem defensible. But what Khrushchev's speech had described was not the convulsions that followed in the immediate wake of the revolution but rather a deliberate policy of torture and murder that lasted for decades. I had been very impressed with Jackson until then, but I never regained my respect for him afterward. In contrast, Ben Davis was very shaken by the report and said that thinking back over the history of our own Party, it seemed to him that had we come to power we might have committed the very same crimes. I was reminded of my vote to expel Roy Hudson in the early 1950s when I knew full well that the charges against him had been nonsense. Would I have voted the same way if we had been in power and it had been a question of life or death? The very fact that I was unsure as to the answer left me with a queasy feeling.

> What should we, as Marxists, have been saying all these years? We should have stated frankly that the building of Socialism in the Soviet Union was not the establishment of Paradise on Earth. . . . We Marxists should not have ever had such illusions for ourselves, nor passed them on, as we did, to others. ■ Dorothy's May Day speech, 1956.

That afternoon I flew back to California. I was scheduled to make a speech at our annual May Day meeting, and I didn't know what I was going to say. We had been sworn to silence about the contents of the Khrushchev report; it would be another five weeks before the *New York Times* printed the text. (There are all kinds of theories as to the source of that text, which was never officially released by the Soviet government; I've always maintained that the U.S. government obtained its copy from the FBI, who could have gotten it from someone like Morris Childs, or could have bugged the auditorium of the Jefferson School where the report was read.) I couldn't just stand up and give the usual speech celebrating the growing strength of the international working class, with the implication that everything was just fine in the Soviet Union as far as I was concerned. So I tried, very cautiously, to prepare my comrades in Los Angeles for the shock I knew that they too would soon receive. I said something to the effect that those who pioneered in building a socialist society were bound to make some tragic mistakes and that we should not expect to find perfection in those societies.

The reaction to my very guarded comments was a foretaste of things to come. People came up to me after the meeting just heartbroken: "How dare you say such things?" They did not want to hear the truth. I was in a difficult position, because on the one hand I was the Party leader and I had the responsibility of holding the Party together. On the other hand, I was in the midst of a tremendous reevaluation of everything I had believed and had a responsibility to myself to come to a new political understanding. It was not an easy conflict to resolve. I made a lot of mistakes in the next few months. Temperamentally, I simply could not understand people who didn't want to look facts in the face and draw fresh conclusions from them. Even when the Khrushchev speech was printed, first in the *Times*, and then in the *Daily Worker* and the *People's World*, there were Communists who refused to read it, who just dismissed it as capitalist propaganda or a CIA provocation. Many had a similar reaction to Gene's "New Look" report. They didn't want to hear that the policies we had followed were wrong; it astonished me to realize that they would rather have been able to have taken the onus on themselves for having shown insufficient zeal in carrying out those policies. This kind of "New Look" challenged the essence of what had enabled them to hold on during those terrible years, that belief in the infallibility and righteousness of the Party. Now Dennis was telling them "we've been wrong," which to many in the Party meant that the sacrifices they had made during those years were in vain. I was ready to begin living without that blind faith, though it had taken me a long time to do so, and I had no sympathy for others who had yet to reach that point. Perhaps I should have been more patient with them. Khrushchev, Dennis, and I were all tarnishing their faith, but I had nothing comparable to offer them to take the place of lost illusions.

One of the most important concepts that Marx developed was the distinction between what he called class consciousness and false consciousness. He used it to explain the dynamics of revolutionary working-class movements. Just because workers are exploited under capitalism doesn't mean that they will understand their real interests and unite to overthrow capitalism. As he described the "fetishism of commodities" in *Capital:* "the relation of the producers to the sum total of their own labor is presented to them as a social relationship, existing not between themselves, but between the products of their labor. . . . [I]t is a definite social relation between men, that assumes, in their eyes, the fantastic form of a relation between things." The task of revolutionaries was to demystify capitalist relations of production, to strip away that false consciousness, that ideology based on a partial truth. Ideology is not a lie; it is a distorted version of reality. Communists did not prove immune to their own variety of false consciousness. We developed our own fetishisms and substituted abstract categories for actual human relations. Thus we decided, "This person is a liberal" and felt we knew all about liberals and their weaknesses, or "This comrade shows revisionist tendencies" and felt we knew about how revisionism would eventually lead you into the enemy camp. We never stopped to consider that the liberal or the revisionist might have something to teach us, that they were seeing a part of reality obscured to us. We ignored anything which challenged our version of the truth. What sustained us all those decades in our quest to change the world was an unreal set of notions about the world. Faith in the inevitability of victory and the purity of our own cause had always been our greatest asset. Paradoxically, our illusions strengthened our commitment even as they weakened our chances of ever reaching our goal.

The Khrushchev speech had the most positive impact, at least initially, on those of us who came from the YCL and who had in a sense grown up with the Party. We were on the verge of inheriting the Party's leadership positions, and by and large we were willing to consider making dramatic changes in the Party's outlook and structure. The generation that came after us, the young people who had joined during the Wallace campaign or immediately afterward and were now in the Labor Youth League, were also very responsive.

Others proved resistant to change. The maritime workers, for example, were very hard-line, as had always been the case. For them, politics was shipboard politics, class struggle in its most naked form, and they weren't about to make any concessions to those of us who had to deal with a more complicated political world. Some Blacks in the Party regarded the whole debate as the preoccupation of whites and a diversion from more pressing issues at home (Doxey Wilkerson, Abner Green, Claude Lightfoot, and Howard "Stretch" Johnson were notable exceptions to this rule). The Yiddish-speaking old-timers in the needle trades also couldn't see the need for change. What they had learned in the past was all they knew, and they didn't even remember that too accurately. I remember shocking them terribly in a speech I gave. I wanted them to look at the question of why we kept talking about how great we'd been in the 1930s but would never confront the fact that we weren't so great in the 1950s. So I told the story of the eighty-year-old Catholic woman who'd gone to confession and said, "Oh Father, forgive me, I have sinned." And he said, "What have you done, daughter?" She said, "I slept with a man and I wasn't married to him." "Oh my," he said, "that's terrible. But before I give you absolution, when did this happen?" She said, "Forty years ago." "Well," he asked, "why do you come and tell me about it now?" And she replied, "I enjoyed it so much I like to keep talking about it." The 1905ers were just outraged. They went all over town saying "Dorothy is telling dirty sex jokes at Party meetings."

In the course of 1956 and 1957 my role as a Party leader underwent a qualitative change. Instead of simply being concerned with keeping things running smoothly in Los Angeles, I was now directly involved in national Party debates. I began to shuttle back and forth every three months between Los Angeles and New York. In February 1957 at the national convention, I was formally elected to the National Committee. The following year I was elected to the National Executive Committee—usually referred to as the National Board—which was ostensibly the Party's top policy-setting body (in truth, real policy was generally determined by the Political Bureau or Secretariat, composed of a few full-time national leaders in New York, the smallest body but the one actually determining day-to-day policy.) Also in 1956, the long-simmering debate over whether the state headquarters of the California Party should remain in San Francisco or be moved to Los Angeles was resolved, in truly Solomonic fashion, with a decision to simply divide the state into two separate districts. But that took months and months of meetings—all held in San Francisco, naturally—and that was a further drain on my time. And even when I was in Los Angeles there were meetings vitually every night throughout the year to prepare for the district convention and to let people know what was going on at the national level.

The pressures and tensions were incredible for me, and I'm sure they were very hard on Richard. We lived on a merry-go-round. Richard had just entered his teens when the de-Stalinization crisis began. For the next few years there were a lot of meetings in our house, with these long, loud, passionate arguments going on as to what to do and where to go from here. I think that hearing all of this going on in his living room reinforced his own conclusion that he wasn't ever going to join the Party. I remember about this time he was reading Simone de Beauvoir's *The Mandarins*, and I asked him what he'd thought of it. The book goes on in some detail about her sexual activities, bouncing from bed to bed, and I thought maybe that was what would stick in his mind. On the contrary, he was most taken by her account of the debate between Sartre and Camus over the Soviet Union. He asked me, "What was your position on the question of Soviet slave labor camps?" And I said simply that I hadn't believed that they existed. "How could you not believe it?" I told him all the reasons why I hadn't believed in them. He looked at me awhile and then said reflectively, "You people really deserve what's happening to you today."

In 1956 I got to go to New York and spent two weeks there while my mother was fighting in those climactic national committee meetings. Every night she'd come back to the hotel and tell me what a son of a bitch Foster was and how Dennis waffled again. I had a very personal sense of who these people were. ∎ Richard Healey.

In the aftermath of the April National Committee meeting, a power struggle began in the Party leadership. The three main contestants were Eugene Dennis, William Z. Foster, and Johnny Gates. Of the three, Dennis could have done the most to hold the Party together—had he been up to the challenge. He was the Party general secretary and had begun the year by playing a bold and innovative role. He occupied a middle ground between the extremes represented by Foster, who wanted to change nothing, and Gates, who wanted to change everything. I have many positive memories of Gene. Unlike so many others, he never to my knowledge used his political post to punish those who disagreed with him. He and his wife Peggy lived in very modest circumstances; he would never use his position for personal aggrandizement. And his political thinking was worth serious consideration. But I was very disappointed by the role he played in the next few years.

It is, in theory, possible to hold the middle ground decisively; one can play an honorable role as a compromiser and conciliator and avoid the onus of being a vacillator. Dennis, unfortunately for us, was unable to pull it off. Instead of genuinely representing the middle, the majority, and what I regarded as the true interests of the Party, he vacillated, first leaning to the "right" and to Gates, the leaning to the "left" and to Foster. In the turbulent battles from 1957 to 1959 he was overwhelmed by his fears: on one side, of the danger he felt from what he thought was anti-Sovietism; and on the other, of the danger he felt from the Foster's camp's dogmatism. And, though no one yet knew it, he was beginning to weaken physically due to cancer.

I got to know William Z. Foster well after the war and found him an impressive man in many ways. I would drive him around to his meetings when he came to Los Angeles, and that gave us a chance for long talks. He spoke quite freely. I remember his telling me when I first met him in 1946 that the biggest mistake he had ever made was agreeing in the late 1920s to have the Trade Union Education League, which tried to work within the AFL, transformed into the Trade Union Unity League, our none-too-successful attempt to create an independent revolutionary federation of unions. All his life he had fought against dual unionism, and he regretted having given in to the pressures from the Comintern to form TUUL. Foster was a man of strong views and was not usually so self-critical, but he was always very honest in expressing his views. He could be utterly ruthless in inner-Party battles, but you always knew what he believed and what he was up to.

For a man his age, and with his history of heart trouble, Foster was still extraordinarily energetic. We'd get a lot of national Communist leaders out in Los Angeles, because we were an important center of Party strength, a good place to raise funds for national campaigns—and because a trip to the city could be a kind of vacation junket: sunshine, the chance to meet Hollywood stars, that sort of thing. Foster was not oblivious to the attractions of the place. It may seem a little out of character, but he turned out to be a devoted fan of cowboy movies. He had watched a lot of them in the 1930s when he was recovering from his heart attack and could tell you everything about the plot, the director, and the stars of any cowboy movie you might think of. I once took him to a meeting at Dalton Trumbo's house, and he was very excited about it beforehand. When we got there it was a big disappointment for him, all screenwriters and no stars. He didn't care about writers. But Foster was not just out for a good time. He put in his hours. One of his attributes I particularly envied was his facility in writing, which was never my strong suit. Foster had a regular column in the *Daily Worker*, which he would keep up while he was on the road, so I got to see him at work in our office. He could sit down at the typewriter and in fifteen minutes have a letter-perfect column which required no further editing and contained not a single typing error.

I saw Foster regularly in New York City in the late 1940s at National Committee meetings. It was at those meetings that it became clear that as much as I admired his personal qualities, we were not of one mind on political questions. At one of those meetings in 1949 there was a big battle over the line we should take within the Progressive Party. Gene Dennis and Fred Fine were leading a fight to have us soften our position that there could be no criticism of the Soviet Union from within the Progressive Party. The defeat of the "Vermont resolution" at the Progressive Party's nominating convention in 1948 had been a major setback in the Wallace campaign, and Dennis and Fine argued that it was self-defeating nonsense to insist that the Progressive Party mirror our own interpretation of the international situation in every detail. Foster was inflexible; any softening of our position within the Progressive Party would be an abandonment of our principles. I was sitting next to Marion Bachrach, who was one of the top party strategists in electoral work and a very bright woman. I remember her leaning over to me in the middle of Foster's remarks and saying in a low voice, "As if the Soviet Union wouldn't be grateful for a strengthened Progressive Party, even if it were to criticize Soviet as well as American foreign policy." Foster had become a prisoner of the past who simply kept repeating the old concepts, slogans, and approaches.

Johnny Gates was Foster's best-known opponent in the 1956–1957 power struggle. Like me, Gates was a product of the YCL and the Popular Front days. He had fought in Spain with the Abraham Lincoln Brigade, and in Germany with the U.S. army. After the war he became the editor of the *Daily Worker* and a top Party leader. Gates's prominence and the fact that he had the *Daily Worker* at his disposal to promote his ideas gave outside observers the misleading idea that he was the undisputed leader of all the forces favoring change in the Party: in fact the term "Gates faction" came into use in 1956 as a generic description of the proreform camp. There was widespread sentiment for some kind of change within the Party, but outside of New York and a few other places the "Gates faction" was a myth.

In southern California we were convinced that Foster and Gates were writing each other's speeches: Foster served Gates's purposes by offering an intransigent defense of outmoded ideas, and Gates served Foster's purposes by the self-serving recklessness with which he argued for his counter-positions. Gates's main proposal, which was to return to the "political association" of the late Browder period, and Foster's fierce counter-attack against that proposal served only to distract the Party from a sober examination of the real problems it faced. The main difference I saw between Foster and Gates was that basically I liked Foster as a person, and I could not stand Gates. He was a supreme egotist; everything he said was just "I, I, I, I, I." In southern California the only "Gatesite" who comes to mind was Don Wheeldin of the *People's World*. In northern California Gates counted a few prominent supporters, including Louise Todd, Oleta O'Connor Yates, and Mickey Lima. Mickey wanted to bring Gates out on a speaking tour, but Al Richmond and I opposed that proposal in the state board—to the surprise of some of those to our "left" in the Party who also tended to regard those favoring change as one undifferentiated revisionist mass. We were unhappy with the way in which he used the *Daily Worker* to promote his own views. Here we were, supposedly fighting against the kind of bureaucratic dictation that had been so characteristic of the way that the Party made its decisions in the past, and Gates in his own way was just as great a bureaucrat as Foster: the lyrics were different, but it was the same old song.

Until the Hungarian events of the fall of 1956, the Los Angeles leadership remained fairly united in its view of the Party's crisis. We wanted to change the way the Party operated in some fundamental ways, but we also wanted to preserve the Communist Party and not see it dissolve. There were some disagreements, but we strove to find a consensus. We had worked together a long time, and there was a kind of mutual respect for one another's opinions. With the Soviet invasion of Hungary, the consensus disappeared. The arguments grew shrill and the forces pulling the Party apart increased geometrically.

The Hungarian Party leader Imre Nagy had succeeded the heavy-handed Stalinist Matyas Rakosi as Hungarian premier in 1953. Nagy wanted to loosen the grip of the Soviet Union over Hungary's internal affairs, but he went too far too fast in criticizing past policies and was removed from office at the end of 1955. Rakosi was reinstalled in power, but only briefly. The reforms in Soviet policy promised or implied at the Twentieth Congress had a dramatic impact on popular aspirations for change in Eastern Europe. When rioting broke out in October 1956 Nagy regained the premiership. He wasn't able to restore order and made the fatal error of announcing that Hungary was going to withdraw from the Warsaw Pact. That provoked a Soviet invasion, the suppression of the rebellion, and Nagy's arrest and eventual execution.

> From the start, a majority of our County Committee felt that the terrible errors and perversions of Socialist approaches on the part of the Hungarian Communists and the Soviet Union, were responsible for the disintegration of the Hungarian Party and the demoralization of the working class, thereby providing the basis for the uprisings. Nevertheless, we think that the action of the Soviet army on November 4th was a tragic necessity, a necessary action on behalf of the interests of the adjoining Socialist countries, and a necessary action on behalf of the basic interests of the Hungarian workers, peasants, students and intellectuals. . . . We know that it was American dollars that assisted the Horthy, Mindzenty forces in corrupting the demands of the honest Socialist workers, intellectuals and students who were fighting. . . . However, we do not feel that we have said the last word on this question, nor even that our opinion is necessarily the only correct opinion to hold. We do not feel that Comrades who do not share our position are thereby automatically anti-Soviet. . . . ■ Dorothy Healey, "Report to Southern California District Convention," April 12, 1957.

I defended the Soviet invasion on the ground that the Communist Party of Hungary had practically dissolved, and as a result there was both a danger of Western intervention and of a restoration of reactionaries and even fascists to power. That was the position which Foster and Dennis took; Gates condemned the invasion, as Al Richmond did in California. The events in Hungary thus helped undermine the already tenuous unity which existed within the Party's reform caucus. My only difference with Dennis and Foster is that I still insisted that the cause of the problems in Hungary was the great-power chauvinism of the Soviet Union combined with the mistakes of the Hungarian Party leaders under Rakosi. Their position was that the whole thing had been somehow engineered by the CIA.

> I was opposed to the Soviet intervention in Hungary. I wrote an article for the *People's World* in which I presented the contending arguments, and at the end I injected my own personal opinion. Dorothy thought that the intervention was justified. In retrospect I find it somewhat surprising. But there it was. There are very few people that I know who are politically consistent. ■ Al Richmond.

My position didn't win me friends in either of the contending camps within the Party, being equally unacceptable to those who felt that under no circumstances should the Soviet army have invaded and those who felt that I was downplaying American responsibility for the uprising. The National Committee met in mid-November to discuss our position on the invasion, and it was the scene of a violent dispute. Eventually a compromise resolution was patched together which left us neither condemning nor condoning the invasion. I now question the certainty with which I spoke in 1956 about the necessity of the Soviet invasion. My views began to change when I read an article by Mao, written during the years when the Sino-Soviet split was becoming apparent, where he revealed in a footnote that the Soviet Union did not want to send the Red Army back in on November 4 but did so when China threatened to "expose" them before the world communist movement as betraying socialism in Hungary. The 1968 Soviet invasion of Czechoslovakia gave me further reason to think back on Hungary, though the two events are not strictly comparable. The changes taking place in Czechoslovakia before the invasion were initiated by the new leadership of the Communist Party, whereas in Hungary the Party was in a shambles, and power lay in the streets, ready to be grabbed by whoever came along.

> Dear comrades:
> We are writing to inform you that, with profound regret, we are leaving the Communist Party. We have reached this conclusion reluctantly and only after a considerable period of time in which we, with others, hoped that the Party would move in the direction of overcoming its isolation from the American people. . . . We believe that the Party no longer has the resources with which to overcome its isolation: in our opinion its reserves have been exhausted. . . . Nor do we believe it possible to seal off local party organizations from the effects of this total national state of affairs. . . . ■ collective letter of resignation from twenty-six leading California Communists, including Oleta O'Connor Yates, Louise Todd, Frank Carlson, Celeste Strack, Lil Carlson, Don Wheeldin, and Henry Steinberg, dated March 26, 1958.

We might have weathered the Dennis report and gotten the Party to look at the weaknesses of past policies objectively and been the stronger for it in the end. We might have weathered the Khrushchev speech on Stalin and gained a new independent perspective in international affairs, as well as a new respect for democratic safeguards against the despotic use of power in socialist societies. And we might even have weathered the Hungarian invasion, though that raised very difficult issues for the Party and certainly would have cost us the allegiance of many members. Any one, perhaps even any two of these events we could have survived. But when we had to undergo all three blows in rapid succession in less than a year, it was just too much, and the Party was gravely weakened.

> Every time another comrade who wants "change" to guarantee the Party
> as a more meaningful instrument for winning Americans to Socialism leaves

our Party, he is helping to prevent change from taking place. . . . Did anyone seriously believe that the Party could change overnight? Did anyone believe it could change without the most extended struggle "against our main adversary—the habits of the past"? ■ Dorothy Healey, "On the Status of the Party," *Political Affairs* (March 1958).

An ever-heavier burden of expectations was being placed upon the upcoming sixteenth national convention of the Communist Party, scheduled for February in New York. This would be the Party's first national convention since the late 1940s, and many hoped it would mark the decisive triumph of the reform forces. In our preconvention discussions in the Party clubs in Los Angeles, we focused on the question of how to interpret "democratic centralism," how to guarantee that in the future it would not function as all centralism and no democracy, how to guarantee the rights of dissent in the Party, and how to allow the views of dissident leaders to be made known to the membership as a whole.

Because Los Angeles had suffered relatively smaller losses during the McCarthy era, and because delegates to a national convention were allotted on the basis of membership, our district now loomed larger in importance than we ever had before, the second largest district after New York. With the distance and expenses involved, we had seldom sent as many delegates to national gatherings as we were actually entitled to. In November Herb Wheeldin, a supporter of Gates and the brother of Don Wheeldin, came out to Los Angeles to offer us funds to enable southern California to send a full delegation to the national convention. Gates knew that we were not supporters of his full program, especially his call for liquidating the Party, but he figured that since we were anti-Foster our presence in strength at the convention would be to his advantage. We indignantly refused the offer. If money came to us to help us send our delegates to the convention, we felt it should only come through normal channels, which would be through the national office. In retrospect, I wish we had bridled our self-righteousness and just taken the money, because the enduring problems the Party would face were not those represented by Gates's positions but those Foster stood for.

Three hundred delegates came from all over the country to meet on a snowy weekend in mid-February in a dismally cold hall with the misleading name of Chateau Gardens on the Lower East Side of New York. The FBI was out front snapping pictures of everyone who entered or left the hall, a reminder if we needed one that the spirit of Joe McCarthy was still alive, even if the man himself was in disgrace and soon to die. In a symbolic gesture, the convention agreed to seat a delegation of outside observers, including A. J. Muste; it was the first time that outsiders had ever been allowed in to see the workings of a Communist Party convention. The convention was the most democratic that the Party had ever held, with all viewpoints being heard. The full proceedings of the convention were published in a booklet, which meant that for once our members could find out exactly what their leaders stood for and how they differed among themselves on the issues facing the Party. (Ordinarily all that would be published were the formal reports from the most important leaders, which often concealed as much as they revealed.)

Superficially, the convention seemed unified, partially because all sides had agreed beforehand that it was best that the explosive issue of Hungary not be discussed. The draft resolution proposed by the national committee the previous fall, which embodied many of the proposals for a more independent, more democratic Party that had been made since Dennis's "New Look" report, passed without much difficulty. At the end of the convention Gates, Davis, Foster, and Dennis all stood together on the platform holding their hands linked together above their heads to symbolize the unity of all the factions. But it was made clear to me even before I could leave the convention hall just how shallow that unity really was. I was heading for the door and walked past Foster, who was standing in the back of the hall with a small group of his followers around him. I overheard him say to them, "Well, we may have lost this convention, but we'll win the next one." I froze, looked at him, and said, "Bill, you know what you're doing is like the line from Oscar Wilde, 'Each man kills the thing he loves the best.' " I told him about all the old-timers in Los Angeles who already had one foot out the door, people like Celeste Strack and Frank Carlson, who were waiting to see if the Party would live up to the spirit of the resolutions passed at this convention. He replied, "Let them go, who cares?" And then he added, "You must understand, Dorothy, that even if the Party goes down to only fifty members, if they are true Marxist-Leninists, staunch people, it doesn't matter. It is better to have fifty true members than fifty thousand who are not genuine Communists."

Foster almost got his wish. By the end of the 1950s the Party nationally would be reduced to about three thousand, considerably fewer than we had had in Los Angeles alone a decade earlier. In Los Angeles, by 1959, we could count fewer than five hundred members left. That was my generation that was leaving, the generation that had grown up in the Young Communist League, that had a great deal of experience in both mass work and Party leadership, the people who had done the writing and organizing. It was a terrible blow in terms of the competence of the Party, just to be able to continue to do the ordinary kinds of things that preoccupied us 90 percent of the time in our daily political work.

If anyone thought that peace and stability were now about to descend on the Party, they were quickly disabused of that notion. When I returned to Los Angeles I was elected chairman of the new southern California district, or as the post was formerly called, the district organizer, or "D.O." I was one of the very few women in the Party who had ever held a D.O.'s position. In northern California everyone expected that Bill Schneiderman would continue as chairman, but he refused the post. Partly, he was miffed that he had so recently been the leader of the second-largest district in the country and was now going to be left with only a rump. But he was also angry at the Party for a more important reason. Boris Ponomarev, a member of the Soviet Central Committee responsible for relations with foreign Communist Parties, wrote an article for *Kommunist*, the theoretical journal of the Soviet CP, in which he denounced Bill by name for some articles he had written the previous year. Bill had criticized the absence of true democratic centralism in the Communist movement and taken on some other sacred cows, and now he was being attacked in the vilest language as if he were a capitalist agent. All the California Party leaders were outraged and demanded that Eugene Dennis, as general secretary, publicly respond to the charges. Dennis, cautious as always, and more and more preoccupied with the so-called right danger in the Party, refused to do anything. It was a terrible blow to Bill. He lived in Moscow in the 1930s when he was American representative to the Communist International, and the idea that he was being denounced by the Soviet Communist Party, and that his own comrades would not take up the cudgels on his behalf, left him devastated. He stepped down from the leadership, and Mickey Lima replaced him as chairman of the northern California district. Lima also took the seat on the National Board that would otherwise have gone to Schneiderman, which was significant because shortly afterward he moved into the old guard's camp, where he became one of the most rigid defenders of ideological orthodoxy.

When I went to New York in those years for National Board and National Committee meetings, there was a caucus of sorts of like-minded board members that I attended. It was there that I met Gates's close associates (Johnny himself only came once, which was a good thing because otherwise I would have stopped attending). Carl Ross, Fred Fine, Sid Stein, Mike Russo, Dave Davis, Mickey Lima, Claude Lightfoot, Martha Stone and Jack Stachel were in regular attendance at these meetings, which would be held just before a National Board meetings (those on the other side were having their own private meetings at the same time, of course). It wasn't much of a caucus: we found that we could only agree on what we were against; we could rarely find agreement on what we wanted to offer as an alternative to Foster's policies. And that, of course, is what finally defeated us. You can't fight something with nothing. The main value of those meetings was that those of us from out of town could be told by Fred and Sid what was going on in the national office, the "who-shot-Johns" that took place during our absence. Otherwise we'd have no idea of what we were facing, what the real differences were within the national leadership, or what policy faits accomplis were being cooked up behind closed doors.

In the aftermath of the convention a fierce factional battle resumed within most Party districts. Only one-third of the members of the new National Committee were elected at the convention; the remaining two-thirds were to be elected at district and state conventions to follow. But the strength of reform-minded Communists had peaked at the sixteenth convention (which, among other measures, had adopted important new provisions for inner-party democracy, including the right to dissent from Party decisions, and the establishment of a discussion bulletin to report to the membership regularly on debates within the National Committee). The New York District was the most important post-convention battlefield, as Gates's followers began pouring out of the Party and Foster's followers saw the chance to reassert control. Proponents of the changes mandated by the sixteenth convention, like New York district chairman George Charney, were left alone, without allies. George and I were very close friends and had great regard for each other. We always sat next to each other at National Board meetings, and he would pass me surreptitious notes mocking the solemnity of the debaters. In the midst of one particularly heated exchange he slipped me a note I still have proposing a three-point program for the board to consider: "(1) cease fire; (2) exchange of the wounded; (3) both sides retire to the 32nd ideological parallel."

Unfortunately, because we were so close, George chose to listen to my advice when I approached him on behalf of the National Board and asked him to agree to share the leadership of the New York district with Ben Davis. Davis, initially shaken by the secret speech, had soon returned to Foster's side. Charney was asked to give the chairmanship to Davis and accept the post of district org secretary, with the understanding that power would be shared equally between them. It was an absurd proposal, I realized later, because in an organization like the Communist Party you can't divide up that kind of position, particularly when the coleaders shared diametrically opposed views on most questions. George yielded to the request, and all it did was prepare the way for the Fosterites' triumph and his own rapid departure from the Party.

. Foster scored another coup by destroying the *Daily Worker* and driving Johnny Gates out of the Party. The Foster camp controlled funds left over from the underground period but refused to make them available to the newspaper, which was suffering financially from our rapidly declining membership. Out on the west coast the *People's World* had already been forced to cut back to weekly publication, and now the Fosterites proposed that the *Daily Worker* suffer the same fate. Despite my personal dislike for Johnny, I was completely opposed to these maneuvers. It was a subterfuge, using organizational means to settle a political question. Gates was no newspaperman, and from Slim I had picked up a healthy dislike for these commissar types with which the Party was always saddling newspapers. Still, the staff of the *Daily Worker* held Johnny in high regard, because he was willing to fight on their behalf. But the balance of power had by late 1957 shifted decisively against Gates. In early January the *Worker* was forced to cease publication as a daily, and Gates announced his own resignation from the Party.

When the National Committee reassembled to meet in February 1958, the ultraleft had regained control, reflecting the continued exodus of reformers from the Party. Dennis continued his alliance with the Foster forces, and now that Gates was gone they concentrated their efforts on attacking Fred Fine and Sid Stein, who had become the symbolic leaders of the reform forces. The committee elected a new National Board, which dropped Fred, Sid, and me. The proposal for the antireform slate was read to the National Committee by Gene Dennis. I was nominated from the floor by Mickey Lima for the board. I declined to stand for election because I felt it was going to be a waste of time, but I later accepted appointment as one of a number of members added from the most important districts. Our district board decided that someone from southern California had to be on the National Board so that we could have some idea of what was going on with the leadership in New York.

When the National Committee next met, in June, the dwindling group of reformers within it staged a fight on the question of the Party's reaction to Imre Nagy's execution. His death was announced in early June, though he had been killed by his Soviet jailers some time earlier. I was not an uncritical admirer of

Nagy, but the execution of a dissident Communist leader by a Communist government was more than I could stomach. Just before the meeting of the National Committee, the *Worker* (now a weekly four-page sheet) printed an editorial by the Party journalist Joe North applauding the execution. The surviving reformers on the national committee were outraged over both the execution and the fact that the *Worker* was presenting the National Committee with another policy coup d'etat. When Johnny Gates had used the *Daily Worker* as the mouthpiece for his own views, Dennis and Foster had climbed up on their high horses to condemn him; now that the paper reflected the views of their own supporters, they had no problems with the practice. We could only muster eleven votes for a resolution condemning the execution, which was voted down by a three to one margin. I made a speech in favor of our resolution in which I quoted my mother, who had asked me, "How do you account for the fact that Rakosi could live through eighteen years of imprisonment in a fascist prison in Hungary, but Nagy couldn't live through a year in a socialist prison?"

That infuriated the Fosterites. Ben Davis stood up and demanded that the National Committee take a vote and go on record that the Los Angeles Party should remove me as chairman. Davis may have been emboldened by the recent resignation of twenty-two prominent California Communists, including Oleta O'Connor Yates and four other Smith Act defendants. Just as the Fosterites had been able to regain control in New York state because of the resignations of so many of Gates's followers, so some now hoped that the resignation of reform-minded Communists in California would present a similar opportunity. But cooler heads prevailed, and the resolution failed. They just weren't all that sure what would happen in Los Angeles if they had made such a recommendation. Since Los Angeles was the second largest district, they couldn't afford to take the chance of completely wrecking the Party there. When a motion was made at the next meeting of the district council in Los Angeles in July that I be removed from office, it was tabled by a vote of sixty-eight to six.

This was, however, only the beginning of the efforts the national office made to remove me from office. I cannot think of another occasion when the Party's national leaders decided that a district leader should be dumped and then were unable to achieve their goal. It must have been enormously frustrating for them. They sent Lou Weinstock out to Los Angeles to organize against me. Lou was an old Party leader who had spent many years in the leadership of the AFL Painters Union and was a staunch Fosterite. I had to admire his forthrightness. He came into the Party office, sat down across the desk from me, and said, "Dorothy I'm here representing the Foster caucus and I'm here to get you removed." I said, "Try your best." Meanwhile the FBI, seeing a chance to further disrupt the L.A. Party, did their best to undermine my leadership by means of planting rumors and printing phoney "opposition" leaflets.

COMRADES: REMOVE DOROTHY HEALY [sic] FROM LEADERSHIP BEFORE FURTHER DAMAGE IS DONE

DOROTHY HEALY HAS IN THE PAST AND NOW IS TRYING TO CAUSE FRICTION WITHIN THE NATIONAL COMMITTEE; Why has DOROTHY continued to confuse the issues? cause friction? and disunity in our Party?. . . . REMEMBER THIS: The House Unamerican Activities Committee receives information from those who talk before it in closed sessions as well as open sessions. DOROTHY HEALY TESTIFIED RECENTLY BEFORE THIS BODY IN LOS ANGELES, IN A CLOSED SESSION FOR MORE THAN FOUR HOURS AND FORTY FIVE MINUTES. She says she told them NOTHING. THIS COMMITTEE DOES NOT KEEP PEOPLE ON THE STAND FOR SUCH A LONG PERIOD, UNLESS THEY SAY SOMETHING. ARE WE TO BELIEVE DOROTHY'S WORDS ON THIS TO THE PARTY? WE DON'T BELIEVE HER STORY. . . . DO YOU???? ■ anonymous leaflet produced and distributed by the FBI at a Communist Party meeting on October 3, 1958. [According to an FBI memo dated October 15, 1958, "the success of this operation [should] be taken into consideration by the LAO [Los Angeles FBI office] in submitting its justification for commendation of the Agent supervising the Counter-intelligence Program" in Los Angeles.]

My opponents from the national office decided that their best bet was to line up behind Bill Taylor, with whom I had long-standing differences. Taylor ran against me for the post of district chairman. An alliance of convenience was formed between the national office crew and a leftist tendency in the Party that included some people who would eventually split off to form the Progressive Labor Party.

Though they raised the issues of "white chauvinism" and "revisionism" against me, their challenge proved unsuccessful. Weinstock and the others could not understand why Ben Dobbs and I didn't organize our own caucus. Here they were running around, holding private meetings and electioneering, and we were simply carrying on with Party business as usual. But we had been in the district leadership for fifteen years. We were a known quantity. If people wanted us, they'd vote for us; if they didn't, they wouldn't. We found that even among those sections of the Party where the disagreements with our approach ran the deepest, as in the case of the 1905ers, there was a kind of grudging admiration for the fact that we kept the Party so busy. We were certainly one of the most active districts all through the 1950s and 1960s, involved in all kinds of issues. We provided a framework of activism that reminded people of why they became Communists in the first place. I think that at some level even the hardest-liners knew that with a more ideologically "correct" leadership, there was going to be a falling off of that kind of activism. And I think that many Communists, even our critics, were pleased that we brought the Party as much visibility as it enjoyed in Los Angeles.

[It's] interesting to learn that Mrs. Dorothy Healey, party chairman here, is in difficulties with the national leadership and some local Red talent.

National Commie bosses are reportedly sour on our home-grown Mme. Defarge because she didn't enthusiastically endorse the murder of Imre Nagy in the Hungarian massacres. . . .

Mrs. Healey happens to be one of the very few female Reds who doesn't look like an irrefutable argument for celibacy. . . . As long as unappetizing

frumps resent gals who don't curdle milk, she'll create dissension.
■ " 'Haybag War' Rends Red Junta," Los Angeles *Mirror*, 1958.

Around this time I started appearing regularly on television talk shows, usually the kind where the moderator is a neanderthal right-winger who makes a speciality of insulting his guests. In Los Angeles Tom Duggan pioneered that kind of show on Channel 13. Only an ultrareactionary would dare to invite a Communist to appear on his show; a liberal would have been driven off the airwaves for doing it. I always enjoyed those shows. They were very free-swinging debates. The commentators would try to make me lose my temper, mixing personal insults in with their political comments, but after all those years of debates in the CIO Council I knew the wisdom of never losing my temper with enemies, only with friends.

I felt it was important to appear in public whenever asked, to end our pariah status. Most Americans had never seen a Communist, and it's so much easier to hate the unknown than the known. The first time I went on Duggan's show my son was off with some of his high school buddies playing poker. When I got home he mentioned to me some point I had made in the show. I said, "How'd you know about that if you were playing poker?" He said, "Oh, I made them stop playing and watch it." Remembering all that he had gone through a few years earlier I asked, "Richard, why did you do that?" I thought he was going to lose yet another set of friends because of me. But he replied, "How often does someone's mother appear on television? Of course I made everyone watch it. Everybody liked you." It's a strange thing about American culture how notoriety can shade off into celebrity, and Richard's comment made me realize it was beginning to happen to me.

In 1959 KPFK, an affiliate of the Pacifica radio network, began broadcasting in Los Angeles. The Pacifica Foundation, which had been started by a group of pacifists who had been imprisoned during World War II, launched its first FM station in 1946 in San Francisco, KPFA. Throughout the 1950s KPFA had played an important role in the Bay Area as a center of alternative culture and politics, offering programs of jazz and folk music and the kind of radical news analyses that you simply couldn't find on any commercial radio station. It was a sign of the changing political climate when at the end of the 1950s and the start of the 1960s Pacifica was able to open up two new stations, KPFK in Los Angeles and WBAI in New York City. A few months after KPFK went on the air, its station manager Gene Marine asked if I would be interested in doing a regular program. I jumped at the opportunity. It started out as a fifteen-minute program known as "Communist Commentary" (after I left the Party I changed the name to "Marxist Commentary"). Fifteen minutes is a very hard slot to fill. You can't afford to waste any time, so you can't be very informal: when I started, I just filled the quarter-hour by reading a written statement. Before long the show became quite popular, even in that cramped format, probably because the times were getting so interesting and people wanted to hear what a Communist would have to say about the civil rights movement, the peace movement, and so forth. For awhile we tried to rotate the job of doing the broadcasts among other leading Los Angeles Communists: Ben Dobbs and Nemmy Sparks took turns with me. But Gene told us we were losing our audience, because people wanted a greater degree of continuity when they tune into that kind of program. So we decided that I should take it on as a full-time responsibility.

As the show became more popular it was moved to Sunday morning (a prime listening time for a station like KPFK) and enlarged to an hour. I think my chief competitor for ratings on KPFK was a show telling people how to fix their automobiles. The new format gave me a lot more freedom to vary the style of the program. Sometimes I would do interviews with people, sometimes I would just give my own views on some question of topical or theoretical interest, but the most popular part of the show was when I would take telephone calls and answer questions or get into arguments with the people who called in. I knew, both from the calls and from the letters I would receive afterward, that much more than just the Left listened to the show. When I talked about why I was an atheist I got a bulging mailbag full of replies from outraged fundamentalist Christians. I always remember one letter I got out of that controversy which began, "Dear Mrs. Healey: I wonder if you realize what trouble you're in? If I'm right about there being a God then when I die I'm all right. And if you're right about there not being a God, then when you and I die, we're both all right. But if you're wrong, and I'm right, then when you die, boy are you in trouble."

There was a phrase that Communists habitually used about the necessity of "showing the face of the Party." In Los Angeles, it was my face that was shown most often; my voice that was heard. Our members were used to it, they liked it, and they expected that I would continue to play that role, however much the national office would have liked to undermine my leadership.

> In the pre-convention period, everyone united in criticizing the leadership for failing to report on past differences in leading committees. Today, many are unhappy at hearing such reports. They say: leave the national debates back in New York, and let's discuss only our local problems. But ours is a national party, and one area or another cannot solve its problems by hiding the nature and content of the status of the national Party. ∎
> Dorothy Healey, "On the Status of the Party," *Political Affairs* (March 1958).

I always had to juggle my local committments with the demands of fighting for the minority position within the National Board and National Committee. I never doubted it was something that had to be done, distasteful as it got to be. I could not understand those Communists who could show such courage in fighting outside the Party against anything that could be thrown at them—FBI harassment, Smith Act trials, physical attacks—and yet could not tolerate being in the minority in the Party. The more I learned about it, the more I was intrigued by the kind of socialization process that goes on in the Party, a revolutionary organization which trained people for conformity, where you value the opinions of your peers within the party more than your actual ability to influence anyone outside the Party.

I remember a discussion I once had with Rose Chernin, who in private conversation could offer absolutely scathing judgments of Party leaders, but who would seldom stray beyond the safest platitudes in Party meetings. I said to her, "Rose, you're such a frank woman. Why when you get up at district committee meetings do you always lard your speeches with phrases like 'as our general secretary says.' Why don't you say in public what you say to me privately?" And she said, "Dorothy, you simply don't understand the Party. If once in a meeting you're heard questioning or challenging the leadership, you will never be trusted after that. Everyone's going to say 'Ah ha! Keep an eye on her.' You just won't be included in the 'inner family' of the party if you do that." She was absolutely right. But I was unable to do it. Here again the big influence was my mother, who never tried to be more than a dedicated rank and filer in the Party and who retained a healthy measure of the old Wobbly suspicion of leadership. When leaders walked out onto a platform at a big Party meeting they would inevitably be greeted with a standing ovation before they spoke. Mama would never rise. I asked her once, "Why don't you stand?" And she said, "Why don't they stand for people like me? We're the ones who keep this party going. We raise the money, sell the literature, carry out the assignments." That left a big impression on me.

10

[T]he late Elizabeth Gurley Flynn, a longtime CPUSA official, once remarked that Healey was a good leader in her District but was afflicted with a psychosis when she attended national meetings, because she insisted on challenging the leadership. ■ FBI memorandum, August 6, 1969.

I had seen many women in the Party who worked very hard and were intelligent and developed theoretically and politically, but I hadn't seen anyone with quite Dorothy's energy and charisma. I do remember very clearly certain Party conventions that I was at in the sixties where I saw her as the "embattled female." It was like this sea of cigar smoke, and she smoked these little cigarillos, and there was something about that, her being little, and she'd barge into these circles of men conversing on something or other, whatever caucus it was, she'd barge in there, and I just loved it. I thought that was great, just great. I didn't care what she said. ■ Bettina Aptheker.

In 1959 Gus Hall was released from prison. Hall was the son of Finnish immigrants in Minnesota who had been charter members of the American Communist Party. He joined YCL in the late 1920s, worked as a CIO organizer in steel mills in Ohio in the 1930s, and after his service in the navy during the war, he joined the Party's national leadership. He was one of the Foley Square defendants and wound up serving five years for his Smith Act conviction and an additional three years for having jumped bail.

Because he had been in the navy during the Teheran period and in prison during the de-Stalinization crisis, Gus had not been forced to take positions during those contentious times that would have antagonized one or another tendency in the Party. After his release from prison he began to travel around the country, ostensibly on vacation, but in reality to line up support for a bid to replace Gene as general secretary. Gus can be a very charming man when he wants to be. He and his family stayed in our house for two weeks while he was politicking. At a meeting of our district board we told him bluntly that to us the decisive question facing the Party was establishing its independence from Soviet direction. We would never acquire the capacity to really understand our own country as long as we were under the tutelage of the Soviet Union. "Not only do I agree with you," he said, "But as a matter of fact I'm convinced that for the Soviet Union's own good we have to maintain our independent outlook."

When Gus Hall first came out here in '59 he charmed me completely. Oh yes! And he was so self-critical. "We're going to have a critique of the Soviet Union. They should have checks and balances, oh, absolutely." Just lied like a bastard. Dorothy and I were completely behind him. ■ Ben Dobbs.

All of us were very impressed. We were also concerned by charges he made about Gene Dennis. Gus accused him of cowardice and violation of Party discipline for failing to go underground as ordered in 1951. (Dennis was, in fact, supposed to have joined Hall and the others in the underground, but apparently there was some mix-up involving a clandestine meeting, so when the time came to surrender to federal authorities he had no choice but to do so.) Gus also accused Gene of financial irregularities in handling funds for the underground, the implication being that he had appropriated Party money for his own use. I should have known better than to believe him, but it just didn't occur to me that he would deliberately spread what proved to be false and scurrilous tales about Gene.

A TOUGH LADY RED is giving the U.S. Communist Party a facelifting and a new confidence.

She is the mysterious mastermind behind the recent dumping of Kremlin-approved Eugene Dennis as boss of the Red movement. . . .

She hand-picked Gus Hall, a hardened but flexible-minded Red, to become the American "Khrushchev."

Who is this generally unknown woman who staged a successful internal revolt in the face of hopeless odds, and is furthering Red aims behind a deceptive "new look"?

She is Mrs. Dorothy Healey. . . . ■ Jack Lotto, "Lady Behind New Red Look," *New York Journal-American*, January 30, 1960.

We gave Gus a sympathetic hearing, though not an endorsement. Later on I learned that when Gus continued his national tour he went around telling people that the Los Angeles district board was in full support of his becoming the new general secretary. At the "showdown" meeting of the national secretariat where Gene finally gave in, Gus told the other Party leaders that I was backing him. A few years later, after a horrendous National Board meeting when Gus and I were at dagger's point with each other, Claude Lightfoot came up to me and said, "Gee, I don't understand why you and Gus are always quarreling. After all, you're the person who put him into office."

At the Party convention in December Gene acquiesced in Gus's election as general secretary to avoid a knock-down fight. Gene was given the post of party chairman, which is supposed to carry coequal weight with that of the general secretary. But he was already very sick and wasn't even able to attend the convention. A five-member secretariat was set up to run things in the national office, consisting of the general secretary and the chairman, along with Ben Davis, James Jackson, who was now editor of the weekly *Worker*, and Hy Lumer, who was serving as the Party's educational director.

This was a moment of generational transition for the Party. My generation, though decimated by the de-Stalinization crisis, was coming to power in the Party. Gus was part of this generation but was an unlikely representative of it. Although Gus had briefly held the post of acting general secretary in the early 1950s when Dennis was imprisoned on a HUAC contempt sentence, I don't think many people in the Party regarded him as a major contender for leadership until 1959. Once, in the early 1960s, I heard Gus himself acknowledge his own surprise at finding himself in this position. I was standing with Gil Green and Henry Winston at a birthday party being given for Elizabeth Gurley Flynn. Gus came over and after some casual conversation said completely out of the blue, "Who would have ever believed that I would be the one on the top, instead of you two guys? You were the important ones in the YCL, not me." The two of them just stood there, looking at him, and neither said a word.

Many of the older leaders were dying off. Gene died in 1961. Foster, Ben Davis, Jack Stachel, V. J. Jerome, Clarence Hathaway, and Elizabeth Gurley Flynn would all be gone by the mid-1960s. Flynn succeeded Gene as Party chairman. She was the first woman to be elected to that post. She had been a compromise candidate; Ben Davis was also campaigning for it and many people in the Party, including a good section of the Black leadership, were terrified by that prospect. Liz seemed the best alternative.

Elizabeth enjoyed a very positive reputation in the Party. When she rejoined in the 1930s (she had been a member briefly and secretly in the 1920s), she moved directly into the top leadership. She didn't need to adopt that fierce demeanor that was required of other women who were battling their way up in the hierarchy. She was genuinely concerned about people in a way that most Party leaders were not. Whenever I went to New York I would try to visit her down in the Chelsea Hotel, where she lived. She was worth listening to for her political views and because she had very acute opinions of her coworkers in the national office and wasn't afraid to express them. She adored Gene Dennis but was always very critical of Foster. Evidently the antagonism went back many, many years. She wasn't taken in by all the glamour of his heroic past as a union organizer. After all, she had her own credentials which were at least as impressive as his. She was very effective in the role of a public face for the Party, as well as a link with the historic past of the Wobblies, the "Bread and Roses" strike in Lawrence, and the free speech fight in Spokane. She had a remarkable ability to speak in plain language before a large audience and establish immediate rapport. That was something that the old-time agitators in the Party had, people like Flynn and Foster, and Clarence Hathaway, much more than my own generation. But over time I developed very mixed feelings about Liz. In Party meetings she was always very careful not to say anything unacceptable to Gus or to the Soviet Union. She was worried about me and the bad end to which my politics would lead me.

Flynn died in 1964 in Moscow, where she was visiting when she fell ill. Foster also spent his final days in Moscow. On my first trip to the Soviet Union in 1961 I went to visit Foster in a sanitarium shortly before his death. He asked me, "How's the party in Los Angeles?" I said, "Oh, it's improving." And he replied, "You have nowhere to go but up," which was certainly true. Then he asked me about Celeste Strack, who was one of the California Party leaders who had resigned in 1958. He was very fond of Celeste. And he said in a kind of sad voice, "Well, we are losing some very wonderful people, irreplaceable people." I was surprised to hear him say that, considering the attitude he had expressed at the end of the party's sixteenth convention.

Gus and I got off on the wrong foot almost immediately. It wasn't my "revisionism" in any abstract sense that made Gus dislike me so. The real problem was that my political differences led me to challenge the prerogatives he claimed as general secretary.

Naive as always in these matters, I was slow to shake off the initial impression I had gained of him in 1959. After a National Committee meeting in 1960 I went up to him privately and said that I was disturbed by the way the sessions had gone. I thought he would welcome my observations, that maybe he wasn't aware of what was happening. I told him that he had made a mistake in choosing to give all the reports to the National Committee; every single meeting had consisted of a two- or three-hour report by him. And I warned him that he was surrounded by sycophants in the leadership who had nothing but praise for anything he said. That could prove dangerous to his own judgment. The way things were going, I told him, "If you said 'the sun rises in the east,' someone would stand up and say, 'What an original thought. Nobody ever thought of that before.' " He didn't say a word in reply; he just flushed a deep shade of purple. I don't think he ever forgave me for that remark.

Gus was not the first person to occupy the post of general secretary of the American Communist Party who was swept away by a vision of his own brilliance. That had certainly been true of Browder. You needed a certain amount of self-regard to pursue the office in the first place, but there was something about holding the post for any length of time which transformed normal vanity into something quite different. There is an atmosphere surrounding the general secretaryship in most Communist Parties around the world with which I'm familiar such that the occupant of the position would have to be a very special kind of person not to feel that he is the repository of all wisdom. The main exception I know of to this rule is the Italian Communist Party, where since Togliatti's time people with dissenting views have been included in Party leadership as a matter of course. In most Communist Parties, everyone defers to the opinion of the general secretary, no one challenges him, and you only have mock debate. General secretaries never have to test their ideas in an atmosphere of genuine controversy and challenge. So how could they be expected to retain any facility for critical judgment and thought? That this remains true down to the present is a measure of how little the Communist movement has done to throw off the effects of Stalinism and return to the original promise of its Leninist origins. People forget that Lenin was a staunch advocate of Party democracy, even though it often worked against him. Time and again Lenin was voted down by his colleagues in the leadership of the Bolshevik Party, but he never tried to purge his opponents.

The general secretaryship of the Communist Party is usually a lifetime sinecure The internal power dynamics of the Communist Party at the top are more akin to feudalism than socialism. The general secretary is the lord; he surrounds himself with loyal vassals, each in charge of a minor fiefdom which is his to keep as long, and only as long, as he enjoys his lordship's continued favor. When things proceed smoothly, the lord doesn't interfere with the minor fiefdoms surrounding him. So the editor of the *Worker* could run it as he saw fit, and the various district chairmen could run their own local operations as they saw fit, as long as they didn't rock the boat, which was a great incentive for staying on good terms with the general secretary. There are all kinds of subtle and not-so-subtle ways in which Gus has learned to reinforce his power. There are extra funds available for vacations for Party leaders, and he gets to decide who gets those. When Party delegations are made up to travel to the Soviet Union or Cuba, his choices will get first priority. If you want to publish a book Gus can make it very easy for you to do so, through International Publishers or by finding you a ghost-writer if that's what you need. It's a very effective patronage system. And it's worth noting that Gus Hall has been in leadership longer than any other American general secretary. Most Party members don't remember any other leader, and there is now a generation of "Hallites" in the Party, just as there were once Browderites and Fosterites. I knew young people in the Party in the 1980s who would come back from a national convention and say, "Oh my God, I sat right next to Gus Hall at a meeting!" Gus is not without charm, but he's just not *that* thrilling a personality. The glamour with which the post of general secretary had been imbued swept people away.

I wouldn't want to give the impression that I was totally alone in standing up to Gus. Jim Allen, the head of International Publishers and always one of the abler thinkers in the Party leadership, had little respect for Gus from the very beginning. And there were others who would probably prefer not to be singled out. Sometimes I found allies among people I previously had written off as hopeless hard-liners, such as Bob Thompson. I regret that a lot of people who left the Party in the de-Stalinization crisis never knew about the enormous change in him in the 1960s. All their memories were of the intransigent Fosterite Bob had been in the years when, along with Foster and Davis, he had presided over the Party's repudiation of Browderism. George Charney's description of Bob in his autobiography as "a man of inexorable will, who viewed hesitation or doubt as signs of fatal weakness," is representative (and accurate as far as the period he was describing). Bob's training was certainly a hard one. He had attended the Lenin school in Moscow, fought and been wounded in the Spanish Civil War, and won a Distinguished Service Cross for his exploits in the South Pacific during the Second World War. He was convicted in the Foley Square trial, spent two years underground and then five years in prison, where he was attacked by a right-wing prisoner who fractured his skull with an iron pipe. After he got out of prison in 1960 he underwent a profound transformation. He was appalled by many of the things he saw in the Soviet Union on a trip there in the early 1960s and impressed by what he saw of the Italian Communist Party after a trip to Italy. We became close friends. And as he opened up to me, he told me how much he regretted the role he had played in the years just after the war. Bob had been absolutely devoted to Foster, so I was astonished when he told me that it was tragic that Foster had not died ten years earlier than he did, because then he would have been remembered as a hero of the party rather than as the man who had done so much to damage it.

> [Bob Thompson] was a man of indomitable courage and single-minded purpose. This was his strength, but it also proved his undoing, and ours. It was an inflexible, Stalinist strength that could be ruthless, that relied on sheer power more than argument and persuasion. ■ George Charney, *A Long Journey*, p. 137.

Among other things prodding Bob to reexamine his ideas was his disgust at what Gus was doing as general secretary. Bob had been a hard-liner, but he had never been a conniver, which was what you had to become if you were going to get along under the new regime. He wouldn't be a part of it, and as a result Gus hated him with a passion—perhaps more than he hated me, if that's possible. One incident in particular stands out in my mind. There was a national board meeting in 1964 sometime after the Gulf of Tonkin bombings. Gus had obviously gotten some kind of signal from Moscow, because he went out of his way to criticize the Vietnamese Communists for their failure to compromise with the United States. They were too intransigent, their slogans were not the proper ones, and so forth. (The Soviet Union was not eager to see the Vietnam War turn into a major conflict.) Bob was fit to be tied and tore into Gus for what he was saying. He could not understand how the leader of a Communist Party in a country that was in the midst of attacking another country would dare to presume to dictate tactics to the Party that was under attack. He knew exactly what Gus was up to, and why, and he was outraged by it.

Betty Gannett underwent a similar transformation. She was a very intelligent and gifted organizer. She was also probably one of the most unpopular people in the Party, particularly among other women. The things that made her so unpopular were not simply a product of her personal idiosyncrasies. Almost all women leaders acquired a certain abrasiveness, because the only way you could be heard was to talk louder and more assertively than the men. When someone wanted to insult me, they would say that I was the "Betty Gannett of the west"— the designation suggesting that, like Betty, I was an impersonal "unfeminine" character.

> Ours is, I believe, the only district where many women are in one or another leading post. Their absence in any important number is notable both nationally and in the states. I was asked by a national visitor whether the fact that I was a woman accounted for the presence of other women in responsible posts. My first reaction was to say: what nonsense, I don't even think about it when it comes to making recommendations on leadership. But that almost involuntary reaction is in itself significant; it is quite probable that with the dominance of male supremacy in our culture, men comrades may react as involuntarily in the opposite direction. ■ Dorothy Healey, Report to the Southern California District Convention, June 12, 1966.

If any man had had one-tenth the ability Betty had he would have been on the national secretariat from the beginning, but she was always relegated to subordinate positions. The only time she was on top was in the period of the the underground when she and Pettis Perry were left in charge of the open national leadership. After the trials and the underground period, she was bumped back downstairs to become editor of *Political Affairs*, which was not a particularly highly regarded post. She always resented the male supremacy at work in the Party, although it wasn't until shortly before her death in 1970 that she was able to define it for what it was.

> Certain kinds of articulation and assertion which are tolerated in men, and even celebrated in men, are not accepted in women. I think women like Dorothy were patronized (this applied to a number of women, like Peggy Dennis, who was basically seen as the difficult widow, a classic female role.) When there was political disagreement, it took the form of patronization, which is extremely irritating, really hard to deal with. . . . If you tried to raise "personal" issues in the Party, they were seen as trivial. "Why are you arguing about the dishes?" I wouldn't be surprised if informally within the Party there were "women's caucuses," private meetings where women tried to figure out how to sustain personal relationships with men or whatever. But what women lacked was any validation that what they were saying was anything more than being personally "cranky." ■ Bettina Aptheker.

I often found myself in disagreement with Betty, sometimes very sharply as in the white chauvinsim campaign of the early 1950s when she wreaked a lot of havoc. But I always had great admiration for her. In the last years of her life I saw her change. She started to question the Party's attitudes toward people outside its ranks and its undemocratic practices within its ranks. But this new understanding came to her very late in her life. I remember a meeting of the national board in 1969 just before the national convention. This was the meeting where Party leaders were supposed to engage in self-criticism, summarizing the mistakes and shortcomings of their stewardship of the Party in the years between conventions. Jim Tormey, Betty's husband and a member of the Party secretariat, said that he wanted to raise two very disturbing questions in regard to the way that Gus functioned as general secretary (that was very remarkable; I had never known Jim to show that kind of audacity before). The first criticism he made concerned the way that money was being handled in the Party. In the past, there had always been some leader other than the general secretary who took care of the Party's financial business, but Gus chose to handle certain funds himself. Jim thought that was improper. The second issue he raised, which turned out to be a tactical mistake, was the fact that when Gus was out of town the secretariat could not function. Everything had to wait for Gus to return because they didn't dare make a decision in his absence. Sitting next to Jim at that table was Henry Winston, who as national chairman ran the secretariat in Gus's absence. And that was Jim's undoing, because to suggest that Winnie, who was Black, did not have equal authority with Gus, who was white, left Jim open to the charge of "white chauvinism," and all of Gus's supporters on the board just piled onto him. The issue of how Gus handled money got lost in the melee. Betty was sitting opposite me at the meeting. For some time she had been suffering from throat cancer and had pretty much lost the use of her voice. She got redder and redder. I thought she was going to explode just from having to hold her feelings in. That was the last time I ever saw her.

We were taken in 2 limousines to Moscow and then to our hotel. It's brand new and beautiful. I have a bedroom and living room and bathroom—it's really charming. . . . This is a place reserved for visiting delegations—everyone should only have it so good. We feel like heads of state. ∎ letter from Dorothy to her mother, April 27, 1961. [The CIA intercepted and opened all of Dorothy's letters to her mother sent from the Soviet Union.]

In April 1961 I went with six other American Communist leaders to the Soviet Union. It was the first "official" delegation to go since before the Second World War and hence was treated as a big deal by both the American and the Soviet Parties. Before we left we were briefed by Gus, Jim Jackson, and Helen Winter. The big thing they said to us, I suppose mostly for my benefit, was that we were to remember we were guests. I remember the expression they used: "Don't look under the rug to see whether there's any dirt swept up." In every delegation, even if it only consists of two people, there has to be an official chairman. That's very important in the world movement, because whoever becomes the chair is automatically considered a dignitary, the one who makes the speeches or responds to toasts at banquets, and that sort of thing. As a matter of course, the person designated chairman is the one who holds the highest Party office. On this particular delegation that should have been me, because I was the only one there who was a member of the National Board. That, of course, was unthinkable, because who knows what I might have blurted out at some big official shindig, so Arnold Johnson, who was a member of the National Committee, was named instead. I received the designation "responsible secretary," which in the jargon of the Soviet Union and other parties abroad implies someone with political clout. It caused a lot of headaches for the Soviet comrades in terms of just what the proper etiquette was. Because both Arnold and I had titles we always got the largest suites in the hotels we stayed at, while the others had to make do with single bedrooms. This went on for two months, and I needled the young woman, Gali Udina, who accompanied our tour and with whom I became good friends, about the absurdity of it. "Why do I and my title need more rooms than my poor comrades without titles?" Gali would sometimes share my two- or three-room suite at my insistence. When we got back to Moscow at the end of two months, in the middle of a heat wave, they gave me the tiniest, stuffiest room in the hotel, as if to say, "Okay, comrade, this is what you want, this is what you get."

I live at such a dizzy pace I don't have time to write. Yesterday was the Big Day—following the parade we had a party, then went to the Bolshoi Ballet. Today the subway, then a soccer game and then the Belshoyza dancers. Tomorrow, the Kremlin, etc. ■ postcard from Dorothy to her mother, May 2, 1961.

We saw a lot of the Soviet Union: Moscow, Leningrad, Stalingrad, Georgia, Azerbaijan. Every time we went to a factory, a collective farm, or a city soviet, we would immediately be shepherded to a groaning banquet table. That's what happens with every delegation—it's the Soviet conception of how to show hospitality to visitors. It's also a good way to keep you so preoccupied with seeing things and meeting new people that you don't really have time to think or look or analyze or hear anything. It was overwhelming and exhausting after the first few days.

There's no doubt [Leningrad is] the loveliest city—its relationship to Moscow is much like L.A. to S.F.! After a massive breakfast (including 5 vodka toasts!) we went on a sightseeing tour, then to the Hermitage Museum, a quick dinner and then to a new ballet. ■ letter from Dorothy to her mother, May 7, 1961.

I wish there were a 7 hour day for delegations. . . . ■ letter from Dorothy to her mother, June 7, 1961.

This was, of course, seeing socialism through a limousine window. I was aware at the time that this meant that there was much concealed from us. I was critical of the way that we were shepherded around, and I was critical of some of the things I did manage to discover on my own. But there were also things about the Soviet Union that were genuinely impressive. People who think of life in the Soviet Union as just a dreary totalitarian prison are being deceived. The Soviet Union has known an immense amount of tragedy and suffering, some of it due to the decisions of Soviet communist leaders, much of it due to the hostility of the nonsocialist world. And in the years since the war, life improved dramatically for most Soviet citizens. In the factories we visited we were impressed by the cultural and educational programs that were provided for the workers. Factories would have their own libraries, and they were obviously very well used. In every city there was an enormous amount of space devoted to parks, and in the parks they would have free theater, and concerts and puppet shows for the kids. We also visited a session of what was called a "comradely court." These served as an adjunct to the regular legal system and dealt with what would be classed as misdemeanors in the United States. Instead of having your case heard before a judge, you'd go before a court of your peers, elected from a particular work place or neighborhood, and they would essentially be used to bring the weight of public opinion to bear on issues like drunkenness, wife beating, or child neglect. In the Soviet Union, which is so top-heavy with bureaucracy, here at least was one small example of the "withering away of the state" which Marx had predicted.

That was one side. But there was another side that I found more disturbing. In the factories we visited there was certainly no problem of "speed-ups." There were very few supervisors, and the place of work was very leisurely—so much so that it was easy to understand why the Soviet Union has been faced with a continuing problem with low industrial productivity. There is a big difference between a working class whose basic attitudes have been shaped by capitalism—where the first lesson to be learned is that if you don't work hard, you get fired—and a working class that has gone directly from a preindustrial rural existence to socialism. Soviet workers have never had a chance to internalize that capability for sustained and regular hard work which was developed over several centuries in the western industrial world. They know that they aren't going to get fired for poor work, and no other material or socialist incentive for sustained hard work had been devised other than a kind of heavy-handed reliance on propaganda exhortation which didn't do the trick.

When I saw it, the Soviet Union was in many ways still a very backward society. When the Soviet state applied itself to an issue, as it did to the question of keeping the streets and parks clean, it could put the West to shame. We never saw litter scattered about as you would in Los Angeles or New York. But when you got behind the scenes it was a different story. I was struck, in the factories, and particularly on the collective farms, with the complete filthiness of the toilets. At one of the collective farms we visited—a very beautiful farm—there was a banquet table set up outdoors about ten feet away from the most primitive outdoor privy imaginable. The flies were swarming around it and then coming over to investigate the food on the table. I mentioned it to the local minister of health, and she said that she knew of no instance of sickness that came from this lack of proper sanitation, which I found hard to believe.

I brought it up again later with one of the people from Moscow who was accompanying our delegation, and he said, "You must understand that we are responsive to the pressures of our people. Historically they've never known modern methods of sanitation. It's not a priority for them. We get pressure on other things. And we allocate our social funds where the pressures are." I didn't accept that either. Why do you have a Communist Party if not to provide education about what steps were needed to provide for the common welfare? I got the same response when I asked Party officials why the Soviet Union had just reinstated the death penalty for economic crimes. "The people demand it. We are acting in response to the mass demand by people who are outraged that socialist property is being stolen." I replied that I was glad that the people were indignant, but shouldn't the Communist Party convince them that capital punishment was a barbaric vestige of the past and that rehabilitation rather than punishment might be a preferable strategy? That just got me blank looks.

But just before we left Moscow, Gali asked me to go outside and then told me that her mother—a veteran of the 1905 Revolution—agreed with me about capital punishment.

Another thing I noticed in the Soviet Union was that while the formal equality of men and women is guaranteed, real equality was absent. Time and again we'd meet with the leaders of a factory or a collective farm or a soviet, and they would all be men—despite the fact that there was a large female majority as a result of the disproportionate number of men killed in the Second World War. After one all-day meeting in Stalingrad, when once again we had only met with men, I said to our guide Gali, "Where are the women?" She said: "Dorothy, why don't you understand that women have children, and when the children get sick the women have to stay home and take care of them. We can't have our leaders taking time off to take care of children." I looked at her in amazement. "Gali, children have fathers, too. Maybe the father should stay home when they get sick." She was nonplussed; the idea had never crossed her mind that this was not automatically a woman's responsibility.

Finally, it was obvious that as a society like our own that was made up of many different racial, ethnic, and religious groups, the Soviet Union had not solved problems of discrimination and prejudice. John Pittman, who was the *Worker*'s Soviet correspondent, visited me while I was staying in the Party hotel in Moscow. He told me how the Soviet comrades had asked him to travel around the country in order to write a pamphlet on the solutions they had found to the "National Question." When he finished the trip, however, he was unable to write the pamphlet because he found no such solution. Instead, he was appalled by what he described as the "Russification" going on in the various Soviet republics. One of the leaders our delegation met with in Moscow was M. A. Suslov, a member of the ruling presidium of the Soviet Party. In response to our insistent queries about the treatment of Jews in the Soviet Union he said: "There is no longer a Jewish Question in the Soviet Union. We have solved it; now, there are only the Soviet people." Jack Kling, a member of our delegation who spoke Yiddish, would come back to us after a day spent in various cities talking to Soviet Jews, horrified by the widespread examples of anti-Semitism they told him about. On his return to the United States, however, he not only refrained from any criticism of Soviet anti-Semitism but actually spoke in terms reminiscent of Suslov's position.

In mid-June I left the Soviet Union for Bulgaria, where I saw my stepfather Fedya for the first time since his deportation in 1956. He had set off with such eagerness, but now I found him a sadly disillusioned man. He took me to one neighborhood of fancy homes with barred windows and said, "That's for the Red bourgeoisie, that's where they live." And he showed me shops where only the Party leaders could buy goods. Things like that just broke his heart.

So without making much effort but just by asking some simple questions I did get a look at some of the dirt under the rug. Still, I could understand why so few foreign Communists who visit the Soviet Union come back disappointed. None of us were used to much luxury or honor in our own country, but in the Soviet Union we stayed at the best hotels, we never had to worry about our luggage getting lost, we were wined and dined and given all these private conferences and briefings. Wherever we traveled a doctor accompanied us, just in case one of the precious American comrades developed a cold or a stomachache. All this can go to one's head very easily. And most corrupting of all is the little thought that I suspect creeps into the back of some people's minds, "If I can just stick with it long enough, then perhaps all this will someday be mine to enjoy back home as well."

One of our number who was clearly swayed by all the attention being lavished upon us was the delegation chairman, Arnold Johnson. Arnold was a kind of political valet for Gus, an old-time Party leader who knew Gus from the 1930s when they both worked in Ohio, part of the "Ohio gang" Gus brought with him into the leadership. In the Soviet Union Arnold was overwhelmed with a sense of self-importance. As chairman he gave all the speeches for our delegation at these banquets and meetings, and he would just glow as the translators spoke in Russian (which he did not understand) after he was finished. The rest of us just suffered through his grandiloquent speeches. One day on board the *Aurora*, the revolutionary battleship which had fired the first shot at the Winter Palace in the Bolshevik revolution, Arnold went all out in a ludicrous display of self-regard. Some of our dismay and embarrassment must have shown in our faces, though none of us, of course, said anything. That night Gali and another Soviet comrade who was accompanying us knocked on my door, and the man said to me, "Comrade Dorothy. Tell your comrades not to be upset about your comrade Arnold's speeches. We don't translate what he says, anyway."

When I went to Moscow I looked up all my mother's friends. She met all kinds of people. I spent the most time with Freda Lurie, a woman who was one of the high cultural people, Deputy Secretary of the Writers Union, who was friends with Sartre, Camus, and Simone de Beauvoir. She was very critical, very honest with me, about what was wrong. And yet she still believed she had a right to read that stuff and other people didn't. I was outraged by that. And then I broke off from the tour and went to Bulgaria to see my grandpa. I stayed with him for a couple of weeks. Sofia was very repressive. The streets were clean, but there were guns and soldiers everywhere. It was not hard to pick up on what life was like there. So I came back to the U.S. much more critical. There was no way I was ever going to join the Party. I told my mother my reactions, and she agreed. It was at that point I started asking her why did she stay in the Party. This was '63, '64, and she'd say, "Look at the young people joining, look at the fights going on, we can win, we can change the Party." ■ Richard Healey. [Richard toured the Soviet Union after visiting the Communist-organized World Youth Festival in Helsinki in the summer of 1962.

A new decade brought new opportunities. In the United States things began to move very quickly in 1960. The southern student sit-ins of February and March, the sympathetic response they received in cities and campuses across the North, and the demonstration by thousands of students against the House Un-American Activities Committee when it came to San Francisco in May all signaled a qualitative change in the political climate, at least among young people. The Communist Party had been greatly weakened in the decade just past and had all kinds of internal problems, but as the sixties began we looked forward to rebuilding our movement. In Los Angeles, where we had bottomed out at about five hundred members in the late 1950s, we began to see young people join again. We felt as though we had survived the worst setbacks that could possibly befall us and could now reap the rewards due us for our patience and endurance.

> Woe unto the aging who insist on superimposing their memories, their concepts, their blue-prints on a new generation, for they shall be rejected. ■ Dorothy Healey, "Old leftie relates to the new lefties," *Los Angeles Free Press*, January 23, 1970.

Not surprisingly, there was a tendency in the Party to look back to the 1930s as the great revolutionary model from which all lessons about how to build and develop movements should be drawn. The events of the 1930s were formative ones for my generation, and it was people my age who were in charge in the Party by the time the 1960s rolled around. But the start of the 1960s was a reminder, not always heeded by my comrades, that history was constantly offering up new lessons and new models. In retrospect it is obvious that something had been going on beneath the surface of the so-called silent generation of the 1950s to have produced this eruption at the start of the 1960s. I've seen many people committed to social change, even many Communists, whose training and tradition constantly stresses the need for the "long view," grow discouraged in times of reaction. Either they don't look beneath the surface to see the kind of tensions inherently present in society that can and will erupt, or they keep looking desperately for the wrong kinds of signals and portents.

> No other generation has grown up with the threat of nuclear annihilation hanging over them. No other grew up under the whiplash of McCarthyism. And, no other grew up in a period when the adult movement was not a powerful, growing, and stabilizing influence upon it. . . . ■ Dorothy Healey, Report to the Southern California District Convention, June 12, 1966.

Take the case of Caryl Chessman, who after being convicted for rape had spent eleven years on death row in San Quentin and who by no stretch of the imagination could be called a political prisoner. Because his case was so protracted, it began in the late 1950s to attract the attention of a small group of opponents of the death penalty. Suddenly in the spring of 1960 his plight grabbed the interest and enlisted the sympathies of Berkeley students, and hundreds of them stood vigil every day asking the governor to grant clemency. When Chessman was finally executed, it proved an important milestone in the radicalization of the early New Left, confirming what they already suspected about the inhumanity and impersonality of the justice system and bureaucratic politics. The Party had no involvement in the case; it would not have occurred to us to have gotten involved in a case of this sort where there was no direct question of racial or class oppression. We thought in terms of what we remembered from Sacco and Vanzetti or the Scottsboro Boys, and Chessman didn't fit that model. But there was something about his case that spoke to the concerns of young people. The real lesson there was that almost all great movements are spontaneously generated. They rarely come as a result of someone sitting down and thinking, "This is how we'll build a movement." Real political leadership lies in being able to understand the significance of these events as they appear and then deciding, "Well, where do we go from here? Here is a new movement, what do we do with it?"

[Y]ou have [Party] youth clubs and then you have DuBois clubs. And 90% of your youth during the height of the DuBois clubs were in the DuBois clubs and you would meet in your Party clubs and decide policy and then you would meet in your DuBois clubs and discuss the same policy and the discussions would be already dry and flat. And you would have your position already and the people coming into the organization who were not in the Party felt they were being "used." They were in to watch a debate that had already taken place. ■ Jim Berland, "Report to the District committee and Youth Panel," Southern California pre-convention *Discussion Bulletin*, March 1969. [Jim Berland was active as a young Communist in Los Angeles from 1964 through 1969, when he left the Party. He later went on to become station manager at KPFK.]

The Party's hostile attitude toward the New Left was probably the greatest political liability we had to contend with in the 1960s. Our muddled response to the new opportunities opening up in the early 1960s was not only a question of organizational inefficiency, although that was part of it; it also reflected a political estimate made by the national office. Gus regarded the New Left as a distraction or a threat to our own political prospects rather than as a fertile field for our young people to work in. (The Progressive Labor Party, which originated as an ultraleft "Maoist" split-off from the Communist Party, was not so squeamish; by the end of the 1960s they had grown very influential within Students for a Democratic Society—to the complete detriment of SDS.) Gus's notion was that we should create our own youth organization, controlled by the Party but not explicitly Communist in its politics. For all practical purposes, that strategy kept us isolated from the most significant outbreak of youthful radicalism in thirty years. By 1964, when the Party got around to organizing the W. E. B. DuBois Clubs, we had decided in southern California that the main focus for our young members should be within SDS, which had already established itself as the most significant group among white radicals on campus. Only in Los Angeles, Boston, and a few other places did Communists go into SDS in any systematic way. In most places young Communists found their time and energy drained by the burden of staffing and maintaining their separate "mass" organization.

Healey's only child, Richard Erle Healey, . . . attended forums sponsored by the CPUSA when he was only 13 years of age. In 1962, while a student at Reed College, Portland, Oregon, he attended the Eighth World Youth Festival, an international communist affair, in Helsinki, Finland, and also toured the Soviet Union and East Germany. In 1963 and 1964, he attended and participated in W. E. B. DuBois Club meetings in Berkeley, California and Portland, Oregon. In 1965, he was a participant in a demonstration in Portland, Oregon against the Subversive Activities Control Board. He has also been a leader and spokesman in demonstrations protesting United States policy in Vietnam. ■ FBI memo, August 6, 1969.

The DuBois Clubs had all the disadvantages of a group clearly tied to the Communist Party, yet it wasn't free to act as though it were a Communist youth organization. It was supposed to be a mass organization but never found any masses interested in joining. If the DuBois Clubs ever grew to be much more than a thousand members nationally, I would be very surprised. Its one great moment came in the spring of 1966 when the Subversive Activities Control Board labeled it a Communist organization, and there was a sudden influx of students who wanted to join as a gesture of either solidarity or irreverence. But the clubs' leadership had no idea of what to do with this opportunity and made no permanent gains from its brief popularity. In northern California the DuBois Clubs played a modest role in civil liberties struggles, but in the rest of the country they served very little purpose, except perhaps as the temporary organizational home for some "red-diaper babies." Richard went to some DuBois Club meetings but never joined. Richard was more active politically than the children of almost all of my contemporaries. There are a few very well known examples of the children of Communists who went on to become Communists themselves, like Herbert Aptheker's daughter Bettina—though she wound up quitting the Party in the mid-1970s. But there were some children of Communist leaders— like Gus Hall's own kids, for example—who would have nothing to do with their parents' politics or the Left in general.

> In junior high school I rebelled against things like going to mass meetings. I got sick of people coming up to me and pinching my cheek, and saying, "Ah, little Ricky, when are you going to follow in your mother's footsteps?" A little of that goes a long way when you're thirteen. I liked parts of it, like the singing. I also enjoyed going to my friend Bonnie's fundamentalist church for that reason. Same spirit. Sometimes even the same songs, with different lyrics. ■ Richard Healey.

Richard went off to Reed College in Oregon as a freshman in 1960. I gave a deep sigh as he departed, one part concern, the other relief. This was the first time in so many years I could just be myself. I wasn't a wife, I wasn't a mother. I could just concentrate on doing what I needed to do. I think that's when I became absolutely convinced of the virtues of living alone. While Richard was at Reed I made the mistake of sending him a book on the fundamentals of Marxism-Leninism edited by the old Communist International leader Otto Kuusinen, which had just been published in an English-language edition in the Soviet Union. It was being touted as the definitive work on the subject. Richard promptly sent the big volume back to me, saying that any book starting with the quotation, "Marxism is omnipotent because it is true—Lenin," was not worth reading. It didn't bother me that he had no interest in joining the Communist Party; in fact we were entering a period when I would take more of my politics from him than he would from me.

> Reed was one of the earliest schools to have a hippie influence, and already by 1960 there were beards and sandals. I became active immediately in the demonstrations supporting the British antibomb marches, all-night vigils for peace. I remember arguing that men had to shave, women had to wear dresses, their hair had to be up, we had to look respectable to appeal to a broad constituency. The photographers from the local paper, the *Oregonian*, would always run pictures of a demonstrator with a beard, with a caption like "Fuzzy face, fuzzy mind." What I called my "mass approach in cloth-ing" was something that came out of the Old Left. Even during the height of the sixties I was never a cultural eccentric. It was too deeply ingrained in me, you want to look like other people, don't do things that make your politics harder to get across. Finally about '65 we managed to get a march in which everybody looked impeccable, and the *Oregonian* ran an editorial saying that these Reed College kids spend so much time worrying about their clothes that they obviously aren't serious about their politics.
> ■ Richard Healey.

I had always pushed Richard to concentrate on the hard sciences in his studies, despite the fact that my own interests in school had been in history and literature, because I figured his livelihood would not be as likely to be jeopard-ized for political reasons as it might be if he was a teacher in the humanities or social sciences. After he graduated Phi Beta Kappa from Reed College in 1966 with a BA in mathematics, he went on to Tulane University for graduate study on a National Science Foundation fellowship. When he got to Tulane he dis-covered that his fellowship had been canceled, partially because of his political activities at Reed, but mostly because he was my son. The FBI had leaked the news of the fellowship to their pet newspaper columnists.

> The third day I was at Tulane my mother called to say I had gotten a telegram saying my fellowship was pulled. I go see the dean of students, and he's a fascist. He says you're a liar, you're a Communist, and I want you out of this school. So I go see my department chairman just to say good-bye. I tell him the whole story. He says, "Son, don't you worry, I will get you money, I will keep you in this school, and if you don't get money I'll get you into Harvard with money." I later asked him why he did this for me. He had been at the University of Michigan in '53 when Chandler Davis had been kicked out of the mathematics department for refusing to testify at a HUAC hearing. He had vowed that that would never happen in his department. ■ Richard Healey.

Richard appealed the decision to the Department of Health, Education and Welfare, which was the granting authority, and after a hearing in Washington the examining board decided to restore his grant. I found it a remarkable decision. The HEW hearing officers decided that it wasn't fair to hold Richard guilty by association with his mother's politics, and that his opposition to the Vietnam War, which he explained was based on the principles established by the Nuremberg trials, was a legitimate position for him to hold. Who could say whether the future would not validate his judgment? Their ruling reinforced my own sense of how complex American political institutions are in their functioning: here was one branch of the government displaying no scruples about employing the lowest kinds of dirty tricks to punish Richard for his background and beliefs, and here was another branch of the government deciding, in the middle of the Vietnam War, that Richard was entitled to his beliefs because the U.S. government might eventually be found guilty of war crimes.

> The following comments are furnished relative to the possible effects of a news story which if published will imply that a fellowship for study at Tulane University was awarded in payment for information furnished to the government by _____and DOROTHY HEALEY, Chairman, Southern California District Communist Party (SCDCP).
> It is not believed that such a newspaper article would jeopardize DOR-OTHY HEALEY's position as Chairman, SCDCP, as far as the Party on the West Coast is concerned. . . . There has been no wavering of the loyalty of the membership of the SCDCP to HEALEY. . . . GUS HALL, General Secretary, CPUSA, has indicated from time to time that he is displeased with HEALEY but has done nothing about it. . . . Consideration of the news sources in Los Angeles who would consent to publish this fabricated story reflects that there are one or two who might consider the printing of such a story. However, it is the feeling of the Los Angeles Division that on this particular story little of counterintelligence accomplishment could be achieved. ■ FBI memo, November 30, 1966.

Our ability to recruit new members, young or old, was not helped by the fact that until 1966 we did not hold any open meetings under our own name. During all that time we were involved in the struggle against the McCarran Act. The McCarran Act, also known as the Internal Security Act, was the major piece of McCarthy-era legislation which survived the gradual liberalization of the political and judicial climate in the late 1950s. Its most notorious provision authorized the Justice Department in the event of a loosely defined national emergency to round up people judged to be "security risks" and hold them without benefit of trial or normal legal rights, along the lines of the Japanese relocation during World War II and in fact making use of the same camps. The act's constitutionality was challenged in the courts, and some of its provisions were held unconstitutional by the Supreme Court. But one of the clauses that did survive required leaders and members of "Communist-action organizations" to register as agents of a foreign government. Because this judicial legacy of the early 1950s affected only the Communist Party and not the Left as a whole, many people in the 1960 and too many historians since have assumed that McCarthyism was dead and buried by the time John F. Kennedy took the oath of office. The dividing line between two political eras is not that neat. It was a liberal Democratic administration under John F. Kennedy that enforced the decision of the liberal Supreme Court under Earl Warren upholding the registration provisions of the decidedly illiberal McCarran Act. Despite the radical truism that the courts follow the election returns, it is sometimes the case that laws and court decisions reflecting the priorities of one era will have an impetus that carries them over into a very different era.

"Unable to send [Dorothy Healey] to prison as a criminal, the government is trying to send her to prison for failing to register as a criminal," Abt said. ■ "Hearing Seeks to Prove Party Officer a Red," *Los Angeles Times*, November 8, 1962. [John Abt, lawyer for the Communist Party, defended Dorothy in her appearance before the Subversive Activities Control Board.]

In 1962, along with thirteen other Communist leaders nationwide, I received a letter from Attorney General Robert F. Kennedy ordering me to register as a member of a proscribed organization. In separate proceedings Gus Hall and Ben Davis were ordered to register as leaders, and the Party itself was indicted for violation of the McCarran Act. In November the Subversive Activities Control Board came to Los Angeles, where it was proved to the board's satisfaction that I was indeed a Communist and thus subject to imprisonment and fines if I did not register with the government. "The only surprise" in the hearing, as a pamphlet we put out on the case declared, "was what vast machinery it takes and what considerable expense is required for the government to make public what was already public." I had no objection to telling all and sundry that I was a Communist; what I objected to was being required to register with the government as a member of a "Communist-action organization," which was defined in the Subversive Activities Control Act as "an organization which in effect is a participant in a world-wide criminal conspiracy under the control of the Soviet Union to destroy the Government of the United States by espionage, terrorism, sabotage, and other violent and criminal means." To register as a Communist would mean accepting the definition of Communism promoted by these McCarthyite laws, and that I was not about to do.

"So you gave a fund-raising affair for "The People's World," you invited people to come to your house, is that it?"
"Yes sir."
"And you fed them coffee and cake, I suppose?"
"Not always a cake, sometimes a good pie."
"And then you would report all their names to the FBI, is that right?"
"That is correct."
"And you did the same thing with the Independent Progressive Party affairs, is that right?"
"Yes sir."
"You would say to people you know, 'Why don't you drop around tomorrow night? I am having an affair for the IPP,' didn't you?"

"Only such people I knew would be interested in such things."

"So they came and you would turn their names in to the FBI?"

"That is correct." ■ cross-examination of Lulu Mae Thompson by John Abt at Subversive Activities Control Board hearing, November 7, 1962. [Thompson joined the CP as an FBI informant in 1953 and remained a member until March 1962. She received a stipend of $225.00 a month for informing.]

The notion behind the McCarran Act would have been laughable if it were not undertaken with such complete cynicism. If we were a bunch of spies, terrorists, and saboteurs, were we likely to single ourselves out for arrest by obeying the McCarran Act? If the Soviet Union wanted to maintain a conspiratorial fifth column in the United States, the last place it would recruit its agents would be within the ranks of the Communist Party, since it was no secret that the FBI kept tabs on virtually every single one of its members. The whole point of the registration law was to make the Communist Party illegal without having to own up to the fact that constitutional rights to free speech and free association were being tossed into the trash can. So here we were in the early 1960s, just barely past the trauma of the Smith Act trials, once again faced with a legal challenge to our very existence as an organized political movement. Given our experience with the *Yates* appeal, we had some hope of ultimate vindication. But in the meantime our political rights continued to be curtailed.

County college trustees stood by their guns yesterday and refused to cancel the appearance of Communist leader Mrs. Dorothy Healey on the Ventura College campus tonight.

At the end of a 3½ hour emotion-packed session, the board left its speaker policy unaltered. This gives a student-faculty committee the authority to approve speakers. . . .

Said R. V. Leis, Ventura: "They (the students) are breaking the hearts of their parents and of those boys who are dying overseas (by insisting on having a Communist speaker on campus). If this is education, I'm glad I'm dumb!" . . .

Ralph Cook, minister of the Unitarian Universalist Church [said]: "The college has a special function. By the practice of freedom of speech it is educating the community. We must not teach our young people to run and hide from controversial ideas."

When Rev. Cook asked: "Who is to decide what is dangerous?" a voice from the back of the room said: "The FBI!" ■ "Red Speaker on Campus Ok'd After Hot Session," The Ventura County *Star-Free Press*,

Another battle we had to fight—and that in the end we won—was for the right to appear as invited speakers on college campuses. In December 1961 I was invited to speak at UCLA by a group called PLATFORM, which was a student political party similar to the better known SLATE at Berkeley. Since 1951 no Communist speaker had been allowed to appear at any of the UC campuses, and the Regents reaffirmed that ban to keep me from speaking at UCLA; it wasn't until 1963 that it was finally lifted. One of the main arguments advanced in the editorial pages of the Los Angeles *Times* and elsewhere against allowing me to speak at UCLA was my refusal to register under the provisions of the McCarran Act. When I finally did get to speak on campuses again, I usually felt I had to begin my speech by talking about the McCarran Act. The bulk of my speeches would always be about pressing contemporary issues like civil rights and Vietnam, but I couldn't ignore the civil liberties question. If the Party often seemed hung up on old issues in the 1960s, as our critics on the New Left charged, it wasn't always our own fault.

The McCarran Act hearings sparked a debate within the Party, with a faction led by Milt Rosen (who later organized the Progressive Labor Party) insisting we had no alternative but to dissolve and start over secretly and underground. That position was rejected out of hand; too many of us still had vivid memories of our underground misadventures in the 1950s. The Party leadership came up with its own two-pronged strategy, which was put into effect. Part of it was quite sensible. We would refuse to register and then fight the issue through the courts. This was not a decision to take lightly, because there was a cumulative penalty of five years in prison and a $10,000 fine for each day you refused to register, which could add up to a life sentence and a lot of money in a short time, but we thought we could win. I spent two months in New York in 1964 organizing a national campaign against the McCarran Act, meeting with people from churches and civil liberties groups and journalists, and finding a very sympathetic response in general. A lot of people were beginning to feel it was time that the country put this embarrassing legacy of McCarthyism behind it.

The part of the leadership's strategy for countering the McCarran Act that caused us problems lay with the decision to curtail public activities until the issue was settled in the courts. That turned out to be a very long period, because it wasn't until 1965 that the Supreme Court finally reconsidered its earlier decision and found the registration provision to be a violation of the Fifth Amendment guarantee against self-incrimination (it was, by the way, the third time I had been involved in a case appealed all the way to the Supreme Court, each time successfully). Some of the measures taken to protect the Party were of little consequence. We no longer used official titles: I was now described as a "spokesman" rather than as chairman of the Los Angeles district. National Committee meetings were now described as "legislative conferences" and other euphemisms. But other measures were more harmful. The Party decided that its clubs would no longer function as official Party organizations but would instead consist of "readers' groups" of the *Worker* or the *People's World*. It was a little silly, because if the government decided that it really wanted to arrest Communists, it wasn't going to let the distinction between club and reading circle stand in its way. Worse than that, the organizational changes loosened the bond of identification that kept our members loyal to the Party. They stopped paying dues, they stopped meeting regularly, and many just drifted away. In southern California we were able to hold down the losses, because instead of instituting the new policy as a blanket measure we tested it out first on our lawyers' club and one industrial club. Within six months we could see its disastrous potential and went back to our regular form of organization. But we still had to be very cautious about holding publicly identified Communist meetings, which was particularly frustrating in a time when political opportunities were expanding.

One of the worst consequences of the nearly five years in which we operated under the constraints imposed by the McCarran Act was that we were unable to hold a national convention in all that time. It was only in a preconvention discussion that all of the disagreements and debates within the Party leadership could be brought before the membership in a systematic way. Of course in the past it often didn't work the way it was supposed to, but the preconvention discussions before the 1957 and 1959 conventions were very open and democratic, and we hoped they had set a precedent for the future. Without those Party-wide discussions, there was just no way to hold the leadership accountable. We didn't hold another national convention until 1966, following the Supreme Court's reversal on the McCarran Act. I think it was in that long interval between conventions that it dawned on Gus and the others in New York just how easy life would be for them if this became a more or less permanent state of affairs. In the 1970s they succeeded in rewriting the Party constitution so that instead of having to hold a national convention every two years, the normal interval between conventions was expanded to a full four years.

> Al Richmond's report on the Italian Party Congress in *Political Affairs* describes how, long before the national convention opened, the membership of the Party had been fully involved in prolonged debate on questions of policy and inner-party life. This was an example of inner-party democracy and democratic centralism as it should be. Ours is an example of how it should not be. ■ Dorothy Healey, Report to the Southern California District Convention, June 12, 1966.

In my report to the southern California district convention in 1966 I had to cover a lot of territory, because a lot of disagreements had piled up in the meantime. I made a serious error in Party etiquette in the very first paragraph of the report when I paid tribute to "the courage of our membership [and] its determination to defend the principles of Marxism-Leninism and the Bill of Rights," during the McCarran Act struggle. When we got to the national convention later that year the whole southern California delegation was called before the secretariat. They demanded that we repudiate my report, which had been passed with only two opposing votes in our district convention. They were furious, of course, over the criticisms the report offered of national policies, but the very first thing they found objectionable was that opening paragraph. "How dare you start off a report acclaiming the heroism of the membership and make no mention of the leadership of Gus Hall during this period?" Within the Party and in the international movement it was a virtual reflex for Communists to begin their remarks with praise for the "brilliant and inspired leadership" of Comrade Hall, or Comrade Khrushchev, or whoever the particular general secretary happened to be. To depart from that custom already marked you off as unreliable, no matter what else you had to say afterward. The FBI, ever alert for opportunities to do mischief, ran an advertisement in the *Los Angeles Free Press*, the local underground newspaper, offering copies of my report to the district convention, describing it as "Banned by the Communist Party National Secretariat."(It wasn't, in fact, "banned"—although when some young Communists from Los Angeles brought copies to a national training school run by the Party in New York, they were confiscated.) Readers were asked to send fifteen cents in stamps to "Ivanova," care of the *Free Press*. Those unfortunate enough to do so had their names entered into the FBI files, but the main point of this charade was to convince the national office that I was actively organizing a cabal against them. When I saw what they were up to I put my own ad in the paper offering a free copy of the report to anyone who wrote directly to me. The national leadership, typically, fell for the FBI bait, believing that I had inserted the original advertisement. Henry Winston sent me a letter asking me to "repudiate" the report, which, of course, I refused to do.

> Los Angeles is authorized to place the advertisement . . . in the local left-wing newspaper "Free Press" using a Russian-speaking Special Agent and the Russian-speaking experienced clerk you recommend. If the newspaper should ask for identification of the persons placing the advertisement, be prepared to furnish the names and addresses of appropriate local Communist Party members. Choose members who would be compromised should the Party check back on the ad. . . . Los Angeles and New York should be alert for other methods of distributing this report that make it appear dissidents within the CPUSA are responsible. This suggestion by Los Angeles appears most imaginative and should have disruptive results.
> ■ FBI memo, January 3, 1967.

Although the "inner Party struggle" looms large in my memories of the sixties, the bulk of our time and energy was devoted to more valuable pursuits. The Party, for example, played a central role in the peace movement in southern California, particularly through the Peace Action Council. Irving Sarnoff, who initiated the group, was a very dedicated man who had been active in the Railway Brotherhood. In Los Angeles, the Peace Action Council was the primary source of education and mobilization during the war in Vietnam, and Communists were an accepted part of the anti-war coalition. I think I attended almost every demonstration held against the war in the city, including the one at the Century Plaza Hotel where Lyndon Johnson was greeted by tens of thousands of protesters. That demonstration was broken up with incredible police violence. I was also at the Chicano moratorium demonstration on the east side, which was the largest anti-war demonstration in the history of L.A., where Reuben Salazar, columnist for the Los Angeles *Times*, was murdered by the police when they attacked the peaceful marchers.

In my campus appearances I always talked about Vietnam. At an appearance at UCLA in 1963, as the U.S. was just beginning the escalation of the war, I quoted from the plaque to the British soldiers at the Concord, Massachusetts, battlefield, "They came three thousand miles to die to keep the past upon the throne," and I said that's what we Americans were doing in Vietnam. I also used the word "imperialism" to describe what we were doing there and ended the speech with the slogan "Bring our boys home alive!" Some of my younger comrades were very critical of me afterward, saying that using such language made me sound like a middle-aged relic. No one but Communists used a word like "imperialism," and young people would never respond to a slogan about bringing the boys home. It wouldn't be too long before such language was the common currency of antiwar rhetoric; in fact is was pretty mild stuff compared with what was to follow. It was a lesson in how quickly political moods can change, and with them the concepts and language which are considered acceptable.

> The problems of taxation are integrally involved in all serious social and economic problems in our country. An example: our illegal and immoral war in Vietnam costs the taxpayers millions of dollars. This drain increases public and private squalor in our land. ■ Healey for tax assessor campaign flier, 1966.

Freed at last from the burden of fighting the McCarran Act, the Party in Los Angeles decided that I should run as a candidate for public office, which was a first for me. So in the spring primaries in 1966 I entered the race for county tax assessor. Bill Taylor had run for the county board of supervisors the previous year; other than that race, no one had campaigned for public office in Los Angeles as an open Communist since the late 1940s, when Henry Steinberg had received 55,000 votes running for a seat on the board of education. We put out two buttons for my campaign, one which said "Vote for Dorothy Healey for a radical alternative," and the other which said "Vote for Dorothy Healey, Vote Communist." We sold them to raise money for the campaign; unlike most campaigns, this one didn't cost the Party anything because we made it a principle to raise all the money for it from outside sources. The buttons cost fifty cents each, but when we discovered how popular the "Vote Communist" one was, we raised its price to a dollar.

I didn't appear on the ballot as a Communist candidate, because it was a nonpartisan race, but all of my campaign literature noted that I had been a Communist since 1928 and listed my role as a Party leader as one of my qualifications—along with the more conventional items of campaign biography, like the fact that I had been a homeowner in south Los Angeles for the past twenty years. I don't think that there was anybody in Los Angeles who owned a television set or subscribed to a newspaper who didn't know exactly who I was and what I stood for, because of my appearances at college campuses and on television debate shows. I made headlines right at the start of the campaign thanks to Howard Jarvis, who sued to get my name off the ballot. Jarvis was an oldtime anti-Communist crank, president of the right-wing California Republican Assembly and close to the John Birch Society, who in another decade would become famous as the organizer of Proposition 13, the conservative tax initiative.

He filed suit on the grounds that as a Communist I had no right to sign the loyalty oath that was required to run in the election. He said that should I be elected county assessor I would be a great security risk because I would gain access to information about defense industry contracts in the county. The loyalty oath I had to sign was a relatively innocuous one that didn't mention the Communist Party by name but simply said that you were not an advocate of the violent overthrow of the government. I had no problem with that. As for defense contracts, overlooking the obnoxious implication that the only reason I sought public office was in hopes of acting as a Russian spy, all the information I would have access to was a matter of public record. In any event, after a week of hearings before Judge James Tante of the Los Angeles Superior Court, during which time the news that Dorothy Healey was running for tax assessor was the lead story every night on the news, Jarvis's complaint was thrown out of court. The Judge said he knew of no law prohibiting Communists from running for public office. Jarvis did us a big favor in obtaining publicity we never could have afforded to purchase.

I didn't know much about property taxes at the time I decided to make the run, but I did an enormous amount of research, aided considerably by Charles Kramer, and learned how it was that poor homeowners paid a higher percentage of the property tax than wealthy homeowners. I proposed that low-income families be exempted from the assessment rolls, that low-income elderly tenants receive a 25 percent rebate on their rents, and that assessments on business and industrial property be increased to make up the difference. I appeared before dozens of audiences, including some which were basically front groups for the John Birch Society. I got a very sympathetic hearing from otherwise conservative homeowners, and the Property Owners Association met with me privately to hear what I had to say, even though they wouldn't endorse me publicly. By this time I had become a kind of local institution, and I think I got the votes of a number of people who had simply stopped thinking of me only as a Communist and instead voted for me as Dorothy Healey, the local troublemaker. In this instance familiarity bred a measure of acceptance, or at least an absence of the fear and loathing that is usually elicited by the label "Communist."

Dear Mr. Watson:

The following information is being brought to your attention as a matter of possible interest to the President.

Semiofficial returns in the June 7, 1966, primary elections in Los Angeles County, California, disclosed that Dorothy Healey . . . received an impressive 86,149 votes in an unsuccessful effort to become Los Angeles County Tax Assessor.

Although this was a nonpartisan election, Healey openly proclaimed her connection with the Communist Party and distributed hundreds of pins with the designation "Vote Communist." Her total of 86,149 votes is the highest number received by a Communist Party member in a public election in the past 16 years.

The fact that Healey was able to receive over 86,000 votes tends to substantiate recent public observations by Gus Hall. . . . He has boasted that the greatest mass upsurge in history is currently taking place and that communists are being increasingly accepted and listened to by noncommunist groups. Hall cited this as a symbol of the emerging "legality" of the Communist Party achieved by "certain victories over the McCarran Act."

This information is also being furnished to the Attorney General. . . . ■ letter from William Sullivan, head of the FBI Intelligence Division, to Marvin Watson, Special Assistant to Lyndon Johnson, June 15, 1966.

I didn't win, nor did I ever dream I had a chance of doing so. But when the polls closed I had received over 86,000 votes, more than any Communist candidate had gotten in an election in the state since the 1930s—more, in fact, than Earl Browder had received nationally as the Party's presidential candidate in 1936.

> President Lyndon B. Johnson called. He stated he saw on the ticker an item regarding "Puerto Ricans" and proceeded to read the following:
>
> "The FCC said today it is looking into a report that a Spanish-speaking announcer for a radio station in Chicago urged Puerto Ricans to join the riots that erupted in the city earlier this week. . . . "
>
> The President said that in line with the report he read last night about the woman in Los Angeles, he wished my man in Chicago would take a good look at this and see if anything like that did happen and he would like him to keep his ears open.
>
> I told the President I would take care of it right away. ■ memo from J. Edgar Hoover to "Mr. Tolson, Mr. De Loach, Mr. Sullivan, Mr. Wick" in FBI headquarters, June 16, 1966.

These were encouraging if not exactly earth-shaking results: I came in third, in a field of four, with 5.6 percent of the total vote. But that was enough to send off alarm bells ringing all the way to the Oval Office, where Lyndon Johnson was being kept apprised on "the woman in Los Angeles" by J. Edgar Hoover. This was the only occasion that I can think of that the Left in California waged a public campaign on the issue of taxes—an issue which, unfortunately, we all but ignored afterward and thus ceded to the Right. Howard Jarvis's success with Proposition 13 in the late 1970s turned out to be one of the key events paving the way for the arrival of the "Reagan Revolution" in 1980.

11

At UCLA during the Cambodia strike there were these mass meetings where thousands of people would be there. I remember one where the leader of the Black Student Union spoke. And he gave a harangue against the Soviet Union, and against the Communist Party, against the Communist youth on campus, he quoted Stalin, I think he even mentioned Dorothy by name as a revisionist, all this kind of stuff. Afterward I went over to Dorothy's house to talk over with her what had gone on, and there he was. He was getting advice from her, asking her what to read. She was his teacher too. ■ Terry Kupers.

Comrade Dorothy,
 . . . We won the case contesting my solitary confinement, so my spirits are especially high at the moment. I should be moved into population sometime soon—there are some truly beautiful sisters behind these vile walls.
 I love you all. What I would do to be able to talk to you now, Dorothy.
 Love & Power,
 Angela   ■ letter from Angela Davis
                                       to Dorothy, November 5, 1970.

Ronald Reagan's march to victory in the 1980 presidential election began in California in the 1960s. Unlike many on the New Left, and even some of our own comrades elsewhere, the Party in Los Angeles never made the mistake of underestimating the potential danger of the far Right. The early 1960s saw the emergence of the John Birch Society as a significant force in southern California politics. From the perspective of radicals in other parts of the country the thunder on the sun-belt Right may have seemed like it was coming from a marginal bunch of kooks, but I had debated those guys often enough that I had no illusions about the seriousness of their intentions or their potential. In the 1960s Birchers and like-minded conservatives went into the Republican Party and moved it dramatically rightward while building up their own independent organizational strength outside the framework of electoral politics. It was, ironically much the same strategy we had attempted to carry out (with less success) vis-à-vis New Deal Democrats in the 1930s.

The central fact that must be recognized in any discussion of political tactics today is that Goldwater's nomination in 1964 pushed all politics to the right. . . . The Ultra Right is working for a political realignment on its terms, based upon the appeal to hysterical anti-Communism and to the "white backlash." ■ Dorothy Healey, review of Irving Howe's *The Radical Papers* in the *Yale Law Review*, July 1966.

The Republican primary battles in California in 1962 foreshadowed the Goldwater presidential nomination of 1964, just as Goldwater's campaign led to Reagan's rise to power, first in California and then in national politics. Three Republican congressional nominees in 1962 publicly identified themselves as members of the Birch Society. All three went down to defeat in the fall election, as did Richard Nixon in his race for the governor's seat against the incumbent Democrat Pat Brown (which prompted Nixon's famous promise to the press, later reneged on, that "You won't have Dick Nixon to kick around any more"). On the surface, liberals had much to cheer about in those results, but in fact they marked an ominous new development. From here on, in order to win a Republican primary in California, a candidate would have to satisfy the ideological demands of the far Right.

Traitors Beware

See the old man at the corner where you buy your papers? He may have a silencer equipped pistol under his coat. That extra fountain pen in the pocket of the insurance salesman who calls on you may be a cyanide gas gun. What about your milk man? Arsenic works slow but sure. . . . These patriots are not going to let you take their freedom away from them. . . . Traitors beware! Even now the cross hairs are on the back of your necks.

Minutemen

■ printed card
sent anonymously
to Dorothy in 1965.

The Communist Party remained an obsession to the far Right in the 1960s, despite our great reduction in numbers and influence. In January 1962 a bomb exploded in the ground floor doorway of the building that housed the Party office in Los Angeles, demolishing a tobacco shop on the ground floor but sparing our office, which was on the fifth floor. Fortunately no one was hurt, but our lease was canceled after the bombing and it didn't help us any when we tried to rent new office space in later years. My living room functioned as the de facto Party office after that, which I was never happy about. When people come to see you in your office, they know you have other responsibilities, so they do their business and leave. When they see you at home, there is a more informal atmosphere, and business meetings had a tendency to turn into more lingering personal visits.

The phone used to ring at Dorothy's house all the time. People were always there. I've never ceased to be amazed at the different kinds of people with whom Dorothy had a close working relationship, or at least a relationship where they would come to her to use her as a sounding board or to ask her advice. Sometimes it got to be too much for her. She'd call me and say, "Call me at two o'clock and say you need me to pick you up at the airport." So I'd call and she'd say, "Hello," and I'd say, "I'm at the airport." "You are?" And we'd go through the whole charade. She'd hang up and say to whoever was there, "I have to pick up Donna at the airport," and so they'd leave. That was her way. She just could not say no to people. ■ Donna Wilkinson. [She was a member of the Communist Party in Los Angeles from 1966 through 1974.]

We faced another threat that year in the form of Proposition 24, an initiative measure on the fall ballot which would have amended the state constitution to outlaw the Communist Party. When a similar bill had come up before the state legislature the previous year, civil libertarians managed to bottle it up in committee, so its supporters tried to get it passed as an initiative measure instead. The initiative had few respectable supporters; even Richard Nixon came out in opposition on the grounds that it was so patently unconstitutional that it was bound to be thrown out by the courts. The measure went down to defeat that fall by a two-to-one vote, but again it was a measure of how the Right was beginning to bring its own issues to the fore, even if it meant opposing the established Republican Party leaders.

One cannot issue ultimatums to the worker or the Negro or the Mexican-American that he should promptly cease and desist from his allegiance to the Democratic Party. Nor will he learn this solely through the education provided by independent candidates (as we learned from the Progressive Party). . . . ■ Dorothy Healey, "California Ends the Nixon Era," *Political Affairs*, February 1963.

In an article I wrote after the election, with the somewhat premature title "California ends the Nixon era," I celebrated the defeat of Proposition 24 and that of the three Bircher congressional nominees. But I warned against complacency, pointing out that "the ultras have become an *organized* sector of the Republican Party." I took issue with those on the Left who derided the Nixon-Brown race as a meaningless choice between two cold warriors and defenders of capitalism. I had been through all this before, starting with the Upton Sinclair EPIC campaign in 1934, and then again with the Progressive Party campaign in 1948. I felt that the mistakes we had made in the past might have some value and meaning at long last if we were able to use the lessons they provided to prevent the Left from once again falling into the same sectarian traps. The question of whether there was any point in supporting a "lesser evil" candidate would come up repeatedly in the next few years, and never with greater long-term significance than in the 1966 gubernatorial election, which pitted Brown, running for a third term, against Ronald Reagan.

One of the most important lessons Dorothy taught us was what it really meant to govern, that is, what the effect of who was governing was in a practical sense. She talked from her own experience. She had been appointed as a deputy labor commissioner by Culbert Olson. She'd talk about all these boards and committee assignments and judges, you know, the real stuff where the social tilt comes from, and how important that was. It wasn't irrelevant who was elected. ■ Jim Berland.

When Reagan was nominated in 1966 by the Republicans it marked a qualitative turn for the worse in California and national politics. Now the Right was not simply an organized force within a major party but had actually gained control. Johnson's landslide victory over Goldwater in 1964 had not discouraged the ultra-Right, but only increased its determination to dig in for the long haul. A defeat for Reagan in 1966 would not have ended the Right's hopes for ascendancy—Lyndon Johnson had seen to that by tying the albatross of the war in Vietnam around the neck of Democratic liberals—but it might have spelled an end to Reagan's prospects as a Republican standard-bearer. And without Reagan as its amiable front, the Right would have had a great deal more difficulty in selling its agenda to the country in the 1980s. A lot more rode on the 1966 elections than just the question of who would be running things in Sacramento for the next four years.

It's time for a change. You can sense it. Or, you can read about it any day of the week in the newspaper.

Beatniks, taxes, riots, crime, delinquency, drug addiction, pornography. Our state is a leader in *each* of these areas . . .

Common sense . . . says helping those who are unable to help themselves does not include taxing hard working men and women who are busy providing for their own families, in order to provide for lazy freeloaders who make welfare a way of life.

Common sense wouldn't allow a few rabble-rousing malcontents to totally disrupt the campus of one of the greatest educational institutions in the world. . . .

VOTE FOR REAGAN-FINCH TEAM ON NOVEMBER 8!

■ Reagan campaign flier, 1966.

There were good reasons for the Left to be critical of Pat Brown. He had taken a crude "law and order" position in opposition to the Berkeley Free Speech Movement in 1964; he was a loyal supporter of the war in Vietnam; and most recently he had engineered the removal of Si Casady, the leader of the California Democratic Council (CDC), because of Si's opposition to the war. Nevertheless, in terms of appointments and policies, his was a generally progressive administration and was responsive to pressures from his Left. In the primary race, Brown was being challenged from the Right by my old acquaintance Sam Yorty, mayor of Los Angeles. The Party's strategy, which I think was a good one, was to support Carlton B. Goodlett, the Black publisher of the San Francisco *Sun-Reporter*, in the primary race. We thought of the Goodlett candidacy as a way of increasing pressure on Brown from the Left, so he wouldn't be tempted to make too many Right-leaning gestures to potential Yorty voters. When Brown, as expected, won the primary, we argued that liberals and radicals should swing behind him to forestall the obviously greater threat represented by a Reagan victory.

> Dorothy Healey actively encouraged all CP members to attend the Statewide Conference on Power and Politics. . . .
> She outlined the policy to be followed by CP members at this conference as:
> 1. Convince the conference participants that a boycott of the November 1966 California election will only serve to elect Republican candidate Ronald Reagan who is a member of the extreme right.
> 2. To show the danger of the extreme right.
> 3. To prevent the adoption of a resolution that a boycott of the election be conducted. The participants of the convention must be shown that although the Communist Party favors Governor Edmund G. Brown, it does not mean that they actually support his policy but that it is the only way to prevent candidate Reagan from gaining control of the State of California.
> 4. Try to unite all forces with a view toward the selection of candidates for the 1968 election.
> ■ FBI memo, January 3, 1967.

There were other important political developments that spring. Bob Scheer, an editor of the New Left magazine *Ramparts*, mounted a very well-organized antiwar campaign in the Seventh Congressional District in Berkeley and Oakland, which was then represented by the Democratic Congressman Jeffrey Cohelan, who was a hawkish liberal. Scheer's campaign was endorsed by CDC, one of the reasons why Brown had turned on Si Casady. Cohelan also had the strong backing of the White House but was only able to win the primary by a very narrow margin of victory. Scheer's ability to draw 45 percent of the vote in a campaign against a prowar incumbent was one of the factors that persuaded liberal activists in the Democratic Party that Johnson was vulnerable in the 1968 presidential election. It also helped pave the way for Ron Dellums's later successful run for that Congressional seat. There were clear parallels between Scheer's achievement, what Upton Sinclair's EPIC campaign had done in 1934, and what we had been doing through Labor's Non-Partisan League in the years leading up to Culbert Olson's victory in 1938.

> There were a few Party people and a lot of old Progressive Party people in this group called Californians for Liberal Representation. It was a mass outreach vehicle, and its strategy was to select districts where progressive coalitions could be built and good candidates could win. I was hired as staff person to organize [CLR's] '66 conference. It was without question the most

broadly representative grassroots coalition that had been established since the thirties. The liberal and radical leadership from every community that you could envision—teachers, Chicanos, Blacks, liberal Democrats, peace groups—was there. Everything went pretty smoothly until the floor fight over the issue of whether to boycott the election. ■ Jim Berland.

By the time I first encountered Robert Scheer, at the Conference on Power and Politics in East Los Angeles in September 1966, he seemed to me to have undergone an unfortunate change of heart in electoral strategy. This "New Politics" conference was organized by Californians for Liberal Representation and was an attempt to draw together all the progressive and anti–Vietnam war forces that had been in ferment both within and outside the Democratic Party that year. Communists had played an instrumental role in pulling the conference together. It was the first time since the late 1930s that you had so many people, both the Left and liberals, together in the same room at a statewide conference. Hundreds of people turned out, representing the antiwar movement, unions, Blacks and Chicanos, and the Left, so it was a very exciting moment, full of potential. But it turned into a long, debilitating wrangle between those of us who thought there were some very good reasons to prefer a Brown to a Reagan and a group centered around Scheer, who called for a boycott of the Brown-Reagan race.

> The San Francisco Chronicle, surveying the California primary election barnyard, used a phrase which describes the increasing polarization of American politics: "power on the right, militancy on the left, chaos in the middle." That's the story in California: the liberal center bringing chaos on itself—purging the Casadys, clobbering the students, killing the Chessmans—and then wondering why an increasingly disillusioned left won't help it to gain power. . . . [An] increasingly large number of Democrats . . . feel that their causes—from civil rights to farm labor to the freedom of the university at Berkeley—have as little chance for survival in the Brown compromise machine as under the principled opposition of a Reagan administration. ■ "Golly gee, California is a Strange State!" *Ramparts*, October 1966.

Communists didn't call for the conference to endorse Brown; our position was simply that it should keep away from divisive issues like the boycott proposal and consider the long-range role it could play in state politics after this particular election was over. That way alliances could be maintained between the "New Politics" people and those more deeply entrenched in the Democratic Party. It was perfectly obvious that nobody in that hall was going to vote Republican, so a boycott would only mean taking votes away from Brown and thus objectively providing votes to Reagan. Part of the problem with the conference was the way it had been organized, on a "one man, one vote" basis. That sounded democratic but in fact favored a very manipulative kind of politics. Everyone who showed up was entitled to one vote on conference resolutions, which meant that someone who came from a union with ten thousand members carried exactly as much weight as someone who came from some little ultraleft sect with two dozen members (in fact, knowing how those sects operate, all two dozen of their members were probably in the hall).

Scheer made a very impassioned speech in favor of the boycott, condemning anyone who wanted to work with the Democratic Party as an opportunist and sell-out. I taunted him about it from the floor: "Why was it all right for you to run as a Democrat in the spring, but now it's a dirty terrible thing to do?" But Scheer's speech carried the day, and the conference voted for a boycott resolution by a small margin. At that point all the people who represented genuine mass organizations, like the United Farmworkers, walked out, because they were under no illusions about what a Reagan victory would mean for their members. The Communists stayed, although I was sympathetic with those who decided they had to leave. Scheer had known, or at least should have known, that if he forced through the boycott vote, this was going to be the inevitable result. But the temptation to make a thrilling gesture of defiance toward the Democratic establishment overcame more strategic concerns. In the end, of course, Reagan was an easy victor in the gubernatorial race.

> The outcome of the conference probably didn't make any difference in terms of Reagan's victory but I think it did make a difference in terms of the direction the Left went in California. The objective we had set out with was to define an independent position that was neither in nor out of the Democratic Party, an issue-based framework for a coalition that could inject its issues into electoral politics when it seemed appropriate. Who knows how it would have developed, but what developed instead was the Peace and Freedom Party, which became a splinter that never went anyplace seriously. ■ Jim Berland.

In a public debate I had with Scheer and with historian Eugene Genovese in Los Angeles some months later after Reagan's victory, on the topic "Which Way for the Left?" I tried to draw the lessons I saw in the New Politics debacle. I warned against the mistaken optimism so prevalent on the New Left that the country's ruling circles had made a permanent decision to rule through the co-optive politics of liberalism rather than the coercive politics of reaction. Bob's position was, basically, that the Old Left had nothing to teach the New Left. I didn't expect the New Left to sit obediently at the knee of the Old Left, but I did think there were a few valuable things that could be learned from our experience and mistakes. If I had learned anything in four decades of political activism, it was that expectations that victory was going to be quick and easy could be disastrous.

> We know that politics can be dull and tedious. We know in our bones that you cannot win on issues without the difficult, grueling, and, alas, often boring day-to-day work of organizing. Politics is not a hit-and-run affair, no splash rhetorical jab and *away we go*—although some of this may be

---

necessary. It means working with, and staying in, communities and in people's organizations, year in and year out, building around issues. It means developing radicals who stay that way, regardless of blunders, defeats, or "combat fatigue." ■ Dorothy Healey, debate with Scheer and Genovese, December 2, 1966.

I was surprised when shortly after the conference collapsed I read a report on it in the *People's World* by Carl Bloice which in effect approved of the position taken by Scheer and condemned the people who walked out as the ones who had split the conference. Bloice had acted as Scheer's campaign manager in the Democratic primary that spring, which partially explains his position, but he was also speaking for a tendency present both in the northern California CP and in the national office to downplay the idea that there was a meaningful choice between Democrats and Republicans. I sent in a response to the *People's World* and soon got a call from Mickey Lima. Mickey was very concerned, saying that if I insisted on having my article printed, he was going to have to write a response defending Bloice's original position. He didn't think it was a good idea to have the leaders of the southern and northern California Party districts fighting in public. I said I thought it was a great idea. This wasn't our private disagreement: we should let other people, especially other Communists, hear and participate in the debate and clarify their own thinking in the process. My article did come out, as did Mickey's response, and so for the first time since the late 1950s there was actually a public debate on an important issue going on in the pages of an American Communist newspaper.

The theory of "the-worse-the-better" is political LSD—hallucinatory politics. ■ Dorothy Healey, "New Politics meet; still another view," *People's World*, October 22, 1966.

In October I went back to New York for a meeting of the National Board. It was much more congenial than usual, for the simple reason that Gus Hall happened to be in the Soviet Union that month. After a good discussion, the board took a vote on the debate that Mickey and I had had in the *People's World* and wound up endorsing the position of the southern California Party. In December, when Gus was back in the country, the National Committee met (I arrived a day late, because my debate with Scheer coincided with the first day of its meeting). When I got there, I learned that Gus's report to the committee the previous night had consisted almost exclusively of an all-out attack on the southern California district's position on the 1966 election. Gus argued that we should have run an independent candidate against both Reagan and Brown in the fall election. Under no circumstances should we have offered support to Brown, however critical, because of his backing of the war. As far as Gus was concerned, Reagan's victory in itself was inconsequential; the reason that Brown had lost was not because of the growing appeal of the Right, but because the voters had disliked Brown's support for the war. This was typical of Gus; everything, properly interpreted, was always a victory. I started calling him

"Dr. Pangloss" after that, because he kept imagining that the working class was growing ever more united and class conscious, and the people's movements were going from victory to victory. I remember once in the early 1960s he came out to Los Angeles and visited some of our clubs and told the members that the Sino-Soviet dispute was ending. After the meeting I asked him where he got such information, as everything that I was reading from both countries seemed to indicate an intensification of the battle. "Yes, I know," he replied. "But it makes the comrades feel better." Gus's philosophy was one of positive thinking, which is a fine approach for authors of self-help books but not so useful a trait for those who aspire to revolutionary leadership.

> HEALEY believed that there is a difference between capitalist candidates running for office. . . . During any other time of war, in the United States the Party has always found repressive legislation. This is the first time during a war that the CP has made gains. For example, the Supreme Court's five to four ruling on the question of the CP [ruling the McCarran act unconstitutional], one of the court justices who made a difference in the five to four decision was an appointee of President JOHNSON. A GOLDWATER appointee would have voted the other way. HEALEY continued that the Party will further attack and criticize President JOHNSON but the Democratic Party does represent an opposition to the JOHNSON policy. . . . HEALEY believed that they should criticize their allies and those who form new political parties. New politics have led many individuals into a march into the wilderness. ■ FBI report on the southern California Communist Party district convention, held February 24, 1967, report dated June 27, 1967.

In September 1967 I took part in the national New Politics conference which met in Chicago. The conference drew together several thousand activists from the civil rights, peace, and other movements from all over the country to consider a plan of action for the following year's presidential election. There was a big California delegation, including Si Casady, who served as the convention's co-chair. No one yet dreamed that Lyndon Johnson would decline to run for reelection. With Johnson seemingly having the nomination sewed up, we wanted to explore the possibility of running independent candidates on an anti-Vietnam war platform. Communists didn't want to see a third *party* take the field, since it would have no chance of attracting significant union support or support from the most significant Black or Chicano organizations—we had learned something from 1948. But we did want to explore the possibility of launching a third *ticket*, so that people who considered themselves loyal Democrats could stay within the Democratic Party yet still cast a protest vote against the war. Our dream ticket would have been one consisting of Martin Luther King and Benjamin Spock, linking the issues of civil rights and peace.

The delegates at the New Politics conference found little to agree upon. The SDS people were hostile to any kind of national electoral strategy, favoring an exclusive concentration on local community organizing projects. Trotskyist groups were pushing for the immediate creation of a third party. We wanted a third ticket. But the major divisions proved to be racial rather than tactical. The issue on which the conference foundered was the demand by the Black Caucus, an amorphous group that was influenced by Black nationalism, that before anything else could be decided they would have to be awarded 50 percent of the votes and the convention would have to embrace a long series of other political positions—some reasonable and some not. The Party people present, myself included, supported the Black Caucus's demands. We understood why Blacks would seek some kind of dramatic gesture from the white Left proving that it didn't simply intend to use them as window dressing in a white-run organization. But the way in which the demand was presented killed off any possibility of compromise. Some of the caucus's demands, like the one condemning Zionism, can only be described as mischievous—designed to measure how far they could push the convention, without any concern for the effectiveness or even survival of the New Politics movement. Much later it was revealed that the primary motivator at the caucus, a Black student from Cal. State University, L.A., was an FBI plant. When rhetoric becomes so inflamed it is hard to discern a provocateur. The Black Caucus was not representative of all the Blacks present (Martin Luther King, Julian Bond, James Bevel, and Ralph Abernathy all showed up for the convention but stayed away from the caucus's meetings). The spirit within the convention that weekend was all too reminiscent of the anti-white chauvinism campaign of the early 1950s. People were unwilling to challenge anything that a Black speaker said, no matter how outrageous. In such a highly charged atmosphere it was almost impossible not to get caught up in the sense that no matter what else happened, white radicals had to meet the demands of the Black militants. Rather than laying the groundwork for common action, the wholesale capitulation to those demands represented a retreat into a kind of symbolic politics that had nothing to do with political realities.

In the end nothing was accomplished. A resolution was passed allowing each state to launch an independent presidential challenge, which was something you hardly needed a national convention to decide. That led the following year to the creation of the Peace and Freedom Party in California (a development we had mixed feelings about, both because of our memories of the Progressive Party campaign and because the new party nominated Eldridge Cleaver as its presidential candidate, a man addicted to the most irresponsible rhetoric). After the convention was over I went on to New York City for a meeting of the National Board. James Jackson just tore into those of us who had been in Chicago for having gone along with the 50 percent demand—and for once, I have to admit, he had the better part of the argument.

As things turned out, the main electoral challenge to Johnson in 1968 came from within the Democratic Party, in the form of the Eugene McCarthy and, later on, the Robert Kennedy candidacies. The huge antiwar demonstrations of 1967 encouraged and gave a base to McCarthy. Rather than see the McCarthy campaign as an attempt to co-opt the peace movement, as some on the Left did, Communists in Los Angeles saw it as an opportunity to open a new front against the war through the ballot box. We were part of a left-of-center alliance at the nominating convention of the California Democratic Council in the fall of 1967 that insisted that the McCarthy delegate slate run as a "peace and equality" slate, linking domestic and foreign policy issues. (McCarthy never did bridge the gap between the two and as a result failed to attract much support among Blacks and Chicanos, whereas Bobby Kennedy proved he could go into the ghetto and get a tremendous response.) Because we were so involved with the CDC and the Democratic Party insurgency, we were reluctant to put too many of our forces into the Peace and Freedom Party, though in the fall Ben Dobbs did run as its candidate in a Los Angeles congressional district. At the same time, we did think there would be some political benefit in having the Party run its own candidate in the 1968 election, and at the National Board meeting after the New Politics convention I proposed that we start thinking about launching a presidential campaign. We had gotten out of the habit of running our own candidates (the Party had not offered a candidate for president since 1940), but based on my own positive experience the previous year running for tax assessor in Los Angeles, it seemed to me that it made sense to run candidates under our own banners. Naturally we couldn't expect to win, nor should we pull all our supporters out of other, non-Communist campaigns. Still, there were few enough times when the American public was willing to listen to a Communist, even out of curiosity. Election campaigns offered us a chance to speak to others outside of our normal circle of influence. The degree to which we would campaign in 1968, what our emphasis would be, and how we would present the candidate would all need to be decided once we saw what was happening on the broader political scene. But in order to be in a position to mount any kind of campaign, we would have to get started early on in planning for it.

Any idea I favored was going to have rough going with the other members of the National Board, and the proposal was overwhelmingly voted down. But by January it occurred to Gus Hall that if there *was* a Communist presidential campaign, he would most likely be chosen as our candidate. So the word came down that, yes, the Party might mount a campaign after all, and a nominating convention was scheduled for August 1968. It turned out that Gus wasn't the only Communist who had an eye on the nomination prize. Charlene Mitchell was bitten by the same bug, and she completely out-organized Gus that spring and summer. When we had our district convention in Los Angeles, Charlene's sister-in-law Kendra made a very emotional speech about how this was the year that Communists could make history by running a Black presidential candidate, and how Charlene was obviously the best possible choice as that candidate. The motion passed unanimously. At the national CP convention in August, Charlene easily beat out Gus for the nomination. He was outraged, but he couldn't very well challenge the Party's nomination of a Black woman without opening himself up to charges of white chauvinism. The Party put almost no resources into Charlene's campaign. She was only able to get on the ballot in a couple of states. Don Hamerquist and Mike Meyerson, acting on their own initiative, served as Charlene's campaign staff, but they were hindered as much as they were helped by other Communists. Southern California was one of the few places where we managed to turn out decent crowds when Charlene came through on her campaign tour.

Within the national office there was a great deal of hostility to the new Black revolutionary movements of the 1960s. Except for a brief moment in the late 1960s when the Party forged an alliance at the top with the Black Panthers and helped them stage their "United Front Against Fascism" conference in Oakland, Black militants were regarded by important Party leaders as demagogic and dangerous. James Jackson, who was by then editor of the *Daily Worker*, developed an absolute hatred of Malcolm X. The paper came out with front-page stories attacking Malcolm as a bourgeois nationalist, spreading ideas which threatened the unity of Black and white workers. In Los Angeles we tried to be more sympathetic. Cyril Briggs, an L.A. communist who had played an important role in launching the "Black Belt" thesis back in the 1920s, argued that the Muslims were an extremely significant movement within the Black community that deserved the respect if not the unqualified support of the Party. What we had to do, he said, was to find an approach that allowed us to encourage individuals within the Muslim movement like Malcolm to realize their best potential instead of just standing by self-righteously and shaking our heads over their sins. (It's worth remembering that in the last months before his assassination, Malcolm changed his perspective and recognized the possibility of working in alliance with sympathetic whites.)

I carried Cyril's argument from Los Angeles to the National Committee. I met with little public support but a good deal of private agreement, particularly from Black comrades. At the 1966 CP national convention Jackson completely outraged our younger Black comrades and others when he spoke at a press conference and criticized the Lowndes County, Alabama, Black Panther Party (which was a precursor to, but separate from, the Oakland Black Panther Party started by Bobby Seale and Huey Newton), saying that he wished they had adopted the symbol of the American eagle rather than that of the black panther. The young delegates demanded that the Party issue a public retraction of Jackson's statement, since it catered to the most backward kind of national and racial chauvinism.

In Los Angeles we benefited from having a particularly talented core of youthful Black cadre. Charlene Mitchell had been active since the 1950s and was elected to the National Committee in 1957. Her brothers Deacon and Franklin Alexander and Franklin's wife Kendra became key local activists in the 1960s. They helped recruit and develop around them a group of several dozen Black Communists by the late 1960s. They were highly visible and involved in the Los Angeles Black community. I was very close to Franklin and Kendra, both personally and politically, all through the 1960s. On questions of domestic strategy, Party democracy, and relations with the Soviet Union, they sided with me all the way until I left the Party leadership. In fact when they came back from a trip to the Soviet Union in 1968, they were very proud of the fact that they had resisted the blandishments of their Soviet hosts to accept the official explanation of the necessity for the invasion of Czechoslovakia.

In 1967 the Los Angeles Party organized an all-black unit, the Che-Lumumba Club, chaired by Charlene. James Jackson was outraged. He denounced the club at a National Committee meeting, which passed a resolution supporting his position. He argued that the Che-Lumumba Club violated Party principles, because the Party had always insisted on integrating its Black and white members and to do otherwise was to capitulate to Black nationalism. We went ahead with the club anyway. Since we had many more white than Black members, there was no way that we could guarantee that a club based in a particular neighborhood, or representing a particular industry, or organized within a profession would necessarily have any Black members. The Party had never insisted that when the Jewish Commission met a Gentile had to be present. Why should this hard-and-fast rule be applied only to Blacks in the Party? Internationalism, we insisted, was not form but content. It was perfectly possible to have an all-Black group committed to a politics that transcended a narrow nationalism. The presence or absence of a white face wasn't going to make much difference in terms of the politics represented. But it might make a huge difference in terms of our ability to recruit and hold on to Black Communists.

One thing I came to realize about Black life in this country is that no matter how "integrated" the individual may be, there is a great difference in the way Blacks interrelate and relax among themselves and the way they do in mixed company. Once I drove Paul Robeson to an all-Black party and stayed for a few minutes. And I noticed how Robeson, an enormously sophisticated Rutgers graduate, immediately began using Black English colloquialisms in this crowd in a way he never had when I was with him in groups with whites. The ease of communication among an all-Black group is simply impossible to create within a mixed group in a society as racially divided as our own. The formation of the Che-Lumumba Club allowed Black Communists to play a role within the Black community and among Black students on campuses in Los Angeles that they never could have pulled off as a mixed group during that period of intense pressure from Black nationalism. I doubt very much that Angela Davis, for one, would have come into the Party in 1968 were it not for the Che-Lumumba Club.

Since the 1930s we had always held on to a base of supporters in the Black community. Blacks were never as caught up in the anti-Communist hysteria of the 1950s as whites—something which I knew from very direct experience because for three decades I lived in a neighborhood on the border of Watts. When I bought the house it was still in a somewhat mixed neighborhood, but by the time I left I was the only white for blocks around. And in all that time, even in the worst days when the FBI cars were staking out the house, my Black neighbors were always cordial. It was not that they shared my politics, but they saw my beliefs as ones which a reasonable person could hold. As a matter of fact they even liked having those FBI cars sitting out there with their motors running all night—in a neighborhood which ordinarily had a high crime rate, the number of break-ins and muggings on our block dropped dramatically as long as I remained an object of intense interest to the government.

When the Watts riot broke out in August 1965, I happened to be in San Francisco for a Party meeting. I immediately flew back to Los Angeles. The next day we held an emergency meeting of the district leadership at Bill Taylor's house. Black Communists who lived in Watts reported to us that the riot had an almost festive atmosphere to it, involving a wide section of the community, not just the street cats. The feeling seemed to be "By God, we're doing something on our own." The looting and burning of stores that went on was selective, aimed at businesses which had a reputation as gouging or cheating the community. Black-owned businesses, and even white-owned businesses that were known to be fair, were spared. We thought that the riots were a self-destructive but understandable response to intolerable conditions, and we put out a leaflet addressed to the white community explaining how poverty and police brutality had led to the disorders. The Party also helped organize collections to bring food into the neighborhoods that were worst hit. One thing I was surprised to learn was that Blacks were welcoming the National Guardsmen sent in by the governor to restore order. Our first reaction had been to oppose calling out the National Guard, but our Black comrades from Watts said, "You just don't know what you're talking about." The Guard was viewed by people in the community as a disciplined multiracial force, while the L.A. police were virtually all white and out of control, just shooting at random at people on the streets. I was home alone during the riot, living in a neighborhood that was unaffected but close to the riot zone. I kept getting calls from friends urging me to leave, but I thought that the safest place for me to be right then was in a neighborhood where all the people knew me.

After Watts, the nature of the new Black recruits attracted to the Party and the political mood they represented changed dramatically. Previously our appeal had been to those groups that represented the most stable forces in the Black community: industrial workers, trade unionists, people who might have belonged to a church or to the NAACP, people whose sense of grievance and whose language reflected the fact that they had been shut out of a society they wanted into. In the late 1960s the grievances and the language of our new recruits reflected the anger of those who were on the outside looking in, in the Black community as well as in the larger society, the "brothers on the block" as the rhetoric of the time had it, or as we would have called them, the "lumpenproletariat." Although few of our new Black recruits were themselves "lumpen" (many were college-educated), certainly the style of politics they represented derived from the mood on the streets. It was a somewhat diluted version of the kind of politics represented by the Black Panther Party—and some of our Black members held dual membership in the CP and the Panthers. (Many of our young white recruits, like their counterparts in New Left organizations, were also very taken with the example and style of the Panthers.)

> One of the things I'd say about Dorothy is that she has a great capacity to listen sympathetically and to be able to see the other person's point of view. She might have disagreed with ideas that people were articulating (not just these young Black people; it was true of many people that she would encounter), but she could see from the point of view of their culture and who they were personally why they were saying the things they were. At the same time she would be able to articulate alternative ways of thinking. That's a great gift. It's very helpful to people. It allows them to see things in a different way than if you come at people with your line and bash them

over the head with your pickax and say, "You're wrong, you're counter-revolutionary, you're petit bourgeois." You do that with people and they say, "Bye." ■ Bettina Aptheker.

I admired the personal courage and commitment of individual Black Panthers I got to know, but I was not a fan of their politics. With the Panthers you found this curious mixture of selfless dedication and some of the worst aspects of street culture. They maintained discipline in their party "with a stick," as their own phrase had it. In Los Angeles they would run classes every Saturday in "political education" in which their members had to memorize sections of Mao's little red book. If they failed to memorize their assignment, they were beaten up. The same thing would happen if they failed to sell their weekly quota of their party newspaper. The Panthers picked up the Maoist slogan "All power grows out of the barrel of a gun" and made an ideological fetish out of it. That phrase has to be one of the stupidest things Mao ever said, because what power really grows out of is the organized consciousness of millions of people. At some point guns may become important tactically in the revolutionary process in some countries, but that isn't where power comes from—and a good thing, too, because revolutionaries are always going to be outgunned by the forces defending the old order.

On the issues of black nationalism, where the Party took a knee-jerk, re-actionary position, the young people joining the Party tended to react more like the New Left. SDS tactics, flying squads, violence—while we might struggle for a broader view, a lot of young people in the Party were attracted to that as well. . . . The streets were very rough in L.A. It scared me to death. We got a call one morning that Panther headquarters was under attack from the police, "All you white people come down and be present." So we went. There were bullets whizzing by. ■ Jim Berland.

One of the problems the Panthers faced was that their founding leaders, Huey Newton and Bobby Seale, were either on trial or in prison for most of the late 1960s and early 1970s. That left control of the party pretty much in the hands of Eldridge Cleaver, an unstable character who led it close to the brink of destruction. After Huey and Bobby got out of prison and broke with Cleaver, they shifted their emphasis from "self-defense" to "survival programs." The place where they did most to implement the new strategy was in Oakland, the only city where they were able to build any kind of a base. There they functioned as a kind of free-lance social welfare agency, providing free food, clothes, and health care services to the community. We obviously didn't have anything against people receiving those kinds of services, but our idea had always been that the role of radicals was to organize people to demand that such benefits be provided by the government. Radicals shouldn't be in the position of competing with the churches as dispensers of charity. At the height of the Panthers' "serve the people" phase, Bobby Seale came down to Los Angeles to speak at a fund-raising event in some wealthy white supporter's house. He was standing up at one end of the room explaining why this free-groceries strategy was the key to political success, and the rest of us were literally sitting at his feet. I think I was one of the few skeptics in the room, and I asked him, "How is the Black Panther Party different from any church running a soup kitchen?" He didn't know who I was, and when he turned to me he said, "I'm afraid I can't explain it to you because you don't understand dialectical materialism." That got a big laugh. The problem with the Panthers' approach to politics, in both its early and later stages, was that they were always substituting themselves for someone. When their emphasis was on military confrontation, they were substituting themselves for mass revolutionary activity, and when their emphasis was on free handouts, they were substituting themselves for the welfare department.

> Dorothy wasn't into armed insurrection. She didn't think that the way to be a revolutionary was to go get a gun and shoot people. She didn't foster that. At the same time she didn't stand up and say, "It's stupid you're carrying guns around, you're going to get yourself killed." That wasn't Dorothy's task. She felt that if she could educate people on what a mass struggle was all about, what organizing really means, rather than getting your kicks carrying guns, that would have an effect. She didn't have direct contact with the Panthers, but she had a huge influence on the Black Student Unions, which were the recruiting grounds for the Panthers. When she spoke on campus, they were all there taking notes. The effect she had was to knock some Marxist sense into some really crazy people. ■ Terry Kupers. [Kupers, a medical student in Los Angeles, was a member of the CP from 1969 through 1971.]

As much as I disliked the Panthers' rhetoric and feared its consequences, I also had to recognize the genuine appeal that their militarist posture had for young Blacks. I would have preferred it to be otherwise, but for young people guns became a symbol of revolutionary commitment. It drove many older Communists crazy to see that even our Party youth were involved in this enthusiasm for carrying guns and practicing with them. For people in the national office this was regarded as cause for expulsion. I knew we couldn't take that hard a line, because first of all, there were instances in which armed self-defense was legitimate, as in the voter-registration projects in the South when some SNCC organizers began carrying guns to defend themselves against the incredible level of racist violence they had to face. And I also knew that young Communists were under tremendous political pressures from others in groups like the Panthers and various New Left groups, who regarded the Party as a group of stodgy reformist sell-outs. If we simply denounced anyone who talked about guns or carried one, we would lose most of our members under the age of thirty.

> I think that socialist democracy requires *its own equivalents* of what we term checks and balances. I emphasize the phrase *its own equivalents*, because we Americans have the bad habit of believing that our forms are universally valid for all countries . . . But if, for instance, in the Soviet Union the trade

unions and the Soviets played a genuinely independent role, there would be a built-in safeguard against the idea that the Communist Party (and particularly a current leadership) was the alpha and omega of all wisdom. Lenin suggested this, I think, in his sharp debate with Trotsky as to the role of trade unions in a socialist state. Trotsky urged that the unions should be, in effect, a semimilitary formation. "No," said Lenin, "the unions must defend the workers against *their own* state." He was emphasizing the to-be expected differences between the immediate needs of the workers and the long-term planning policies required by the workers' state. Extend this premise to all of socialist society, workers, farmers, intellectuals, etc., and it is possible to perceive the framework for Socialist checks and balances. There are public organizations in each field which could express and defend their needs and policies and which, in turn, could express its responsibility to society for its own sector. ■ Dorothy Healey, KPFK radio broadcast, February 21, 1968.

In the 1960s the Soviet Union had little or no appeal to young people—Black or white—as a model of revolution or of a desirable socialist society. It seemed old, staid, repressive, even counter-revolutionary to young activists. The Cuban revolution, however, had an enormous appeal. And because Cuba was a Communist society, led by a Communist Party, some small amount of its prestige rubbed off onto the American CP. I wouldn't say that we gained many recruits on the basis of our fraternal ties with the Cuban CP, but for those young people who did join the American Party the identification with the Cuban revolution was a very important part of their political consciousness as Communists. Something little known even within our own ranks was that American Communist leaders were not at all well disposed toward Castro until 1968. Before that he was regarded with much suspicion, as he was by the Soviet leaders, because he was pursuing a very independent path politically and theoretically. This was the period of the tricontinental conferences in Havana, where the major Latin American CPs were denounced for clinging to "parliamentary illusions." The Cubans were encouraging the creation of guerrilla foci in the mountains of a number of Latin American countries, policies which culminated in Che Guevara's ill-fated adventure in Bolivia in 1967. The Cuban Communist leaders were often mistaken in their political estimates, but the fact that they were acting on their *own* political estimates was something I had to admire—and something which naturally made them suspect in the eyes of both Soviet and American Party leaders.

I had my own criticisms of some of Fidel's policies. In a KPFK broadcast early in 1968 I talked about the arrest and trial of Anibel Escalante, an old Cuban Communist leader from the days before the *Fidelistas* had taken over the Party. He was sentenced to fifteen years in prison, according to the Cuban Communist newspaper *Granma*, for such offenses as holding "meetings and study sessions where the Party line and the measures taken by the Revolution were criticized and revolutionary leaders maligned." I used Escalante's case (which, ironically, had an anti-Soviet twist—he was also accused of distributing materials "obtained at TASS and Novosti agencies") as an example of why socialist societies needed a strong system of checks and balances to protect against arbitrary abuses of power. "Once again," I said, "as in the Stalin era in the Soviet Union, inner-party disagreements are first defined as heresy and then as criminal actions against the state." Inner-party democracy, I argued, was not a luxury to be dispensed with lightly: "It is an absolute necessity if there is to be a growth of ideas and of humans commensurate with the objectives of a new society."

After Che's death, Castro shed his illusions about the imminence of revolutionary victory in Latin America, just as the Bolsheviks had drawn some hard lessons from the failure of a European revolution in 1919. Cuba was going to be isolated for the foreseeable future, and I think that realization made Fidel more amenable to pressures from the Soviet Union to toe the ideological line. That became apparent after the Czechoslovakian events in 1968, when Fidel, despite some initial criticisms of Soviet actions, reversed himself and endorsed the Warsaw Pact invasion. That was enough to return the Cuban revolution to good graces in the eyes of Party leaders in the United States. These developments had an unfortunate effect on some of our younger comrades. If Fidel was adopting the same international line as Brezhnev and Gus Hall, then the line must be correct. I think this had a big effect on the thinking of young Communists like Mike Meyerson, Carl Bloice, and most important, on Angela Davis.

> I began to pay visits to Dorothy Healey, who was then the District organizer for Southern California. We had long, involved discussions—sometimes arguments—about the Party, its role within the movement, its potential as the vanguard party of the working class. . . . I immensely enjoyed these discussions with Dorothy and felt that I was learning a great deal from them, regardless of whether I ultimately decided to become a Communist myself. ■ Angela Davis, *An Autobiography*, p. 188.

I first met Angela in 1967 at a meeting to discuss how radicals should respond to the increasing level of violence directed against the Black Panthers. Angela was a young Black woman not yet twenty-four years old, strikingly beautiful, intelligent, articulate, and poised. She clearly had the potential to be anything she wanted to be, a scholar or a political leader. But she was confronted with a dilemma: she had these genuine intellectual gifts, yet had to prove herself at a time when anti-intellectualism was running rampant in the movement, when the only thing that seemed to count was proving yourself a tough street cat, able to stand up to the Man with the gun. Angela had grown up in Alabama and New York. Her mother had been involved in the campaign to free the Scottsboro Boys in the 1930s. Angela had been a brilliant student at Brandeis University, where she studied under Herbert Marcuse, and had then gone on to graduate studies at the University of Frankfurt—all of which had prepared her for a political role as a Marxist intellectual that seemed tame and irrelevant in the heated atmosphere of the late 1960s.

Angela came to southern California in 1967 to work on her PhD in philosophy with Marcuse, who by then had moved to the University of San Diego. She got involved in local Black radical circles, joined the Los Angeles chapter of SNCC, which the Party was very influential in, and attended some meetings of the Che-Lumumba Club. She worked closely with Charlene, Franklin, and Deacon. In June 1968 she attended the southern California CP convention as a special invited guest. Deacon Alexander took her to my house for the first of several long conversations we had about whether she should join the Party. I told her that she should not join if she expected to find perfection. "If you come in with those illusions, you will go out very quickly, because the Party is not like that. It has many weaknesses." I told her that building a party is always the most complicated and important task confronting a revolutionary; it requires the greatest amount of courage and self-sacrifice, because it means you have to be willing to fight with your comrades and not just with the ruling class. She joined the Party in July, and for the first couple of years she was critical of many aspects of its line, even in the midst of her subsequent legal difficulties.

Angela spent the next year dividing her time between La Jolla, where she was preparing for her oral exams, and Los Angeles, where with Party permission she and Deacon Alexander joined the local Black Panther Party. (The Panthers, because of some shift in their own internal politics, soon decided to expel Deacon, and Angela dropped out afterward of her own accord.) After spending the summer of 1969 in Cuba, Angela returned to Los Angeles to begin a one-year appointment as an instructor in the philosophy department at UCLA. Before she returned, however, an FBI informer named Bill Di Valli sent a letter to the UCLA student newspaper saying that an unnamed newly hired instructor in the philosophy department was a member of the Communist Party. The Board of Regents responded by sending her a letter demanding to know her political affiliations. Angela arrived home to find herself a cause célèbre.

Angela came to my house to decide what to do. She was understandably unhappy with being forced into this martyr's role just as she was beginning her first teaching job. Her comrades in the Che-Lumumba Club were pushing her to defy Reagan and the Regents by openly avowing her Party membership and daring them to do their worst. I had seen too many people pressured into doing something that they really didn't want to who later felt that they'd been betrayed. I didn't want Angela to go through the same experience, so I just stated her alternatives as clearly as I could and told her she had to make her own decision. She and I went down to talk with John McTernan. There was still a law on the books prohibiting Communists from teaching in the UC system. John told her that if she decided to take the Fifth Amendment she could probably hold on to her job. If, however, she were to take the position, "Yes, I am a Communist, and so what?" then she risked losing the job, but her case could serve as a test of whether or not Communists should have the right to teach. She decided to come out openly as a Communist. She was able to continue teaching while her case worked its way through the university administration and then the courts and eventually won her case—although the Regents prevented her reappointment for a second academic year, this time on the grounds that her statements supporting Black political prisoners were a "breach of professional ethics."

About Angela generally, she's a Symbol now, and it's very tough to be one. Given this awesome burden that's been thrust upon her I can understand why she would be reluctant to say anything in haste without a deep inner conviction that's based on knowledge or experience. And her political experience thus far, along with all the conflicting pressures to which she has been subjected, have reinforced, I assume, a sense of responsibility in making choices. With all that, and granting a period of grace, she's still [going to] have to make the difficult choices. If you can help her, fine. ■ letter from Al Richmond to Dorothy, August 4, 1972.

Throughout that school year Angela's case received extensive news coverage. By this time the public had lost its previous consuming interest in the question of domestic Communism; the battle the Party fought against the McCarran Act never received a tenth of the attention paid to the Smith Act cases in the media in the 1950s. With Angela it was a different story. Because she was not simply a Communist, but a Black in a time of racial upheaval, and because she was not simply a Black Communist but a beautiful woman, the media turned its full focus on her, and for the next few years she was never long out of the headlines. Without any effort on her own part, she became a kind of pop icon—even appearing as the heroine in a Rolling Stones song. From 1969 through the mid-1970s all you had to do was say the word "Angela" and people instantly knew who you were talking about. It was not a role she was ready for, emotionally or politically, nor was it a role she welcomed: as she wrote in her autobiography, "I loathed being stared at like a curiosity object." That in itself distinguished her from many other movement "stars" who fascinated the media in the 1960s, like Jerry Rubin, Eldridge Cleaver, and Huey Newton, all of whom relished, courted, and in the end were corrupted by the attention they received.

In early 1970 Angela made a fateful decision to get involved in a campaign organized to defend three Black prisoners, George Jackson, John Clutchette, and Fleeta Drumgo, who were accused of murdering a prison guard at Soledad prison. The prison had been in an uproar for weeks since a white guard stationed in the gun tower above the prison yard had shot and killed three Black prisoners. When a grand jury ruled the killings were "justifiable homicide," a prison rebellion broke out. Someone pushed a white guard over a railing, and he fell to his death. Jackson, Clutchette, and Drumgo became the scapegoats, even though there was no way of knowing who was actually responsible for the guard's death (they would finally be acquitted of the charges in 1972). The case began to attract outside attention, and the phrase "Soledad Brothers" became a well-known one in radical circles.

Angela found herself personally drawn to one of the Soledad Brothers, George Jackson, who had been in prison for more than a decade for taking part in the armed robbery of a gas station when he was eighteen. George grew into manhood in prison, educated himself, and became a revolutionary. The publication of his prison letters in 1971 would make him famous because of his keen intelligence and gift for self-expression. To the extent that it was possible, given the iron bars that separated them, Angela and George became lovers. She also took his younger brother Jonathon, a seventeen-year-old high school student, under her wing. Jonathon worshipped his older brother and devoted himself without stint to his defense. I met him on several occasions at defense committee meetings and when he was acting as a bodyguard for Angela. George had asked Angela to look after Jonathon: in an all-too-accurate prophecy he warned her that Jonathon "is at that dangerous age where confusion sets in and sends brothers either to the undertaker or to prison."

The Soledad Brothers campaign never succeeded in drawing much support outside radical circles. That was in some measure Angela's fault, because she fell into the all-too-common trap of substituting militant rhetoric for the humdrum work of organization. The whole atmosphere of the movement, Black and white alike, was by this time suffused with the violent rhetoric of the Panthers. To the extent that Angela indulged herself in "pick up the gun" rhetoric, she was neglecting her responsibility to the young Blacks for whom she was a heroine. Jonathon was still a very young man who did not know the difference between what was said for atmospherics and what was really being advocated by the leaders he admired.

Angela had bought guns and ammunition for the Che-Lumumba Club to use for target practice. Jonathon knew about the guns, and on August 1, 1970, he took them out of the closet where they were stored. He already had a shotgun in his possession that Angela had given to him to take to the Soledad defense committee office. On August 7, he burst into a courtroom in San Rafael where James McClain, a Black prisoner from San Quentin, was on trial for involvement in another prison disturbance. Two other prisoners, Ruchell Magee and William Christmas, were also in the courtroom as witnesses for the defense. Jonathon armed the prisoners and took the judge, the district attorney, and several jurors as hostages and tried to escape in a van he had parked outside. The van never made it out of the parking lot. When the guards finished firing, the judge, Jonathon, McClain, and Christmas were all dead.

If I had known what Jonathon was up to, I would have done anything in my power to keep him from throwing his own and others' lives away. But I could also sympathize with his feelings of desperation. His brother would never have had to spend all those years in prison if he had been white, and Jonathon had come to believe that George would never again be allowed to walk the streets as a free man. When I talked about the events in San Rafael at public meetings, I would always compare what Jonathon did to the actions of the McNamara brothers in 1910. J. B. and J. J. McNamara were AFL organizers who dynamited the Los Angeles *Times* building in the midst of a bitter labor dispute. The blast killed twenty-one people, and the McNamaras were the subject of near-universal condemnation, from employers as well as many of their fellow unionists. But Eugene Debs had come to their defense, even though he was appalled by the bombing. Debs argued that it was the violence and repression unleased by the ruling class in the "open shop" drive in Los Angeles that had driven the McNamaras to their desperate act. I thought that Communists could do no less for Jonathon Jackson than Debs had done for the McNamaras: we had to make it clear that we didn't think that was the way to go, but we should not disassociate ourselves from the motives that had led him into the courtroom that day in 1970.

Angela fled as soon as she heard the news from San Rafael. When the police traced the guns Jonathon had carried into the courtroom to Angela, she was charged with murder, kidnapping, and conspiracy. Her disappearance added a charge of interstate flight to the list and made it easier for the authorities to portray her as a desperate terrorist. She managed to avoid the FBI for just over two months when she was captured in New York and brought back to California to stand trial.

Communist Parties around the world launched campaigns on Angela's behalf in 1971. There were huge demonstrations organized around her case in the Soviet Union, in the Warsaw Pact countries, and in Western Europe. Ironically, the "Free Angela" campaign in the United States was probably the most poorly organized of all of them. Although the National United Committee to Free Angela Davis (NUCFAD) was able to raise a lot of money for Angela's defense, for a long time it proved unable to perform even so elementary a task as producing a bulletin that would keep the local defense committees regularly informed as to what was happening in the case, let alone reaching out to a broader audience. When I joined the campaign I hoped to see it develop into something more than one of these amorphous defense committees in which a few Communists make a lot of speeches and the names of non-Communists appear on the letterhead, but no one outside the Party ever really does anything. With Angela's case we began with the enormous advantage that her name was already widely known. Usually you have to spend months and months of effort just to get a case into the newspapers, but television had already made Angela a household name. Among Blacks there was overwhelming sympathy for her, uniting the militants with the most mainstream Black leaders and public figures. They regarded her prosecution as an attack on the Black community as a whole. Many whites were also supportive. The problem was to turn that awareness into meaningful support, to get people to become actively involved in her defense.

> In New York they had very little understanding of the Soledad Brothers case. Their tendency, because they didn't know about the struggles, was to try to separate Angela from all of that. The comparison they used was to compare Jonathon to van der Lubbe in the Reichstag fire. It wasn't just Angela who objected. I wrote a long piece for the *National Guardian* about the case saying that was the wrong way to characterize this. Jonathon was no van der Lubbe. I think it's accurate to say that Angela was quite concerned about how the Party was characterizing the defense. ■ Bettina Aptheker.

Franklin, Kendra, Charlene, and Bettina ran the national office for Angela's defense out of San Francisco. I worked closely with the Los Angeles "Free Angela" campaign. I played one other role which only a few people knew about at the time. Angela carried herself in public with impressive dignity, and her statements to the press and in the courtroom bristled with militancy, but she was not free of private doubts. There were things she could discuss with me that she felt she could not raise with Franklin or Charlene or the others. Some months before the trial began, I got a message that Angela wanted to see me. I flew up to San Francisco and drove out with one of Angela's attorneys, Margaret Burnham, to the Marin County jail. When Angela and I were alone in her cell she told me that she was thinking of resigning from the Communist Party. She was upset about a number of things about the defense campaign, but she was particularly angry that the national office of the CP kept trying to build a wall between her case and what had happened that day at San Rafael. The *Daily World* repeatedly condemned Jonathon Jackson's actions as "adventurist." Angela felt that by repudiating Jonathon, the Party was betraying his memory and the Black liberation struggle. She asked me what she should do. I told her unequivocally that she couldn't leave. If she wanted to resign after her trial was over, that would be one thing. But to resign now would make it seem as if she was trying to curry favor with the government, and it would have a devastating impact on her supporters. And in practical terms, it would certainly guarantee the Party's withdrawal from her defense campaign, and it would be very difficult for others to step in and pick up the pieces. I don't know whether she was just letting off steam that day, or how seriously she weighed my words, but there was no more talk of her quitting.

> I also argued for a long time with Angela to stay in the Party. The issue came up after George Jackson was killed [in August 1971]. That was a terrible blow. She was very depressed, totally disheartened, just hanging on, trying to keep her sanity. One of the options she considerd was to leave the Party, but I think it has to be seen in that framework. I think there's a tendency that is not just Dorothy's to project onto Angela their own political concerns. I think it would be more honest to Angela to place it in terms of the agony of that time. Dorothy did come up to Marin, and I think she was a great source of comfort personally to Angela. Angela had great personal feeling for her. ■ Bettina Aptheker.

Angela's eventual acquittal was due to both the skill of her own defense team and the ineptness of the prosecution. Leo Branton, the chief attorney for Angela's defense, did an absolutely outstanding job. Through a pioneering use of jury selection techniques, the defense managed to seat a sympathetic jury. The contrast with the kind of jurors we had faced in the 1950s could not have been more dramatic. The "foreperson" of Angela's jury (she wouldn't allow herself to be called "foreman") had a son who was a conscientious objector; she came to court some days wearing a peace button. Even a less open-minded jury might have had a hard time with the government's case. The government went to some length to prove that Angela had purchased the guns used in San Rafael. The defense readily conceded the point, because it actually worked to undermine the case against Angela. Why would this highly intelligent woman openly purchase weapons for such a purpose, making no attempt at all to disguise her identity? In one case, she actually signed an autograph for the storekeeper who sold her the gun. There was no other credible evidence linking Angela to a conspiracy.

At the celebration in San Jose almost all of the jurors were present and they were manifestly pleased with what they had done. Even proud of it. . . . Listening to jurors, it was apparent that if they were ideologically motivated at all, it was by what is broadly called the American democratic tradition. But somehow we manage not to identify ourselves with it (or, more to the point, with what is positive in it).

The problem is not new. But here it was in an especially dramatic form. Sure, we talk in the abstract about the democratic tradition, about the defense of democracy against fascism, but when these abstractions assume tangible expression we are horribly inept in dealing with. . . . It is part of the problem of confronting American reality, and our woeful lack of so-phistication in doing it. It is all right to pour cold water on illusions, but the trick is not to dampen at the same time the positive impulses that underlie the illusions, and to establish some bond with the people motivated by these impulses. ■ letter from Al Richmond to Dorothy, June 7, 1972.

In June 1972 Angela was acquitted on all counts. She returned to Los Angeles a few days later. My happiness in her acquittal was alloyed only by my exasperation at a comment she made immediately after the trial. When a reporter asked her, "Did you get a fair trial?" she replied, "No, a fair trial would have been no trial at all." She should have acknowledged that she received a fair trial; that's what we were fighting for, after all. The fact that we could win a legal victory like this one had political significance in how we judged American society and its contradictory character. A Communist and Black militant *could* get a fair trial in 1972, which was something that it would not have been possible to say a decade or two earlier. I said to Angela when I saw her, "You've got to learn to be able to deal with victories as well as defeats." It was a mistake to trivialize what she and her defense had just achieved.

Angela told the audience "It was no accident that I began my tour of many countries by coming first to the Soviet Union, the first land of so-cialism."

She said that were it not for the Soviet Union it would not be possible to build socialism in other countries.

She thanked the Soviet people for their aid to the campaign to free her. . . . ■ Joseph North, "Women of 30 Nations hail Angela in Moscow," *Daily World*, August 31, 1972.

The Angela Davis defense campaign had been the biggest Party-initiated movement of the entire decade, and it was the one occasion on which the Party was really attuned to the political mood of the younger Left. It had a big effect on the Party and brought in a number of young recruits. Indeed, whatever political credibility the Party has had to draw upon from the early 1970s was largely a product of that campaign. Certainly nothing else it has done since compares with the importance of Angela's defense campaign in terms of image and the ability to interest outsiders. Angela Davis, not Gus Hall, has been the most attractive public face the Party has had to offer. But one of the sadder aspects of the whole episode was the impact it had on Angela herself. She felt that it was the Party and the Soviet Union which saved her life. She became unwilling to consider any criticisms of those she regarded as her saviors. When she was released from prison, the first thing she did was embark upon a tour of the Soviet Union, eastern Europe, and Cuba to thank them for supporting her during the trial.

Miss Charlene Mitchell, a close friend of Miss Angela Davis, the black militant, said today that Miss Davis would not be responding to the appeal for help from Mr. Jiri Pelikan, one of the leading figures in the "Prague Spring" now living in exile.

Miss Davis, she said, did not think that people should leave socialist countries to return to the capitalist system. This was a retrograde step, and even if such people said that they were communists they were still acting in opposition to the "socialist system," objectively speaking.

In his appeal, which was published in *The Times* today, Mr. Pelikan asked Miss Davis to call for the release of political prisoners in Eastern Europe as well as in capitalist countries.

Miss Mitchell, who said she was acting as a spokesman for Miss Davis, took the line that people in Eastern Europe got into difficulties and ended in jail only if they were undermining the government. ■ [Manchester] *Guardian*, July 29, 1972.

While Angela was on her tour and not always available to western reporters, Charlene and other Communist leaders sometimes put words in her mouth, denying that there was any political repression within the Soviet bloc. Not that Angela was willing to do anything to challenge that view. In fact, within the next few years, she accommodated herself to the stalest clichés in the Party's outlook. She remains to the present an important public figure, able to attract larger audiences than any other Party leader. But rarely if ever in her speeches and writings today will you see evidence of the kind of fresh thinking of which she was once capable. Whether she is capable of breaking free from Party orthodoxy is a question still to be answered.

12

Marta Goldstucker: You see, the longer you go on believing and working for the Party, believing everything is good, the longer it takes. Just to show you how deep our faith was, Edward was arrested and imprisoned. I didn't see him for a year and a half until he was sentenced to life imprisonment. The first week after his sentence, it was his fortieth birthday, I was allowed to see him in prison. And the first words we exchanged were that our attitude toward the Party hadn't changed. So in spite of all theses blows, which we didn't understand . . .

Edward Goldstucker: There was always the urge to explain away the unpleasant things and to cling to every little bit of hope. There were hopeful things, the great victory in the war, there was the renewal of the Czechoslovak state, our return from exile. There was the Twentieth Congress. There was the Prague Spring. We hoped that the movement could be directed into a channel toward the goal we dreamed of, that is, socialism with freedom. ■ [Marta and Edward Goldstucker joined the Czech Communist Party in 1933. Edward was imprisoned during the purge trials in 1951 and released in the early days of de-Stalinization in 1955. He went on to become vice-Rector of Prague University and chairman of the Czechoslovak Writers Union. He played a key role in the "Prague Spring" of 1968, and he and Marta were forced into exile in the aftermath of the Soviet invasion. They met and became friends with Dorothy in California in 1971.]

[T]he need for military action by one's Socialist neighbors in defense of Socialism is the exception to what is the rule between such countries. . . . It is not going to destroy Czechoslovakia's sovereignty—it is going to strengthen it. . . . One must see things as they are and then say it as it is. ■ Gus Hall, *Czechoslovakia at the Crossroads* [August 1968].

In the spring of 1967 I made my second trip to eastern Europe. This time I went, along with Hy Lumer, as a fraternal representative to the Communist Party Congress in the German Democratic Republic (GDR). I was chosen, I suspect, as part of a carrot-and-stick strategy on the part of the national office: they might have hoped that sending me to the GDR would serve as a reminder of the perquisites available to those who remained within the fold. But the trip had a quite different impact on me.

Hy and I were briefed by Gus Hall before leaving on the main issues that were to come before the congress. The central issue concerned trade with the West, and particularly West Germany, by the eastern European countries. The GDR and the Soviet Union were both insisting that none of the eastern European countries should enter into individual trade agreements with the West; they wanted to use such trade as political leverage to bring about recognition of the GDR by the Western powers. Most of the speeches to the congress by the fraternal delegates from socialist countries dwelt on the need for united action of the East Bloc on this question. During the same briefing Gus handed me a report from the Soviet Union on Soviet Foreign Minister Andre Gromyko's recent trip to North Vietnam. En route Gromyko had stopped off in China for a meeting with Mao. Gromyko was urging that in spite of the strong polemics then being exchanged between China and the Soviet Union they should strive for unity to support the Vietnamese struggle. "Not in 20,000 years," said Mao. "Can't you cut that figure in half?" replied old frozen-faced Gromyko. I was the only one who found that hilarious.

The GDR Party Congress was the least interesting part of the trip, full of canned rhetoric and decisions announced from the top. At one point the East German general secretary, Walter Ulbricht, announced how the wages of the workers were to be raised, and the head of the East German trade unions then stood up to thank Comrade Ulbricht on behalf of his members for this generous decision. What kind of trade unions were these? Would that union leader have stood up and denounced Comrade Ulbricht if no wage increase had been forthcoming? The only moment in the congress when there was a spark of warmth and spontaneity was when Hy and I met with the Vietnamese delegation. For once there was no strict adherence to hierarchy; the Vietnamese all treated each other as equals, speaking freely among themselves and with us, not drawing the usual distinctions between Hy, the "chairman" of our delegation, and me as the subordinate who was supposed to remain silent.

I spent May Day evening at the home of Grete Witkowski, who was deputy minister of finance in the GDR. I had not been looking forward to the occasion, fearing it would be taken up with the usual boring protocol, but I soon discovered that she was very free-thinking. Grete had spent the years of her exile in the West, which had made her the target of suspicion within her Party. She asked me what I thought of the May Day demonstration we had attended earlier in the day, and I told her how distressed I was to find that the GDR's soldiers were still using the Prussian goose step. She told me, "Those of us who were in the West during the war know what the goose step represents to other people. Communists who were in exile in the Soviet Union, or who joined after 1945, don't realize it. They hope that by retaining the goose step they will show the continuity of the history of Germany. But I can't stand it either." Then she asked me what were my other impressions of East Germany. I said it seemed very prosperous compared with what I had seen in the Soviet Union in 1961, but it still seemed a very dreary place, particularly in terms of the official culture. Earlier I had met the son of the woman who was acting as my guide. He was a student in his early twenties and a folk singer. This was at the height of the folk song craze in the West, and many young people in eastern Europe had taken to playing the guitar and singing the same songs you could hear in American coffeehouses. It amounted to a very mild form of generational rebellion: the songs these young Germans were singing were "western" but they were also left-wing in pedigree. The government didn't like it and had just passed a regulation that folk singers could only sing a certain proportion of western folk songs in any given concert. Eighty percent of the songs had to be of German origin, and you had to report at the end of each night what percentage you had sung. Even the use of the term "hootenanny" was forbidden. That struck me as just about the most absurd thing I had ever heard. When I mentioned my concerns to Grete she said, "Oh, you must go over and talk to Gerhart Eisler about this because he's in charge of radio and television."

I told her I wouldn't think of doing that. Eisler was a well-known and respected figure in the Communist movement who had lived as an exile in the United States during the 1930s and 1940s. After the war he returned to East Germany, where he held a series of important posts. I didn't feel like I should intrude on him. But Grete said, "Oh, you must. He'll want to talk to you." She called Gerhart, who readily agreed to my coming over. He spoke excellent English and we talked for a long time. He was clearly unhappy with the cultural restrictions in East Germany but was unable to do anything to change the situation: he too was something of a suspect of character because of the years he had spent in the United States. He was also keenly interested in the fate of the American Communist movement. Why, he asked, couldn't the Party come up with more thoughtful analyses of the problems it faced in overcoming its isolation? Weren't there any intellectuals in the Party leadership? "Well," I said, "Hy Lumer has a PhD." "No, no," he replied, "I mean *real* intellectuals. What about Herbert Aptheker?" Aptheker was widely known as the Party's "theoretician," but inside the Party everyone knew that his opinions didn't count for much in determining policy. The main problem, I told Eisler, was that whatever Aptheker's personal abilities might be, the only role the Party leaders permitted intellectuals to play was that of providing a rationale for whatever the current Party line might be. Gerhart nodded. I obviously wasn't telling him anything he didn't already know all too well from his own experience. It was an interesting evening for me, because it showed that underneath the surface unanimity that prevailed in even the most orthodox Communist parties, like that of the GDR, there were people with doubts and a capacity for independent thinking.

I decided not to accompany Hy on a tour of East Germany after the end of the congress, because I had already had my fill of official pomp and circumstance. Instead I went on to Czechoslovakia, where two friends of mind, Paul and Yvette Jarrico, were living at the time. Paul had been a highly successful Hollywood screenwriter. Blacklisted in 1951 after he refused to name names for HUAC, he went on to produce the movie *Salt of the Earth*. He later moved to France and then to Czechoslovakia, where he continued to write screenplays for European films. He and Yvette met me at the airport in Prague with a banner reading "Healey is Our Leader." I was quickly dragged off to a Party hotel in the center of the city by a Czech Party representative (as a member of the CP's national board I couldn't avoid all the demands of protocol), but I made it clear to my hosts that I could get around quite well in the company of my friends without an official guide or itinerary.

> I gather there was a big contrast between the May Day parade in Berlin and the one here. That in Berlin was a goose-stepping military parade with a not too exciting civilian parade following. Here, my friends tell me, it was very gay with singing, etc. ■ letter from Dorothy to Richard, May 4, 1967.

Paul's wife Yvette was a Frenchwoman who had lived in Czechoslovakia for many years. She had served as a translator during the purge trials that had led to the execution of Rudolf Slansky and other leading Czech Communists. It had been a terrible, disillusioning experience, but she still considered herself a Communist and still hoped that out of the tragedies of the past a decent democratic socialism could emerge in Czechoslovakia.

> Czechoslovakia was the only democratic country in all of central Europe in the interwar years. Everything around us went fascist or semifascist. We were subverted only when our friends joined our enemies: western democracies joined Hitler at Munich to destroy Czechoslovakia. Czechoslovakia was the only place where a Communist Party existed from its inception, which was 1921, uninterrupted practically, as a mass party, with its own traditions. It built up founts of experience. We didn't realize until very late that strong democratic tradition would be a bone of contention in the eyes of the Soviet leadership. They had to suppress it by brutal terroristic means. That is why the political show trials in the fifties were most cruel in Czechoslovakia. . . . ■ Edward Goldstucker.

This was a time of great excitement within Czechoslovakia. Of course, the official Party leadership was still dominated by Antonin Novotny, who had succeeded Slansky in the post of general secretary. There was a joke told in Prague after the Soviet Twentieth Congress that went, "The reason Czechoslovakia has escaped the cult of personality is because we don't have a personality around whom to have a cult." Novotny was a dull and cautious hack. But there were new forces at work within the Czechoslovakian Party. Unlike the other countries of the Soviet bloc, Czechoslovakia had a long history of democracy behind it. It had a large, well-disciplined, and quite radical working class, who had made the country's Communist Party into the most genuinely popular of the Parties in postwar Eastern Europe. And it had a substantial body of intellectuals who took their commitment to Marxism quite seriously and who were not content with the role of acting as apologists for the official line.

> Sunday, I went to the Writer's Castle . . . where I had a meeting with a philosopher, sociologist and economist (who was at Berkeley one term) on the NEW thinking and objectives, the most exciting and stimulating and

hopeful I've heard. Added to that was an earlier meeting with constitutional lawyers who are exploring the *realities* of power and what to do about it. Believe me, there is not one question which we skeptics raise that they're not dealing with in the most sober and realistic manner. ■ letter from Dorothy to Richard and her mother, May 9, 1967.

Through Yvette I came in contact with an interdisciplinary research team of Czech intellectuals set up by the Academy of Sciences to discuss the problems of power in a socialist society. She introduced me to a sociologist named Ota Klein, part of this research team. Ota first showed me the tourist sites—which I was quite delighted to see because Prague is one of the most beautiful cities I have ever visited. Then he took me out to the Writers' Castle, some miles outside of Prague, where the Academy of Sciences research team was holding its sessions. The head of the team was a man by the name of Radovan Richta, who was staying at a tuberculosis sanitarium not far from the castle. He and the others laid the intellectual groundwork for the Prague Spring of 1968 through a document they were then in the process of writing, *Civilization at the Crossroads: The Social and Human Implications of the Scientific and Technological Revolution*. The basic question they sought to answer was whether and how a Communist society, such as the one in Czechoslovakia, could be run in a truly democratic fashion. How should the Party be reformed to prevent its leaders from simply dictating policy to the rank and file? What kinds of checks and balances could be built into the system to prevent the arbitrary abuse of power and the denial of individual rights that had occurred in the past? How can you build an egalitarian society and still reward people for education and professional achievement?

> Until the beginning of the sixties the Novotny leadership of the Party succeeded in suppressing any reform movement. But then the economic situation worsened to such an extent that the Party leadership had to listen for the first time to ideas of economic reformers. The economic reforms were watered down and adopted only half-willingly, but nevertheless it started. And as the years went on it was more and more evident that you cannot realize successful economic reform in a regime like that without political consequences, without changing the political status quo. That culminated in Prague Spring in 1968. Czechoslovakia in 1968 was the only example where the reform, the democraticization initiative, came not from the streets but from the Central Committee of the Party. ■ Edward Goldstucker.

I spent an entire day listening to their debate, absolutely stunned. Here I had just come from East Germany, with its Prussian-style Communism, which had led me to the brink of despair. And now I was in a neighboring Communist country where these Communist intellectuals, who had decades of Party experience behind them, were freely debating the same kinds of questions that had so disturbed me ever since the Twentieth Congress. Radovan, who had played the leading role in the discussion for othe past several hours, turned to me at the end of the day and said, "Well, Comrade Healey, do you have any questions you'd like to ask us?" I felt very self-conscious and at a distinct intellectual disadvantage. There were serious scholars who had devoted much time and thought to these problems. But I put two questions to them. First I wanted to know how they were going to convince the Politburo of the Czech CP to surrender its excessive powers? "When did any ruling committee ever voluntarily give up its authority?" And second, I asked them how they proposed to construct a democratic Communism in Czechoslovakia without the approval of the Soviet Union? "Will they stand by and let you do it?" They burst into laughter, and I instantly reddened. I thought, "Oh dear, now I've shown how provincial I am; I've just said something to reveal my ignorance." When the laughter died down Radovan said to me, "Dear Comrade Healey, would you mind asking us any other two questions? Those two are the ones that we ourselves don't know the answers to yet."

After I left Czechoslovakia I went on to the Soviet Union and then to Italy, France, and England. I was very excited by what I had seen in Czechoslovakia, though it was hard to retain that feeling intact in the sober atmosphere of Moscow. I did meet a number of Soviet intellectuals on this trip, including one who had been imprisoned in the Stalin era, who told me that a thaw was on in Soviet internal affairs. It seemed obvious to me that the presence of thousands of such "rehabilitated" exprisoners would provide a yeast in Soviet society, leading to changes in consciousness with long-term consequences.

From Moscow I flew to Italy, where again my spirits were buoyed. Czechoslovakia was a model of Communists coming to grips with the limitations of the Soviet model in a society where they already held power; Italy showed me just how open and innovative a Communist Party could be in a country where it was still contending for power. The thing that struck me in all my dealings with the Italian Communists was their absolute candor. There were no forbidden questions as far as they were concerned, and also none of this nonsense about protocol which I so disliked.

One of the intriguing characteristics of the PCI was the fact that it had a "non-Leninist" organizational character. There were many thousands of Italian Communists whose sole obligation to the Party was to pay annual dues, without the usual burden of working within a Party organization or carrying out assignments. In conversations with PCI leaders, I asked them about this, and they told me that Italy had a tradition that at the age of eighteen people enrolled in a political party. If they had not accepted these young people in such an openhanded way, they would have just drifted elsewhere. One of the major tasks the PCI faced was to guarantee that there was a constant flow of new recruits from that periphery to the inner core of the Party, where the responsibility of members was similar to that in other CPs. Similarly original was their approach toward industrial clubs, where they always tried organizationally to link together the workplace and the community. I ask them, "How do you keep a revolutionary élan within this large party, when you're always poised on the brink of victory but never quite strong enough to actually come to power?" They admitted it was a very difficult problem. "What we have tried to institute," one of them replied, "is an emphasis on Party education so that Marxism stays alive within our ranks—combined, of course, with constant open debate about the issues which confront the Party." And that was, in fact, exactly how they functioned. When the Central Committee had a debate they printed the details of it on the front page of the Party newspaper. The contrast with the American CP's attitude toward such things could not have been starker. It meant that in Italy the Party members could actually learn to think for themselves. They could differentiate between the positions of various leaders. The Party's line was not something created by demigods through some mysterious process that mere mortals could never understand: it was the product of argument and persuasion and choice by real live fallible and improvable human beings.

> The recent statements by some of the leading cadre of the Italian and Spanish Communist Parties explicitly and implicitly contain just about every fabrication, mystification, distortion, and vile slander that the reactionary forces have been spreading against socialism, and especially the Soviet Union, for over sixty years. There is no basic difference between the statements by comrade [Enrico] Berlinguer, "It is necessary to go beyond the criticism of individual mistakes [in Poland] and look for the errors in the system" and [U.S. Secretary of State Alexander] Haig, "The communist *system* itself is in trouble." ■ Gus Hall, speech to *Political Affairs* forum, February 28, 1982.

The leaders of the American CP frowned upon the PCI—which I don't imagine caused Italian Communists too many sleepless nights. After the Italian Communists criticized the suppression of Solidarity in Poland, Gus Hall wrote a long analysis for the *Daily World* denouncing them as "revisionists." But to me the PCI represented the essence of the genuine Leninist tradition—the Leninism of the early days of the Bolshevik revolution when the Party openly debated its differences and even Lenin could be voted down after the issues had been debated. This was how democratic centralism was supposed to work.

> [Healey's] conception of socialism . . . is that it is a democratic world system designed to suit the desires and needs of the specific people it proposes to serve and not those of one master socialist nation. Accordingly, she vigorously opposed Soviet intervention in Hungary in 1956 and in Czechoslovakia in 1968. . . . For several years, Healey has openly manifested serious and organized political opposition to the policies of Gus Hall. ■ FBI memo, August 6, 1969.

I was heartened by the role that young people were beginning to play in the Party in the late 1960s. The fact that in 1968 Gus was denied the nomination he so clearly wanted as the Party's presidential candidate was symbolic of a much greater discontent among young delegates to the Party's nominating convention. On issue after issue the young people were really pressing forward, and the more orthodox national leaders like Gus, Carl and Helen Winter, Jim Jackson, and Hy Lumer were being forced to retreat, the first time anything like that had happened since the mid-1950s. If that 1968 convention had been a regular Party convention, charged with electing a new leadership, I suspect that most of those around Gus would have been in danger of losing their seats on the National Board. But once again, as in the past, an international issue arose which cemented the power of the old guards.

I followed events in Czechoslovakia in the spring and summer of 1968 with growing excitement and apprehension. I was tremendously enthusiastic about Prague Spring, because for the first time I could see all the issues I was concerned about being tackled by those who lived inside a socialist country. When the new Czech Communist leader Alexander Dubcek came into the leadership that spring, the Soviet Union launched a campaign within the international Communist movement against the ideas of the Czech reformers. Many Communist Parties ignored or resisted that campaign, but American Communist leaders played a servile role in promoting every lie and calumny being spread by the Soviets. The Party's New York–based newspaper, the *Daily World*, launched a journalistic onslaught against Prague Spring, without ever having consulted the National Board. The newspaper's coverage of Czechoslovakia was designed to create an atmosphere of hysteria, spreading wild and nonsensical stories that the West German army was waiting for the signal from Dubcek to cross the border into Czechoslovakia. George and Eleanor Wheeler, two American Communists who had lived in Czechoslovakia for many years, wrote frequently to the *Daily World*, *Political Affairs*, and the American CP's leadership that spring and summer, trying to correct some of the most ridiculous misconceptions and distortions promoted by the Party press. George was an agricultural economist, the only foreigner who had been accepted as an official member of the Czechoslovakian Academy of Science. They were both very knowledgable about the real state of affairs in the country, but their protests were ignored. Gus was holding meetings on the east coast and in the midwest to spread the official line about Prague Spring. The southern California district sent a resolution to the national office demanding that the National Board meet to debate the Czech issue, but to no avail. So we had our own mass meetings in Los Angeles to discuss events in Czechoslovakia. The majority sentiment was very much in sympathy with what Dubcek was trying to accomplish.

> I was glad to have your letter, Dorothy. I'd like to thank you for the courage in defending our policy. I am so sure as I never was of anything that you defend a good cause. It is by far not a won battle, I am sure. People are too unpatient and they will be disappointed, because the real progress cannot come so soon as they would like to have it. You know me and you know my skepticism: this is the only chance we have and even if I would be still hundred times more pessimist I would try it and I would engage myself in this, because this is *my* cause, and this is, in my mind, the first real and serious attempt . . . to transform the Communist movement into a modern political and human movement which corresponds to actual needs of young

people, too, and which at least in Europe, transcends the old-fashioned pattern. . . . I was glad to hear of Margulies (?) [Ben Margolis] how successful and beloved you are, in Calif. and I was very proud to listen to that and consider myself your friend. I am well aware of the fact, that it is hundred times more difficult to do what you do in the States than here.

■ letter from Ota Klein, Prague, August 19, 1968.

In early August Czech leaders met with leaders of the other Warsaw Pact powers, and it appeared that they had won the right to continue their reforms unmolested. We were very encouraged by the news and scheduled a meeting for Friday evening, August 23, to continue our local discussion of the Czech situation. But by then everything had changed. Soviet troops crossed the Czech border in the early morning hours of August 21; the next morning at seven o'clock my telephone began ringing with calls from the L.A. *Times* and the local television stations asking if I had any comment on the invasion. My first reaction was disbelief until they read me the wire dispatches. I told them that I didn't have any comment to make, but when our staff had a chance to meet later in the morning I would give them a statement. Then I called Gus in New York. He sounded very cheerful. "Oh, don't worry about it, Dorothy," he said, "it's going to be over in a couple of hours." He named three particular leaders in the Czech Party, all members of the Party presidium, who he said were going to be placed in power in place of Dubcek. As it turned out he was absolutely correct, which suggests that the invasion did not come as the same surprise to him that it did to the rest of us. Gus promised that he would call me with an official Party statement as soon as the Secretariat had finished its morning meeting. Three hours later when I still hadn't heard from New York, I called back. Gus had left the office, so I talked to Helen Winter instead. She told me that the Secretariat had been unable to agree on a collective statement, and that Gus would issue an individual statement instead. She read Gus's statement to me, which said that he was sure that the Warsaw Pact powers had good reasons for what they were doing.

> The central issue in Czechoslovakia is the defense of socialism against the threat of counter-revolution. It seems clear that what has happened, in the course of a process of vital democratic reform, is an upsurge of anti-socialist elements, supported by the forces of subversion of U.S. and West German imperialism. . . . We do not yet have all the facts necessary to make clear whether or not there was any other alternative to the action taken. However, from the vantage point of a party existing within the world center of imperialism, it seems to us the most fatal error would be to underestimate the subversive powers of imperialism or the dangers of an anti-socialist takeover in Czechoslovakia for the entire socialist world. ■ Gus Hall, statement to the press, August 21, 1968.

The District Committee of the Communist Party of Southern California has reaffirmed its position of support for the complete independence and

autonomy of each Communist Party. The draft program of the Communist Party, USA, has contained this principled position. Under the circumstances, the military invasion is, therefore, a violation of these principles.
■ Dorothy Healey, statement to the press, August 21, 1968.

Meanwhile my phone was ringing every few minutes with callers demanding to know our position. Inasmuch as the Party had not yet adopted an official position and Gus was releasing a statement that reflected only his personal opinion, the L.A. district board decided that we were free to do the same. In our statement we denounced Lyndon Johnson's hypocrisy in deploring the Soviet action, pointing to American military intervention in Vietnam. But then we quoted the program of the American Communist Party, which talked about the sovereignty of nations and the equality of all Parties in the Communist movement and the guarantee that none of their rights would be interfered with by other Parties. We didn't feel we had to say anything else to condemn the invasion. Later on, that statement to the press would be cited by Party leaders as evidence of our continued disregard for democratic centralism, even though we did no more than quote our own Party program.

A meeting which had been scheduled previous to the Russian takeover of Czechoslovakia to be held August 23, 1968, at Baces Hall, 1528 West Vermont Avenue, Los Angeles, California, was held as scheduled. At this meeting both DOROTHY HEALEY and BENJAMIN DOBBS spoke and criticized the invasion of Czechoslovakia by the Soviet Union and encouraged members of the SCDCP to openly speak against Soviet intervention. ■ FBI memo.

Our meeting on August 23 was jammed; there must have been six hundred people there. I defended the Czech Communists' right to create their own vision of socialism and denounced the whole notion of a counter-revolutionary plot and West German intervention as ludicrous: if the Soviet Union could guarantee the security of Cuba, half a world away, did it seem likely that Czechoslovakia, bordered on three sides by Warsaw Pact nations, was in greater danger? The real reason the Soviet Union acted when it did was because the Czechoslovak Party Congress was scheduled to meet on September 9, and without question that congress would have removed the remaining leaders, like the three Gus mentioned, who were willing to act as stooges for the Soviet Union. The delegates, who had already been elected, were committed to the program of democratic reforms that Dubcek and other Party leaders had initiated that spring. What the Soviet Union feared was not a military invasion from the West, but rather the example that the Czechs would set for people in other Eastern European countries and in the Soviet Union itself.

In Czechoslovakia you had a reform movement that was led by the CP. It wasn't like Hungary or Poland where the initiative came from outside the Party, and the Party responded to one degree or another. Here the thing matured inside the Party, and you had the Party as the leading force in outlining this program. And then you had that god-damned intervention, the tanks rolled into Prague, and the first thing they did was surround the Central Committee building. It was counter-revolutionary, an armed coup against the CP of Czechoslovakia. So here we were in the United States committed to the struggle for reform within the framework of the CP, and it's being done in Czechoslovakia, by all the rules, and then that happens. That's why it was so shattering for us. ■ Al Richmond.

When I finished speaking I opened the meeting up to comments from the floor. Again, as in so many instances in the past, the pull of loyalty to the Soviet Union overcame any other consideration for some of those in the audience, who were just furious with me for having dared to criticize a decision of the Soviet leaders. But the majority mood was still very much in favor of my position.

A meeting of the District Committee, SCDCP, was called for August 25, 1968 at Los Angeles, California. At this meeting the District Committee, SCDCP, reaffirmed the District Executive Board's position that no Communist Party has a right to interfere with the functioning of any other Communist Party. The District Committee, by vote of 19 to 1, adopted a resolution to this effect. . . . A motion was passed by a vote of 13 to 4 that the Soviet Union should withdraw all military troops from Czechoslovakia and release all Government and Party people now confined. ■ FBI memo.

Thanks to Al Richmond the *People's World* adopted a very critical attitude toward the invasion—Al was soon to leave for a long-planned trip to Czechoslovakia which he took at my suggestion, and he sent back an excellent series of first-hand reports on the postinvasion mood and situation in the country. The *Daily World* continued to offer complete endorsement of the Soviet actions, and in doing so took a markedly different line than that of the newspapers of most of the western European Communist Parties like the French, the Italians, and the British, all of whom had reporters in Prague, and all of whom condemned the invasion. Meanwhile I was being barraged by calls from younger comrades, including Charlene Mitchell, Don Hamerquist, Michael Meyerson, and Carl Bloice, who were outraged by the invasion and who wanted me to demand that a meeting of the national committee be held to debate the issue. Gil Green called me up; he too had spoken publicly in condemnation of the invasion and wanted to see the issue debated as soon as possible.

The week before the military action by the Warsaw Pact countries, there were ten to twelve thousand West Germans in Czechoslovakia . . . there were three to four thousand Americans in Czechoslovakia, besides the large numbers of Italians, French, and British. Of course, most of these were students on vacation; of course there were businessmen amongst them, but one would have to be totally blind not to see that there was a worldwide mobilization of the ideological and political cadre of imperialism in Czechoslovakia. . . . Arms have been found in the basements of 11 Ministries. . . . There were secret printing shops—all set up. They set up full scale gallows in town squares—for practice, they hung Communist leaders in effigy. . . . It is clear the situation was headed for an explosion. ∎ Gus Hall, *Czechoslovakia at the Crossroads* [report to the National Committee of the CPUSA, August 31, 1968].

When the national committee met over Labor Day weekend it voted by a five-to-one margin to endorse Gus Hall's report, which laid out the case for the Warsaw Pact invasion. Gus's report was filled with lurid nonsense about how a hangman's gallows had been erected in the central square of Prague where all the loyal Communists were going to be hanged, and so forth. It was subsequently published in full as a special supplement of *Pravda* and reprinted in eighty languages and distributed all over the world. When Al Richmond was in Prague that September, a Czech Communist remarked bitterly to him that *Pravda* had allotted more space to one Hall report than it had to all the speeches, reports, and documents of the Czechoslovak Communist Party over the previous eight months. Under Gus's leadership the American CP had picked up the dubious distinction of being the chief ideological sheepdog in the international Communist movement, barking on command when any of the other lambs threaten to stray from the fold. The Soviet leaders would contact Gus and tell him what they wanted him to say, he would say it, and then *Pravda* could run a story declaring that embattled American Communists speaking from the heartland of world imperialism had thus-and-such to say about whatever issue was of particular concern to the Soviets at the moment. I have no doubt that the "facts" in Gus's report, and perhaps even the report itself, were provided to him directly by the Soviets.

One particularly poignant aspect of the debate within the American CP's National Committee was that it pitted Bettina Aptheker, who denounced the invasion, against her own father, Herbert Aptheker. Bettina was one of the liveliest of the young people who rose to prominence in the Party in the 1960s, and also one of the warmest human beings I've ever met. She adored her father, so it could not have been easy for her to oppose him that day. Herb, endorsing the invasion, claimed that Czechoslovakia was particularly prone to counterrevolution. "What we must remember," he declared, "is that unlike the other eastern European countries, Czechoslovakia had a developed bourgeoisie." Of course it did; that's why it had a developed working class, which had been very pro-Communist in the past. Turn his argument on its head and you had a good explanation for why Czechoslovakia should be playing a vanguard role in the creation of a "socialism with a human face." Herb also criticized the Czech Communist leaders for having praised Tomas Masaryk, the first president of the Czechoslovakian republic, despite the fact that he himself, as a historian, has always been devoted to establishing the continuity between past American heroes like Jefferson and Lincoln and our own movement. One thing I found particularly discouraging in the meeting was seeing how some of those who had initially been so upset by the invasion, like Charlene Mitchell, had been "gotten to" in the meantime; Charlene abstained on the final vote.

A District-wide meeting of members of the SCDCP was held at 7213 Beverly Boulevard, Los Angeles, California, on September 8, 1968. This meeting was called for the purpose of members of the SCDCP to hear the results of the National Committee meeting held in New York City over the Labor Day weekend. . . . At the Los Angeles meeting, HEALEY, DOBBS, and [Sam] KUSHNER all spoke in opposition to the HALL statement [backing the Soviet invasion] and were soundly backed by the members of the SCDCP. WILLIAM C. TAYLOR, Negro Affairs Director, SCDCP, was the only SCDCP leader who endorsed the statement of HALL. It is believed by the sources that this will tend to widen the disagreement in policy between TAYLOR and HEALEY which has been previously very much in evidence. ■ FBI memo.

Although the district leadership mostly held firm against the invasion, in its aftermath the national office succeeded in turning the district membership against me for the first time. They sent a team of national leaders out, including Carl Winter, Lou Weinstock, and Danny Rubin to organize against my position and found allies among some local Communists, especially Bill Taylor. I was accused of being anti-Soviet and of having violated democratic centralism for having issued my own statement about the Czechoslovakian invasion. All my sins against orthodoxy over the past fifteen years were raked up. Everything else ground to a halt in the Party in Los Angeles except the all-important campaign against Healey and her friends.

I had been in Czechoslovakia two weeks before the Red Army moved in. I spent a week in Prague. I came back telling everybody, "I've seen a new kind of socialism; this is what the socialism of the future is going to be." It was free. People were talking. Al Richmond had gone to Czechoslovakia just after the invasion and wrote some articles critical of the Red Army. He was the main speaker at the annual banquet in Los Angeles to raise money for the *People's World*. I was chairperson in 1968, as I was every year. He came back and made a speech, and the audience went crazy, booing and shouting "liar," and so forth. I went home and canceled my subscription to the *People's World*. Some of the Party people came and talked to me. I told them that if they were ever attacked again, for violation of the Smith Act or whatever, I would certainly consider defending them, but on any other level I didn't want to have anything to do with them. I've never resubscribed to the *People's World*, although Dorothy told me I was wrong. She said you should read everything. ■ Ben Margolis.

The first public manifestation of the campaign came in mid-October when Al Richmond spoke before a large audience gathered in the Miramar Hotel for a *People's World* banquet. As in his reports from Prague, Al was very sympathetic in his comments to the Czech reformers and very critical of the Warsaw Pact invasion. Midway through his speech, an organized chorus of boos started up. Al finished the speech, but was so shaken by the experience, as he reports in his autobiography, that he subsequently decided it was time to step down from his post as *People's World* editor. One hard-liner who led the booing at the banquet, Sid Harris, went back to his club and declared that Al ought to be taken up to the top of a thirteen-story building and thrown out the window.

GUS HALL was present at both the first and second sessions of a general membership meeting, SCDCP, which were held on November 7 and 8, 1968, at 7213 Beverly Boulevard, Los Angeles, California. The purpose of this meeting was to hear HALL's report concerning the position of the CPUSA on the situation in Czechoslovakia. . . . [Hall] denounced HEALEY for making a public statement to the capitalist press giving her viewpoint on the invasion of Czechoslovakia by the Soviets. . . . HALL summarized the general membership meeting, stating that he welcomed debates, and that he was not angry with the SCDCP or with the individual members who had spoken. He denounced AL RICHMOND, Editor of the PW, for his editorials in the PW and for RICHMOND's speech at the Annual PW Banquet in October 1968 at Los Angeles, all concerning the Czechoslovakian situation. Hall said that dissenting opinions are welcome, but that it is up to the CP District leadership to direct these opinions toward the decision of the National Executive Board, which decision must be carried out. ■ FBI memo.

The invasion of Czechoslovakia was the beginning of the end of my years of involvement in the Communist movement. The southern California district held its annual convention in April 1969, followed in May by the national convention in New York. At the L.A. convention I gave my last report as district organizer. I was fed up with the internal bickering and despondent about the possibility of ever making any real change in the Party's outlook. I no longer wanted to have the responsibility of leadership. I decided I would remain on the district committee for the time being, which mainly functioned as a kind of sounding board for the district leadership, but would not stand for re-election to the smaller and more important district board. Nemmy Sparks, Sophie Silver, and a number of others who shared my views made the same decision.

My report to the district convention was the longest I ever gave to a Party meeting. I was trying to summarize what I'd learned over the past few decades. I wanted to get away from the impression that I was just dueling with Gus Hall in some kind of personal vendetta, so I deliberately took examples from before his administration to try to point out some of the enduring problems the Party faced in the way it went about making and carrying out its decisions. I wanted to show that there was a connection between the way in which decisions were made and the problems that developed once the decisions had been made—a connection between form and content. Using World War II as my primary example, I asked why we had been unable to offer a balanced, nuanced strategy, like the "Double V" campaign advocated by some Black groups that called for both "victory over fascism abroad" and "victory over Jim Crow at home." For us the only acceptable slogan had been "everything for victory against fascism," and if that required the postponement of the struggle for Black rights or the well-being of the labor movement, then we were all too willing to pay that price.

We went from one one-sided estimate of the war in 1939–1941 to another in 1941–1945, never seeing what should always be apparent to Marxists, which is the contradictory strands that make up any given historical moment and situation. Yes, it was a necessary war, but it was also a war that was at the same time strengthening some undemocratic trends at home and consolidating America's postwar role as the guardian of western imperialism. Maybe you can't always do justice to the complexities of a given issue when you're trying to mobilize thousands or millions of people to support this or that candidate or policy, but there's no reason why the Party itself had to abandon all sense of complexity in its analysis. That's what gave us the deserved reputation for flip-flops. And the reason why we were never able to see more than one side of an issue had to do largely with the Party's undemocratic internal functioning. Once the leaders handed down a line it was impossible for others to speak up to correct the exaggerations that a one-sided emphasis could lead to.

> I get exasperated when I hear the same comrades who denounce us for violating democratic centralism on Czechoslovakia speak of Browderism. Why did we have to wait for a French Communist to tell us we were following a revisionist policy? Because those who could have challenged it including Comrade Foster remained silent, bound by these military ideas of democratic centralism which developed during the Stalin era. Our Party was almost destroyed as a revolutionary instrument—but we sure defended democratic centralism during that period! Which, dear comrades, was the greater evil? Liquidating the Party, or violating democratic centralism? Both the term "Browderism" and "cult of the personality" represent a major departure from Marxism-Leninism, in that the individual is everything, the Party is nothing. From this flows the nonsense that an individual leader can be wrong, but the Party is infallible. It is the opposite side of the concept which believes that a leader can *never* be wrong; when the "wrongness" is exposed, the leader is dismissed—as with Browder or Stalin, later Khrushchev—but the reason why mistaken policies were uncritically accepted at the time of their leadership is never questioned. ■ Dorothy Healey, "Report to Southern California District Convention," April 4, 1969.

Gus, who wanted to be in on the kill, came to Los Angeles for our convention and at the conclusion of my report stood up and declared, "There is nothing that the Communist party has ever done that Dorothy Healey approves of." When we got to the national convention, the mood of dissent and opposition to Party leaders so prevalent at the previous summer's convention had evaporated. Southern Californians were absolute pariahs. No delegation even wanted to sit near us. I remember at one point taking out a cigarette and finding that I didn't have any matches. I asked a delegate sitting across the table, "Have you got a match?" and the answer was "Not for you."

> [Hall] confirmed that Gilbert Green, controversial former leader of the New York party, had been re-elected to the party's ruling national com-

mittee. But he also said that Dorothy Healey, chairman of the Southern California party and an ally of Green's opposing the party's support of the Soviet occupation of Czechoslovkia, had been dropped.

Hall said Miss Healey "has been released so that she can spend a year's sabbatical leave for study." ■ "Top US. Red Says His Party Seeks Only Panther Talks," *Oakland Tribune*, May 7, 1969.

When I got back from the national convention I was just a rank-and-file member of the Party, the first time that had been true since 1945. I joined a Party club, known as the Venceremos Club, which consisted mostly of young people. Some of them were Red Diaper babies; others recruited out of the civil rights and anti-war movement. They were a very creative and independent group of activists. We used to refer to ourselves as the "workers and peasants club" in jest. Bill Taylor had hoped to succeed me as the new district organizer, but the national office, not completely oblivious to his incompetence, passed him over. A man named Lou Diskin became the new district organizer—a nice enough man, but somewhat over his head (his previous experience had mostly consisted of running a Party bookstore in Chicago), and he didn't last long. His replacement, Arnold Lockshin, was a rigid dogmatist, utterly convinced that Party history started in 1967, the year he happened to join. (He later gained considerable publicity for his "defection" along with his family to the Soviet Union on the eve of the Reagan-Gorbachev summit meeting in Reykjavik in 1986.)

Lockshin closely monitored my activities in the Venceremos Club, building a case against me should the Party decide that I was to be expelled. I knew what he was up to: in fact, one of the reasons I joined that particular club was because the Party constitution read that a person could only be expelled if their club brought charges against them and voted to expel them. I knew that the young people would at least be willing to listen to my side, if it came to that, though they were by no means all supporters of my position.

After all those years of being in leadership, it came as a relief to be able to set my own pace of political involvement. It was also a relief to be spared the burden of going off to New York every few months for another National Board meeting. I had always tried to avoid taking things personally in internal battles. In the early 1950s, for example, Bill Schneiderman really cut loose at me in state board meetings, but we remained good friends. It was different with Gus, because unlike Schneiderman, he was sneaky and snide in his attacks. I realized later that my personality was starting to change, that I was brooding over the little nasty things he did and said, which I had never done before, and growing nasty and short-tempered myself as a result.

MARTA: It must have been a terribly hard thing for Dorothy after spending all her life in that movement just to break with it. It must have seemed to her at first as treason.

EDWARD: She struggled with that very intensely, the breach of loyalty. But American Communism had become something horribly grotesque.

> Gus Hall was the first to publicly approve and welcome the Soviet invasion of Prague. He was the first to go and preach to the Czech Communists how counter-revolutionary they were. And then Angela Davis was the next ambassadress. I asked Dorothy, how many members does the Communist Party have in America? She told me something that I found surprising. She estimated that the membership was about three and a half thousand. If the proportion of Communists to total population was transferred to Czechoslovakia, then the Czech Communist Party would have a total of 233 members, instead of its one and a half million. The American Party is nothing but the leadership. Some individual members can be very bona fide, probably they are. But the leadership sees its function as the mouthpiece of Moscow. ■ Marta and Edward Goldstucker.

Freed of the pressures of leadership, I was able to catch up on my reading. I also made some new friends when I met Edward and Marta Goldstucker, former Czech Communists living in exile. Edward had been one of the leaders of Prague Spring. He came to California as a visiting fellow at the Center for the Study of Democratic Institutions in Santa Barbara. We had long talks about the situation in Czechoslovakia and in the international Communist movement. It was startling to find two people from a country with such a different history than the United States who had been shaped by a political process so similar to the one I had undergone. They had joined the Czechoslovakian YCL the same year I joined the YCL here, 1928, and they joined the CP at the same time, in the early 1930s. Their individual experiences had been different from mine, but underneath those differences we had really been shaped in fundamental ways by the same international movement. Our ideas, our responses to current events, and our loyalties were virtually identical. Discovering these political kindred spirits was a revelation of the power of a common ideology in forming character.

> I kept urging my mother to leave the Party. I kept saying, "Why are you staying in? What's in it any more? You've lost." Before that I could see the relatively good work it accomplished on specific reform issues, peace, labor, civil rights, and say, "All right, I understand that." But not after the invasion of Czechoslovakia. The best young people left after the '68 convention. It had become a battle of Don Quixote against the windmill, a self-defeating, de-energizing activity. I didn't press hard. She knew it. ■ Richard Healey.

It was clear that my time in the Party was limited: sooner or later I was going to be presented with some totally unacceptable ultimatum from New York, and I would have to tell them "no" and accept the consequences. I just could not bring myself to initiate the break. I had been in the Party too long, put too much into it, and gained too much from my association just to hand it over to Gus and his cronies. The Party belonged to me as much as it did to them. I still felt, as I had since the mid-1950s when I first went into active opposition, that the Communist Party was something greater than the sum total of its parts. You couldn't judge it by what it was at any particular moment. Since the 1950s I had tried always to keep in mind the Party's potential for becoming something other than it was, even when I had no illusions about the immediate prospects for meaningful internal reform. Now, for the first time in my years as a Communist, I was no longer proud of being in the Party and no longer tried to recruit people for it. How could I take the responsibility for encouraging people to become Communists when I couldn't even read an issue of the *Daily World* or *Political Affairs* without feeling ashamed of the nonsense they featured?

> Gus Hall in his report [to the National Committee] dealt with elections and the new initiatives required of the Communist Party. . . .
> Disaffection with the two major parties of monopoly capital is high among the people, he said, adding the moment is ripe for active steps towards organizing a mass, working class-based antimonopoly party. . . .
> Hall pointed to the "lesser evil" pattern of voting as the main factor imprisoning the electorate in the two-party trap.
> Now, however, after the fiasco of the McGovern campaign, and the purge of even pale liberals from the leadership of the Democratic Party, masses of people are ready to make a clean break, he said. . . .
> Hall sharply criticized the tendency to believe that the Democratic Party can be taken over by the people's forces, and he said that the Communists had to some degree fostered this illusion by an electoral policy that was not well enough formulated. ■ Rick Nagin, "Communists Call for End to 2-Party Grip on U.S. Elections," *Daily World*, December 12, 1972.

After Nixon's landslide victory in November 1972, Gus made a report to the Party's national committee on the presidential election, later published as a pamphlet called "The Lame Duck." In it he threw out the window the analysis and electoral strategy we had held for the past three and a half decades. No longer, Gus declared, would we seek to influence the Democratic Party in a progressive direction; to speak of any meaningful distinction between bourgeois candidates was revisionism; from now on we would run our own Party candidates, while encouraging the growth of "antimonopoly" third party. There had been absolutely no debate within the Party over this major shift in policy. The "Lame Duck" had not been approved by the Secretariat before being sprung on the National Committee. Some Party members probably didn't even notice the change: if Gus said it, then it must be all right. For those of us who were aware of what it represented, it fell like a bombshell. I know that privately some other Party leaders were aghast. Gus's new analysis was soon abandoned, again without explanation. The general secretary could spout any nonsense he chose to, without any responsibility to the Party, and it didn't seem to make any difference.

Perhaps the hardest thing for me to accept was that so many of the young people I had been close to in the 1960—Angela, Kendra Alexandra, Carl Bloice,

Mike Meyerson—after years of standing up to and criticizing the national office, had decided to make their peace with Gus. They saw no future for themselves in remaining critics of the Party's status quo. Certainly the rewards for acquiescence were much more tangible. After her acquittal, Angela emerged as one of the Party's leading spokespersons, while Kendra became district organizer for northern California, Carl became editor of the *People's World*, and Mike Meyerson became head of the U.S. Peace Council.

> Self-serving books attacking the Communist Party, written by people who have left it or have been expelled from it, are not uncommon. But in the newly-published book by Al Richmond we have . . . a book of this character written by an individual who is still an active member of the Party. . . . The direction in which he is moving, it is clear, is out of the Party. This book, written and published without the Party's knowledge, is a long step on that road. ■ Hyman Lumer, "A Subjective View of the Left," *Political Affairs*, May 1973.

I might have drifted indefinitely had matters not been brought to a head by the Party's reaction to Al Richmond's autobiography, *A Long View From the Left*, which was published late in 1972. Al's book was an open and honest attempt to understand the meaning of his own lifetime of revolutionary commitment, emphasizing those aspects which he hoped would be relevant to a new generation of revolutionaries. He did not hesitate to draw critical conclusions about his own earlier activities, in the hope that old mistakes would not be repeated in a new guise. And, of course, he talked about the 1968 events in Czechoslovakia, which had been a watershed in the development of his ideas, as they had been for me.

> Dear Dorothy,
>   Your call last evening (or rather the content of it) was not unexpected, and yet it came as something of a shock, as you might have surmised from by fumbling reaction. . . . Until I see the Lumer text it is difficult to work out the precise forms and content of a response. But the characterization of the book as "anti-party" already poses questions that involve the relationship with the party. And on these questions I'd appreciate your thoughts.
>   The basic issue, it seems to me, is one of perspective: is a rupture avoidable? And, under the circumstances, should it be avoided? And if a rupture cannot or should not be avoided, then, to the degree that I can influence the issue, what precise form is preferable?
>   I pose the problem in these sharpest terms because, it seems to me, that once they characterize the book as "anti-party," they are virtually obligated to proceed with administrative-organizational measures. And they cannot offer me an Ambassadorship to Mongolia. . . .
> ■ letter from Al Richmond
> to Dorothy, April 27, 1973.

The first blow was struck by Hy Lumer, who reviewed *A Long View from the Left* in *Political Affairs*. He characterized the book as "anti-Party" and "racist." As evidence for the latter, Lumer cited the fact that several leading Black Communists were "merely mentioned in passing" in the book, and Henry Winston, William Patterson, and Benjamin Davis were not mentioned at all. Al noted in his response, never published by *Political Affairs*, that William Z. Foster had failed to mention a single Black Communist by name in his autobiography *Pages from a Worker's Life*, but no one accused him of racism for the omission. What was really at issue was, first, Al's outspoken sympathy for the Czech reformers, particularly his conclusion that "workers overwhelmingly supported the Dubcek leadership," and second, his insistence throughout the book that the cause of American revolutionaries could only prosper through "an independent confrontation with American reality in the spirit of Marx and Lenin, without borrowed spectacles or dogmatic preconceptions." Al had already left the editorship of the *People's World*; now the national leadership decided that he and all those who stood by him had to be driven from the Party.

The alternatives look like this to me.

A. If you stay (for the nonce) your reply is that of a party member refusing their urging that you leave. If you (& we) leave now their job is made much easier; it is no longer a question of inner-party differences but The Party vs. ex-s, always a simpler rallying cry.

B. If you (we) go now, it dispenses with much that is totally time-wasting and irrelevant inasmuch as there isn't the slightest prospect of any significant debate. . . .

■ letter from Dorothy to Al Richmond
[late-April, early May 1973].

I knew where I stood on the issue. Al had been sending me chapters of the book as he wrote them over the last few years for my criticisms and suggestions, and I helped him organize book parties in Los Angeles when his book came out. And when Hy's review appeared I mentioned it on my radio broadcast, told people where they could find it, and also told them where they could find reviews expressing a very different interpretation, in *Ramparts* and other publications.

GENERAL MEMBERSHIP MEETING
All Comrades Invited

Discussion of certain ideological questions harmful to the Party. MONDAY— July 2nd—Hungarian Hall, 1251 S. St. Andrews Pl. at 8 p.m. sharp.
■ flier sent out by Southern California District Committee of the Communist Party, June 1973.

Events moved quickly after that. In June Gus Hall made a report to the meeting of the national committee in New York in which he reiterated Lumer's charges and labeled Al's book "a weapon in the hands of the class enemy." The southern California district committee, at the instigation of the national office, adopted a resolution endorsing the national office's characterization of Al's book and requiring "each comrade to reflect the Party's position when speaking and writing among masses." Any member of the district who publicly disagreed with the charges against Al would be subject to disciplinary action up to and including expulsion. It was a provision tailor-made for me because I was the only Party member who regularly and openly spoke in a public forum as a Communist, through my program on KPFK.

A special meeting of the district membership was called as part of an "educational campaign" to complete the ritual disgrace of the views expressed in *A Long View from the Left*. The meeting was like something in *Alice in Wonderland*: "verdict first, trial later." George Morris, an old Party warhorse, stood up and said that the fact that Al's book had been brought out by a "bourgeois publisher," Houghton Mifflin, was proof of his anti-Party attitudes, because clearly they wouldn't have published a book by a Communist if it wasn't going to undermine the Party. The fact that Angela Davis, Herbert Aptheker, and many other Communists had, at one time or another, had books brought out by other "bourgeois publishers' didn't seem to occur to him. Bob Klonsky stood up and denounced the book as racist because it didn't deal with the mass deportations of Mexican workers from California in the 1930s. (Klonsky had been one of the California CP leaders who resigned in 1958 to protest the stifling of reformers within the Party; in the 1960s he rejoined and embraced the most orthodox views in order to do penance for his earlier sins.) Klonsky ignored the fact that Al had not even come to California until 1938, several years after those deportations took place. It wasn't just the old people who were capable of such stupidity. When I spoke up to defend Al, a young woman, Evelina Alarcon, who had been in the Party for all of six months, stood up and attacked me as a "white middle-class liberal racist."

> My meeting with the "old folks" last Thursday was depressing. They are all solidly in agreement with our position but as I listened to them I kept wondering what they had learned in the 35–50 years they'd been in the outfit. In short, my allies are that because they regard me as their leader and simply transfer to me their need to "believe" in and follow a leader. I found the whole experience sad. What they'd like is for me to meet with them regularly as a kind of "board-in-exile." God forbid. ■ letter from Dorothy to Al Richmond [late June 1973].

There was no question that I would go along with the denunciation of Al's book. I had the choice of either ignoring the directive and being expelled, or simply resigning. Some people, including my friend Gil Green, urged me to make my fight within the Party. But I knew, first of all, that it was a fight I could not win. Second, if I did wage an inner-Party battle, it would wind up in a split, with a whole group of people following me out of the Party. I was not anxious to see that happen for a number of reasons, most important because I knew that if people followed me out of the Party then I would be placed in a position of political responsibility to them. I had no desire to be a guru of a little splinter group. I never called on others to leave the Party; if they wanted to do so, as far as I was concerned they should do it only on the basis of their own considered judgment and not out of sympathy for me. The anti-Richmond meeting was held July 2; I resigned July 9.

> The specific question of Richmond's book is secondary in my decision to resign. The primary question is the lack of party democracy and the use of a distorted version of democratic centralism to compel approval of decisions made without prior discussion among the membership. And it is precisely on the question of how decisions are made, how policy is decided, that I have been in such long and frequently public disagreements with the national leadership of the Communist Party. ■ Dorothy's statement of resignation on KPFK, July 9, 1973.

I decided that I would read my resignation statement on my KPFK show that evening. Bill Taylor tried to persuade me not to make a public issue of my resignation, but after so many decades as the public spokesman for the Communist Party in Los Angeles, I knew that there wasn't any way that my departure would not be noticed. And I wanted to make it perfectly clear that I was not leaving in a "God that failed" mood or embracing capitalism. I was not repudiating the movement I had belonged to or the beliefs I had held for the past forty-five years.

> My resignation from the Communist Party will not bring comfort to anti-Communists on either the right or the left. My hatred of a capitalism which degrades and debases all humans is as intense now as it was when I joined the Young Communist League in 1928. I remain a communist, as I have been all my life, albeit without a party. . . . ■ KPFK radio broadcast, July 9, 1973.

Bill called Kendra Alexander and told her of my plans. She flew down from San Francisco that same afternoon. When I finished reading my statement of resignation, she called KPFK, and for the remainder of the hour we debated Al's book and the problems of democratic centralism in the Party. I handled her very gently, as perhaps Bill had counted on when he called her. Here was a woman whom I had recruited into the Party many years earlier and kept in the Party in years when she was upset about the same issues of the lack of internal democracy that so disturbed me. As late as 1971 she had been attacked for her close association with me. But like many other young Communists, she finally made her peace with the national office. In earlier years Kendra and I had had almost a mother-daughter relationship. After my expulsion Kendra would warn her own mother that if she remained in contact with me, she would refuse to see her on her visits to Los Angeles.

> Dorothy Healey and Al Richmond have engaged in struggle against the Marxist-Leninist norms of the Party's political policies, organizational principles and such fundamental ideological concepts as proletarian interna-

tionalism over a long period of time. . . . Well known is Richmond's persistent championship of the threatened counter-revolution in Czechoslovakia. . . . [His] writing also contains slurs and slanders of the experience and role of the Communist Party of the Soviet Union. . . . Healey's opposition to the Party's position on Czechoslovakia and on other Party decisions is also well known. . . . Thus, the challenge of Healey and Richmond to basic tenets of Marxism-Leninism has taken on a more openly anti-working class, anti-Soviet and anti-Party course. . . . Therefore, the Central Committee of the Communist Party, USA characterizes the position and role of Dorothy Healey and Al Richmond as anti-Party and adopts this resolution for their expulsion. ■ statement issued by the Communist Party, December 21, 1973.

I resigned from the Party in July 1973; I was expelled from the Party in December 1973. Whether one can be expelled from an organization one no longer belongs to is an interesting metaphysical question. But the Party had its reasons for pursuing this apparently absurd course of action. Over the years hundreds of thousands of people have quit the Communist Party, sometimes out of principled disagreement, sometimes out of fear of the consequences of staying in the Party, sometimes out of sheer boredom. If someone simply resigns from the Party there is nothing in the Party constitution to prevent Communists from associating with them. But if someone is expelled, then it's a very different story. Then it becomes a breach of discipline to consort with the "class enemy." So when the Party expelled Al and me in December, there was a perverted rationale involved: they could then expel anyone who continued to be seen in our company. And they did expel people for just that. It wasn't enough that I was no longer around to raise those embarrassing questions at Party meetings: I had to be turned into some kind of monster, the latest in a long line of bogeymen, from Browder to Gates to Healey, in order to frighten the faithful of the consequences of the slightest dissent from the gospel according to Gus.

Dear comrades:
. . . You take exception to Healey's self-designation as "a Communist . . . albeit without a party." In your narrow, bureaucratic visions this declaration is demeaned into just "another fraudulent attempt to sustain contacts with party members. . . .

This capacity you display for so quickly reducing things to the mean and petty measures of your own factional obsessions tells more about you than it does about us. That self-designation is validated by a lifetime of conviction, struggle and action.

We stand by that conviction. We continue the struggle for the revolutionary transformation of society, for the creation of a more rational, just and humane social order. The privilege to do that is not yours to grant or deny.

Comradely yours,
Dorothy Healey
Al Richmond   ■ letter to the Central Committee,
                          Communist Party USA, January 22, 1974

EPILOGUE

[O]ne observer has stated that Healey's proposed solutions to Party problems are based on reality and frequently collide with standard and sectarian Party approaches. . . . Her political views are too deeply based to expect them to be changed in any fundamental way. ■ FBI report, August 6, 1969.

Marx said capitalism degrades and debases men; socialism has debased and degraded the language of Marxism. So, whether in the realm of theory or politics, we no longer have a common language—and, I suppose, that means that the common ideology we shared is a patchwork quilt of symbols drained of agreed-upon content. . . . How does one get away from the paradox of total reliance on the "Marx wrote on page 3" school or the bowdlerizing of what He or his first disciple V. I. said? How reconcile a decent regard for their seminal accomplishment with a recognition of their historic limitation? . . . [M]y thoughts are as cluttered as my house. ■ letter from Dorothy to Al Richmond, June 18, 1972.

It was a tremendous relief to find myself for once with no organizational affiliations or responsibilities. Now, I thought, I could be like all those other "independent radicals" who enjoyed the luxury of standing above the fray, criticizing what other people on the Left were doing without actually having to do anything themselves. Although I had no intentions of plunging back into organizational work, I did join a discussion circle, which referred to itself jokingly as the "Forty Socialists Without a Party," made up for the most part of young people who had been in or close to the Communist Party. When emissaries from a new, nationally organized radical group known as the New American Movement (NAM) visited Los Angeles and tried to recruit the "Forty Socialists" into their ranks, my first impulse was to say, at least as far as I was concerned, "No, thanks."

I told myself that the new organization was my son's generation's thing, and that we old people ought to get out of the way. Richard, who had been one of NAM's founding members in 1971, convinced me to reconsider. He thought it was just preposterous that I, of all people, should talk about remaining above the organizational fray: "What's the significance of anything you've done before if you're now going to retire and be an onlooker from afar? Who needs them?" NAM drew together many former New Left activists who since the breakup of

245

SDS had no national organizational home, though like Richard many of them belonged to locally organized radical collectives. Purely local organizations are very difficult to sustain. Without something to join, much of that generation was going to be lost to the Left—just as, after 1956, much of my own generation drifted away from active political commitment. Most of the "Forty Socialists" were very attracted to NAM, and the more I thought about it, the more it seemed to me that Richard's arguments were right. I had something to contribute—and something to learn—and it would be irresponsible to hold myself apart.

> NAM's politics in its early days functioned on both a conscious level and an unconscious level. On the conscious level, our self-conception involved the creation of a healthy, native, socialist project, based on our own traditions, which incorporated a strong concern with feminism and racial issues, that was interested in working-class politics and yet aware of the fact that America had an unusual and diversified, sometimes conservative working class. That was explicitly what we were about. On the unconscious level we brought in our own history with us, as people do. So that in spite of intentions of starting anew we still looked remarkably like a 1960s style New Left organization, with very great emphasis on "process" and terrible fear of leadership. And we also had our share of one of the abiding problems of American politics, intense localism, loyalty above all to the local project, the local idea. That created very great difficulties for us in coming together. ■ Richard Healey.

Despite NAM's early promise, it never fully realized its potential. The group came along a little later than it should have. It started with about a thousand members, which was a pretty good base on which to build. But NAM got started just at the moment when the great mass movements of the sixties, with the exception of feminism, were winding down. NAM's founders assumed that in the vacuum created by the absence of any other credible national organization it would inherit all the tens of thousands of people who had been sent into motion by the civil rights and antiwar movements. That was not to be. By 1975 NAM had dwindled to perhaps 350 members, and its leadership realized that it was not enough just to say, "We're the nice American socialists; we're for democracy."

For a long time NAM found itself paralyzed by what Richard called its "perfect program" syndrome. Local chapters searched for the proper "nonreformist reform" they could organize around in the community, one that had the right racial, class, and gender dimensions to it. At the same time they viewed any proposals for national programs and strategy with great suspicion. In 1974, at the first NAM convention I attended, there was a proposal to work on an "impeach Nixon" campaign, but it caused a big political fight because even impeaching Nixon was seen as an acknowledgment of bourgeois legality which would just restore people's faith in the system. One of the things I found most difficult to adjust to in NAM was how much emphasis there was on "process."

No one seemed to care much about the finished product, the final decision, just how you had arrived at it. The flip side of that was that no one felt much responsibility for carrying out those decisions once they were made.

Another problem NAM had to face was competition from the so-called new communist movement in the early 1970s. Several small Marxist-Leninist would-be vanguard parties grew up out of the wreckage of SDS.

Rival groups like the "October League" and the "Revolutionary Union" took the most sectarian period of the American CP's history, that of the late 1920s and early 1930s, and glorified it. They embraced "industrial concentration" and sent their cadre of former students out to work in the factories; they embraced "democratic centralism," and if anything applied it in an even more authoritarian fashion than it had been used in the CP; they were determined to be "antirevisionist" and succeeded to the extent that they never had enough contact with people outside their own ranks to have to worry about accommodating their long-term principles to their short-term needs. But in a time of confusion and drift on the Left, they promised certainty, which made them appealing to some. Three of the best NAM locals, in Minneapolis, Boston, and Chapel Hill, were captured by one or another new communist sect by the mid-1970s.

> I learned from my mother that sometimes the only thing you can provide your members is education. It's something they will value. It's something you can give to them, which makes them feel better about themselves and therefore about the organization. So it had an intrinsic value apart from whatever impact it has on their ability to do outside work. ■ Richard Healey

When I joined NAM in 1974, these problems were beginning to be recognized. NAM created a new political committee to give the organization some sense of national direction. Richard was one of its members. One of the innovations that the political committee introduced to the organization was an on-going program of political education which explored the Marxist tradition and tried to salvage what was best in it. They put out literature, organized classes in local chapters, and held national training schools before each national convention. NAM members read everything from Gramsci to the new socialist-feminist literature. And in contrast to the New Left, they had some interest in learning from the achievements and mistakes of past radical movements. By the later 1970s the organization reversed its decline and began to grow again.

I spoke at a lot of NAM gatherings on my experiences in the Party. I found that my big problem, which I was aware of but couldn't always avoid, lay in telescoping my own experiences. It was easy for me to present the conclusions I had drawn from my years in the Party but much more difficult to make them understand the process through which I had formed my ideas. And without that, or without comparable experiences of their own, it wasn't easy to make it clear why I felt so strongly about certain issues. At national conventions I kept giving the same basic speech, pointing out the paradox that a group like NAM faced. With an organization that doesn't claim to have a monopoly on truth and doesn't inspire its members with the belief (even if it's an illusion) that no matter how irrelevent you are today tomorrow you're going to be the vanguard, how can you inspire people to make the necessary commitment and sacrifices that will keep the group alive and growing? You can't keep members enthused and willing to sacrifice their time and energies on the basis of an amorphous perspective or on one that says "I don't know the answer, but hopefully we'll all find out together." That's a very good attitude for the already committed to have, but it's not one that will inspire newcomers or the less committed to give of themselves. No organization can grow without self-sacrifice: some people *have* to be responsible for thinking about an agenda for a meeting ahead of time. Even a PTA can't function without some people giving their time and energy to that kind of drudgery, and it's all the more true for a radical political movement where the rewards are very distant and remote, if at all realizable.

The main thing I emphasized in the classes I taught for NAM was that theory only works as theory when it is constantly renewed. Marxism had been taught as a set of formulas, and most Party members had neither the time nor interest to look beyond those formulas. I know from my own case that it took nearly two decades of practical experience before it occurred to me that the "theory" I was reading in books by Marx and Lenin had much of anything important to do with my practical activity. That was in part my own fault, but it was also the fault of the intellectual atmosphere within the Party. We weren't encouraged to think of Marxism as a *methodology*, as an open system of thought that could change in a changing world.

There is an important lesson to be learned in the way that Marx dealt with contemporary thinkers. Marx is remembered as a fierce polemicist, which he was, but that's only half the story. Even when he dismissed other theories as nonsense or invalid, he was still able to extract some valid kernel of truth from what he was reading and make it part of "Marxism." The disciples and descendants who followed him, for the most part, lost that ability. Either we attacked our opponents at their weakest points, or ignored them completely. If they weren't Marxists—and Marxists of our own persuasion, for that matter—we felt we could just dismiss what they had to say with a wave of our hand, ignoring whatever empirical data or new theoretical conclusions they might have drawn. In contrast, treating Marxism as a methodology means having the ability to look dialectically at contemporary reality and not to be contented with one-sided arguments or formulas from the past. I still call myself a Marxist, although I respect other revolutionaries who do not. The Japanese Communists, for example, took the word Marxism out of their Party constitution. They say they are guided by "scientific socialism," which of course is what Marx and Engels called their own theory. I really don't care what it's called. When I say that I'm a Marxist, what I mean is I see the value in continuity in the spirit in which Marx approached his own world.

Her fears that somehow her perspective, her experience, would dominate too much with the cold hand of the past, just did not prove true. No one accepted her answers, *per se*. What they accepted and learned from was the kinds of questions she asked. That seemed interesting. That people accepted. ■ Richard Healey.

In 1975 I was elected to NAM's national interim committee (which, in terms of organizational structure, was the equivalent of the CP's national board). I was reluctant at first to accept, because I felt it wouldn't be fair to some of the young people already involved in leadership, including Richard. When I mentioned this to some of the delegates at the national convention, one of them, a young man from Antioch, said, "You know, Richard was a leader in this organization before you ever came around, and we don't have any prohibition against our leaders recruiting their parents." So I went on the committee.

In 1979 the Democratic Socialist Organizing Committee (DSOC), led by Michael Harrington, approached NAM with the idea of exploring the possibility for a merger of our two groups. Although many in NAM were sympathetic to the idea of a merger, it seems to take a lot more time and energy to bring radical groups together than to split them apart. The NAM-DSOC merger negotiations took two years to complete. There were three main issues under contention, concerning our attitude toward the Democratic Party, the Middle East, and the Soviet Union. There was some compromise on both sides, but on the last issue the DSOC people insisted on a position denying that the Soviet Union is a socialist country. There were a number of people in NAM like myself who came out of Party backgrounds who found the DSOC line on the Soviet Union difficult to swallow. But younger people in the NAM leadership whose judgment I respected, like Roberta Lynch, persuaded me to give way.

The bottom line was that we really didn't have much of an alternative. NAM had some good local chapters but little national presence. DSOC had a national presence but little local organization. We needed each other, we were relatively close politically in the overall spectrum of things, and it was worth some compromises and burying some old animosities to achieve unity. When the merger came in 1982, NAM had about 1500 members. Two or three hundred split off to form a splinter group. The rest of us joined the merged organization, Democratic Socialists of America (DSA), in which I have held the nominal position of vice chair since 1982.

I wish you much happiness in your new role of practicing grandmother, and much satisfaction in realizing such opportunities as Washington offers for your other interests and talents. Having sent Nixon and Reagan to Washington, it is about time that California made some atonement for its sins. ■ letter from Al Richmond to Dorothy, March 29, 1983.

One of the problems I faced after stepping down from Party office in 1969 was that for the first time since 1945 I was off the Party payroll. Fortunately I have never had expensive tastes, and I got by with some odd jobs and eventually Social Security. I also enjoyed a modest financial windfall when I sold my library and papers to California State University in Long Beach, which set up a special collection in my name. Like Mama before me, I don't think I ever threw out a pamphlet, so between the two of us we had amassed quite a collection.

Mama died in November 1979. Although even the Socialist Party, which she had left in 1919, sent me a letter of condolence noting her lifelong activism, the Communist Party, of which she had been a charter member (and remained a member even after my resignation), offered no official response to her death. The *People's World* did feel obliged to run an obituary, which noted that Mama was survived by a daughter, but didn't mention her name (actually she had three surviving daughters). A number of Party members in Los Angeles got together to publish a memorial notice for her in the *People's World;* I was pleased by their decision but dismayed when Rose Chernin, who had long been Mama's close friend and my Smith Act codefendant, withdrew her name from the list of sponsors. She called me up tearfully to explain that even at this late date she couldn't take this small decent step, because it might be interpreted as a criticism of the Party.

After Mama's death I had to make up my mind about what to do with our two houses on 84th and Western. For a few years I lived in the front house where she had lived and just left the back house empty. That seemed a waste, but I wasn't about to become a landlady. My neighbors were starting to worry for my physical safety. By this point the neighborhood had developed one of the highest crime rates in the city, and I was the last white person living in the area. The neighbors came by one day in 1982 and said, "Look, we're getting real worried about you. Nobody on this block would ever let anything happen to you, but the people three blocks away don't know anything about you." I thought their worries were exaggerated, but it was true that I didn't need the two houses, so I finally decided to move into an apartment in a housing project in a "safer" neighborhood. Five days after I moved, someone broke into my new home and raped me. So much for security. A few months after that I decided to make another and larger move. Richard by then had married Debbie Goldman, a woman he met in NAM. They had just had their first child, my grandson Benjamin, and were moving to Washington, D.C., where Richard was starting a new job. They asked me to share a house with them and help care for Benjamin—just as Mama had lived with me and helped raise Richard—and I agreed. (Richard and Debbie have since had a second son, and in caring for Benjy and Joshua I've discovered that being a grandmother has its special reward: one has all the fun of being a parent but little of the responsibility.) In July 1983 I left Los Angeles, fifty years after I first arrived in the city as a YCL organizer.

At the age of twelve I decided I wanted to be what I later came to call a "professional revolutionary," that is, someone who was totally dedicated to the fight against capitalism. I don't feel any differently today. When I read stories in the newspaper in the morning about the homeless, or about industrial pollution of the environment, or about the racism that is endemic to our society, I still get just as outraged and indignant and furious as I did fifty years ago. But while I have never felt tempted for a moment to abandon that one central and motivating belief of my life, I look out at a world today that in many other respects would have seemed unimaginable a few decades ago.

The greatest changes in the world today are those taking place in the Soviet Union and eastern Europe. The reforms undertaken by Soviet President Mikhail Gorbachev in the name of *glasnost* and *perestroika*, along with the turn toward a more open and pluralist social, economic, and political order in Poland and Hungary, are causes for rejoicing by socialists. I do not believe that they are the omens of the final and inevitable triumph of capitalism, as so often proclaimed in the American media. Gorbachev along with other reform-minded leaders in the Soviet Union and Eastern Europe have returned to the project to construct a "socialism with a human face" that the Czechoslovakian Communist Party was forced to abandon in 1968.

Particularly in the Soviet Union, the reformers do not face an easy task. The demand for fundamental change in the Soviet Union thus far has come largely from the top, rather than from the bottom of society. Millions of Soviet citizens who will ultimately benefit from the realization of *perestroika* and *glasnost* are fearful of change. This is because of the deadening and depoliticizing impact of long years of Stalinist tyranny and Brezhnevite stagnation, during which the notion of any kind of meaningful reform was a fanciful—and often dangerous—illusion. Gorbachev faces many other challenges, from the wave of nationalist resentments spreading through many Soviet republics, to resistance from Party bureaucrats reluctant to surrender their privileges. But he does enjoy one great advantage that Alexander Dubcek did not have in 1968: the armies of the Warsaw Pact are unlikely to come pouring across his borders to reestablish the old order. Gorbachev has made a brave start toward genuine reform. At the same time it would only be repeating the mistakes of the past to fashion around him a new "cult of personality." He is neither infallible nor omniscient, and there will always be a need for independent and critical assessments by both Soviet citizens and *glasnost*'s foreign well-wishers.

The U.S. Communist Party, after so many years of tailing along after every twist and turn of Soviet policy, has responded to the arrival of *glasnost* and *perestroika* with confusion and, in some cases, barely hidden hostility. On the one hand, American Communists have benefited politically, if only to a mild degree, from Gorbachev's popularity in the West. They have, quite properly, hailed the lessening of Cold War tensions that have resulted from the bold Soviet initiatives in foreign policy. On the other hand, Gorbachev's constant calls for the reinvigoration of Soviet leadership by means of replacing old worn-out Party hacks with young people who have new ideas cannot have much appeal to the ruling gerontocracy that surrounds Gus Hall as he enters his fourth decade as the U.S. CP's general secretary.

Careful readers of *Political Affairs* have noticed the way American Communist leaders are signaling their disenchantment with Gorbachev, and their sympathy for the remaining hard-liners in the Soviet leadership. In the international movement the American CP has lined up with the Cubans, the Czechoslovakians, and the East Germans—although that too may have changed before this appears in print—as opponents of Gorbachev's reforms. Within the ranks of the present-day CP there are some young people—and some of my own generation—who support Gorbachev. They have not, however, had any appreciable impact on the Party's official policies. The Gus Hall regime's cult of mediocrity remains in full force within the Party; reading current Party publications puts me in mind of a saying by Heinrich Heine that Lenin on occasion pointedly quoted when he grew exasperated with some of his contemporaries: "I have sown dragon seeds and have reaped fleas."

For all the problems the American Left has had to contend with in recent years, I still retain my optimism about its future. The bogeyman of the "evil empire" is losing its ability to terrify, which has led to a loosening of the paralyzing grip that anti-Communism has had on the American political imagination for so many years. Americans are once again beginning to look at the problems they face at home, as they did in the 1930s and the 1960s. And while the revolution is certainly not coming around the next corner, I think there will come a time in the not so distant future when the "S-word"—socialism—will again be discussed and debated and attract a new generation around its banners.

What would a socialist society look like in the United States? When I was a teenager in the YCL that would have been an easy question for me to answer, for I could have pointed to the Soviet Union as the model to emulate. Today it is a more difficult question.

I'm mindful that one of the smartest things that Marx did was to reject the temptation to provide a blueprint for utopia. He was not a dreamer; he understood that different countries and future generations would have to find their own way to a socialism shaped by their own histories, cultures, and economic resources. And even without Marx's cautionary example, no one could have lived through this much of the twentieth century with their eyes open without developing a healthy respect for history's habit of taking sudden unexpected turns, invalidating the predictions of wise men and fools alike.

Still, I didn't put in all those many years in the Communist Party, in the New American Movement, and in the Democratic Socialists of America, without giving the question some thought. It seems to be that Lincoln's definition of democracy, "Government of the people, by the people, and for the people," is as good a summary as any of an essential element of the kind of socialism I would like to see established in the United States. Socialist democracy means democracy in the economic as well as in the political sphere. Those who create the real wealth of the country must have ways of participating in the decisions that affect their own and the nation's welfare. When powerful corporations are free to destroy a community by shutting down a factory, or by pouring toxic chemicals into the air and water, they may be acting in ways fully consonant with the principles of the "free market," but they are denying democratic choice to those affected by their decisions. The challenge for American socialists will be to come up with ways to make use of modified market principles and coordinated (rather than "central") planning to guide decision making under circumstances vastly different than those faced by the pioneers of 1917.

In the political sphere, a socialist United States will have to guarantee a system of checks and balances that maintains but goes even further than the present-day separation of the legislative, executive, and judicial branches of government (after watching the L.A. Board of Supervisors operate over the years as both an executive and legislative body, I became convinced that Marx was wrong in lauding the combination of these functions in the Paris Commune.) The diverse organizations of civil society that represent labor, farmers, racial and ethnic minorities, women, gays and lesbians—all the associations that get labeled as "special interests"—will need to be preserved and strengthened under socialism, in defense of their own needs. Socialist politics should mean more not less debate; socialist democracy will involve an ongoing debate over all the important issues confronting the nation.

Genuine democratic debate requires a genuinely free press. My travels to Eastern Europe and the Soviet Union convinced me of the necessity for the independence of the mass media from state and Party control. Most people did not believe what they read in the official press or saw or heard on radio or television. Their daily lives belied the "official" facts. A socialist America should not only ensure a free press, it should guarantee as well something that does not exist today under capitalism, and that is the widest possible access to popular communication for individuals and groups. Real democracy is impossible unless people know the facts behind proposed policies, unless they hear all the relevant arguments pro and con—which is something that our own corporate-dominated media has almost as little interest in promoting as the Party-dominated media in the pre-*glasnost* Soviet Union.

I won't see socialism in my lifetime; I don't know if my son will see it in his, or even my grandchildren in theirs. There is no way to foretell what kind of political developments and issues will galvanize a future generation to turn towards socialism. The model I embraced in my youth, the vision of a vanguard party of the working class seizing power in the midst of a great social and political crisis like the one that had overtaken Russia in 1917, is no longer relevant. But I still believe that working people must be at the center of any real movement for socialism, for they are the majority for whose well-being that government "of, by, and for the people" should be concerned.

Ultimately I have faith that people, given the understanding of how they can help bring it about, want to live in a better world. People *can* change the world, but they can't do it as individuals alone. They have to join with others to do it. One thing I have not changed my views on over the years is the belief that organization is the key to winning victories for social change. That's why it was such a tragedy that so little in the way of organized radicalism survived the collapse of the New Left.

The Sixties changed many things in American society for the better. Those years represented an enormously important shift in popular consciousness. I think the New Left won some remarkable victories, especially in building a popular, sustained resistance to the war in Vietnam and in helping to create new frontiers for people of color. The impact of the sixties continues to be felt today in the lives and careers of tens of thousands of people who have followed through on their convictions as organizers, as teachers, as lawyers, as doctors, and in many other fields. They haven't given up the struggle. It is true that some New Leftists believed that they were going to show all us old people how to totally change society, and when that didn't happen they became discouraged and disillusioned. Still, the overall impact of the sixties has been a positive one. But the problem we face—and by "we" I mean both the generation of the thirties and that of the sixties—is that two decades later, in the absence of organization, either of the Left or of mass social movements, it has not been possible to develop new ideas, new tactics, and new programs to revitalize American radicalism.

People must have a channel through which they can express themselves if there is to be any hope that they will transcend the sense of powerlessness and apathy encouraged by our dominant ideological myths. Jesse Jackson's Rainbow Coalition has come closest in recent times to serving as this kind of channel. One could see a glimmer of the possibilities for the future, watching the young people who were Jesse Jackson delegates at the Democratic conventions in 1984 and 1988. Many had never participated in any political movement before, and you could see how the Jackson campaign had opened things up for them and gave a whole new dimension to their lives. The Rainbow Coalition has had its share of internal problems, but it has been far more successful than any of the more explicitly ideological groups on the Left in teaching people to give an affirmative answer to the old Biblical question, "Am I my brothers [and sisters] keeper?" One keeps oneself only by keeping others. That means we have to learn to look upon the societies of this world as things which have been created by humans and which are therefore subject to being changed for the better by humans.

> Arise, ye pris'ners of starvation!/Arise, ye wretched on the earth,/For justice thunders condemnation./A better world's in birth./No more tradition's chains shall bind us,/Arise, ye slaves, no more in thrall!/The earth shall rise on new foundations,/We have been naught;/We shall be all. ■ The International.

I have had the great good fortune throughout my life of being part of a warm and supportive family. All my siblings and their mates suffered to some degree from the attacks that came as a result of my political activities. Yet none of them ever reproached me for the hardships they and their families had to go through because of the fall-out from my notoriety. None ever suggested that I curtail my activity because of its impact upon them; on the contrary, whenever I needed their help they were always there to give it. All of them, each in their own ways, shared Mama's passionate feelings about the need to challenge injustice and oppression.

I have never understood the bitterness that some former members of the YCL and the Communist Party feel about their years in the movement. As the poet Johann Schiller admonished Don Carlos, "Bear respect for the dream of one's youth." For all of my own criticisms of the Communist movement, I retain a great feeling of gratitude that those of us who were in it gained knowledge that we never could have gotten any other way. My respect for thousands of people with whom I worked in the Communist Party, including some who have remained in it, remains undiminished. But my loyalties are to a vision of socialism, not to a particular organization. There's a phrase I've always liked in the revolutionary anthem "The International." It goes, "No more tradition's chains shall bind us." As Communists we argued that the survival of capitalism depended on the false consciousness of the majority of the people who weren't able to perceive the reality of their own lives. Ironically, the Communists also found themselves bound by "tradition's chains," and substituted a false consciousness for a real understanding of the world around them. The challenge that faces the Left in the future—if it is to have a future—is to base itself on the knowledge of what collective action by human beings can mean, rather than on faith in the infallibility of either its dogma or its leaders. If I were allowed just one piece of advice to give a new generation as to how to sustain a life-long commitment, I would suggest the cultivation of those two essential virtues of a good revolutionary, patience and irony.

INDEX

Neukom, Norman, 143
New American Movement (NAM), 245–49, 252
New Deal, 39, 72, 77, 105, 108, 197
New Left, 183–85, 191, 197, 201, 202, 210, 245, 246, 253–54
Newman, Carol Jean, 15, 17, 19, 20, 21, 23, 24, 25, 35, 38, 56, 86, 87, 89, 122
New Politics Conference, 205–6
Newspaper Guild, 65, 95
Newton, Huey, 208, 211, 216
New York Journal American, 173
New York Times, 155, 156
Nieto, Frank, 44
Nixon, Richard, 75, 111, 198, 199, 239, 246, 249
Noral, Alex, 37
North, Joe, 167, 220
Novotny, Antonin, 225
Nylander, Dr. Towne, 78

October League, 247
Office of Strategic Services (OSS), 131
O'Halloran, Cy, 106
Olsen, Jack, 60, 61, 62, 64
Olson, Culbert, 59, 69, 72, 77, 78, 85, 200, 201

Party Organizer, 96
Patterson, Lt. Governor Ellis, 78–79
Patterson, William, 241
Peace Action Council, 193
Peace and Freedom Party, 203, 206
Pearl Harbor, 86
Peet, John, 82
Pelikan, Jiri, 221
People's Educational Association, 87, 105
People's World, 29, 30, 43, 86, 99, 125, 135, 144, 148, 156, 160, 161, 166, 189, 204, 232, 234, 235, 241, 250
Perry, Pettis, 41, 125, 127, 133, 178
Pittman, John, 182
Political Affairs, 104, 163, 170, 178, 199, 228, 229, 238, 240, 251
Ponomarev, Boris, 164
Popular Front, 57–58, 59, 75, 76, 81, 82, 113, 131, 160
The Progressive, 107
Progressive Labor Party, 168, 185, 191
Progressive Party, 109–10, 112, 126, 151, 159, 201
Proposition 13, 196
Proposition 24, 199
Purge trials,

Rabin, Emile, 25, 30
Rakosi, Matyas, 160–61, 167
Ramparts, 201, 202, 241
Reagan, Ronald, 196, 197, 199–00, 201, 202, 215, 237, 249
Red Scare, 105

Red Squad, 39, 40, 78, 80
Reed College, 186–87
Republican Party, 85, 197–00
Reuther, Walter, 106–7, 110
Revolutionary Union (RU), 247
Richmond, Al, 29, 59, 68, 86, 93, 101, 103, 134, 135, 137, 140, 146, 154, 160, 161, 192, 216, 219, 232, 233, 234–35, 240–44, 245, 249
Richta, Radovan, 226–27
Robeson, Paul, 154, 209
Roosevelt, Franklin, D., 57, 77, 79, 86, 91, 92, 108
Rosenblum, Bernard, 19, 20, 22, 25, 26, 27, 36, 39, 55, 56, 62, 139
Rosenblum family, 15–16
Rosenblum, Frances, 17, 19, 20, 25, 36, 39, 56, 64, 87
Rosenblum, Helen, 19–20
Rosenblum, Joe, 15–16, 18–19
Rosen, Milt, 191
Ross, Carl, 165
Roybal, Ed, 136
Rubin, Daniel, 234
Rubin, Jerry, 216
Russian War Relief, 87
Russo, Mike, 165

Salazar, Reuben, 193
Salgado, Tony, 76
San Francisco Examiner, 85
San Jose Mercury-Herald, 48
San Rafael shoot-out, 217–18
Sarnoff, Irving, 193
Scales, Junius, 141, 147
Scheer, Robert, 201–4
Schneiderman, William, 38, 59, 65, 76, 90, 92, 93, 112, 120, 131, 134, 137, 139, 141, 142, 151, 154, 164–65, 237
Schulman, Alex, 136
Seale, Bobby, 208, 211–12
Sherman, Lou, 38, 39, 66, 86
Shachtman, Max, 148
Shafran, Eva, 91
Shapiro-Bertolini, Ethel, 124
Shapiro, George and Joseph, 69–70
Shaw, Mayor Frank L., 78
Silver, Max, 96, 98–99
Silver, Sophie, 235
Sinclair, Upton, 25–26, 40, 56, 77, 199, 201
Slansky, Rudolf, 225
Sleepy Lagoon Case, 91
Smith Act, 3, 114, 123, 131–32, 133–47, 151, 167, 170, 172, 190, 234, 250
Socialist Party, 22, 23, 148, 250
Soledad Brothers, 216–17
Soviet Union (USSR), 27, 33, 34, 57, 58, 60, 61, 62, 80, 81, 82, 83, 85, 87, 122, 127, 130, 135, 137, 148–49, 151, 152–53, 154, 155, 159, 160, 172, 173, 174, 176, 177, 178–83, 190, 197, 208, 212–13, 220–21, 223, 227, 230–34, 249, 251, 252, 253